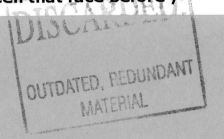

MARY WICKES

HOLLYWOOD LEGENDS SERIES
CARL ROLLYSON, GENERAL EDITOR

MARY
WICKES

I KNOW I'VE SEEN THAT FACE BEFORE

STEVE TARAVELLA

University Press of Mississippi • Jackson

www.upress.state.ms.us

The University Press of Mississippi is a member of the Association of American
University Presses.

Copyright © 2013 by Steve Taravella
All rights reserved
Manufactured in the United States of America

First printing 2013

∞

Library of Congress Cataloging-in-Publication Data

Taravella, Steve.
Mary Wickes : I know I've seen that face before / Steve Taravella.
pages cm. — (Hollywood legends series)
Includes bibliographical references and index.
Includes filmography.
ISBN 978-1-60473-905-3 (cloth : alk. paper) — ISBN 978-1-60473-906-0
(ebook) 1. Wickes, Mary, 1910–1995. 2. Actors—United States—Biography. I.
Title.
PN2287.W45875T37 2013
791.4302'8092—dc23
[B]   2012050083

British Library Cataloging-in-Publication Data available

To Lillian (1907–84) and Victor (1903–97) Taravella,
my paternal grandparents, whose generosity enabled me
to start this project

and

to Tim Reagan, my partner, whose patience and support
enabled me to finish it

CONTENTS

PREFACE

I REMEMBER LETTING OUT A LITTLE GASP.

I was reading the *Los Angeles Times* one October morning in 1995, as I did every morning in the years I lived in California, and turned the page to see Mary Wickes peering up from the obituary section. I had never met this character actress and had no relationship with her, yet I immediately felt a sense of loss.

I reacted as I did because of the characters that Wickes brought to life so vividly. Whether nurse, nun, or housekeeper, she was always the wry observer peering into a world that she did not entirely belong to. Intimately a part of whatever was taking place on screen or stage, she was at the same time an outsider—and it was clear to everyone that she had made her peace with this status. Although she was almost never the lead, she was the one who held my attention. Her persona resonated with me.

I soon learned I was not alone. Some years later, having decided to produce this biography, I immersed myself in Mary's papers in the archives of Washington University. Among them, I found stacks of fan letters that had arrived in the months following her death from people unaware she had died. I was astonished by the number of letter-writers— from as far afield as Australia, Belgium, Spain, Turkey, and the United States—who revealed the same thing: Most of them tell Mary that she is the first celebrity they ever wanted to write. Maybe these people, too, were outsiders of sorts. Certainly, she touched them in some way other performers had not.

Mary did not try to be funny or clever. In fact, when she occasionally gave seminars later in life, she reminded participants that her class featured "Acting in Comedy," not "Comic Acting." She had a natural sense of where the laugh was, of what would work and what would not. She didn't push for the laugh or nudge the audience, but rather left a gap between herself and audience members, inviting them to reach out and receive the laugh—which they did with uncommon ease. Take the episode that opened the 1972 *Here's Lucy* season, "Lucy's Big Break," in which Mary plays a nurse caring for a hospitalized Lucille Ball. The story is no standout, but Mary elicits guffaws with the most mundane dialogue. Uncovering the meal tray for her reluctant patient, Mary says, not very convincingly, "There, doesn't that look (pause) *tasty*?" On paper, this line looks lifeless. In Mary's hands—with an inflection that suggests she knows better, with eyes that are slightly rolled, with a voice resting on "tasty" just long enough that its two syllables become two words—it brings a powerful laugh.

That power could instantly awaken a moribund production. In the film *Half a Hero*, Red Skelton and Jean Hagen mope through an insipid story that breathes only during the scene that features Mary. Her very entrance signals us to sit up straight because we are about to be entertained. And we are.

Mary's comic gifts extended to writing, an aspect of her talent I would like to have explored more in this book. Poring through scripts she had written decades ago, I began laughing uncontrollably in the quiet Special Collections reading room at Washington University, where she donated her papers. (This is why I can't bring a David Sedaris book on an airplane.)

Every biography of a figure from the recent past is a race against time, and Mary's story is no different. By a matter of months, I missed many people I believe could have helped illuminate some aspect of Mary's life. Political advisor (and college classmate) Clark Clifford, actress Mary Jane Croft, singer Annamary Dickey, and actor E. G. Marshall all passed away while my interview requests were with them. Some I missed by even less time. When I phoned girlhood friend Melba Seay in St. Louis to request an interview, the woman who answered couldn't stay on the line because she was rushing out to Seay's funeral. I did reach Irving Rapper, the distinguished Warner Bros. director, but at one hundred years old, confined to the hospital wing of the Motion Picture and Television Home, he was not lucid enough to speak coherently. Then there was the death that wasn't. In search of actor Elliott Reid, I called the Screen Actors Guild locator service—a reliable gateway to contact information for performers—only to be told he had passed away just two weeks earlier. Reid had known Mary across a span of years, working with her in the Mercury Theatre in the late 1930s and again in television in the 1970s. Since his family might be sorting through his things, which could include correspondence from Mary, I phoned back the following morning to ask SAG if it had contact information for next of kin. I was asked, "Why? We have no record of his death." The first representative had been mistaken. I phoned Reid, who met with me twice in Los Angeles, providing many observations that helped shape this book.

Not everyone's memories were as reliable as Reid's. One longtime friend of Mary's offered a detailed recollection of how Mary had been affected by Lucille Ball's death. A few months later, this friend sat down for a second interview, and I asked a follow-up question. "So when Lucy died," I began—only to be interrupted by a shocked "*Lucy died?!* When?" On another occasion, I was quick to travel out of state to meet a woman who shared a house with Mary for a summer in the 1940s in Stockbridge, Massachusetts. But the two of us began to realize during the interview that she had been mistaken: Although she knew Mary, Mary was not in Stockbridge that summer.

I had yet to talk with anyone who worked with Mary in her Little Theatre days, the period after college and before she left home in search of an acting career. One of the last boxes of Mary's memorabilia to be opened at Washington University contained Little Theatre cast photos. One photo had the actors' names penciled on the back. Having already learned that many of Mary's generation never left the area, I took the names that were still legible to my hotel room and pulled out the phone book. The "Louis Westheimer" in the book was in fact the man of that name in a cast photo, taken fifty-six years earlier. Choked up, he said he had always known he had stories to tell, that he had hoped one day to receive a call like this, and that he was very glad he was still living when the call came. I met with him twice in St. Louis and a third time in northern California. After he died, I was privileged to speak at his memorial. St. Louisans of Mary's generation engendered that kind of fondness.

Few were as complicated as Kitty Carlisle Hart, who would certainly have had interesting recollections about the 1930s and '40s, when Mary was part of the Kaufman and Hart circle. I had three brief conversations with Hart, but nothing was on the record because she would agree to a proper interview only when I could produce a book contract, which I did not secure until after her death in 2007. In other seemingly unsuccessful interview pursuits, serendipity intervened. After countless paths turned up nothing, I had reluctantly given up trying to locate Iris Mann, the former child actress who would be the only living member of the original cast of "Mary Poppins," in which Mary starred for *Studio One*. Having moved on to other interviews, I was listening to a National Public Radio

report in the background at home one day (a sensitive story about an actor with a spinal cord injury), when I thought I heard the on-air reporter
sign off as "Iris Mann." Could it be? Fifty-one years after this groundbreaking TV production, could the voice in my living room belong to the
woman I had been searching for? It could, and it did. Mann, who had
given up acting for journalism, has a reporter's keen observation skills
and provided two revealing anecdotes about Mary.

By coincidence, it was another former child actor who helped me understand Mary's technique. When I reached out to Johnny Whitaker,
who had charmed audiences as the adorable redhead in *Family Affair*
and *Sigmund and the Sea Monsters*, he was running his own entertainment agency. He had deep affection for Mary, but it was easier for him
to show me why she remained important to him than tell me. Over
dinner, Whitaker began making dramatic, exaggerated gestures, the sort
that draw attention in a quiet restaurant. Craning his neck, contorting
his mouth, feigning shock, he was sharing methods Mary had taught
him as a boy. With names like the "Butterfly Double Take," these movements had been staples of Mary's professional repertoire, and she wanted
to share them with a younger generation.

But perhaps Lucie Arnaz best illustrated the spirit that I hope I've captured in this book. Blow-drying her hair the morning of our interview,
Arnaz reflected on what she might share with a writer about Mary, who
had been like family to her since childhood. She thought of a consumer
marketing campaign of a few years ago. She grabbed pencil and notepad
and scribbled, "Mary was like a great pair of No Nonsense, Control Top
panty hose—firm, strong, flexible, held you up and never failed to make
you look a little better than you really were."

"That's her as a person and as an actress," she told me a few hours
later. "I just loved being around her. I miss her terribly."

ACKNOWLEDGMENTS

WHEN I BEGAN EXPLORING MARY WICKES AS A BIOGRAPHICAL SUBJECT in 1998, three years after she died, a friend in Los Angeles surprised me by saying, "My friend Bill went out with Mary Wickes all the time. You need to speak with him." He introduced me to Bill Givens, Mary's friend and frequent escort, who became one of the first people I interviewed. Bill is also an author—he wrote the *Film Flub* series—and had considered writing about Mary himself. I appreciate the support he offered me and the doors he opened for me.

Mary's trustee, the Rev. Canon M. Gregory Richards, had some anxieties about this project. Mary was a private person and Canon Richards— initially Mary's pastor, later her close friend, and finally the guardian of her estate—was not at all sure that she would have welcomed a book about her life. Although she recorded anecdotes on tape for a possible autobiography, she never made a decision to go through with the project. For the trust he placed in me to present her life fairly, to treat her papers respectfully, and to put private letters in context, I am deeply grateful.

I extend special thanks to Lucie Arnaz. Because of her parents' continuing popularity, Lucie receives many requests to discuss elements of their lives and relationship. I appreciate her making time to discuss Mary with me and trusting me with so much of the unpublished correspondence between her mother and Mary. Lucille Ball was such an important part of Mary's life that telling Mary's story without benefit of this correspondence or Lucie's reflections would have been difficult.

I cannot imagine a more helpful group of archivists to work with than the Special Collections team at Washington University Libraries, the St. Louis repository Mary chose for her papers and memorabilia. By chance, I initiated this process while University Archives was still cataloguing this new collection, whose contents ranged from Mary's baby book, first locks of hair, and grammar school report cards to her scripts and correspondence with a who's who of twentieth-century pop culture. The archivists opened new boxes between my visits, and I found myself discovering Mary's world just a few steps behind them, so to speak—a researcher's dream. Mary's medical and financial papers were closed to me, but the archivists helped me navigate everything else. For organizing Mary's material so carefully, for their patience during my nine visits to St. Louis, and for the help they gave me at every turn, I am indebted to archivists Carole Prietto and Sonya Rooney, archive assistants Jay Kempen and Miranda Rectenwald, and graduate student assistant Ashley Eckhardt.

Mary's papers were invaluable, but her story could not be told without the recollections of those who knew her. Chronicling Mary's life took me to Boston, New York, Los Angeles, St. Louis, and Washington, D.C. In addition, I traveled to Dayton, Ohio, Granite City, Illinois, Stockbridge, Massachusetts—and to Chester, Roxbury, and Washington, Connecticut. I interviewed more than two hundred and fifty people, from the women who played dolls with Mary when they were girls in St. Louis, to the men who were her pallbearers in Beverly Hills—and scores of writers, producers, directors, and friends who were a part of her life in between.

I am particularly grateful to a retired paper salesman named Brooks Adkins. After finding his name in several of Mary's files but not understanding why it was there, I phoned him in Ohio. At eighty-seven, he was puzzled by this unexpected interest in his life, and more puzzled to learn that documents related to his childhood and guardianship were among the effects of a woman whose name he did not know. Agreeing to discuss long-buried family secrets is brave at any age—even more so with a stranger. His willingness to dig deeply into his own history produced what I think is one of the most interesting chapters of this book. I regret that he is no longer here to read it.

For their help in understanding aspects of Mary's family history, I thank Jim Alexander, Bill and Janice Dorsam, and Sally Alexander Higginbotham, all of St. Louis; Ruth Alexander Stubbs of Edwardsville, Illinois; and Edward L. Wickenhauser of Godfrey, Illinois.

For their help in understanding Mary's childhood, college years and lifelong connection to St. Louis, I thank the many people in St. Louis who opened their homes, scrapbooks, and memories for me, especially Helen Margaret Aff-Drum, Amy Jane Harrison Ax, Jerry Berger, Bill Carson, Dorothy Calkins, Bill Danforth, Elizabeth Danforth, Stella Koetter Darrow, Gene Fincke, Alfred Gellhorn, Edmund Hartmann, Judy Sutter Hinrichs, Virginia Weber Hoffmann, Nelson Hower, Sharon Huffman (St.

Louis Public Schools Archives), Dorothy Wagner MacCauley, Marcella Wiget MacDermott, Barbara Mahon, Lois Haase Mares, Mary Jane Roach Masters, Herb Metz, Julian Miller, Mary Jane Moise, Dorothy Conzelman Nash, Archer O'Reilly, Richard Palmer, Selwyn Pepper, Jack Pirozzi, John Scott, Cyrus St. Clair, Betty Sutter, Jane Sutter, Harriet Switzer, Mary Beresford Vahle, and Louis Westheimer. *The Streets of St. Louis* author William B. Magnan kindly consulted old maps to explain changes in street names so that I could find Mary's birthplace.

For helping me understand the life that Mary built in New York and Los Angeles, I am grateful to many who shared personal or professional stories, especially Rod Amateau, Arthur Anderson, Clinton Atkinson, Richard Baratz, Paul Barselou, Sheila Bond, Tom Bosley, Hal Broderick, James Brown, Nancy Thomsen Brown, Gordon Chater, Wanda Clark, Rosemary Clooney, Lester Coleman, John Corey, Anna Crouse, Emily Daniels, Joan Darling, Madelyn Pugh Davis, Ted Donaldson, Nanette Fabray, Terry Faye, Mary Flynn, Ruth Ford, Bill Frye, Betty Garrett, Michael Germain, Virginia Gorski Gibson, Janet Fox Goldsmith, Malcolm Goldstein, Laurence Guittard, William Hammerstein, Bonnie Happy, Christopher Hart, Mary Healy, Paul Henning, Bill Herz, Alan Hughes, Barnard Hughes, Marsha Hunt, Mary Jackson, Lamont Johnson, Hal Kanter, Andrea King, Don Knotts, Wendy Borcherdt LeRoy, Janet Lewis, Laurence Loewy, Marjorie Lord, Arlene Ludwig, Adrian Luraschi, Sheila MacRae, Delbert Mann, Iris Mann, Martin Manulis, Patrick McGoohan, Janie Miller, Helen Morgan, Paul Nickell, Jack O'Brien, James O'Rear, Lenka Peterson, Rita Pico, Harv Presnell, Mary Grant Price, Lee Roy Reams, Marge Redmond, Elliott Reid, Gene Reynolds, Joe Ross, Aaron Ruben, Anne Kaufman Schneider, Barbara Sharma, Warner Shook, Max Showalter, Ira Skutch, Lewis Stadlen, Mary Kay and Johnny Stearns, Jenny Sullivan, Dolores Sutton, Bill Swan, Alice Urist, Dolly Reed Wageman, Peter Walker, Bob Wallsten, Jeff Warren, Johnny Whitaker, Anne Whitfield, Max Wilk, Stewart Williams, Eleanor "Siddy" Wilson, Elizabeth Wilson, Ethel Winant, Jane Withers, Iggie Wolfington, and Jane Wyatt.

I appreciate those who have allowed me to quote from previously unpublished letters, which have helped me illustrate Mary's life. For their permission, I thank Edith A. McGrath (granddaughter of Howard F. Baer), Lucie Arnaz (daughter of Lucille Ball), W. Wyatt Walker Jr. (nephew of Patricia Collinge), Victoria Lucas (granddaughter of Michael Curtiz), Michael Merrill (son of Bette Davis), Doris Day, Diane Massell (niece of Robert Fryer), Jane-Howard Hammerstein (widow of William Hammerstein), Christopher Hart (son of Moss Hart), Walter Anthony

Huston (great nephew of Robert Edmond Jones), Jerrold Gold (executor, estate of Garson Kanin), Anne Kaufman Schneider (daughter of George S. Kaufman, widow of Irving Schneider), Benn Clatworthy (grandson of Gertrude Lawrence), John Bard Manulis (son of Martin Manulis), Dianna Wittner (daughter of Sherman Marks), Louise Newdall (niece of Clifford Newdahl), Mia Farrow (daughter of Maureen O'Sullivan), Steven Rehl and Bradley Strauman (executors, estate of John Patrick), Shannon Fifer of Warner Bros. Entertainment (for Irving Rapper), Lynne Rayburn (daughter of Gene Rayburn), Ruth Roberts (widow of Charles Donald Roberts, executor, estate of George Seaton), Susan Rodd (daughter of F. Cowles Strickland), Nancy Thomsen Brown (co-executor, estate of Robert Thomsen), Warren Steinhauser, Carter Lodge Productions (for estate of John van Druten), Andrew Wald (son of Jerry Wald), and Peter A. D'Auria Jr. (son of Barbara Wolferman).

In securing photographs, I again benefitted from the trust placed in me. For their permission to use photos in this book, I thank Michelle F. Amon (daughter of Gloria Swanson), Edmund R. Rosenkrantz, Gloria Swanson Inc., and Steve Wilson (at the Harry Ransom Center at the University of Texas at Austin), Max Klimavicius of Sardi's restaurant, Peter A. D'Auria Jr., Anne Kaufman Schneider, Barbara Olsen (daughter of Barbara Luddy), and the studios and licensing agencies named in the credits. Every effort has been made to identify the proper copyright holders of all photographs and previously unpublished letters used in this book, but a few could not be located. In the event that a piece of text or a photo has been used improperly, the copyright owner should contact me, c/o University Press of Mississippi.

Other important assistance was provided by the Library of Congress Division of Motion Pictures and Television (Madeleine Matz) and Division of Manuscripts, which houses the papers of Ruth Gordon, Garson Kanin, Joshua Logan, and Vincent Price; the New York Public Library for the Performing Arts, Billy Rose Theatre Collection (Charles Perrier); the New York Public Library, Genealogy Division (Philip Sutton); the Museum of the City of New York (Marty Jacobs); the Paley Center for Media, New York; the Missouri History Museum Library and Research Center, St. Louis; the Municipal Theatre Association of St. Louis (Laura Peters); the Howard Gotlieb Archival Research Center, Boston University, which houses the papers of Whitfield Cook, Bette Davis, Sumner Locke Elliott, John Patrick, and Alexander Woollcott (Sean Noel); the University of California at Los Angeles Film and Television Archive (Laura Kaiser); the Warner Bros. Archives, School of Cinematic Arts, University of Southern

California; the Margaret Herrick Library at the Academy of Motion Picture Arts and Sciences, Beverly Hills; the Stockbridge, Massachusetts, Library Association (Polly Pierce); the Vanderbilt University Special Collections and University Archives, Nashville, which houses the papers of Delbert Mann (Kathleen Smith); and the American Heritage Center at the University of Wyoming (Carol Bowers).

I appreciate additional help from Bill Munn, historian for the Berkshire Theatre Group in Pittsfield, Massachusetts; Justin Pettigrew at Turner Classic Movies; Martha Wilson, the resourceful assistant to Garson Kanin; Lysna Marzani at Samuel French; Craig Pospisil at Dramatists Play Service; Stephen Bowie, who runs the popular *Classic TV History Blog* but who when I began this book was just a nice guy sharing hard-to-find copies of *Alfred Hitchcock Presents*; the St. Louis and Los Angeles public libraries; the Ira and Leonore Gershwin Trusts Archives, San Francisco (Michael Owen); the St. Louis Mercantile Library and the Western Historical Manuscript Collection, both at the University of Missouri at St. Louis (Zelli Fischetti); the Gardiner, Maine, public library (Anne Davis); and Margie Tompros, who introduced me to perhaps the only surviving member of the original *Hollywood Pinafore*.

I thank Caitlin Ryan for pulling me into the Washington Biography Group, a vibrant source of encouragement over the years. I thank many colleagues for their advice, including: Bill Finger, Pat McNees, Henry Neiger, Naphtali Offen, Jim Parish, Harvey Solomon, Jan Stuart, Jon Thompson, Curt Wagner, and Ginny Young. I especially thank Tim Reagan for his keen editing eye. For those who put me up so I could conserve funds for additional research travel, I thank Bill Araiza, Taylor Burke, Ken Haller, Paul Serchia, Jeff Skorneck, Barbara Reagan, Chris and Robyn Reagan, and Evelyn and Eddie Whitcomb.

I started this project in Washington, D.C., but completed it while living in Rome. For carrying material across the ocean for me (saving me countless sums in international courier costs) I thank Leighla Bowers, Steven Cohen, Janine D'Angelo, Devin Gangi, Hally Mahler, Monica Marshall, Julia Pacheco, Nancy Roman, Andrea Stoutland, Kye Young, and others.

Finally, I thank Leila Salisbury at the University Press of Mississippi for recognizing that a character actress who never stopped working has a place in the pantheon of Hollywood legends, and Lisa Paddock for her many helpful edits.

MARY WICKES

CHAPTER ONE

Pardon Me Lady,
But Did You Drop a Fish?

ALTHOUGH THEY LIVED ONLY ABOUT TWO MILES APART, WORKED IN the same industry, and were fond of each other, Rosemary Clooney and Mary Wickes had not seen each other once in the forty years since they appeared together in *White Christmas*, the most popular film of 1954. That changed on Christmas Eve of 1994, when Clooney attended midnight mass at All Saints' Episcopal Church in Beverly Hills, which had been Mary's church for decades. Clooney's son Gabriel Ferrer had become a rector at the church, and he was officiating that night. As Clooney turned to leave after the service, she was delighted to spot Mary sitting a few rows behind her—the angular features that defined Mary's appearance were unmistakably hers even at eighty-four. "I almost knocked over two pews leaning over to give her a big hug," says Clooney. But Mary's reaction puzzled her. "She gave me a kiss and a hug . . . but she didn't talk." At first, Clooney wondered if Mary had been momentarily silenced by sentiment, so choked up at seeing her former co-star—on Christmas, no less—that she could summon nothing to say. "It was certainly moving to me, and maybe it was to her, too," says Clooney, a singer and recording star of the 1940s and '50s (who may be better known in younger circles today as actor George Clooney's aunt). No, Clooney ultimately concluded, a medical problem must have affected Mary's speech.

In fact, Mary was silent simply because she could not identify Clooney as the person greeting her. Certainly, Mary never had trouble talking; she had been a boundless stage and screen presence for half a century. But macular degeneration had robbed her of so much of her sight that she could not clearly discern images in the center of her vision, especially up close. "It really bothered her when someone got in her face and started talking to her and she couldn't recognize them," says Bill Givens, a close friend in the last ten years of Mary's life.

Mary's deteriorating vision was not her only health problem, but it was the hardest for her to accept. By the time she appeared in *Sister Act*, the 1992 film that brought her a new generation of fans with her portrayal of the sarcastic Sister Mary Lazarus, Mary was legally blind. "I don't think anybody knew it except us," says Dolly Reed Wageman, another member of Mary's small circle of confidantes late in life. "How the hell she managed those last two or three movies, finding her way around a set with cables on the floor, I will never know."

By this point in her life, Mary was one of the most recognizable character actresses in the United States. Though the general public might not have been able to recall her name immediately, generations of moviegoers, television viewers, and theatre lovers delighted in her distinctive presence. She helped create countless significant moments in film, television, theatre, and radio history. When silent film star Gloria Swanson decided to host a live talk show on this new thing called television, Mary was one of her first guests. When Lucille Ball made one of her first TV appearances anywhere, Mary appeared with her—and became Ball's closest friend for more than thirty years. On stage, Mary appeared with Montgomery Clift in his first stage role and with Grace Kelly in hers. On film, Mary performed with Frank Sinatra in his first lead film role. She played opposite a who's who of twentieth-century movie stars. She was the animator's model for the villainous Cruella De Vil in Disney's *One Hundred and One Dalmatians*, and was the original Mary Poppins long before an umbrella carried Julie Andrews across the rooftops of London. And the night that Orson Welles recorded his earth-shattering "War of the Worlds" radio broadcast, Mary was waiting on a soundstage for him, oblivious to the havoc that was taking place outside.

After such a career, many actresses might have retired. But Mary was not like many other actresses, and she was not satisfied. Health obstacles—encroaching blindness, breast cancer, a pacemaker, debilitating arthritis, and more—never prevented her from working, which was her driving passion. It was a passion evident from her earliest years, years shaped by doting parents in turn-of-the-century St. Louis who allowed her to pursue a career that was unavailable to most women at the time— and unthinkable for women who looked like Mary.

Mary's father, Frank August Wickenhauser, was an only child, born to August and Mary Marshall Wickenhauser in St. Louis in 1880. When Frank's father died two years later, his mother took a job as a cook at

Memorial Home for the Aged, a historic nursing home dating to the 1860s and known today as Beauvais Manor on the Park. Later, she married Andrew J. Hetherington, a marble and stone dealer of German and Irish heritage who was one of nine children in a prosperous family.

Young Frank grew up with his mother and stepfather and began working a succession of jobs in his late teens. He was a clerk at Glaser Brothers, a furnishings and notion store, until it was destroyed by fire in 1898. He then worked at the Simmons Hardware Company, a popular business whose Keen Kutter tools are collectible items today. For four years, he was a salesman at Hargadine-McKittrick Dry Goods Company. Always drawn to numbers, in 1904 he became a bookkeeper at American Central Trust Company.

As a young man, Frank was tall, thin, and slightly bent over, with dark hair, dark eyes, and thick glasses worn low on his nose, like a pince-nez. He smoked a pipe, as did many men at the time. He was quiet and generally took a back seat to whatever was taking place around him. Those who knew him are challenged to come up with descriptions that impress. They remember a man who was simple and uncomplicated: "amiable," "ordinary," "pleasant," "nice," and "an enigma." "He just really withdrew from conversations," says family friend Sally Alexander Higginbotham. His reserve was physical as well. "Frank was not a very warm person, where he'd come up and hug someone. I don't think he'd make any public display," says Jim Alexander, Higginbotham's brother.

One reason for this seeming reticence is that Frank was profoundly hard of hearing. For most of his life, he wore a hearing aid, the conspicuous sort with wires connected to a small instrument in his shirt pocket. It did not seem to help much. His hearing impediment created an isolation that no doubt influenced his personality. Frank "always seemed so much older because of his deafness. He was always sort of a spectator, just kind of along for the ride," says Ruth Alexander Stubbs, Sally and Jim's sister, who was a few years younger than Mary. "He was interested in everything going on and you could count on him for being there, but as for making an impression, especially with strangers? He didn't add much." But Frank found comfort in Masonic activities, and it was at a dance of the Order of the Eastern Star in January 1904 that he met Mary Isabelle Shannon.

Isabella, as she was called from an early age, was the daughter of James T. Shannon, who emigrated in 1873 from County Clare, Ireland, and Mary "Mollie" Thomas Shannon, of St. Clair County, Illinois. Isabella was born in East St. Louis, Illinois, at 14 South Fourth Street, in

1885. She had one sibling, a sister who was sixteen months older named Hester Margaret, called Hes. Together, they enjoyed a safe, rather conventional upbringing. It was a life shaped by church—Episcopalian and Methodist—and civic affairs. At the time of Isabella's birth, her uncle John J. McLean was mayor of East St. Louis, and her father was clerk of the probate court.

Isabella had a somewhat mousey appearance, and several who remember her as an adult compare her to Edna May Oliver, a severe-looking actress known for her humorless expression. But Isabella was not unattractive. She had softer, somewhat warmer features than her daughter Mary, who would inherit her father's looks and coloring. Isabella was blond, but for many years she dyed her hair red. Her gregarious manner helped her compensate for what she lacked in appearance. "I remember Aunt Isabelle as being very vivacious. She was flirty and entertaining and quite a talker—and all that was kind of lost on Frank," says Higginbotham.

Isabella had simple tastes and homespun values. She was an inveterate clipper of the sort of treacly inspirational truisms one might find in the pages of *Readers Digest* or *Guideposts*. She routinely expressed herself in superlatives. It was never enough merely to wish someone a Happy New Year; instead, she would wish them "the best and happiest New Year you have ever known." She was fond of reinforcing "proper" behavior in public, wearing hats and gloves and—when she became a mother herself—reminding her daughter and her daughter's friends to "Mind your manners!" Expecting certain behavior from those around her did not make her judgmental. When her sister left home at a young age to build a life as a vaudevillian—and turned away from the Episcopal Church to Christian Science, to boot—Isabella stood by Hes. "Isi" and "Hes" were devoted to each other, although they took their lives in very different directions.

Isabella and Frank began dating, and their future in the new century looked promising. In 1905, at age twenty-five, Frank joined Mercantile Trust, and, like many American men of his generation, he would remain at the same workplace his entire professional life. That same year, Frank's stepfather, Andrew Hetherington, died. Frank continued living with his mother, as was common practice.

Isabella and Frank were engaged in April 1906 and married in April 1908 at the Shannon family home in Carlinville, Illinois. The couple took a new apartment at 4275 Maffitt Avenue near Fairground Park in North St. Louis, and Frank's mother came with them. Mary Hetherington lived in the downstairs unit, and Frank and Isabella lived upstairs. This was an industrious area of working-class and middle-class families, mostly Irish and German. When Isabella became pregnant the following year, she and Frank rented a larger, single-family home just off North Kingshighway Boulevard. That home, at 5017 Garfield Avenue, was a two-story, red brick house with a basement, a fireplace, a front porch, and a small front yard. In the back yard, the family raised chickens. The home was built just a year before the Wickenhausers moved in.

It was in this home—which still stands today, though the address has changed to 5017 Lotus Avenue—that Mary was born on June 13, 1910. She weighed a full nine pounds. "I can't get over how large she is. She looks like a little boy, but I love her for that," Aunt Hes wrote Isabella shortly after Mary's birth.

Mary Isabella Wickenhauser would be Frank and Isabella's only child, and they doted on her, documenting every move in a way that might embarrass even today's hyperactive parents. So it is that we know Mary delivered her first laugh at eight days old while on the lap of her nurse, Edna Wheatley. (Isabella could not have known that Mary would spend much of her life producing laughter while playing a nurse.) We know that Mary left the house for the first time at seventeen days old, when Frank took her for an evening walk. We know that three weeks later, she went on her first proper outing, a visit to Grandma Shannon nearby at 3013 Walton Place, with a stop at the doctor's on the way. This visit was likely by horse and buggy, Ford's pioneering Model T having been introduced only two years earlier. We know the day Mary first stood by herself and the day she first wore shoes. We know the date that every tooth came in and the exact location of each. We have a detailed account of her early colic attacks. We know not just that she was christened on November 13, but that for the occasion she wore a petticoat made by Isabella, under a dress Isabella hand-embroidered, with a bib made partly from Isabella's bridal undergarments.

Understanding Mary requires understanding the world in which she grew up. She was a child influenced by the frightening declaration of World War I in 1914, by the horrendous deaths during the 1918 flu epidemic, and by the inspiring news of Lindbergh's safe transatlantic landing in Paris in 1927. Hers was a youth enveloped in stigma, where German-sounding street names were replaced with inoffensive ones (Bismark became Fourth Street), and where whites and blacks were segregated by law. Mary did not encounter African Americans in school or restaurants as a child because black residents were not permitted in the institutions that were part of her life. State-sanctioned segregation shaped the views of Mary's generation forever: Longtime friend Mary Vahle shudders at what Mary's Fairground Park home has become. "You can't go look at it now—it's black, black as can be," she cautions a visitor. It was not until 1949 that the swimming pool at Fairground Park admitted African Americans, an act that provoked a violent riot. Nonetheless, when Mary and her friend Louis Westheimer wanted to save money on touring shows that came through St. Louis, they went to the American Theatre (long since torn down to widen Market Street) and bought tickets for what was shamefully called "nigger heaven." This reference was to the third balcony, because black patrons were not permitted in the main seating areas. There, they saw the Broadway success *Of Thee I Sing*, among other shows.

During Mary's childhood, many homes had no indoor plumbing, cooking was done by coal, and evening activities were conducted first by coal oil lamps and later by gas lights; men would come around at dusk to light them. At home, player pianos and Victrolas provided entertainment. At grand downtown movie palaces, Mary experienced the transition from silent films to talking pictures. She spent her adolescence and young adulthood under Prohibition (1919–33), a restriction that hit St. Louis hard, given its robust brewery industry. The city was home to so many breweries and shoe factories that it was popularly described as "First in shoes, first in booze, last in the American League"—the "last" a reference to the perennially underperforming St. Louis Browns.

Mary grew up in a time and in a town and in a family that were driven by strong German values. She was raised to believe in a sense of propriety, in the notion that manners matter and that appearances are important. She would cling to these values her whole life, causing her to seem to belong to another era, even to many of her contemporaries. "When you're raised in that kind of family—and I've had the same kind of background, only diluted somewhat—a woman is to be seen and not heard. You were polite at all times. You never put yourself forward. You never tell people how good you are; you wait for someone else to tell you. You never nominate yourself for office. You never vote for yourself. Even my generation was raised that way," says Judy Sutter Hinrichs, a family friend who is a generation younger. "Being born in 1910, she was basically a product of the nineteenth century. So an awful lot of that value system stuck with her all the way through. And part of that is the personal reserve. You don't share feelings." College classmate Virginia Weber Hoffmann describes "a very proper kind of existence, with lots of rules, and you didn't question them. You felt that that was right. You can't imagine how different it was. Relationships between men and women were so entirely different. There was no living together—you got married. Mothers stayed home and were there when you got home from school. There were no two wage-earners in the family."

By all accounts, the Wickenhauser home of Mary's youth was a warm, loving household. Mary, who was called Snooky, even benefitted from having three grandparents during her childhood; Grandma Shannon and Grandma Hetherington lived until 1924, and Grandpa Shannon until 1927. "They were the typical, sweet little American family," says Louis Westheimer. Indeed, Mary's upbringing was in many ways idyllic. Frank and Isabella were fond of outings and introduced Mary to as much of the region as they could. They visited a farm where they crawled on haystacks and sunned in hammocks, had picnics at a lake where they played in the water and climbed on rocks, admired animals at the zoo, floated down a river in inner-tubes, got thrills at the Forest Park Highlands amusement park, and posed seriously beside canons at the historic Jefferson Barracks Military Post on the Mississippi River. Mary's favorite outings might have been the family's many excursions on the large riverboats that went up and down the Mississippi. "Everybody took their own lunch in baskets. If you got thirsty, you got a big, wonderful, cold stein of A&W root beer with a big head on it, a lot of foam. And that was lovely, *oh my*. That hurrying down the levy to make the boat before it left was lovely," Mary recalled some eighty years later while recording memories for a possible autobiography.

When she was about three, Mary would sit on the porch of the family's Garfield Avenue home during the warm months, listening to the street vendors calling out their treats like the criers of London. Cries of "wa-ter-melon" and "straw-berries" were common, but what really appealed to Mary was the ice cream treat, "Fro-zen Dain-ties, Fro-zen Dain-ties!" The desserts were not available to Mary because Isabella, ever cautious, felt the vendors' pushcarts were unsanitary. One hot morning, Mary heard the cry but was dismissed again by Isabella: "Oh, now, Mary Isabelle, you don't want any of that old stuff." "I thought that over and the minute I could, I got out of the front porch, down the steps, down the walk and down to the curb where the Frozen Dainty man was parked, and said, 'Give me some of *that old stuff!*'"

At the same age, she played dolls with playmate Josephine Hanlon, and when she was about eight, she organized "My Doll Wedding," where more than a dozen other neighborhood girls each brought a doll to celebrate the wedding of over-sized dolls named Clara and Johnny. Frequent playmates were the nearby Darrow family children, Annabelle, Genevieve, Harold and Raymond, as well as Irma and Marie Schnuck. In early photos, Mary is always the tallest child.

Frank and Isabella's greatest shared passion was theatre, and they introduced Mary to it at an early age. Now as then, St. Louis offers one of the most remarkable performance spaces of any U.S. city, an outdoor theatre that seats more than 12,000 people and always sets aside a section for free seating. Open only in the summer months, the Municipal Theatre Association of St. Louis is a local institution and an important part of that city's cultural fabric. The Muny, as it is called, "was as much a part of my childhood as Sunday school and soda fountains," Mary said. The Muny and other theatres in St. Louis cemented her lifelong affection for acting. "From the time I was able to stay awake without a nap, I was taken to matinees in the theatre and later to evening performances," she said.

The cold months, too, were special, with caroling on Christmas Eve. "I can still hear the dry crunch of snow under my goulashes. I can feel my red angora cap and muffler scratching my neck. And my mittens on a tape that went down one sleeve across my back and down the other sleeve. I remember the thrilling words of those old carols. And I can remember the good hot cocoa Mother made when we got home," Mary said.

Frank and Isabella modeled civic behavior for Mary; in their case, this meant engaging in fraternal lodge activities. Frank was a 32nd degree Mason and active in the Shriners' Moolah Temple in St. Louis, while Isabella was a matron of the Tuscan chapter of the Order of the Eastern Star and active in the Temple Club, which raised money for Shriners Hospitals. She held leadership positions in the Missouri Federation of Women's Clubs, and, since she did not work outside the home, had time for civic affairs organizations like the Good Will Club of St. Louis. Despite their differences in political views, Isabella was friendly with Edna Gellhorn, a liberal community activist and pioneering suffragist. "If there was a party at the Gellhorns, Mary's mother would be there," Westheimer says. Frank and Isabella's Masonic activities rubbed off on Mary, who became queen of her chapter, or "bethel," of Job's Daughters, a social and charitable organization for adolescent girls that is rooted in Masonic traditions.

The Wickenhausers were not people of means, but Frank's job kept them comfortable. "Everything was devoted to Mary, but she was not the kind to want something unreasonable. If it was for Mary, I'm sure her mother would have found the money somehow," says Mary Vahle. At Mercantile-Commerce Bank and Trust Company, where he was for many years an assistant auditor, Frank had mid-level responsibilities for the bank's financial reports. Co-workers affectionately called him simply "Wick." "Everybody liked Wick," says Eugene Fincke, who worked with Frank. "He always had a positive attitude about things. If he was looking for a little joshing around, he'd come around with a smile on his face and ask you a leading question. He was very proud of his daughter, but wasn't one of these fellows who was touting his kid. If somebody said they saw her in a play, you could see a big smile on his face and he'd talk about it, but you had to draw it out of him."

Frank wore an elastic garter around his shirtsleeves while working, as was the custom. His desk was positioned in an open space on a suspended balcony overlooking over the lobby. From this central perch, he could see many parts of the bank at once—and others could get his attention, which helped minimize the effects of his poor hearing. "When I went to the bank, because that's where my safe deposit box was, I'd run up and talk to him. I can remember my voice being so loud as I tried to talk to him. I can see him now on the balcony. He'd lean over and he could barely hear you," says Westheimer, who, at the time, worked for a men's clothier. No doubt growing up with a parent so hard of hearing influenced Mary, who learned early to enunciate clearly and project her voice. If she did not make herself heard, life at home would be more difficult. Later, Frank often assessed Mary's performances by how well he could hear them. One night in 1943, after listening to the *Meet Corliss Archer* show on the radio, he wrote Mary to say, "You were wonderful and I heard every word you spoke."

Across the street from the bank was a little restaurant called Quigley's. In the early 1930s, Westheimer occasionally would try to take Frank to lunch. "I was making eighteen bucks a week, and he wouldn't let me. He'd say, 'This man's money is no good—I'll take care of it.' I liked the old man very much. He and I used to drink a little. Once in a while, if he'd see me in the bank, he'd say, 'Lou, come over and have a drink with me at the Mayfair [Hotel]' and I'd have a drink with him occasionally there. He liked bourbon." Was Frank good company? "Not really. He was sort of a bore. But he liked me, and he knew his wife [liked me]. He admired me so much because I was the only guy taking Mary out in those days, though he never said that."

Frank was a baseball fan who rooted for the Browns and often took young Mary to games at Sportsman's Park, the city's iconic ballpark. She loved the sweet cold drinks she would get there, like Orange Whistle or Green River. On Saturdays, Frank sometimes took Mary to the private St. Louis Mercantile Library, the oldest library west of the Mississippi. Afterward, they might meet Isabella for a chocolate ice cream at the Herz candy and baked goods shop. Those library visits left a strong impression on Mary and inspired a love of reading. "The librarians granted me the great privilege of going back in the stacks and selecting my books. I went right down the shelves from Alcott, Dickens to Tarkington and Walpole, opening doors to vistas I have never forgotten," she recalled. She read the *Bobbsey Twins* books by Laura Lee Hope, the *Five Little Peppers* series by Margaret Sidney, the *Live Doll* series by Josephine Scribner Gates, and Louisa May Alcott's tales. *Little Women* was her first "grown-up book" and remained a lifelong favorite. How fortunate, then, that Mary would one day help bring that story to life on film.

Frank's one real friend was Harvey Alexander, the local funeral director he met through lodge activities. The men's families became close. "In those days, most of the entertaining was done at home and since they had only one child and we had four, they came to our home a lot. They were just lovely people," says Higginbotham, Alexander's daughter.

As the Depression loomed, Frank was forced to take a salary cut and—like so many—lost much of the money he had invested. Mary's thrifty approach to money was forever shaped by this turn of events.

As much as Mary enjoyed her father, it was her mother who was the defining figure in her life. In some ways, Mary and Isabella developed a sibling-like relationship that allowed Isabella to continue to have a sister after Hes's early death in 1920. Mary would become Isabella's constant companion throughout life and Isabella her daughter's trusted source of advice. There was no rebelling against a protective motherly influence here; if anything, Mary welcomed it. "Mary was always very sweet to her father, but she and her mother had a lot more in common. They were peas in a pod—very, very much alike. I think her mother enjoyed Mary's success as much as Mary did," Higginbotham says. Mary herself once observed that Isabella "had a wonderful sense of humor [and] was much younger than I in her outlook. My mother was not an actress, but she could have been."

That Mary and Isabella shared a name caused no end of confusion, especially because they also both used "Isabelle" and "Isabella" interchangeably. Mary's mother went by Isabelle almost as often as by Isabella. Mary was officially Mary Isabella, but until she began working, she was always called "Mary Isabelle," as if her first name were hyphenated.

Later, she used "Isabella" when a middle name was called for. Confusion reigned until the end: Death certificates for both mother and daughter use "Isabelle," but both women chose "Isabella" for their tombstones.

Mary began public school at Cupples School on Cote Brilliante Avenue, only a few blocks from the Wickenhauser home, in the school's first year of operation. She would attend there only a year, as Frank and Isabella decided to move farther from downtown. Even at a young age, Mary demonstrated the resistance to change that would become one of her strongest character traits. When her family moved from her birthplace when she was nine, she wrote a sentimental song about longing for her old home. "Carry Me Back to Garfield Avenue," to be sung to the tune of "Carry Me Back to Old Virginny," was a sweet ode to "playmates," "good times," her "happy baby-hood," and where her "heart longed to go." The Wickenhausers moved to 2104 Harris Avenue, a three-story brick house with an exterior landing of pretty blue and white tiles, right on the edge of O'Fallon Park. That's close to Fairground Park and not far from Sportsman's Park, so Mary could continue enjoying outdoor activities.

While attending Harrison Elementary School from 1918 to 1922, Mary was interested in writing, not performing. Just before her tenth birthday in 1920, she hand made her own edition of the *Harrison Weekly Magazine*, a surprisingly sophisticated fourteen-page effort, complete with an orderly table of contents, colorful cover artwork, an assortment of news and playful writings, and the notation "Mary I. Wickenhauser, editor."

Her knack for performing was evident nonetheless. When the Junior Auxiliary and Ladies Guild was organizing a gala in 1919, a committee member asked little Mary if she would read a verse to entertain the guests. Revealing herself every bit the take-charge woman she would become—setting boundaries, attending to proper appearance, and communicating in a mannerly fashion—eight-year-old Mary responded in writing, "I will gladly recite it only I want to ask you if the first and third verse [only] will be all right. It makes very good sense [as] I have pretty much home work to do and don't see how I can get it in and another thing I have a little Kate-Greenaway dress with a little bonnet will it be all right if I wear that." Mary received a proper reply from the committee member: "It is very sweet of you to add more work to your already fully occupied days and I assure you that I appreciate the extra effort you will make for this. The first and third verses will do very nicely and,

I am quite sure, in the dear little costume you speak of, you will make a picture we will all enjoy." Mary was also a cut-up. Completing school forms in 1923, she identified herself as "Iama Nutt" on 235 Hop Alley, the daughter of "Iwasa Lover," who worked as a street cleaner. Two years later, she became "Iona Ford," the child of "Ialso Ona Ford."

The family lived on Harris for six years, until Aunt Hes's daughter Elizabeth came to live with them when Grandma Shannon died in 1924 (Grandma and Grandpa Shannon had taken Elizabeth in when Hes died in 1920). Mary's family now moved into a three-bedroom, one-bathroom upstairs flat at 4120 Farlin Avenue, just four doors from Fairground Park. Mary lived here through most of her teenage years, but continued child-like pastimes, such as playing with dolls. The father of girlfriend Dorothy McCauley built a large, elaborate dollhouse designed to break into two parts; McCauley played with her dolls in one half while Mary played with her own in the other. The two girls also dressed paper dolls in different outfits.

These years saw more serious pursuits as well. At Yeatman High School—where Mary was teased as Mary "Wicken-trousers"—she especially enjoyed debate. She remained active in Job's Daughters, which entertained at nursing homes and presented community shows to fund Christmas baskets for the poor. Mary was featured in most of the shows. "All that girl had to do was walk across the stage and lean on the piano and we were in hysterics. I don't know why it was so funny, but it was. And she wasn't even trying," says Mary Vahle. With all-women casts, Mary invariably played men. This was the case in *Flood Sufferers* and *Belle of Barcelona* (both 1927), *Sweethearts* (1928) and *Spring Maid* (1929). The weeks Mary spent as a camp counselor during several summers at the Frank Wyman Outing Farm near Eureka, Missouri, fueled her affection for performing. The camp brought underprivileged children from the city to the country for a rural experience. "We had a wardrobe trunk and got all gussied up and dramatized fairy tales for the kids," she recalled fondly.

Mary graduated in 1926 from Beaumont High School, which had opened to alleviate crowding at Yeatman. There was never a question that Mary would go to college. Because Frank and Isabella felt strongly that she should remain in St. Louis, Mary chose to attend Washington University, the premier school in the area. Universities in general did not attract many out-of-town students in those days, so Mary's class was rather close knit. Many of her classmates had gone to high school together, would continue on to college together, and would remain in St.

Louis, where they would build careers and families and belong to the same country clubs. Fifty years after graduating, many still lived within a fifteen-minute drive of one another.

The university offered Mary a scholarship, but Frank declined it, saying he was able to put his daughter through school and someone else might need it more. Perhaps he regretted that generosity a few years later when, like so many others in those tough economic times, he was forced to take a pay cut. Tuition was $250 per semester in 1926 for those who did not live on campus, but even this sum was too great for some of Mary's classmates. Virginia Weber Hoffmann was forced to drop out after two years because her father, who worked for a shoe company, lost everything, and she had to help the family. Helen Margaret Aff-Drum remained enrolled but experienced the strain of the period. "Everyone thought I was in mourning because I had a black coat and black dress and black everything, but it was because we had no money for anything new and this way everything matched," she says.

Mary entered college in September 1926, having just turned sixteen. That's younger that most, but she had been pushed ahead two years in grade school. This practice, used to alleviate crowding, was not uncommon in St. Louis during that period. Others in her class had also been pushed ahead, such as Stella Koetter Darrow, who skipped the third and fifth grades, and Dorothy Hempleman Haase, who skipped two grades and entered Washington University at fifteen.

"She grew up a lot in those several years. She was fairly quiet in the beginning—if you're young on the campus and everybody has more social maturity than you do, one tends to be a little quiet. She was kind of boyish and young and hardy. I don't know if she belonged to the YMCA, but she was that type—the kind you'd think of as playing hockey. Over the next several years, she became more feminine and blossomed and her talents began to show," says classmate Dorothy Conzelman Nash. When Mary came from New York for a visit years later, "I was so struck by how she had a hold of herself and was particularly charming. We saw a slightly awkward young girl develop into a clown—but a sensitive and really very attractive woman," she says. Classmate Mary Jane Moise says, "She was an unusual person, just a little different. I can't say how, exactly. It's not that she was really *mannish*. She just wasn't quite like the rest of the girls." Many students used to clamor up the steep outdoor steps at Kingsbury, which runs beside the university. Mary Jane Roach Masters remembers, "One day we were both rushing to make an eight thirty class, and Mary was ahead of me. She turned around and said,

'Pardon me lady, did you drop a fish?' I just roared with laughter and we went to classes. She was a fundamentally comic person who just made that up at the moment." Off campus, Mary showed the same humor. At the Alexanders' open houses at Christmas, "She was always on," says Ruth Alexander Stubbs, "like picking up a loaf of French bread and acting like it was a baseball bat." Sally Alexander Higginbotham remembers, "Mary Isabelle almost always did a reading or something she had worked up. She was always gracious about it, almost eager to perform."

Mary majored in English literature and political science and intended to enroll in law school. She began performing in plays through the school's dramatic society, Thyrsus, and in musicals through its Quandrangle Club. She became the clubs' most popular actress, far more prominent than she might become today, because the school was then a great deal smaller. Her time in university theatricals was a heady period, although she may not have realized it then. Several of her classmates who were in these productions would become nationally known. Howard Morgens, the son of a St. Louis dry cleaner, became president of household products giant Proctor & Gamble. Clark Clifford became a prominent lawyer and Washington insider, advising U.S. presidents Truman, Kennedy, Johnson, and Carter. Clifford later said his college dramatics had been "invaluable" preparation for his later appearances before juries and public speaking. Kitty Fink, a brash student two years behind Mary, changed her name and became celebrated as actress and nightclub performer Kay Thompson, who also wrote the charming *Eloise at the Plaza* stories.

At the time, these were simply peers who collaborated on theatrical productions—not skits, but proper two- and three-act productions. Among the most memorable was *Si, Si, Senorita*, a two-act comedy with eighteen musical numbers that played at the city's American Theatre in May 1930. Clifford directed the show, Morgens was its production manager, Thompson was its musical director, and Mary played a professor's wife in this story about the antics of geology students studying in Mexico. Mary remained in touch with Morgens but ultimately had little in common with Clifford and even less with Thompson. In many ways, Mary and Thompson seem of the same world: Both were born in St. Louis, developed strong, independent personalities, embarked upon careers as performers, knew many of the same people in the industry, and lived during the same period. (Thompson was born one year before Mary and died three years after Mary did.) In between, their lives could not have been more different. In fact, although they performed in some of the same productions and appear in a 1931 yearbook photo together, they probably socialized little. "Mary was like most of my friends. We were all kind of from a mold in those days, very much alike and very properly brought up. But Kay was very different," says Virginia Weber Hoffmann, a close friend of Thompson. "She was very avant-garde. She was willing to bend the rules, willing to strike out and do as she pleased, rather rebellious. We'd go down to the YMCA together and entertain— Kay would play the piano and we both sang. We had a rollicking time. We'd go to speakeasies and drink beer, and this was during Prohibition. Kay was a musical genius—she could sing and dance and compose music and write books—and a genius, period."

Edmund Hartmann was active in the performing arts at Washington University at the same time, and was also impressed with Thompson. "She was a marvelous pianist, a great musician," he says. She was rehearsal pianist for *Princess Nita*, a production he wrote and Clifford directed. But Hartmann, who later became a screenwriter and producer in Hollywood, found that once Thompson established her career, she distanced herself from St. Louis. Her father was a pawnbroker, a fact she especially did not want known. In later years in Los Angeles, Hartmann often ran into Thompson. "She'd see me coming and beat it fast because she didn't want it known that she was Kitty Fink. Once, about 1950, a friend took me to Lena Horne's dressing room at the Cocoanut Grove and Kitty came in and saw me and got right the hell out. I think she had developed a new personality and new background and tried to make it a realistic one," he says.

As college activities became a greater part of Mary's life, Frank and Isabella looked for a home closer to the university. In 1928, they left North Saint Louis and rented a flat in a multi-unit building at 6180 Pershing Avenue in the more desirable University City (the building no longer exists). The family celebrated with "a little luncheon party for Mary," remembers Mary Vahle. Eight teenagers at two tables played Auction, a popular card game then. Vahle says Mary was sometimes ill at ease around other girls, and that "her mother was trying to get her to relax more and be with other people." Partly, Mary was self-conscious about her appearance. "Some time or other, it always gets around to boys, and there was no boy in Mary's life. She was always tall, and that's a drawback. And Mary had a receding chin and a big nose. Boys that age don't look beyond the surface," Vahle says. When there were dances or other events where boys would bring dates, "She just didn't show up for those things." It's also true that height was a greater obstacle in that era, when most boys would not ask a taller girl to dance. By the time she entered college, Mary was taller than both of her parents.

Mary was consistently a B student, and she threw herself into campus activities. She became president of the freshman commission, president of her Phi Mu sorority, president of Mortar Board and treasurer of the Panhellenic Association. She was on the women's intercollegiate debating team, the women's building executive committee and the junior prom committee. With Mary flourishing in the university environment, the family moved even closer to school for the 1929–30 term—and became homeowners for the first time. Frank and Isabella bought a home at 6830 Pershing Avenue in Ames Place, a private neighborhood of two hundred homes. The move made the university practically Mary's backyard, and it allowed Frank to commute to work easily by streetcar.

This was the family's biggest step up yet. The neighborhood was graced by nice sidewalks, distinctive cast iron street lamps, and attractive oaks and sycamores. Then as now, the home featured sixteen hundred square feet on two floors, plus an unfinished basement, where the Wickenhausers stored coal for heating and cooking. Its exterior is of textured red and gray brick and was adorned in Mary's day with dark green shutters. It is the only home in Ames Place with its particular floor plan, since its developer built no other homes there. Downstairs, the Wickenhausers had a foyer, a living room with a fireplace, a large dining room, and a modest kitchen with an icebox. Ice was delivered to the back door and put in the lower part of the box, keeping food on the upper shelves cool. Upstairs were three bedrooms, a small sun porch, and the home's only bathroom, which featured the white and black porcelain common to early twentieth-century indoor bathrooms. Mary's bedroom window offered an unobstructed view of the campus. The house backs up to Millbrook Boulevard. Washington University was called a "streetcar college" in those years because one of many streetcar lines ran on Millbrook, right beside the school. Mary would cross the track on foot in the five-minute walk to campus.

The house was furnished largely with antiques, not the kind acquired as collectibles, but the kind that become antiques simply by virtue of how many generations they have been in the family. This was the 1834 wedding furniture of Mary's great-great grandparents Milton N. and Mary Johnston McLean, passed down over the decades. Mary lived her entire life with this dark, heavy, traditional American Empire furniture, including mahogany loveseats originally upholstered in horsehair.

Sunday nights were special at the Wickenhauser home that year, Mary's last year of school. Isabella would make a big batch of waffles, a classmate of Mary's would bring homemade sausage from his family's farm in Edwardsville, Illinois, and students would gather for dinner and long conversations. The Wickenhauser home was such a gathering place that the family kept a key to the front door concealed outside the house, "and very often we'd come home to find some of my friends from the dorm waiting for us," Mary said. Frank was the unambiguous head of the home. "He ran that household, I tell you. What Mr. Wickenhauser wanted, he got. Mrs. Wickenhauser adored him, and if he wanted steak for supper, there was steak for supper," Louis Westheimer says. Yet on these evenings, "Frank would just sort of sit there and *beam* on us. He was so proud of Mary and her friends," says Amy Jane Harrison Ax, who became a lifelong friend after she and Mary met in college. She says Frank was "just like a father to us." He joked with Mary's college friends "if he had a chance. Between Mary and me and Mrs. Wick, what could poor Frank say?" More than sixty years later, Ax breaks up in laughter recalling some of the dinner table antics of Mary and her mother. Isabella cooked and Frank made Old Fashioneds "with a good brand of bourbon, not bathtub liquor, and this may have been during Prohibition," she says.

Mary so loved what this house meant—the seamless melding of her home life and her university life—that, over time, she came to describe it as the home she grew up in. During scores of visits to St. Louis over the years, she expressed no interest in her youth in North St. Louis. It was as if she had been born in 1929, the start of her final year of college.

Mary's affection for her parents extended to her family's broader history. She was proud of her family on her mother's side and its role in U.S. history, often referring to two distinguished ancestors. One was William Kinney (1781–1843), who served as lieutenant governor of Illinois from 1826 to 1830. He was Mary's great, great, great-grandfather, and Mary and her mother are named after Kinney's daughter Isabella. The other was John McLean (1785–1861), who served as a U.S. Supreme Court justice for three decades. Mary especially took pride in McLean having issued one of two dissenting opinions in the court's infamous *Dred Scott* case striking down the rights and freedoms of African Americans. In his opinion, McLean, the most senior associate justice at the time, accused Missouri of undermining harmony within the union and criticized racist elements of the majority opinion, saying "the argument . . . that a colored citizen would not be an agreeable member of society" was "more a matter of taste than of law." One scholar called McLean's dissent "solid and powerful" and a strong statement of Northern rights.

But John McLean was not Mary's great, great-grandfather, as she always said: He was her great-great-grandfather's uncle. It's unlikely that Mary intentionally misled people about her tie to one of the court's great dissenters. Instead, perhaps because of limited family records, Mary somehow simply misunderstood. Justice John McLean was married twice (to Rebecca Edwards and, after her 1840 death, to Sarah Bella Garrard), but neither woman has any ancestral connection to Mary. Mary's true ancestor was the justice's nephew, Milton N. McLean (1810–55), son of Nathaniel McLean (1787–1871). It was Milton who married Mary Johnston (1813–77) and fathered Mary's great-grandmother Hester McLean (1838–99). Hester became an important figure in Illinois history after marrying army captain John Randolph Thomas (1836–80), who came from a distinguished family in Belleville, Illinois—in the process uniting the McLeans and Thomases, two prominent midwestern families. Captain Thomas's father was Colonel John Randolph Thomas (1800–94), who served the Union in the 142nd Illinois Infantry during the entirety of the Civil War. His son the captain commanded a company in the 117th Illinois Infantry.

In fact, to understand how Mary's family history influenced her life, it must be remembered that the Civil War preceded Mary by little more than a generation. In 1900, just ten years before Mary's birth, her grandmother Shannon and her great aunt Belle Rentchler each received $25 from the U.S. Treasury, partial compensation owed Captain John R. Thomas, now due them as the daughters of a Civil War soldier. Virtually everything related to the Thomas lineage was special in Mary's eyes, something to be treated reverently. For most of her life, in a red storage trunk, she kept some of her great-grandmother Thomas's clothing, as well as Grandma Shannon's bridal garments.

Strangely, as proud as Mary was of her Thomas and McLean lineage, she displayed no such affection for the Wickenhauser side. "She always talked about the Thomases, and mostly about the captain who was in the Civil War," says Bill Dorsam, Mary's first cousin once removed, the son of Aunt Hes's daughter, Elizabeth. "I never heard her talk of the Wickenhauser side."

Again and again, Mary said she knew of no surviving family on the Wickenhauser side because her father was an only child. A few years before she died, she sent the most minimal reply possible to an inquiring amateur family genealogist, Edward Wickenhauser, of Godfrey, Illinois. It is true that Frank was an only child, but Frank's father, August, was one of about nine children, a brood that resulted in Mary having many Wickenhauser aunts, uncles, and cousins. At least three of Frank's aunts lived in the St. Louis area at the time of Mary's birth, making it impossible for Mary to be unaware of at least some Wickenhauser relatives. Carrie Wickenhauser appeared in the St. Louis city directory as the widow of Edward, Frank's uncle, every year Mary lived there: from 1910, when Mary was born, until 1934, when Mary left home. Alvina Wickenhauser was such a part of the family that she presented Frank and Isabella with a red quilt as a wedding gift and Mary with a gift for her first birthday. Emily Wickenhauser married Ernst Haller, a prominent resident in nearby Highland, Illinois, described as a "well-known fellow-citizen" by a newspaper of the day.

It is possible that Mary wanted to disassociate herself from her German roots, given the strong anti-German sentiment in the United States during her youth. Certainly in St. Louis, with its strong German heritage, most people understood the name Wickenhauser to be German. Her own Pershing Avenue—the street she most enjoyed living on in St. Louis—had long been called Berlin Avenue, but in 1918 anti-German sentiment emanating from the First World War prompted it to be re-named after the general in charge of American expedition forces. Mary was quick to offer up that her father was English and Swiss; in fact, he was German and Swiss. Frank's grandfather Lorenz Wickenhauser and great-grandfather Franz Wikkenhauser were born in 1816 and 1785, respectively, in Nenzingen, in an area of Germany known in the mid-nineteenth century as Grand Duke of Baden. Lorenz immigrated to the United States in 1835 and married Regina Suppiger, who was Swiss. Together, they raised about nine children in Highland, Illinois, one of whom was Frank's father, August.

Mary's introduction to performing outside the university setting came courtesy of a favorite English professor, William G. B. Carson. Carson was on the board of the fledgling St. Louis Little Theatre and encouraged Mary to participate. The Little Theatre, with about two hundred and fifty seats, managed to produce about six plays a year at 812 Union Boulevard. It was an important part of the community in a time of fewer entertainment options than today—to be sure, there was no television. Because the theatre was an all-volunteer effort, rehearsals took place at night to accommodate the actors' day jobs. Most of the performers were not students; Mary was an exception, as was Alfred Gellhorn, a young man from a prominent family who went on to a distinguished medical career in New York. For Mary, the Little Theatre was a dream. It kept her evenings occupied, since boys were not asking her out. It created an important social outlet, since the cast members socialized together frequently. And it cost little as entertainment, a critical factor in those years.

Each season, the Little Theatre brought in a different, experienced director from outside St. Louis. This is how Mary came to know Thomas Wood Stevens, artistic director of Chicago's Goodman Theatre. Stevens was also well known for designing elaborate celebrations called "pageants" for special public events in the early 1900s. He became a mentor to Mary, and, in short order, Mary was involved with most of the Little Theatre productions. "She was very workman-like, all business, and immensely likeable," says Mary Jane Masters, who was also part of the troupe. Between Mary's last year of college (1929–30) and 1934, she performed in *Alison's House* (Louise), *Cock Robin* (Maria Scott), *The Constant Nymph* (Kate Sanger), *Escape* (Dolly), *The Good Fairy* (Karoline), and *The Makropoulos Secret* (Marie), among others. She took any kind of role. In the *Follies of 1934*, she played Jo in a parody called *Little Women—Just Little Women*, but also played a medieval character in head-to-toe, Lancelot-like chainmail.

Frank and Isabella supported Mary in all of this. "Her parents worshipped her. The opening night of any play that she was in, they were *right there*, father and mother," says Westheimer. For Mary, the Little Theatre experience did not end when the curtain came down. The theatre's basement featured a large private room, a gathering place called "the crypt." Once the stage was stripped of scenery and performers removed their costumes and make-up, the crypt became home to after-theatre shows, skits, and midnight parties. "Nobody had any money, and we could put on a party for very little. We'd get a three-piece orchestra to come in there and play, or have a dance," says Archer O'Reilly, who was active in the Little Theatre. Mary often acted-out characters from Helen Hokinson's *New Yorker* cartoons, those plump society women who passed their time at beauty parlours, art galleries, and Lane Bryant. (One of the few non-theatre books in Mary's library when she died was *The Ladies, God Bless 'em*, a collection of Hokinson cartoons.)

She completed college in June 1930, days before her twentieth birthday. Having graduated at the height of the Depression, Mary was uncertain what path to pursue, as law school would require funds her family no longer had. She enrolled in stenography classes, reasoning that at least she would learn a new skill. From the fall of 1930 through June of 1931, she attended classes daily at Hadley Vocational School on Waterman Avenue. "We were all pretty serious about it, wanting to get it [done] and get out," says Marcella Wiget MacDermott, a university classmate who entered Hadley with Mary. Mary took to shorthand and for years used it to make notes to herself; in her papers, it can be found scribbled on the backs of envelopes, letters, notes, and telegrams. But her heart was not in secretarial work.

She used her popularity on campus to secure a job as the university's assistant publicity director. For the next four years, she worked in the school's news bureau, preparing press releases and articles in an office in Eads Hall. The bureau oversaw the yearbook and campus humor magazine, and began the first alumni magazine, *The Alumni Bulletin*. Mary also functioned as liaison between the administration and students on the *Student Life* newspaper. "She was good at taking the bull by the horns," says Dorothy Conzelman Nash, the bureau's secretary, who notes that their boss, Ray Howes, used to say Mary "has the nerve of a brass monkey." Howes sometimes left Mary in charge, says Julian Miller, a *Student Life* editor in that period. "Whenever we would be taking a test, maybe English, Mary would be there as the monitor, the faculty person supervising to see that there was no cheating, no talking. You know, 'No nonsense, keep your mouth shut, write your papers and get done,'" he says.

She did not let the university job prevent her from taking every imaginable opportunity to act, and she did not confine her performances to the Little Theatre. In 1931, she began performing in the radio edition of *Transit News*, which aired Monday evenings on WIL. Attending her sorority's annual conventions in 1929 (Cape Cod, Massachusetts) and 1931 (Colorado Springs), Mary took charge of skits for the big entertainment nights. She developed a one-woman show of monologues based on Dorothy Parker's work, something she would return to during her career. She wrote a comedy skit for a fashion pageant, judged a local oratory contest, performed for the College Club of St. Louis and the Washington University Employees Club, and with the Alumni Players. She presented monologues to the American Association of University Women and was mistress of ceremonies for a League of Women Voters revue. She performed for the National Council of Jewish Women and for the Missouri Federation of Women's Clubs. She performed on the *Heart-to-Heart Club*,

Westheimer's live KMOX radio dramatizations of romantic problems. And when a local dentist asked Mary to write a pageant for the seventy-fifth anniversary of the university's dental school, she accepted.

She so wanted to perform that she continued appearing in school productions even after graduating. Among these was *Rose of Arizona*, a piece of burlesque originally presented in the *Garrick Gaieties of 1926* in New York. In the St. Louis version of 1933, Mary had only a small part, playing a Mexican girl named Pimento, because she also was directing. "She seemed to know what she was doing. I used to kind of wonder, 'Where did she learn all this about show business?'" says Nelson Hower, who played a cowboy. When the play sold out in the law school auditorium, the palatial Fox Theatre invited the show to its stage, where *Rose of Arizona* played for about a week. Because the Fox had money and wanted to do it right, Hower was put on a horse. "I may be the only one who ever rode a real live horse across the Fox stage," he says.

Writing still was never far from her mind, and in July 1932, she enrolled in a newspaper practice course at Columbia University in New York, receiving a B+. Then, returning to St. Louis, Mary was adrift. She had made her peace with life as a university communications officer by day and amateur performer by night because the environment was comfortable, her income enabled her to help her parents, she could walk to work, and theatricals enabled a social life. But should she seek work as a journalist? Should she pursue a law career? She remained uncertain. Her greatest pleasure now came from the theatre, so when an opportunity arose for a paying acting role, she jumped at it. Her first professional appearances were in 1933 as Sophia in *Reunion in Vienna* and Helen Hallam in *Another Language*, both with the Arthur Casey Stock Company. She received good notices, like this one for *Another Language*: "A point of particular interest was the appearance of that natural comedienne, Mary Wickenhauser, of Washington University and the Little Theatre, who played one of the Hallam wives almost as if she belonged to it."

After these two professional experiences, she began to believe an acting career was possible. She found paying jobs with the local Mary Hart stock company and the touring Ben Greet Players. Although she had more than one hundred amateur performances to her credit, she wondered if proper dramatic training would help her go farther. In mid-1933, she turned to Thomas Wood Stevens for advice. "As for further schooling, I'd say No. You have a very special sort of personality to market, and I doubt if further schoolwork would help you to find the part you want. If you don't land anything, and Casey goes on in St. Louis next winter,

I'd say get in as much as you can with him. When the right sort of part comes up for you, you'll have no difficulty with it. The trouble is to find the part—if it isn't in a [good] play, no display of technique on your part will help," he replied. "You're probably doing the very best thing now. I mean, going about the offices is all there is to do. That, and make all the acquaintances you can, pull all the strings you can, follow your hunches, and when you hear a rumor, get there first."

It was an amateur show at the end of the year that finally opened the door. In the Little Theatre's *Solid South*, a farce that opened on December 5, 1933, Mary played the spinster Aunt Geneva, an elderly character role that required her to douse her hair heavily with talcum powder. One local reviewer called Mary "easily the outstanding performer," and another said Aunt Geneva was "delightfully played with a rich southern accent hardly to be expected by a lady bearing the name of Mary Wickenhauser." Mary's work in *Solid South* impressed that season's visiting director, F. Cowles Strickland, who had co-founded the famous Berkshire Playhouse in Stockbridge, Massachusetts. "Strick" saw potential in Mary and invited her to be part of the Berkshire Playhouse company the following season. He was making no long-term promises, but he offered an apprenticeship of sorts because, while he had good instincts about her, he had not yet seen her perform with other professionals.

Although she was twenty-three, Mary was not about to move across the country without Frank and Isabella's permission. They wanted to meet Strick first. "He was invited to dinner and mother and dad asked him where I'd be living, with whom, would I be chaperoned, what kind of set up it was—they put him over the ropes. He told me afterwards that he had never been interviewed before about an actress. He usually did the interviewing," Mary said. Strick passed muster, and Mary made plans to quit her university job, leave home, and embark on a new career— three very big changes all at once for a woman who did not like change.

CHAPTER TWO

From Stockbridge to the Mercury Theatre

MARY ISABELLA WICKENHAUSER BECAME MARY WICKES SO CAVALIERLY that she almost missed it. Some weeks before Mary arrived at Stockbridge in 1934, Strick wrote to keep her abreast of preparations for the summer season—the plays selected for production, rehearsal schedules, costumes and the like—and inserted this casual note: "By the way, you are Mary Wickes. We'll take out the E if you don't like it." Wickenhauser, he later told her, was simply too long for the Playhouse's marquee.

Mary adopted her new name without objection, one of the few times in her life she accepted significant change without a fight. She did so partly because she knew what an opportunity like Stockbridge meant, and partly because Strick had already demonstrated judgment that Mary could trust. But she clung to her middle name in personal contexts and years later would still use "Mary I." when signing letters to friends from her youth. She even asked Lucille Ball's television writers to change her characters' names in a couple of *Here's Lucy* episodes from "Jan" and "Mary" to "Isabel."

A summer at the Berkshire Playhouse was a big boon to any young performer's career. It may be hard today to appreciate the influence of the Playhouse during those years. Before air travel became common, audiences drove from perhaps a hundred miles in all directions to this reliable source of quality productions with skilled actors and a climate considerably cooler than Manhattan in summer. This was the beginning of the era of summer theatres, which were opening in many places, and the Berkshire Playhouse, in a building designed by Stanford White originally as a casino, was by any measure the most desirable house on the circuit—for performers and audiences alike.

Mary was determined to make the most of the experience. Being a member of the Stockbridge company allowed her at least one trapping that the non-paying Little Theatre never had: a proper theatrical trunk, upright with hanging space on one side and drawers on the other. By coincidence, the premier maker of wardrobe trunks for traveling theater folk, Herkert & Meisel, was in St. Louis. "Oh! The big, big, excitement was buying a trunk. I can still remember the day we went down, Mother and I and maybe Dad, too, [to] a funny old place on Washington Boulevard where they sold nothing but luggage and these fine H&M trunks. I selected a lovely tan [one] with an orange stripe around it. And they put my initials on it, oh mercy! It was a real honest-to-goodness wardrobe trunk. So I began to really feel like a professional actress now—I had an H&M."

When she arrived in Stockbridge, Mary went straight into the Playhouse's resident company of eight to ten performers who presented about ten plays over eleven weeks. In 1934, Strick introduced a change at the Playhouse, abandoning a conventional stock format in which one new play was presented each week while another was in rehearsal, for a repertory format that presented a different play each night.

Performers mostly did their own makeup and hair and, recalls longtime Playhouse actor William Roerick, "often helped re-upholster the furniture" on the set. The rigor and discipline of this schedule held enormous appeal for Mary, who thrived on the collaborative nature of repertory, in which the same actors performed together in very different offerings. This meant Mary had the opportunity to play, in one season, everything from a country wench in *As You Like It*, to a German maid in *Biography*, to a puritanical landlady in *Saturday's Children*. And she did so with a stable of talented, capable performers. "When I first came here, everyone in that company could have been either a star or a first featured player in a New York company," she said later. "I had learned by watching very, very, very good people."

Stockbridge became a safe haven of sorts, somewhere Mary felt comfortable returning again and again. The Berkshire Playhouse was her first proper training ground, the place where she honed the comedy skills she would use for the next sixty years. She was never part of the Playhouse's famous apprentice program, where young actors spent their mornings refining the panoply of actors' skills—voice projection, breathing exercises, improvisation, pantomime, dance, handling props—and their afternoons working on scenes from different plays. But it was in Stockbridge that she found pleasure in living arrangements shared with other actors, building lifelong friendships in the process. And it was here that Mary developed an almost puritan work ethic, scrubbing dressing room floors that weren't clean enough, scolding others for not arriving to rehearsals on time, and rolling her eyes at actors who tried to improve the playwright's words.

"It was awfully good to have played at Stockbridge, to put it on your dossier. It was slightly prestigious, as it was much better than any of the other summer theatres. It was run so very, very well, and the whole thing was stylish," says Jane Wyatt, whose career began at the Berkshire Playhouse. "I went to the apprentice school at Stockbridge—a thriving school with lots of courses and very distinguished teachers. You took Shakespeare and pantomime, and all this," she says, noting that George Colouris was one of her instructors. "I did a few little parts on the main stage and the next summer they asked me to come back as the ingénue. I thought, my gosh, if I'm going to be the ingénue next summer, I better go on the stage in New York and get some experience. So I didn't go back to college, although I was president of the dramatic club and everything else. I was at Barnard and they were quite annoyed."

After the 1934 season, in which Mary performed in eight plays, she was invited back the next four summer seasons—and quickly accepted each time, reasoning that doing so would allow her to remain on the East Coast in the summer and therefore positioned to look for stage work during Broadway's fall and winter season. These seasons would be more manageable, for in 1935 the Playhouse returned to a format of presenting a new play each week. The repertory experiment proved grueling for performers, too complicated for a crew that had to move new scenery in and out every day, and too confusing for audiences. Many had been attending regularly on a certain night of the week, and "if they were the Tuesday night people, they would arrive sometimes the following Tuesday and find the same play," remembers Billy Miles, who began managing the Playhouse in 1935.

That season marked a new era, as much for a change in leadership as for a return to a conventional schedule. Miles replaced Strick, who left Stockbridge for a career that would include drama and teaching positions at Wesleyan University, Stanford University, and Arena Stage in Washington, D.C. Miles left a lasting legacy at the Playhouse and, in the process, became as close to being a mentor to Mary as anyone she encountered in her career. It was only due to good fortune that she was there for virtually the entirety of the early Miles years (1935 to 1941), which one historical account says "must surely be considered the heyday of the Berkshire Playhouse." Often, Miles augmented the resident company with a star performer brought in from New York, and Mary had the chance to play opposite greats like Ethel Barrymore and Ina Claire, learning by "watching these live textbooks," she said. Mary was asked to accompany Barrymore one day in her limousine and serve as an escort of sorts. "She told me she thought I had talent, which I appreciated very much. She said, 'I want you to remember one thing, and I'm sure you will. Always admire the theatre in yourself, and not yourself in the theatre.' I wish that could be emblazoned on every stage door," Mary later said.

Bill Swan, who performed in more than fifty-five Playhouse productions, says, "Billy was known for his resident company. He picked and chose very carefully, because he supported his wife and children all winter long with what he earned in the summer. He depended on his resident company to star in things when he couldn't afford a bonafide star. If you do ten shows a summer playing different parts, the audience gets to know you, so then he'd give you a leading role and star you in something and you'd be a *little* star in between the times he could afford Kay Francis, Tallulah Bankhead or Ethel Barrymore. That was Mary's contribution—she became one of his standbys who subsequently became a very, very popular player there." Eleanor "Siddy" Wilson, an actress who briefly served as Playhouse director, says Mary's ability to work collegially also was important "or she wouldn't have been invited back. Billy was very sharp about picking people who got along and were personable." Mary became a favorite of Playhouse audiences, who dubbed her "Sarah Bernhardt of the Berkshires," after the prodigious nineteenth-century actress Sarah Bernhard—and sometimes referred to her simply as "our Mary." A quick scan of newspapers of the day reveals a depth of affection that is hard to imagine theatre writers publicly bestowing on a performer today:

- Mary Wickes, whom F. Cowles Strickland brought from his Little Theatre season in St. Louis last winter, developed into one of the best character comediennes any company could want—or pray for. It will require only "the breaks" to enable Miss Wickes to do big things. (William H. Haskell in *Knickerbocker Press*, August 26, 1934)
- Miss Wickes is one of those people about whom even the most cautious person who knows nothing about the stage can say with conviction, "She's going places." (Kingsley R. Fall in a review of *Mary, Mary Quite Contrary* in the *Berkshire Eagle*, 1936)
- It was the younger Mary Wickes who galvanized the play into life when she was on the stage. (Review of *Mary, Mary, Quite Contrary* in the *Knickerbocker Press*, July 19, 1936)

- The appearance of Mary Wickes in only a third of any production is a matter of regret. (Review of *Mariette* in the *Berkshire Eagle*, June 29, 1937)
- When it is said Mary Wickes is in the cast it is superfluous to add she gives another delightful impersonation. (C. R. Roseberry reviewing *Storm Over Patsy* in the *Albany (New York) Times Union*, 1937)
- She has contributed many outstanding performances to the Playhouse history, but never has she played as she did last night. Clowning with authority, Miss Wickes simply emphasized that she is a star in her own right. ("G. W. E." in a review of *Patience* in the "At the Theatre" column of an unidentified newspaper, 1937)
- The welcome accorded Miss Wickes after the curtain included the stamping of feet, which is probably as boisterous a welcome as any favorite daughter could ask for. [I]f people don't stop calling her a wonderful substitute for Helen Broderick, I hope Miss Wickes will purchase a small but lethal weapon. Substitute, my eye. (Kingsley R. Fall, reviewing *George Washington Slept Here* in the *Berkshire Eagle*, 1941)

Perhaps the Playhouse's own playbill best captured the town's affection for Mary. During the run of *Candida* in 1937, the theatre's playbill said, "This is Mary Wickes' fourth summer at the Playhouse, where her personal following has grown to such status that both the audiences and press object if she isn't in all three acts of every play."

Mary returned occasionally over the years, ultimately appearing in forty-one plays in ten seasons between 1934 and 1982. The nature of small-town living in Stockbridge, with its strong sense of community, drew Mary back as much as any professional opportunity. The town's support for the theatre was so genuine that families—especially the wealthy East Coast families who kept summer homes in the area—routinely lent furniture and housewares to be used as props. On one opening night, actress Ellen Hall, playing a maid and carrying a lovely (and borrowed) silver tea service, "tripped on the door jamb as she made her entrance and the tall coffee pot of the silver tea service flipped over and fell on the floor, and from the audience you heard a *shriek* of pain from the owner!" Mary said.

The summers that Mary spent in Stockbridge certainly were more socially active than the life she was accustomed to in St. Louis. Many prominent Boston and Philadelphia families summered in Stockbridge and nearby Lenox and invited the Playhouse performers to their gatherings.

"I brought seven evening gowns with me that first summer and used every one of them. There was a party almost every night," Mary said. Many were thrown by sculptor Margaret French Cresson in the studio of her late father, Daniel Chester French, who created the sculpture at the Lincoln Memorial. In this milieu, attending a show at the Playhouse was a special occasion. Miles remembers thirty chauffeur-driven cars waiting for their owners after a performance one evening. The theatre took to serving coffee after the first act so that those who had dinner parties before the show would not have to rush the meal.

Actors' salaries at the Playhouse were not high; many were happy simply to have work they could not get in Manhattan. During her first five seasons, Mary never made more than $40 per week. Like most of the actors, she rented a room each season in one of the many large homes where locals took in summer boarders, especially along Main Street. Only big-name stars stayed at the historic Red Lion Inn, the quaint hotel that dates from the 1700s and has long hosted monied visitors. Miles assembled a roster of popular local landladies who charged about $8 per week for a room, including breakfast. It was a charmed existence that spoke of another era even then. A postman wearing a linen duster and hat delivered the mail in town twice a day from a horse-drawn buggy, saluting passers-by with his buggy whip. "I was in heaven," recalls Andrea King, an actress who was part of the 1934 company. "We were all together in a wonderful old boarding house run by an elderly woman, Mrs. Walker, which was great fun. We'd all swim in the quarry, which was about half a mile away."

Years later, many came to view Mary's departure from St. Louis as somehow daring, feeling that injecting herself into the East Coast theatre world was a bold move for a young woman raised in a conventional midwestern family. As classmate Helen Margaret Aff-Drum put it, "That was brave, especially in the middle of the Depression. She was really taking the bit in her teeth." Even in New York, some had that sense: "I had been born in New York and lived here in New York and felt I was pretty savvy about things, yet I remember being amazed that here this girl had been allowed to come to New York and to break into the theatre. She was so independent," says Anna Crouse, who would room with Mary on the road during Broadway tryouts in the late 1930s. "But it was her parents who surprised me . . . It seemed a very courageous thing to do, to send your only child and say, 'Go ahead, do what you wish.'"

The reality was more complicated. Mary never really ventured off by herself to seek an acting career—Isabella almost always accompanied her. For much of Mary's time in Stockbridge, and for many of her stays in New York, Isabella was by her side, part companion and part chaperone. As cousin Bill Dorsam says, with only a little exaggeration, "Every trip she ever took, her mom was with her." In fact, when Miles rented a boarding house for the company one summer and needed a resident chaperone, he turned to Isabella, whom he had come to know during her visits from St. Louis. Frank insisted that Isabella accept. Where many young women might have preferred the freedom of a summer without parents, Mary seemed to genuinely welcome Isabella's arrival. "We had a hilarious summer," she said.

So each summer from 1934 to 1938, this was Mary's life. Wherever she was boarding that season, she would start the day with breakfast, often served on a tray in her room, followed by a stroll through town before arriving at the Playhouse for 10:00 a.m. rehearsals. When Isabella was not with her, her errands might take her to Benjamin's Drug Store to buy postcards, or maybe to Western Union to send a telegram inquiring about a job in New York. Lunches and dinners were eaten with other members of the company at a popular family-run restaurant about six houses from the Playhouse, either on a large screened-in porch or on tables set throughout the first floor.

Beginning in 1935, each summer week Mary simultaneously performed in one play while rehearsing a second. She played both comedy and tragedy; one week she might play someone her own age, while the next she might play a woman of seventy or eighty. Dress rehearsals took place on Sunday evenings for plays that opened on Monday in this modest theatre, which had four hundred and eighty-eight seats at the time. To make the pace manageable, Miles tried to ensure that no cast member was given a principal part two weeks in a row.

"Oh, it was madness! It was great. It was highly challenging and wondrous," says actress Lenka Peterson, who performed with Mary in *My Sister Eileen* and *The Late George Apley*, among other productions. "It just seemed like we ate the lines with lunch. We cued each other at every spare moment, lying in the grass, and walking back and forth, and running through things. Billy just ran things so calmly and quietly. He'd have a read-through and always knew exactly how he was going to stage it. And we always had the same people doing the sets and the costumes."

The actors learned their roles with "sides," a rather mechanical but not uncommon technique in those years. This meant the actors worked not from a full script, but instead simply from half-sheets from the Samuel French Co. Each actor's typed sheet bore the several words of dialogue that immediately preceded his or her own lines, followed by the line the actor was to say next—"just little typewritten lines with a dash, dash and the last five words or something," Peterson says. Actors learned to recognize specific words as their cues and might not know the larger plot; the danger, of course, was that if lines were ad-libbed or flubbed, an actor might not realize his line is next.

"You had to learn the cue for the next person because if you were supposed to say, 'I don't believe so,' and you said, 'I don't think so,' nobody would speak, because it wasn't anybody's cue," William Roerick says. "There wasn't time with this tight schedule to learn the ideas [that were motivating] everything that was going on. You had a vague notion of what it was, but you didn't learn the way one now can learn, which is, what's the impulse, so that if the other person says *think* instead of *believe*, you get the point and you speak. In those days, no matter what else you said wrong, you *had to* know the last three or four words of your speech," Peterson says. "With the sides, I'd have to write in key words of the line before mine because otherwise sometimes the last few words don't give you a clue as to why you're saying the next thing. The first morning of rehearsal, we'd come and open our sides, and that's when we'd find out what people said before other than the last three words. I'll never know how we did it. I don't ever remember a terrible disaster. I remember bigger disasters in the big musicals that I've done since then."

When in her first season Strick gave Mary a part opposite Ina Claire, a true stage star, Mary was awestruck. The play was *Biography*, a comedy about a portrait painter persuaded to chronicle her life in an autobiography. Mary telegrammed Isabella: "I am scared pink. She has always been my favorite actress. We open Monday and part of the New York cast is coming to do it with us." Mary got nice notices, but the most significant outcome was an unexpected career boost from Ina Claire herself. Claire was so impressed with Mary that, in a gesture of generosity to a newcomer, she gave Mary a hand-written introduction to one of Broadway's leading producers, Sam Harris. She compared Mary to a popular comic actress of the day: "Mary Wickes is my idea of a perfect understudy for Helen Broderick! She has the same solemn comic 'pan' and sense of humor. If you can place her, I feel she will more than 'make good.' Anyway, she has my sincere endorsement. I've seen her work and I thought at once of Helen."

As the season came to a close, Mary chose not to return to St. Louis but instead, like the rest of the company, to seek work in New York. Isabella came east for a few days to help Mary settle into the Allerton

Hotel for Women at 130 East 57th Street. Even at this point in her life, Mary's friends saw that Isabella and Mary were a package deal. Later, on an opening night in New York, one Stockbridge pal telegrammed Mary, "Hope you make such a big hit for yourself that your nice mother will dance barefoot in 45th Street. But don't let me catch her at it or I'll point."

Mary had barely unpacked when she began to pursue a promising opportunity she learned of from Patricia Collinge, an actress whose influence extended well beyond the Playhouse. It seems producer Marc Connelly would be directing a Broadway-bound show whose cast included Margaret Hamilton, and Collinge thought Mary would be a perfect understudy for Hamilton. Mary decided the value of Ina Claire's letter was its content, not who it was addressed to, so she telephoned Connelly's office. "I told him I had a letter from Ina Claire and he told me to meet him and his assistant, Bob Ross, in half an hour in the lobby of the Gotham Hotel, where Mr. Connelly lives. I promptly tore over to the Gotham, bribed a bellboy to signal me when Mr. Connelly came in [Mary did not know what he looked like] and when he arrived I bounced up to him like an old friend. He appeared a bit bewildered, but he took the letter and my pictures and said he would get in touch with me." But Mary needed the letter and photos for a Theatre Guild audition the next day. "So I telephoned the Gotham the next morning and he asked me to come over. I explained that I wanted a part in *The Farmer Takes a Wife*, and that I had done the Margaret Hamilton role in *Another Language*. Mr. Connelly asked me to read her part. He liked me, gave me the job of her understudy and a walk-on part," Mary said.

Securing a job on her second day in New York "was undoubtedly not so much dumb luck as a combination of starry-eyed innocence, schoolgirl enthusiasm and effervescent personality," one paper said. *The Farmer Takes a Wife* placed a young Henry Fonda and June Walker on the Erie Canal in an 1850s love story involving a boater who is a farmer at heart and a cook who is reluctant to give up the exciting canal life for a farm. Hamilton's part was that of a cook and gossip of the waterway. The show tried out in Philadelphia, where Mary was unexpectedly asked to go on for Hamilton in the first matinee. When Mary shared the news with the ever-devoted Isabella, Isabella swung into action and alerted everyone she could think of (including Strick, who replied, "Well, we're not dancing on Margaret Hamilton's grave, but it is just the break Mary deserves.")

It's not clear if Mary went on because Hamilton was ill, as news accounts reported, or because Connelly asked Hamilton to step aside to allow Mary to better familiarize herself with the role. Mary's own account over the years was that Hamilton had a touch of the flu. Indeed, Hamilton sent flowers to Mary at the Philadelphia theatre that morning with a note of thanks, as if Mary were doing her a kindness. But Connelly was known for making unconventional gestures to help actors see the scope of their parts. In a newspaper feature published during this period, he said, "I had a most competent understudy play her role for Margaret Hamilton during a matinee, so that she might understand the entire production and her part in it." Most tellingly, Mary received this effusive note from Patricia Collinge: "To have had such a chance at this stage of the game will mean so much. It's like the impossible stories in the *Saturday Evening Post*. Marc must have been delighted with you to send you on when it wasn't really necessary. And now a lot of people know that you can do good work." Clearly, Mary led Isabella to think Hamilton was ill, because Isabella wrote her, "Please tell Miss Hamilton we are so sorry to hear she is sick and I really mean it—and hope she is much better. Your city is full of it and the hospitals crowded but it doesn't seem to last but a few days . . . and should I write Miss Hamilton to say I'm sorry she was sick or not?"

Whatever the reason for Mary's going on, by coincidence the Philadelphia matinee was the very performance a *Variety* critic attended. He mentioned Mary by name and reported that she was "more than okay," her first step toward getting the attention of casting agents. Taken together, Ina Claire's letter, Mary's own gumption, and Connelly's decision to have Mary go on had set Mary's stage career in motion. Though Mary never got to go on in *The Farmer Takes a Wife* once it arrived in New York, the show played one hundred and four performances, giving her regular work through January 1935.

One consequence of taking the *Farmer* gig was that Mary would be unavailable for a Stockbridge show that went direct to Broadway for a much longer run. The final production of the Berkshire Playhouse's 1934 season was *Fly Away Home*, produced by Theron Bamberger as a Broadway tryout. It featured a divorced man who returns home to attend his ex-wife's wedding and is forced to spend time with his unruly children. Mary played Penny, the nurse who has raised the four children. The show was received well by Stockbridge audiences, so in 1935, as hoped, it went to Broadway, the first show ever to use the Playhouse as a tryout setting. Most of the Stockbridge cast went with it, including Andrea King, Thomas Mitchell (the prolific character actor who would later play Scarlett O'Hara's father in *Gone with the Wind*), and a very young

Montgomery Clift in his first stage role anywhere. "Montgomery Clift, the thirteen-year-old boy in his first public performance on any stage, shows surprising poise and ability to act," said one local paper. Because Mary was now committed to *Farmer*, her role was given to Clare Woodbury. *Fly Away Home* played for two hundred and four performances over about six months.

Missing out on opportunities like this mattered to Mary. She wanted work. She began using the Ina Claire letter to open other doors. One newspaper said Mary, having shown the letter to at least twenty-five producers, became known as "the girl with the letter to Sam Harris." Meanwhile, uncertain when her next acting job would surface, Mary took whatever paying work she could. Using her journalism training, she occasionally wrote about theatre for out-of-town papers, such as a piece about the Berkshire Playhouse published in the *Knickerbocker Press* on October 15, 1934. Using her stenography training, she took a part-time job as social secretary for Margaret Huston, sister of actor Walter Huston. Mary worked for Margaret Huston in the mornings so that her afternoons remained free for auditions. To save money, she moved into the American Women's Association Clubhouse at 57th Street and Ninth Avenue, a few blocks west of the Allerton; she would stay here for the next several years.

During this period, Mary took a one-day job that resulted in her first performance on film. On February 15, 1935, Mary signed a contract with the Vitaphone Corp. to appear in a short film starring a former vaudevillian named Bob Hope, who had only a little more experience in film than Mary had. *Watch the Birdie* is an eighteen-minute comedy in which a lovesick Hope annoys passengers aboard a cruise ship with his practical jokes. Mary's character is relaxing in a chaise lounge on deck until she falls victim to one of Hope's pranks. Having peered through his telescope, she pulls away to find black greasepaint surrounding her eye. Her character has no lines. Mary was paid $25 for her part, which was filmed at Vitaphone's studio in Brooklyn. She is called "first old maid" in the contract, but she does not appear in the credits. Released in August 1935, the film appears on none of the detailed lists of credits that Mary painstakingly prepared over the years. Neither does a second Vitaphone short, the nineteen-minute *Seeing Red*, for which she was paid $40 for one day's work opposite Red Skelton on March 21, 1939. Ignoring her own early film work was one way age-conscious Mary could prevent producers from realizing just how early she had begun her career. She always maintained that her first film work was in *The Man Who Came to Dinner*, released in 1941.

Mary found work with the U.S. government, too. When the Works Progress Administration created the Federal Theatre Project in August 1935 to provide work for unemployed theatre workers during the Depression, Mary became a dramatic coach for $24 a week. The overwhelming majority of artists given work by the Federal Theatre Project—actors, choreographers, dancers, designers, musicians, and others—came from the relief rolls. Mary likely did, too, though she never spoke about this episode of her life. Many artists who became well known had been employed early in their careers by the FTP; the Harlem Renaissance writer Zora Neale Hurston was an FTP dramatic coach at the same time Mary was. But for Mary, teaching theatre technique did not last long. She was dismissed in February 1936 when she found paying work in the commercial theatre.

She had been trying doggedly to line up a long-term Broadway role. Her first attempts had met such bad fates that she could be forgiven for wondering if she was cut out for a theatrical career. The first two Broadway-bound shows in which she won speaking parts never made it out of tryouts: *Swing Your Lady* died in Washington, D.C., in November 1935, and *Larger Than Life* died in Springfield, Massachusetts, in March 1936. The former, a comedy about Ozark wrestlers, put Mary in a role that drew comparisons to Margaret Hamilton, while the latter paired her for the first time with Thelma Ritter, who later became Mary's frequent competition for wise-cracking character parts. Undaunted, Mary joined the cast of *One Good Year* in May 1936, replacing Doro Merande. The show marked Mary's first speaking part on Broadway and also revealed Mary's ambivalence about giving up her name entirely—she asked to be billed as "Mary I. Wickes." *One Good Year* had been running for six months, but closed about six weeks after Mary joined the cast. Her fourth attempt, *Spring Dance*, had a lot of promise. Produced by Jed Harris and written by Philip Barry (today known mostly for *The Philadelphia Story*), it emerged from mediocre reviews in out-of-town tryouts strong enough to make a Broadway success seem plausible. It closed after twenty-four performances.

In mid-1936, St. Louis friends Archer and Mary-Margaret O'Reilly were in town to visit the actress Josephine Hull, and O'Reilly arranged for them all to have lunch, thinking Hull might be able to help Mary find something. But Hull, like Mary, was looking for an acting job. Starting in the early 1920s, Hull had worked almost non-stop, but now she was experiencing a slow-down in her career. "We came out of the restaurant and I thought, here's one who's had it and another who wants it. One was over the hill and whether she'd get another play was questionable, and one was just fresh trying to get on Broadway. We hoped Mary would be able to find a job in New York, but we had our doubts," O'Reilly said. But within only a few months, Hull had landed a lead role in *You Can't Take It With You*, a hit that ran for two years and gave new momentum to her career, and Mary had landed something big herself.

For Mary, five attempts were needed before she would experience a Broadway hit. It came in the form of something called *Stage Door*, a smash that gave Mary her highest-profile and longest-running role so far. *Stage Door* was a popular comedy of the 1930s, chronicling the joys and disappointments of a group of aspiring actresses at a boarding house for women. Written by George S. Kaufman and Edna Ferber, it was first a stage show produced by Sam Harris and later a film. Mary's involvement with the play is like something out of the storybooks. One afternoon in June of 1936, she was lunching alone at the counter of Gray's Drug Store, a Times Square institution. A woman approached her, looked her over and asked if she was an actress. Mary said yes. The woman introduced herself as Janet Fox, the playwright Ferber's niece, and said Ferber and Kaufman were around the corner at that very moment casting a play about would-be actresses—but were having trouble finding an especially tall actress. "Of course, Wicksie got up. She wasn't *that* tall, but she was taller and thinner and more angular than most girls. She really was kind of a long drink of water," says Anne Kaufman Schneider, who heard this story separately from Mary, Fox, and her father, the playwright Kaufman. Fox directed Mary to the audition, Mary raced over, and, in short order, got the part. It paid her $75 per week and would open many doors for her, just as another lunch counter discovery that same year would open doors for film star Lana Turner on the other side of the country. (Contrary to Hollywood lore, Turner was discovered at the Top Hat Café across from Hollywood High School, not Schwab's drug store.)

The star of *Stage Door* was the beautiful Margaret Sullavan, playing a serious actress who rejects the promise of film stardom to remain in the theatre. But the show was otherwise an ensemble production, and Mary's part was good. She played half of a comic twosome called Big Mary and Little Mary that roamed through the play delivering wisecracks. Mary was Little Mary, and Beatrice Blinn was Big Mary. The show opened at the Music Box Theatre on October 22, 1936—with Noel Coward and

Gertrude Lawrence sitting in the front row—and from the start attracted generally good notices and even better reactions from audiences.

"The sarcastic shafts are brilliantly handled by Miss Lee Patrick, who once was teamed with Jean Dixon and learned expertly. Most of the other laughs are scored by Beatrice Blinn and Mary Wickes. They're a grand combination, never missing," said the *Hollywood Reporter*. From the *New York World-Telegram*: "The story is trash, but it is an excellent theme—the stage and screen socking it out at footlight ringside. Mr. Kaufman and Miss Ferber only mess with it. The fault of the play is obvious in that its highlights are incidental. The marvelous comedy of Lee Patrick, for example, playing superbly a corrosive blond doesn't mean a thing to the story—but is everything to the audience. It is so with the delightful comedy of Beatrice Blinn and Mary Wickes—a couple of tossed-in olios." In one high-profile review, praise for Mary was accompanied by disappointment. In the *New Yorker*, the popular Robert Benchley complimented her performance but referred to her as "a tall girl whose name I could not untangle from the cast of characters." Perhaps the greatest compliment came from Kaufman himself, who told Mary she had been able to extract eight laughs where he and Ferber had intended none. The actress who followed Mary in the part "got two-minus, which meant that you got ten more than she did," he said.

From *Stage Door*, Mary got twenty-three weeks of work—three in previews and twenty in production—and could certainly have eked out more. But Margaret Sullavan became pregnant with daughter Brooke Hayward and gave notice. In similar circumstances, today's Broadway producers would likely find another star to step in, but Sullavan was so central to the play's popularity, so much of a draw, that they decided to close the show.

For Mary, the show had been a godsend. It meant regular work in a show that was sure to be seen by other producers and casting directors. It meant a chance to enjoy other shows from the audience, since *Stage Door*'s matinee was on Thursday, while most others were on Wednesday. That season, she saw John Gielgud in *Hamlet* and Maurice Evans in *King Richard II*. Most importantly, *Stage Door* marked the beginning of a lifelong relationship with Kaufman, one of the American theatre's most successful playwrights. Mary adored him, learned from him, grew close to his family, and ultimately originated roles in five of his plays: *Stage Door*, *The Man Who Came to Dinner*, *Hollywood Pinafore*, *Park Avenue*, and *Town House*. Over the years, she saved fifty-five pieces of correspondence from him, dating from 1941 to 1961, the year he died. "He was heaven, a wonderful person to work with. He was the kind of person who said, 'If you do so-and-so, [if you] do this, do that, do that, then this will be the result.' You didn't question it, you just did it, and by gum, he was right. Another thing about George that was so admirable—I never saw him correct an actor so you could hear the correction. He always took the actor aside, and said [what he wanted to say] very quietly, and in a minute the actor was back on stage, going about his business," Mary said. "And he was so witty. Oh, dear, he was witty." The last show she did with him was *Town House*. During Boston tryouts, it was clear there were problems in act three. One night, returning to the Ritz Carlton on foot from the Colonial Theatre, Mary and Kaufman cut across the Boston Common. "We were taking a path, and George and I were just walking along, chatting, and he said, 'let's take *this* path for a change, we might find a third act.'"

One benefit of *Stage Door* was that Orson Welles noticed Mary in it. In the mid and late 1930s, Welles's career and creativity were on the rise, after he took the arts world by storm with his groundbreaking Mercury Theatre Company. The Mercury is nearly forgotten today by all but the most devoted stage enthusiasts, but its importance to American theatre of the early twentieth century cannot be overstated. Without exaggeration, it can be said that in the late 1930s this ragtag clique of performers transformed American audiences' expectations of theatre. Born in the wake of the Federal Theatre Project's shutdown of *Cradle Will Rock*, deemed too sympathetic to the labor movement, the Mercury remains a constant in theatre textbooks more than seventy years later because of its presentations of that show, *Julius Caesar* (modern dress, bare stage), *Shoemakers' Holiday*, and *Heartbreak House*.

In December 1937, Welles was casting *Shoemakers' Holiday*, an Elizabethan comedy of mistaken identities, and remembered Mary from *Stage Door*. He offered her a role, but she was performing in *Father Malachy's Miracle*, a Broadway comedy about an Irish monk and a dancehall swept out to sea. *Malachy* was doing well (it would run for about one hundred and twenty-five performances), and she was earning $85 a week—so Mary was unavailable. When Welles began casting *Too Much Johnson* the following August, he again turned to Mary, who was now back at the Berkshire Playhouse with nothing lined up after the summer season. She was eager for work in New York, and so quickly signed a contract that would pay her $50 a week. *Too Much Johnson* would try out at Stony Creek (Connecticut) Theatre before an expected Broadway run and, it was hoped, a national tour.

Too Much Johnson was an unconventional job for Mary and an unconventional undertaking overall. First, Stony Creek was a more secluded setting than these New York actors were accustomed to. "The Mercury wasn't going to put anything on in the summer. When we were still in New York, Orson said that if I had a summer theater and I hired Virginia [Welles's wife], he'd do two plays there. It was simply to get rid of her. He was having a do with [dancer] Vera Zorina—there was always another 'dame' involved in one way or another," explains Bill Herz, the Mercury casting director who was the Stony Creek Theatre's producer that summer. "Also, he said, 'You know she has a car?' I didn't have a car in those days so it was a big help to have somebody with a car. I had to go into New Haven quite frequently, and if it hadn't been for Orson's wife, [those tasks would have been difficult.]"

Second, the venture would be presented only partly on a stage; another part of the story would be conveyed to the theatre audience on film. Welles would direct three short films: one piece of twenty to thirty minutes that would introduce the characters and back-story before the live play began, and two other ten-minute reels to be shown immediately before the second and third acts. *Two Much Johnson* was an elaborate 1890s farce of mistaken identity. It's the tale of cuckolded husband Dathis (Edgar Barrier) chasing a man named Billings (Joseph Cotten), who has been having an affair with Dathis's wife (Arlene Francis). Billings flees by ship to Cuba, where—now also hiding from his own wife (Ruth Ford) and mother-in-law (Mary)—he adopts the identity of a plantation owner named Johnson, who is expecting a mail-order bride. The slapstick production also featured Welles's wife, Virginia (under her stage name, Anna Stafford), and the composer Marc Blitzstein in acting roles.

Welles felt Mary was so right for the part of Cotten's mother-in-law that when she was unable to leave her Stockbridge work to attend early rehearsals in New York, he offered to send a car for her every night after her performance and to get her back in time for her next performance the following day—a four-hour drive each way. "Orson had a one-track mind when he wanted somebody. Billy Miles put his foot down because he certainly didn't want to put Mary through that stress," says Herz. In the end, Orson put the TMJ company into rehearsals in New York and had Mary join the others for the final week when her Stockbridge season ended. Preparations were complicated, partly because the casts were not identical: Some actors were in the film portions but not the stage portion (Arlene Francis, Marc Blitzstein, and James O'Rear among them,) while others were in the stage piece but not the film (like Arthur Anderson).

The film also required a lot of hectic moving about New York for specific scenes and sound effects, including a faux suffragette march, a papier-mâché Cuban volcano, and a saber duel.

Today, if *Too Much Johnson* is remembered for anything, it's for what happened with the film. Welles himself described the filmed portions as "an imitation silent comedy, with a big chase over the roofs of the old chicken market in New York." Not just the chicken market—for some scenes, the cast went to Yonkers, says Ruth Ford. "That's where we set up to photograph on a vacant lot. We set up a scene and got in our costumes. I can't recall how far we got, but the police came and chased us away because we didn't have permission to do this." James O'Rear remembers parts being filmed at a rock quarry in Haverstraw, New York, and a lot of action. "We did it like Keystone cops, with lots of jumping around. We had a wonderful time, a lot of laughs. Orson was fun to work for." Yet the actors were driven "to feats of athleticism far beyond their normal capacities," according to Welles scholar Charles Higham. Cotten, especially, found himself hanging perilously from the eaves of Manhattan buildings and jumping between roofs; in one scene, he lets himself fall two stories into a waiting carriage filled with cabbages. Welles said later that he was much influenced by Harold Lloyd, the silent film comedian known for his physicality.

Mary's part was more sedate. As the rigid, disapproving mother-in-law, she wears floor-length, high-waisted dresses with high starched collars, long sleeves and short, tight jackets. Her hair is pulled back into a bun under a proper hat, and she carries a large handbag. Presumably, she wore the same exaggerated white greasepaint makeup that Welles had the men wear in most scenes. From the few existing still photos taken during production of the film, we know a little of what Mary did. She appeared in one scene with Blitzstein and Ford in an open horse-drawn cab that Welles rented from a Central Park hack-stand. And she appeared in another with Ford, standing at a railing atop a riverboat, directly in front of smokestack, presumably en route to Cuba in search of Ford's errant husband.

For the stage portion, final rehearsals took place at Stony Creek, a small summer theatre that had begun life as a dress factory and presented problems of its own. Everyone in the company had to pay for his or her own lodging, and options were limited. Some of the actors, like Mary, stayed in local homes that took in boarders, but others were left to cope with the Flying Point Hotel, a resort property that had fallen into disrepair and was demolished a few years later. "Really, it should have been declared off limits, even for rats. It was unbelievable—like right out of Charles Adams," says Herz, who stayed nearby with a cousin. Arthur Anderson remembers that at low tide, the hotel stank from the creek's mud. "Every morning when we woke up, my shoes would be green with mold," he says.

During all of the work at Stony Creek, Welles was continually commuting to and from New York for his Mercury Theatre on the Air radio show, because that's what made the money. Amidst this chaotic environment, Mary was given a salary boost. A rider to her August 8, 1938, contract was prepared on August 30, giving her $75 per week for the first three weeks, then $100 week thereafter, plus a percentage of any gross box office receipts above a certain amount (unheard of for today's new performers but the custom for the Mercury). The agreement was made with John Houseman, Welles's theatrical partner. It's not that Mary had any clout to demand more from Houseman or the over-spent Welles than the $50 she had agreed to. She did not. But when Actors' Equity received complaints from a few *Too Much Johnson* film actors that Welles was paying them at stage rehearsal rates instead of performance rates, the union decreed that a film is a performance even if it's part of a play. So salaries were raised. With the promise of a little more money, Mary went out the next day and arranged with prominent theatrical photographers, White Studio, for new publicity photos of herself.

On the strength of Welles's name, the two-week run sold out before the engagement started. There were no other names in the cast (certainly, Cotten had achieved no fame yet). But the Mercury made no money on this production. "They didn't get a cent. Whatever money they would have gotten, Orson spent on the way up to Stony Creek from New York. First of all, he had a chauffeur and a rented car. Then they got arrested for speeding not once but twice," says Herz. "In those days, the only place to stop on the road was Howard Johnsons, and he'd eaten them out of house and home, and he had no money, so all these bills kept pouring in. By the time he got to Stony Creek, all of the money they would have made for the first week [was gone]. He kept charging. When I got done paying the bills, I said to Houseman at the end of the first week, 'You know you're not going to get any money from this engagement?' I showed him what Orson had spent so far. But Orson had always behaved this way. He didn't care very much about money." One scholar observed, "the paradox of the Mercury was that it would consistently play to jam-packed houses and consistently lose money."

Anderson, who had appeared in the Mercury's *Julius Caesar* and *Shoe-makers' Holiday*, was in Stony Creek during this time only because he was vacationing in the area. When Welles saw him, he asked Anderson to be part of the stage component. "It was hectic and crazy," he recalls. Anderson did some walk-ons and took part in what he calls "Orson's conceit," an almost staccato, vaudeville-like routine where a group of actors sang "Way Down Upon the Swanee River" in blackface. Mary was not in this bit. (Some seventy years later, when the film *Me and Orson Welles* was produced, the lead character was loosely based on Anderson, the actor who—in real life, as in the film—accidentally floods the stage by placing a match next to the sprinkler system. He was played by Zac Effron.)

In the end, the film component of *Too Much Johnson* was never shown. At the last minute, the production discovered that the small theatre was not able to accommodate suitable projection equipment and, most importantly, lacked the fireproof projection booth required in the days before safety film. And although Welles worked frantically to finish editing the film segments before the play opened, he could not finish. Finally, having completed the longer opening film but not the important shorter bridge pieces, Welles was obliged to do the unthinkable—present the play without the reels of explanatory footage. When *Too Much Johnson* opened in mid-September, he prepared the audience by announcing before the curtain rose that the play had not yet "jelled." But even with audience expectations suddenly lowered, the result was a colossal failure by any measure, its plot so maddeningly unclear that Ford remembers audience members literally throwing food at the stage. "One of the most vivid things I remember about this is that we never integrated the film with the play, so when we put on the play but didn't show the film, of course the audience had *no idea* what *Too Much Johnson* was all about," Ford says. "They were so furious when it was over that on the curtain call they threw everything in their hands at us on the stage. Apples, bananas—every single thing they had, they threw at us. They didn't understand what they'd seen. We were just all going in and out, opening and slamming doors." Herz sighs in exasperation. "The curtain went up at nine with two intermissions and came down at ten thirty and the audience didn't know what hit them. It was an absolute mess. I had no idea what was going on on that stage and I can tell you, neither did the audience. They were absolutely appalled. The actors were also in the dark."

It's not clear that showing the film segments would have helped much. Neither Herz nor Ford ever saw the segments, which represented Welles's first real effort at storytelling on film—but Mary did. "She said the film made as much sense as the show, which was zilch," Herz said. The film was never shown publicly, then or later. The Mercury had to forfeit its negative to the film lab when cost over-runs left the company unable to pay its bills. Welles kept only a positive work print, which is believed to have been lost in a 1970 fire at his home in Spain. "The play and the film were too surreal for the audience. They couldn't accept it," Welles said later. "It was years ahead of its time."

The show never made it to Broadway, and Welles never brought his promised second show to Stony Creek. Yet during previews one reviewer—still presuming a New York debut was afoot—had an optimistic view of how the show would be received once Welles finished working on it. He praised Cotten's performance and added, "Ruth Ford, as the unsophisticated wife, and Mary Wickes as the brow-beating mother-in-law, make a swell comedy team." "The only positive experience I really remember happening around this," Herz says, was that Katharine Hepburn came to see the show and was so impressed with Cotten that she chose him for the lead opposite her in *The Philadelphia Story*, a high-profile role in a show that lasted for more than four hundred performances and propelled his career forward.

Too Much Johnson may have failed, but Mary was now indelibly part of the Mercury. A month after the Stony Creek disaster, she, Welles, Cotten, and Ford would perform together in a live *Mercury Theatre on the Air* presentation of Booth Tarkington's "Seventeen," and Mary quickly performed twice more with the company. For each radio performance, she earned $25. Next up: She and Welles were the headliners at a November 11 symposium sponsored by the Theatre Education League in New York; Mary performed monologues from Dorothy Parker, and Welles spoke on directing and staging.

After *Too Much Johnson*, the company returned to New York and threw itself into the Mercury's second play of the season. Rehearsals began for *Danton's Death*, a period drama about the French Revolution that opened in November. The presentation would be short—barely an hour and fifteen minutes—but it would feature Welles, Cotten, Barrier, Ford, Francis, Stafford, Martin Gabel, Vladimir Sokolov, and Mary, with songs by Blitzstein. But it wasn't the cast that ensured *Danton* a place in theatre history; it was the play's set. Welles glued some seventeen hundred masks onto the back wall of the Mercury Theatre as part of a dramatic lighting experiment, and replaced the conventional stage with a complex, split-level series of hastily built stairwells, moving platforms, and trap doors. Robespierre made his big speech inciting the populace from a platform that was pulled up manually—and noisily—by stagehands. "Day after day actors fell headlong into the rat-ridden basement [and] leaped on and off erratically moving elevators," one account reads. Herz remembers it as "a death-trap of a set. How we weren't all killed is a miracle—all that rushing around in the dark with these flowing hats and coats. In fact, during the dress rehearsal, the elevator broke and Erskine Sanford broke his leg. Orson was in the back—and I never saw him move so fast to the stage. The others were shaken up but OK."

The dangers on stage would have little effect on Mary. While her part was sufficiently important that she had an understudy, it was also so small that she was never actually on stage. She was off-stage, making crowd noises and yelling things like, "Off with his head!" "Up with Robespierre!" and "Vive la France!" "She and I were down underneath the stage most of the time, making noises," recalls Betty Garrett, the actress whose first job in the theatre was as Mary's understudy in this production. "She had a song that she sang, *Soldier, Oh, Soldier.* I can remember only one time that she was out that I had to sing it." Garrett remembers that the song, which Mary sang off stage, had "bawdy" lyrics, including:

> *Mister soldier, handsome soldier*
> *Play me mild or play me rough*
> *I just can't get enough*

Mary "just sang them with great enjoyment, a lusty kind of wonderful [singing]," Garrett says. This part was unusual for Mary, who later steered away from roles that featured anything remotely suggestive.

It was during this production that Welles broadcast his infamous "War of the Worlds" radio drama. Welles asked writer Howard Koch to present H. G. Wells's story of a Martian invasion as a series of real-time news bulletins for a *Mercury Theatre on the Air* broadcast. The effect of the October 30 CBS broadcast was so realistic that many Americans immediately believed the planet had been invaded. While the broadcast unfolded that evening, Mary and others in the *Danton* cast were elsewhere, oblivious to the mass panic that was ensuing. "We were waiting at the theatre for rehearsal of *Danton's Death,* but the radio cast was delayed at the radio station answering telephones," Mary said. They were also delayed by a dozen New York policemen, who rushed to the radio studio. Mary recalled that when Welles, Cotten, and others finally arrived at the theatre for the dress rehearsal (this was two days before Danton was to open), "I never saw Welles so distressed. Some of us were inclined to laugh at the situation, but he was deadly serious. 'It isn't funny. It may be the end of the Mercury Theatre,' he warned us, and it was several days before we knew whether the reaction would put an end to the theatre as well as the broadcasts." The *Danton* dress rehearsal lasted until early the next morning.

The broadcast made Welles a household name and helped him finally attract a sponsor, Campbell's Soup, for the weekly radio series. Herz (referring to a chic midtown restaurant) recalled that after Welles got the Campbell's contract, "When he got up in the morning, the first place he would go was 21." "Then he'd get a haircut and if he didn't need a haircut, he'd get a shave. He wouldn't come into the office. We'd have to do all these auditions, and if we needed him for anything, we'd have to go to 21. That's where he'd have breakfast, lunch and dinner. A week at 21 before the war, where he spent over $2,000 or $3,000—it was just madness."

Indeed, these were heady days in many ways. Elliott Reid, who appeared in *Julius Caesar* and *Shoemakers' Holiday*, remembers a party given during this period by Ford at the Dakota apartment building, where he encountered silent film star Lillian Gish at one end of the room and fashion photographer Cecil Beaton at the other. Herz remembers one special evening. "Orson adored a Yiddish actor named Menasha Skulnick, who was in a show down on Second Avenue in the Yiddish theatre. It was practically at the end of the era of that kind of theatre," he says. One Sunday night, the Mercury company attended the show together but purposely sat apart in small groups. "They sang a number called 'A Tisket, a Tasket,' in Yiddish. We were scattered all over the theatre, and we applauded so much that they did encore after encore. We made them sing it ten or twelve times. I was in a box with Mary and her mother, this lovely lady from St. Louis who hadn't been exposed to anything like this *in her life*. First, we had gone to a kosher restaurant on Second Avenue, where she ate food that she had never *heard of*. It was really one of the funniest evenings of my life. When we went backstage, he accused us of making him sing it over and over again."

But back to *Danton*. The play received mostly poor reviews and closed after less than three weeks. It was dismissed as "more sound than scene" by the *New York Times* and as "all stunt and no play" by the *New York Post*. "Admirable as *Danton's Death* may be as a technical demonstration, it offers a very dull and confusing evening as a script," said the *Post*. From *Time*: "*Danton's Death* is just as undramatic as it is indecisive. Fatalistic, Hamletesque Danton, bogged in procrastination and boredom, shouts back at Robespierre but never fights back. Everybody shouts, nobody fights. The play consists of great gobs of 19th-century rhetoric; it could do much better with a little 20th-century suspense." *Danton* was the Mercury's final stage production. Years later, Mary would recall her time with the Mercury as "dynamic," "a whale of a good time," "a hectic grind of activity," "a dramatic education," and "just this side of being totally crazy."

With the Mercury experience behind them, Mary and Welles would work together only once again, more than thirty years later, in a 1972 television production. Mary and Houseman would work together again when he directed her at Theatre Group at UCLA in 1962 and 1964. Mary did not stay in touch with either of them, but she and Herz remained lifelong friends. Mary never worked again with Cotten, but the Mercury remained a bond. At the American Cinema Awards in February 1993, "I'll never forget, Joseph Cotten and [his wife, the actress] Patricia Medina came over to speak to Mary," said Bill Givens, Mary's escort that night. "I thought, oh, my god, she's introducing me to Joseph Cotten— this is Citizen Kane in person. It was very warm. They interacted like old friends." Cotten, obviously frail and having trouble standing, died twelve months later; Mary would die a year after that.

CHAPTER THREE

On Stage and On Air

TODAY'S AUDIENCES MAY FIND IT HARD TO IMAGINE THE BROADWAY of the 1940s. It was a time of theatres without air conditioning. It was a time of wartime restrictions on paper, which meant theatregoers were expected to share their copies of the playbill. It was a time when the playbill warned theatregoers to remain in their seats "in the event of an alert," but also carried notes like: "The Alvin Theatre is perfumed with Prince Matchabelli's *Stradivari*." It was also a time when a theatre might brag about its "new asbestos curtain."

For struggling performers like Mary, it was also a time of great togetherness. "We all kind of knew each other. It was a time when you didn't even need an agent. If a play was being cast, you could go into a producer's office and ask for the script and sit there and read it and if you thought you were right for it, they'd want you to come in and read," recalls Max Showalter, a popular character actor who met Mary during this period and would remain one of her closest friends. "Then we'd all meet in the drugstore in the Astor Hotel, and someone would say, 'I was just up to [producer] Kermit Bloomgarden's office and I'm not right for the part, but you would be so good in it, go on up there!' It was really everyone helping one another." Anna Crouse, who met Mary in 1938, says, "There was very much a community. You all met at Schrafft's or someplace for lunch. Everybody ran up and down the stairs of these various offices looking for work. You'd sit backstage and talk to people when the show was going on, and you'd all go out after the play. You knew everyone on the street. The theatres were all lit and full. It was very sad if you didn't have any money and couldn't get work, but if you were reasonably secure, you go to Sardi's and know everybody there at lunch," she says.

It was a camaraderie that Mary embraced. From actress Kaye Ballard, who remembers trying out for the U.K. company of the Broadway show

Touch and Go: "My heart sank when I walked into the audition and saw almost every other character actress I knew. We all tried out together in the same large room. The competition included Elaine Stritch, Pat Carroll, Bibi Osterwald and Mary Wickes," Ballard recalls. "Besides being a terrific character actress, Mary was quite a character herself. That afternoon at the audition, she showed up looking tall, thin and terrific. She announced in her wonderfully blunt manner, 'I have a flower show to attend at Madison Square Garden, so let's get this over with.' We each took our turn and nervously sized up the others as they took theirs. After we finished, Mary got up and apologized for having to leave so abruptly. She went down the line saying, 'Good-bye, Pat. Good-bye, Bibi. So long, Elaine.' When she got to me she said, 'Bon voyage, Kaye.' Somehow she knew I was going to get the part!" Ballard won the part and remained in England with the show for ten months.

So, undaunted by the Mercury's closing, Mary continued plugging away. One morning in 1938, Mary by chance ran into Washington University classmate Mary Jane Roach Masters in Times Square. Mary was making the rounds of theatrical agencies, and Masters was working in Manhattan's fashion industry. "We had breakfast together and a chat," says Masters, who recalls Mary's mood as "perky, upbeat and hopeful. She was excited—New York was the dream place. This was the end of the rainbow." Mary had in fact arrived in New York in the middle of Broadway's heyday, when the performing arts were a cornerstone of American cultural life. The great producers—Vinton Freedley, Max Gordon, Sam Harris, Jed Harris, Guthrie McClintic, Brock Pemberton, Herman Shumlin, Dwight Deere Wiman—were still producing, and Mary worked with many of them. Hit plays came not just from George S. Kaufman and Moss Hart, but from Lillian Hellman, Clifford Odets, Maxwell Anderson, and Eugene O'Neill. It was a grand time to be part of the theatre.

In December 1938, Mary was hired for *Stars in Your Eyes*. Her character was a voice coach to a movie star (Ethel Merman) who inherits a film studio from her producer husband. The play featured Jimmy Durante, Richard Carlson, Mildred Natwick, and ballerina Tamara Toumanova, and its chorus included the not-yet-famous Jerome Robbins and Nora Kaye. Mary's character follows Merman's around on a sound stage, with a Victrola playing atmospheric music to keep her in good spirits. The part was small, but Mary also understudied Natwick's much bigger part as a screenwriter. She earned $65 per week. *Stars in Your Eyes* tried out in New Haven and Boston, and to save money, Mary roomed with Anna Crouse, part of director Josh Logan's team. In New Haven, they stayed at the "ghastly" Taft Hotel, and in Boston, at the Touraine Hotel, which had seen better days even then, Crouse says. "We were both on a strict budget, so we didn't exactly stay in high class joints."

Several things made the early days of this production difficult. One was that much of the action took place on a track of sorts that moved across the performance space, created by set designer Jo Mielziner. Working on this set meant the actors could not easily get help with their dialogue from a stage manager, because they were in constant motion on the treadmill-like walkway. A bigger problem was that Durante, whose part was big, had difficulty remembering his lines. "I would have to type them up but he also couldn't see, so I'd have to type them in caps. And then he'd get upset and rip it up and I'd go, 'Oh, god,' because there were no Xeroxes then," says Crouse. During performances, Crouse sat on a stool in a black dress, script in her lap, in front of the orchestra conductor, so she could surreptitiously prompt Durante if needed. One night, when he lost his place, she whispered his line to him. "He stopped the show and said to the audience, 'Of course she knows it, she's got the book in front of her!' I thought [producer] Dwight Deere Wiman would go through the roof. He went backstage to Jimmy and yelled, 'That's so unprofessional!' But poor guy, he did really well because half the time he made it up and it was as good as what [playwright] J. P. McEvoy was writing," she says. Durante was only forty-five at the time, but "he was a burlesque and vaudeville man, and they're not used to sticking to the script and cues and all of that. He had a lot of trouble." Making matters more difficult for him, lines were regularly changed and scenes rewritten; one night fifty-eight minutes were cut from the long show—and then gradually restored in the coming days.

For her part, Merman at the time was having an affair with the very-married Sherman Billingsley, owner of the Stork Club, and had little on her mind except him. During the Boston tryout, Billingsley sent a catered supper to the entire cast, a generous gesture. On opening night, he gave Merman a gaudy, wide diamond-and-ruby bracelet that spelled out "FROM SHERM TO MERM." "Ugggh," says Crouse, who remembers the bracelet sixty years later. "Even then I knew that was tacky." Merman offered Billingsley $500,000 to leave his wife, but he refused.

No matter. The show did not do well, consistently losing $2,500 to $5,000 per week on grosses of $15,000 to $18,000. Neither a reduction in ticket prices nor a 50 percent pay cut taken by the show's principals helped—not even the tourists arriving for the 1939 World's Fair helped. The show closed on May 27, having run for a hundred and twenty-five performances. Wrote one Merman biographer, "Her songs were lackluster, and the lyrics dirty instead of saucy. Richard Carlson and Mildred Natwick, talented performers, were given little of substance as co-stars. Only Mary Wickes shined, and she could get laughs just walking across the stage."

Notices like this gave Mary the confidence to seek more permanent housing arrangements in New York. She left the AWA Clubhouse, where she had stayed whenever she was in town during the 1930s, for a proper apartment of her own. She moved into 1 Christopher Street, a modest but attractive apartment building at the corner of Christopher Street and Greenwich Avenue, just off Sixth Avenue. Although the apartment was in Greenwich Village, there was nothing bohemian about the building. Her unit on a middle floor was unusually dark, which might explain how she could afford it without a roommate. Although she had many friends in New York by this time, she rarely had guests in the apartment. "Food was very cheap in those days, and we went out. In the thirties, you could have a great dinner for a dollar and a half. Equity minimum then was $40 [a week]," says Bob Wallsten, an actor and later a writer, who would become a friend of Mary's for more than fifty years.

Lester L. Coleman, MD, might be called the head and neck specialist to the stars. Over many decades, his patients included Cary Grant, Sidney Poitier, Louis Armstrong, Barbra Streisand, Yul Brynner, and Quincy Jones. After he operated on Judy Garland, she made Coleman and his wife, Felicia, godparents to her two younger children, Lorna and Joey Luft. Coleman retired from practice at age ninety-one, but in the late 1930s he was just building an ear, nose, and throat practice when Mary came to see him at his office at 160 East 80th Street. She had developed a mild bronchial infection, but she was concerned because she was performing in *The Man Who Came to Dinner*. This comedy, in which she played a harassed nurse tending to an insufferably difficult patient, was not just any play, but the seminal role in Mary's career, and it is explored later in this book. In Coleman, Mary found not only a physician, but one of the most important people in her life during the years she lived in New York.

For Mary, who still missed the strong sense of family she left in St. Louis, Coleman and his wife filled a void. Felicia was a colorful woman who liked to write upside-down and backward. She was also a great cook, and Mary often came to their home at 336 Central Park West for dinner when not performing. "She was a homebody. And she had no home here, until later on when her mother came. She always wanted a home and a family, and she felt we were her protectors," Coleman says. It's easy to see why Mary, with her homespun values, would be drawn to the Colemans. Though he was a man of wealth who traveled the world and enjoyed friendships with people far better known than Mary, "fundamentally, I'd much rather have a hard-boiled egg in my home, listening to a little Bach or Mozart, than eat at Lutece or Le Cirque. I've been there and I don't like the pretentiousness." He and Felicia had a country house in Poundridge, Connecticut, where Mary sometimes visited for the day or weekend. "She was a wonderful guest, non-pretentious and needed no catering. She did not play the *prima donna* with friends," he says.

Through Mary, the Colemans also came to know Barbara Wolferman, a vibrant woman whom Mary befriended in Stockbridge and who, as an heir to the Wolferman baked goods company, was the only truly wealthy person in Mary's circle. (Wolferman would give up acting aspirations, first running Vincent Price's art gallery in Beverly Hills, later working as assistant casting director for Rodgers and Hammerstein, and finally becoming a prominent dog breeder—but the two women remained close.) The Colemans even spent time at the Wolfermans' magnificent winter estate on the waterfront in Carmel, California, making the cross-country drive in a brand new 1941 Chrysler convertible. On a second trip made shortly thereafter, Mary joined them in Carmel, leaving a film shoot in Los Angeles.

During these years, Mary found herself going back and forth between New York and Los Angeles more often than she would later in life. In Los Angeles, she stayed variously at the Villa Carlotta or Chateau Elysee, both on Franklin Avenue, or the Ravenswood Apartments on North Rossmore, as well as with actor Barry Sullivan and his family on Belden Drive in Beachwood Canyon. In 1943, having just finished two films in quick succession—the forgettable *Happy Land* and *My Kingdom for a Cook*—she was still in Los Angeles when Vinton Freedley offered her a prominent role in a Broadway musical. In *Dancing in the Streets*, Mary's character, a gossip columnist named Louella, was to have two musical numbers. The role didn't pay much—even with agents Audrey Wood and Edie Van Cleve in her corner, the most Freedley coughed up was $250 per week, plus transit back to New York—but it had success written all over it. It would star Mary Martin (this was before *South Pacific*, *Peter Pan*, and *the Sound of Music*), feature songs by Vernon Duke and Howard

Dietz, and employ sets and lighting by the pre-eminent designer Robert Edmond Jones. She accepted.

During rehearsals, Jones, a respected presence in the theatre who designed many of Eugene O'Neill's plays, gave Mary some advice: "My eagle eye observes that you have a tendency to hang your head on the stage. Perhaps this is because you are so tall. Anyway, the result is that your eyes can't always be seen—and you need those orbs for your comedy. Just play to the gallery and you'll be all set."

Dancing began tryouts in Boston March 19, 1943, and had trouble from the start. Writers Garson Kanin and Robert Russell were brought to Boston to help salvage the show, but it folded after less than a month and never made it to New York.

This season brought Mary an even bigger disappointment. On June 21, her father Frank died of a heart attack in St. Louis at sixty-three. She was in Santa Rosa, California, shooting *Happy Land*, when it happened. "She was devastated by the loss of her father," Coleman remembers. "It apparently was a very good marriage between her parents." It's true that Mary's parents by most accounts had a close relationship. But Mary had always been the center of the Wickenhauser household, and in her absence, any flaws in Frank and Isabella's relationship became harder to overlook. Just a year before, Frank offered Mary an apology for having treated Isabella harshly during one of Mary's visits home. "I know you are worrying about mother but please believe me when I say I will be considerate of her and do as she wants me to and try not to be cross and ugly to her. I know this must be on your mind all the time and I hated to see you leave us under those conditions. I am sorry that your visit was made so unhappy by me and I realize too what a fool I have made of myself," he wrote her. "You need [not] have any cause for worry. I am going to take care of mother and be more considerate of her. I know mother is very, very nervous and that I am the fault of it." A month later, Mary wrote Frank, "Does mother really seem to be getting along all right? Is she eating properly? Have you kept your word about taking care of her and being kind and thoughtful? Please do. It means so much. If you have changed, as you promised you would, I know how much it must mean to both of you and how much happier the house must be."

With Frank's passing, Mary now asked Isabella to live with her in New York. In an exchange of letters in August, the two women shared their desires and anxieties about living together permanently. It would be a big change for both of them, not just in practical ways, but in how they perceived each other. This was no doubt a greater adjustment for

Mary than for Isabella. Isabella, after all, had never stopped adding items to a "hope chest" for Mary—and Mary was thirty-three. Isabella's recent letters continued offering Mary reminders about the importance of eating well, tips on laundering clothing, suggestions for outfits, and advice on getting proper rest, such as sitting whenever possible between scenes.

"While I said I would devote my life to you from now on, I appreciate that that can be over-done in that it might make it very hard on you," Isabella acknowledged. "Yes, we are two individuals. Dad and I used to say that we tried to think of you as an individual—not as our somebody who had to do [things] our way—and you are an individual and a friend and yet, I think we have proven how close we have been and [how close] we are. I hope to be interesting. I'm not so sure of a career, but I would love to have a try at one of some kind. Time will tell that. The thing I have been trying to say is that you are just as free as you ever were and your happiness is my happiness."

"I am afraid of missing St. Louis. But believe me, I would rather be in California or New York with you than in St. Louis without you. Don't ever forget for one minute, you are the only person I want to be with and I couldn't speak truer words to any one, so I am a mother to be envied and I thank God for you every day," wrote Isabella. "The only reason I mention I may miss being here is because I am not going to begin our time together pretending . . . I won't be torn over going away from Dad any more for I did think of him almost all the time and it was right for me to [make this decision] but that is over. And for his sake, we should look forward to being together and being happy."

Isabella remained in St. Louis until she could sell the family house on Pershing Avenue. The two women hoped to get a good amount to help them start fresh together, but real estate had not recovered from the effects of the Depression. Frank and Isabella had paid $18,000 for the house on September 18, 1929, just a month before the market crash. When Isabella sold it on October 15, 1943, the intervening fourteen years had exacted a toll. The home had been listed at $11,500 and sold for $9,250—only slightly more than half what the Wickenhausers paid. After taxes and payment of an earlier deed, Isabella was left with a mere $5,900. Isabella tried to get as much as she could for household furniture that would not be needed in New York, such as Mary's childhood bedroom suite and a piano. Mary, who was filming *Higher and Higher* in Los Angeles, stopped in St. Louis on her train trip back to New York and helped pack up what remained.

Mary and Isabella arrived together in New York in the last days of October 1943, allowing them to be together for their first Christmas without Frank. They settled at the Park Chambers, a modest apartment hotel on the southeast corner of Sixth Avenue and 58th Street, just east of Broadway and south of Central Park South. The building's chief claim to fame was that silent film star Gloria Swanson had occupied the entire top floor for several years in the late 1920s. Once settled there, Mary intended to focus her job searches on New York and travel less frequently to Los Angeles.

So it was that Isabella and Mary became inseparable for the rest of Isabella's life, a life lived in service of Mary's needs. Isabella kept house, did the shopping, and prepared their meals. While Mary worked during the day, Isabella "waited for Mary. That says it completely," says Coleman. "Her mother was highly protective of her. A portrait of general maternalization—what clothes they wore, where they lived, what they ate. They were *always* together. I don't ever remember seeing them separately after the father died. But Mary had a great love for her mother. And she, too, was very protective. I'm sure she didn't want to leave her alone. I never had the feeling that Mary was imposed on." Says family friend Louis Westheimer, "I don't think it bothered Mary a bit. They were deep companions." Lifelong friend Bob Wallsten says, "These two isolated ladies clung to each other. When Mr. Wickenhauser died, Isabella sort of fastened on Mary, but I think to Mary's delight." Isabella helped Wallsten secure a small unit at the Park Chambers in 1944, when housing was scarce owing to the influx of returning servicemen. "Mary's mother talked to the management at the hotel about getting me a room there right after the war as a civilian," he remembers.

Together, Mary and Isabella set about building a new life. They transferred membership from Christ Church Cathedral in St. Louis to the Church of Saint Mary the Virgin in Times Square (both were Episcopal churches). And now Mary sought to integrate Isabella in her life more broadly. This process happened easily and quickly, both in the theatre world and among Mary's friends. "Everybody who loved Mary loved Isabella. She was a sweet, gentle, non-intrusive, caring person. I don't have a feeling of any intellectual accomplishments—she was just a good mother," says Coleman.

Some evenings, the Colemans came to Mary and Isabella's apartment for simple dinners. Often, the Colemans had Mary and Isabella over for dinner and chamber music, one of Coleman's passions. "Neither of them had any knowledge of chamber music, and they were both very receptive. We had a big, sprawling couch-bed, and we would all lie on top of the bed and listen to chamber music. I would play it and teach it to them." On other evenings, Mary and Isabella joined a large, diverse group at Park Avenue and 48th Street. When singer Annamary Dickey and her husband left their fourth-floor unit there for one two floors up in 1945, eight young men just back from the war jumped at the rental opportunity. They began sharing this unusually large apartment and, pooling their resources, had enough funds left over to hire a cook. Various men came and went as some got married or moved away—but they had a regular Thursday night open house that drew thirty to forty people for casual dinners. One constant among the residents was Jim Gillis, a St. Louis acquaintance and an actor who had small roles in pre-war Broadway hits like *Babes in Arms*. From 1945 to 1950, Mary and Isabella regularly joined Gillis, Dickey, and others at the men's Thursday night gatherings. While the guests were a mix of people, occasionally including visiting parents, many were from the theatre. Dickey herself was an operatic soprano and popular supper club performer who broke attendance records at the Waldorf Astoria's Wedgewood Room across the street. "One night, very early in this, one of the guys brought up the fact that we didn't have enough liquor to entertain all these guests after dinner. So one of them said, OK, we're going to have a game, a dance, the Conga, where you took three steps one way then three steps the other in a long line of people," recalls John Scott, a resident who later built a career in the bottled water business. "He took them out the back door of the apartment, through the bowels of the building, out the door onto 49th Street, then across the street into the Waldorf lobby and said, 'Well, good night, everybody!'"

But even in such settings, Isabella never relinquished her sense of propriety. "Her mother was always there and always wore hats," remembers actor James O'Rear. "If she was spending the evening, or at dinner, her hat was on. Outside or inside. We thought it was odd." Isabella did leave an impression. The actress Mary Healy worked with Mary on two TV series, yet she says her most vivid memory of Mary is not of Mary per se but of an evening spent chatting with Isabella after the two women prepared a simple dinner for Healy and husband, Peter Lind Hayes.

Mary's first job after Isabella arrived was *Jackpot*, a Broadway show for which producer Freedley again convened Vernon Duke and Howard Dietz for music and lyrics and Robert Edmond Jones for set design. To recoup some of the money lost on *Dancing in the Streets*, he re-purposed some of the sets from that show and even a few of its musical numbers.

Mary's agent, Edie Van Cleve at MCA, tried to get Mary more money from Freedley than he paid her for *Dancing*, but Van Cleve was not having much luck. At one point, Freedley asked Mary to split the difference between his offer of $250 per week and Van Cleve's counter of $350, and evidently that is what happened. One difficulty in getting Mary more money throughout her career is that she enjoyed direct interactions with producers and could never give full control to agents, who then found themselves undermined both by Mary's rapport with them and by Mary's desire, first and foremost, to work. Mary was generally impatient with agents and never remained with anyone for long. One of her first agents was Jane Broder, a powerhouse of 1930s and 1940s theatrical casting, who guided some of the most popular careers of the day from the sixth floor of the Times Building. But during the 1930s and '40s alone, Mary was also represented at various times by MCA (first Lew Wasserman and Edie Van Cleve, and later Maynard Morris), by the Liebling-Wood Agency, and by the Louis Schurr Agency. If Mary changed agents so much because she felt they were not advocating enough on her behalf, it's also true that many times she suffered for not having a strong relationship with any one agent, or, at several points, for not having an agent at all.

With contract negotiations for *Jackpot* complete, Mary was eager to work. *Jackpot* was a musical comedy about a war bond lottery whose prize was an attractive young woman (Nanette Fabray). Three men win and vie for her attention (actors Benny Baker and Jerry Lester and singer Allan Jones). For romantic interest, Mary was paired with Baker, Betty Garrett with Lester, and Fabray with Jones—the last pair the most prominent performers in the show. Mary was "bug-eyed with excitement" about this one. The show gave her some very funny lines—and Freedley promised that she would be "glamorized."

As a promotion, Freedley staged a war bond rally at Saks Fifth Avenue on Valentine's Day with the slogan, "Buy a bond and get a date with a *Jackpot* pretty." Winners had to draw the right number with their bond purchase. One of the actresses "raffled off" was Jacqueline Susann, who had only a small part but would later become known as author of *Valley of the Dolls*. But the winner was a woman, something organizers had not counted on. This "was of course wrong—a woman shouldn't win a woman," declared one paper, which reported that when the winner insisted on collecting her prize—a visit to the Stork Club—producers "bought her off" with three tickets to *Jackpot*, and Susann went out with two servicemen.

Gimmicky promotions could not save the show from terrible reviews in New York. "There are few safe bets on Broadway, but a Vinton Freedley musical is usually one of them. Consequently, *Jackpot* is something to sit through in amazement. It is a complete frost, an unmitigated bore, an ocean-crossing of tedium. The completeness of the disaster is hard to understand, seeing how many talented and experienced people are mixed up in it. There isn't much you can do except look at Nanette Fabray—who is still a stunner—when she is on the stage, and snooze quietly when she is off," said one opening night reviewer. Another, after seeing the show a second time, wrote, "I still felt, with the utmost regrets, that the musical was not very good. I was offended by its cheap sex gags in both lines and lyrics, and by the practically pathological obsession that many of the principals had in patting, clutching or reaching for people in the environs of the backside." A third called it "vulgar."

Fabray blames a lot of this on Jerry Lester. "He was a pain in the ass. He was always 'on.' He, singularly, was responsible for the show failing, on opening night. He got 'buck fever' and instead of playing the character he was supposed to play, which was just one of three guys, he resorted to his nightclub personality and was throwing jokes to the audience and coming out of character. It just put an iceberg on the show," she said. "We had been playing out of town for weeks because we couldn't find a theatre to come into town with. But we had been playing to sell-out houses—the show was a big smash hit. When a theatre finally became available, we came in knowing we'd settle in forever. And Jerry ruined the show. It just spoiled the empathy we all had for each other. You don't recover from those kind of notices."

While the show may not have been the greatest, "it was the most fun," Betty Garrett says. While Fabray and Jones had the star dressing rooms on the first floor off the Alvin Theatre stage, Mary and the others were upstairs. "It was a strange situation where you took an elevator to the dressing room. I don't think any other theatre in New York had elevators up to the dressing rooms. So we were up on the second and third floors. But we all had so much fun together that half the time, we ended up with everybody in my dressing room. We called ourselves the Four Bananas. Jerry Lester used to come in, bring his makeup and sit. Jerry had no shame—he'd take his clothes off right in front of you. Mary and Benny would always end up in our dressing room, and the jokes just flew back and forth," Garrett says. "It was a very happy company. Allan Jones was an interesting man. He had this glorious voice, but was stiff as a board as an actor, unless he'd had a few drinks. Then he loosened up and was very charming. But then he sang slightly sharp, which used to drive us nuts. We'd say, '*Well*, Allan must have had a drink tonight.'"

After several disappointments in a row, Mary returned to the safety of familiar territory and cast her lot with George S. Kaufman, who had given her two big successes, *Stage Door* and *The Man Who Came to Dinner*. This time, it was a show called *Hollywood Pinafore*. *Hollywood Pinafore* was based on Gilbert and Sullivan's long-running English musical comedy, *HMS Pinafore*, about love among different classes aboard a war ship. As parodied by Kaufman, the ship becomes a film studio trying to acquire movie rights to Edgar Allen Poe's poem "The Raven." The play starred William Gaxton and Victor Moore, an established stage pairing. Moore played Joe Porter, the bumbling but endearing head of the studio, and Gaxton played Dick Live-Eye, the slick, unpopular talent agent. Shirley Booth played Hollywood columnist LouHedda Hopsons (an amalgam of power gossips Louella Parsons and Hedda Hopper), and Mary's friend Annamary Dickey played a film star. Mary's role—Miss Hebe, Porter's studio secretary—was the smallest of the seven principals, but she was on stage in virtually all of Moore's scenes, and there was a lot of comic business between them. Mary must have been thrilled to find herself sharing a stage with Moore, whom she had seen from the seats of the American Theatre in St. Louis years before in Kaufman's *Of Thee I Sing*.

Pinafore paid Mary $250 per week and, as a promising hit, held out the hope of a sustained salary. But it was not meant to be. Officially the show was directed by Kaufman and produced by Max Gordon, with Arnold Saint Subber serving as "production supervisor." In reality, things were a bit different, recalls Jeff Warren, who understudied the role of Ralph Rackstraw, a hack writer, and also had a small part as a make-up man. "It was a combination of George S. and Saint mixing things up quite a bit. And things got so bad that the last week out of town, before coming in [to New York] to open, Moore, Gaxton and Booth threatened to quit if the show wasn't frozen on the night after their ultimatum. There had been too many changes and the stars were panicking." Tryouts in Philadelphia were especially problematic. "Saint Subber and Kaufman were having big problems in making changes and directions. They'd leave us all on stage and go out into the lobby where they could yell at each other for some rather extended periods," Warren says. During one such period, Booth discovered an old upright piano in the wings and, with Mary seated beside her, started to play some bouncy, old-fashioned numbers as the singers and dancers gathered around them.

Hollywood Pinafore had some big strikes against it from the moment it opened. First, it opened during a heat wave. Second, attempting to keep the theatre comfortable, the Alvin relied upon fans that blew air over several dozen huge blocks of ice—but the ice haulers were on strike the first week of the show. Third, there was also a newspaper strike, which kept theatergoers from reading reviews for six to eight days. "Few theatergoers knew the show was in town," Warren recalls. "Under better luck with strikers, we would probably have made it through for six to eight months as a modest success." Several young women in the show could neither sing nor act. "They were just beautiful, and the last of an almost vanished breed of showgirls whose sole reason for being included in the cast was to keep bored husbands and tired businessmen from going to sleep and snoring the during the performance," Warren says.

The writing was on the wall from the beginning. On July 1, Mary received this letter from Kaufman: "You were wonderful, Wickes—sorry I gave you a flop. Don't go back to Hollywood—unless you like to eat, of course." The show lasted about six weeks, closing July 14, 1945. On closing night, Kaufman posted an announcement on the backstage bulletin board apologizing to the company for not giving them as good a script as he had hoped—a rare public concession from a Broadway playwright. Given the vibrant state of theatre at the time, the short run was indeed a disappointment. The smash *Carousel* had opened about six weeks before and would play for another two years. *Oklahoma!*, which revolutionized American musical theatre, was in the second year of what would be a five-year run.

Mary's next big show presented a welcome change. In *Park Avenue*, a musical comedy about the idle rich, she played a glamorous society woman with a dry sense of humor, dressed in chic gowns by Mainbocher and Tina Leser. She received $350 per week, $100 more than during *Hollywood Pinafore*. The show had a strong pedigree: not only Kaufman directing and writing (with Nunnally Johnson), but Arthur Schwartz creating the music, Ira Gershwin writing the lyrics, and Max Gordon producing. "They said this was going to be the hit of the century. We had all these wonderful people and wonderful sets. But I think we knew it wasn't that great. Something was wrong, but I don't know what it was," says cast member Virginia Gibson. The show ran only seventy-two performances between November 1946 and January 1947.

The biggest problem seemed to be that New York audiences took umbrage at the show's premise: The wealthy denizens of Park Avenue divorced so many times they often did not even recognize their own children. The show got mixed reviews in tryouts in New Haven, Boston, and Philadelphia, but audiences responded well to the story, including the final scene in which neither Gibson's character nor her date (played by the much older Raymond Walburn) realize they are father and daughter. Gibson, in a sexy white angora sweater and tight pants, played a teenager who was searching for the autograph book she brought to a party. "Out of town, they laughed and just thought it was funny, this old guy trying to make out with me," she says. But at the Shubert on Broadway, "Park Avenue people were in the audience every night and did not laugh too loudly. We knew from the opening night reviews that it wasn't going to last." In fact, audiences found the suggestion of father-daughter romance so distasteful that Kaufman removed that entire scene after opening night. This surgery shortened the play by about fifteen minutes and cost Gibson a job, since this was her only scene. But Kaufman soon asked her to return as understudy for Martha Stewart, the singing ingénue. Up to that point, Stewart's understudy had been Betty Lynn, and some confusion arose one night when Stewart took ill. Assuming she would go on in Stewart's place, Betty Lynn arranged for her excited parents to come to the show, but Kaufman had Gibson take the part instead.

Once again, Mary's notices were stronger than those of the production as a whole. The *New York Sun* called Mary, who played Walburn's present wife, "delightfully droll as ever." The *Philadelphia Daily News* called her "indignant and priceless" and touted one of her songs, "Don't Be a Woman if You Can," as a show stopper, in which Mary, Marthe Errolle, and Ruth Matteson recount such troubles as "picking out the right nail polish and most surefire perfume." The *Boston Evening American* praised Mary's mugging as "perfectly underdone" and said, "Mary has overcome—as many of us thought she might never—the Kaufman-Hart sobriquet of 'Miss Bedpan' [from *The Man Who Came to Dinner*]."

Kaufman was a strong presence throughout the production. "He was a fantastic man, but he worked very strangely," Gibson says. "I was waiting to get all this great direction for my scene, but the direction was, 'Come in, this is a party, this is not your house, you're not comfortable, you're looking for your autograph book, which you'd put down somewhere. For the rest, just follow what goes on.' That was it. He'd walk back and forth across the back of the theatre and if the way you were saying it didn't sound right to him, he'd stop. So he probably really loved Mary, because a lot of it was her voice." Kaufman may not have communicated very much, but Gibson remembers him as kind and sensitive. One particular conversation sticks in her mind. During rehearsals, he was auditioning showgirls one day and called her over. "Sit with me while I look at them," he told her. "This is terrible because if they get rejected, it's not because they didn't sing the right notes or dance well enough—they're just rejected on what they look like. I hate this. I just hate to do this. "

This string of high-profile appearances meant Mary soon found herself with competing opportunities. In the spring of 1947, she was offered $400 per week and prominent billing to play Tatiana Kerskaya in *Music in My Heart*, a period piece with a Russian ballet storyline. Mary initially agreed to the part—per correspondence between producer Henry Duffy and Maynard Morris of MCA, representing Mary—but later withdrew. A part in the film *The Decision of Christopher Blake* had been written for her, and filming would conflict with rehearsal dates for *Music in My Heart*. No doubt, she also felt on more familiar terrain with *Blake*: The film was based on a play by Moss Hart, whose expectations she knew well, while *Music in My Heart* would require singing, which was never her strength. When *Music in My Heart* opened October 2, 1947, Kerskaya was played by the musically superior Vivienne Segal and ran for a hundred and forty-three performances. Mary, on the other hand, earned $1,000 a week while filming *Christopher Blake* in Los Angeles—but for a much shorter time.

After *Christopher Blake* finished shooting, Mary stayed in Los Angeles to shoot *June Bride*, which starred Bette Davis. Then she received an offer to return to Broadway in *Make Mine Manhattan*, a collection of skits celebrating New York City. She turned this down for something with even great possibilities, *Town House*. Adapted from a series of *New Yorker* stories by John Cheever, *Town House* was a comedy about three couples of different backgrounds who, due to the post-war housing shortage, try to live together in a large New York home. Mary was the humorless Esther Murray, an intellectual who lacks style or social graces. To reinforce Esther's awkwardness, Mary wore an ill-fitting, mustard-colored dress that she made herself years before but had never worn.

Town House unfolded on a large set of rooms on two levels, with action sometimes taking place in multiple rooms at once. Some theater-goers, especially in the front rows, had difficulty viewing the action on the top floor; others found it all distracting and over-wrought. "I was so fascinated by the upstairs, the downstairs and the ladies' chambers that I often missed what the inhabitants were saying," one reviewer observed. Ultimately, a complicated set was the least of the problems at *Town House*. "Despite the three couples and their neurotic crises, *Town House* remains unoccupied. Nothing happens that a theatre-goer can get interested in," concluded *New York Times* reviewer Brooks Atkinson. The play closed after only twelve performances, a particular disappointment for Mary because this show held real financial promise: Her contract with producer Max Gordon gave her $600 a week, the most she had earned for any stage role so far.

Mary received particularly strong notices from the *Boston Post* ("Her sharp wisecracking thrusts are shrewdly balanced by soft touches of pathos") and the *New York Sun* ("she does a great deal with every line written for her, every bit of business given to her"). But what might have pleased her most was this observation from Cheever himself: "Her voice is like a trumpet, her limbs are uncontrolled, her feet hurt her and she is obviously short of breath, but one never loses the sense that her spirit is magnificent and that somewhere in her odd, loose-jointed carcass there beats a heart of gold," he observed. "The performance seems to me to have a richness far beyond its obvious pathos and comedy, so that Miss Wickes brings to her awkwardness some universality." Even when shows did not last, Mary took great pleasure in them; she genuinely enjoyed being on a stage. But it was the television stage that most defined Mary's future.

Where others were hesitant about working in this new, untried medium, Mary jumped at television opportunities. Her first role was in late 1945, truly the early days. She appeared in an *NBC Dramatic Sustainer*, a Sunday night drama intended to help fill programming gaps. The sustainers were broadcast live from WNBT in New York. Some were thirty minutes and others an hour, while a few, such as a production of the Broadway show *Blithe Spirit*, ran almost two hours. The length varied because, well, it could; often, nothing was scheduled to follow. Many of the segments, like Mary's, were directed by TV pioneer Fred Coe. Mary's was an hour-long story called "Ring on Her Finger," about which we know little—except that it was not very good. "Everything about this production, except the smooth camera work, was amateurish, and it also was out of focus frequently. The cast was big and bad. There were plenty of scenes, from a Mexican mountain to a modern living room. They meant nothing," a newspaper review said. "It was a script stinker to start with, and Fred Coe's direction didn't help an iota. The cast muffed lines and hadn't, for the most part, the slightest idea of the motivation of the characters they were playing. Only one fem, Daisy, played by Mary Wickes, seemed to be alive, the rest weren't even good puppets." This television review would be the first of many to single Mary out among ensemble casts, even when the overall view was not positive. The Dramatic Sustainers were replaced in 1948 by the *Philco Television Playhouse*, which would run for seven years.

Mary arrived when television was in its infancy, a status that showed in ways beyond out-of-focus images. The live nature of performances led to an environment where errors were frequent, reflecting lack of experience with the new technology. Audio was sometimes disrupted by the sound of cables being dragged across the studio floor. Lighting was primitive, albeit inventive: To suggest the passing of a car's head-lights, prop men occasionally walked behind the camera holding a light in each hand. Viewers might sometimes spot stagehands walking across the back of the set while the camera was rolling. Costume changes were awkward: Sometimes an actor would appear in a prolonged close-up so that costumers could literally change the performer's clothing below the camera line, and actors might be dressing in the wings of the soundstage.

All of this activity meant that performers sometimes created comedy where none was desired. "Lots of mistakes went out live. I remember one actor was supposed to pick up a prop at the end of the fireplace and he goes over to it and the prop isn't there, so the stagehand comes run-ning in and hands him the prop. It was live—you couldn't stop," laughs Emily Daniels, a friend of Mary's who was "script girl" on the (live) *Ford Television Theatre* and *Nash Airflyte Theatre* and camera coordinator on (the taped) *I Love Lucy*. "It was crazy and *nobody* knew what they were doing," Daniels says. "We were in Studio 41, CBS, up in Grand Central, on the fourth floor. It was brand new—they were still *building* the damn studios when we were in there." In fact, in this period in New York, the man who would later become head of production at 20th Century-Fox Tele-vision in Los Angeles didn't even have a TV. "The only time I ever saw television was when my wife was on it," says Martin Manulis. Katharine Bard, his wife, performed in many early series, such as *Studio One*, which Manulis watched from a corner restaurant.

This creative environment also paved the way for today's TV "re-run" broadcasts. Elliott Reid remembers that a 1949 live episode of the senti-mental sitcom *Mama*, on which he played a piano teacher, was so well-liked that it was performed a second time a few months later—the exact same story ("The Piano Teacher") with Reid again appearing as guest star.

As television production moved to the West Coast, Mary encoun-tered the same dynamics. "We were all quite a fraternity," says Lamont

Johnson, who directed live episodes of *Matinee Theatre* in Burbank in the mid-1950s. "There were always two or three shows sharing that huge studio at NBC. So we were all mixing together running into each other in the dressing rooms and rehearsal rooms there. It was live. There was no turning back—you were on the air until you were off, which is why we depended so much on theatre people. Mary's theatre background made her desirable because people who were used to doing summer stock—where the curtain goes up and you're on your own with a full length play—were much better prepared for live TV. It was turmoil, a wonderful kind of creative ferment . . . and by golly once you got close to show time, you had had so little real preparation for so many things that could go wrong, that there was a great sense of suspense."

But virtually all who were part of it, including Mary, relished the experience, both at the time and in reflection decades later. "We were all starting together and nobody was telling us what to do or how to do it. We learned from each other. It was a very magical time," says Adrienne Luraschi, who was a script girl and then associate director on many early TV dramas. Lenka Peterson, who performed with Mary both on stage and in live TV, loved live television and benefited from the experience. "Competition is much fiercer now. People who are now dancing in the choruses of Broadway musicals could have been stars in that day and age," she says.

Mary's first live series role was *Inside U.S.A. with Chevrolet*, an every-other-week music and variety show in which she appeared in comedy skits with Peter Lind Hayes and Mary Healy, popular New York personalities and nightclub performers. The 1949-50 series drew major guests, including Lucille Ball, Charles Boyer, Ethel Merman, and David Niven. It featured dancers in big production numbers—which were almost too big to appreciate, since most television screens at the time were no larger than eleven inches. The show was performed at CBS Studio 52, home to the *Ed Sullivan Show* and (more recently) the *Late Show with David Letterman*. (CBS named its studios in the order it bought them; the names do not refer to streets.) "It was a top-of-the-line kind of show—but then there wasn't much of a line in those days," says Healy. "It was tough. If you made a mistake, you were stuck out there with egg on your face." Indeed, in one segment, Mary plays a cranky rooming house operator to lodgers Hayes and Healy, but a silent pause in the performance makes clear that Healy does not realize the next line is hers. Alert viewers clearly see Mary giving Healy a big nudge on camera with her right elbow, prompting Healy to quickly blurt out her line.

Although the job was not Broadway, for Mary it represented steady work for twenty-six weeks, and she jumped at it. "It was just another job, because television wasn't what it is today. We were very snobby in the theatre, and television was a way of making money, to be very honest," says the show's primary dancer, Sheila Bond, who would win a Tony Award a few years later. "When I did theatre, they didn't pay as much, but I supplemented my income with 'guest star' roles. I was on the Sullivan show I don't know how many times. We did a scene from a show or I did a dance or a song. I didn't think of [*Inside U.S.A.*] as being very elegant. Television was a brand new thing. Nobody thought it would be what it is today." The show was a pleasant experience—"a fun, family kind of thing," Bond remembers—but Chevrolet decided its $26,000 budget was too much and did not renew its option to continue, so it ended in March 1950. Because TV programs were relatively inexpensive to produce, there were many of them, so for a time it was more unusual for a series to be renewed than dropped. "It was like, if you do badly, we'll try it with another one," says Lenka Peterson. But in this case, Mary's work with Hayes and Healy continued: When the couple was offered an NBC program a few months later—this one sponsored by Borden—they hired Mary to play their housekeeper. The series was first called *The Peter and Mary Show* and later renamed *The Peter Lind Hayes Show with Mary Healy.* "We all felt we were taking part in something new and exciting. A lot of people were afraid to be on TV," Healy says.

A lot of people, but not everyone. One venerable star who made the leap was Gloria Swanson, whose transition from silent films to talkies may have encouraged her to enter this new medium. The nascent DuMont Network brought viewers *The Gloria Swanson Hour* in 1948, and Mary was one of Swanson's first guests. It was a live chat show, part of a genre that would later be referred to as "women's shows." No visual record of *The Gloria Swanson Hour* exists, so we can only guess that Mary was there to promote an episode of *The Actor's Studio* on which she would appear a few nights later. She and Swanson sat beside each other on a set resembling a comfortable upscale living room. The segment was called "Design for Living," and what they talked about mostly was furniture and décor—an odd topic for a young actress, to be sure, but one Mary was quite comfortable with. She and Isabella lived surrounded by family antiques from Missouri and Illinois, dark, ornate pieces from the 1830s and 1840s. Mary quite possibly never bought a stick of furniture her entire life, preferring to surround herself with these inherited pieces.

Mary appeared on some of the most prestigious programs of the pe-
riod, such as *Studio One*, *Playhouse 90*, *Actor's Studio*, *Philco Television Playhouse*, and *Matinee Theatre*. In fact, in 1948 she was in the debut episode
of *Studio One*, a story called "The Storm," starring Margaret Sullavan.
Mary appeared in three other stories in that venerable series, two of
them as the episode's star. One was "Mary Poppins," the first production
of the story anywhere, and the other "Mrs. Hargreaves," in which she
beautifully plays an unconventional Auntie Mame-like character who
springs to life from someone's imagination. The shows were all broadcast
live from New York. Performers rehearsed for a week before a one-day
camera rehearsal, followed by a dress rehearsal, and then the live performance. In this fast-paced environment, functions sometimes blurred.
For instance, "Poppins" was directed by Paul Nickell, but the performers
also received direction from the producer, sometimes creating confusion.
"A very brilliant man called Worthington Miner was the producer. He
would come in and re-direct it, and then Paul Nickel would come in
and direct it differently," remembers Iris Mann, who played one of the
children. "It didn't bother me, but [child actor] Tommy Rettig got a little
upset. I remember his mother saying, 'When Nickell is there do it the
way *he* wants it but when Tony Miner is there do it the way *he* wants it.'"

Mary's final role in a live series—before TV shows began broadcasting
routinely from videotape—was in *I, Bonino*. In this 1953 series, she runs
the household of a recently widowed touring concert singer, who decides
to return home permanently to spend more time with his eight children.
The singer was played by Ezio Pinza, fresh off his Tony Award-winning
turn in *South Pacific*. But Pinza's character seemed oafish, not likeable
enough to sustain interest. As one reviewer noted after the premier episode, "In future weeks, it must be hoped that the assignment for Miss
Wickes will be substantially enlarged, if indeed not made virtually equal
to that of Mr. Pinza. For she not only could be an admirable foil, but also
could carry much of the action and give the show some distinctive im-
print. Mr. Pinza can hardly go it alone."

Lenka Peterson, who played Pinza's eldest daughter, found strong
support from Mary when a personal dilemma surfaced. Shortly after accepting the role (which Eva Marie Saint had played opposite Mary in the
pilot), Peterson discovered she was pregnant. "I went to Mr. Pinza and
[director] Gordon Duff and said, "I'm sorry. I feel terrible. I really didn't
know until just now, but I have to tell you I'm pregnant." And Pinza
said, "Why do you look so sad? I would be so happy if my wife called
and told me that." And I said yes, but it would interfere with the series,

because they had planned for a long time the courtship [of her character]. So they changed the stories and brought the wedding in pretty close to the beginning. But then I began to show signs of miscarriage. The only thing that scared me to death was that I might accidentally get some blood on the $500 wedding gown. Mary was very reassuring when I was worried about the pregnancy. She'd say, 'Your health is all that matters.' She was that kind of person."

The series was broadcast live from the Hudson Theatre, which had been converted to a TV studio (later used for *The Steve Allen Show*, among others). The Hudson was familiar territory for Mary, who had been there many times during its earlier incarnation. In the 1940s, before NBC took it over, the building was partially owned by Russel Crouse and Howard Lindsay, who moved their playwriting offices there. The offices had been lined with bookshelves, all of them empty. So as a moving-in present, Mary and two friends—actresses Mary Mason and Judy Abbott (daughter of producer George Abbott)—hastily populated the shelves. "They went to some minor second-hand bookstores and bought the damnedest collection of books you have ever seen to fill the bookshelves. Everything from books on sex, to bringing up children—it didn't matter what it was, so long as it was cheap. Probably cost them a quarter a piece," Anna Crouse says.

I, Bonino lasted only thirteen weeks. For Mary, the most lasting benefit of this series might have been a cocktail. It was Pinza who introduced her to the Americano (Campari, Vermouth and soda), her preferred drink ever after.

Between TV, stage, and film assignments, Mary sought whatever other work she could. She needed to support herself, but she also wanted to build a name. She appeared in several short industrial films in New York, mostly concerning civil defense matters. Actor Joe Ross remembers them as "a little extra money, like a touch of dessert. It was a job for maybe two or three days—boop, and you were done." Topics included joining the military, leaving home, using a parachute, lifeguarding, and the like. In one, Mary was Ross's belligerent secretary. Mary turned to radio to fill in gaps, too. It's hard today for many to appreciate how central radio programming was to American life in the 1930s and 1940s. Radio offerings were as popular a conversation topic then as movies might be today. Besides working in *Mercury Theatre on the Air*, Mary had ongoing roles in a few series (like *Lorenzo Jones* and *Meet Corliss Archer*), occasional roles in many others (*Colonel Stoopnagle and Budd* and *Portia Faces Life*), and even did commercials (*Vic and Sade*). The shows were performed live but mostly without an audience. "It was just people standing in front of microphones and reading. We had about two readings before we went on the air. This was not a thing where you had to go to the Stella Adler Studio and grope for the truth. It taught you to be quick. You were in and out in an hour," says Elliott Reid, who performed with Mary in radio. Because Mary was usually paid scale, she never earned much, and radio work was never a big part of her career.

CHAPTER FOUR

Anatomy Is Destiny

LIKE SO MANY NEW YORK ACTRESSES SEEKING STAGE ROLES IN THE 1940s, Mary made the rounds to agents' offices, hoping for a job that would bring in a regular paycheck. She was more tenacious than most, relentlessly putting her name and face before any agent who might arrange an audition. One such agent was Sarah Enright, who cast many of Brock Pemberton's productions and who had a reputation for being patient with actors, often welcoming them if they came in without an appointment. When Mary dropped in, Enright would inevitably say, "Oh, Mary, I don't know what I could send you for—*you're so tall!*" Once, Mary was excited about a particular part and told Enright eagerly, "It's a part I could do, won't you please send me?" On this occasion, Enright picked up the small pad of green paper on which she routinely wrote down for actors the information they needed to give producers to get appointments. "Oh, all right," she said with resignation, tearing off a sheet and handing it to Mary. "Here it is. But Mary, when you get over there, *watch that height*!"

This admonition ultimately made it into the annals of Broadway history. Some twenty years later, at a casting session for *UTBU*, a 1966 Broadway comedy about a secret society that tries to do away with disagreeable people, casting agent Terry Fay casually relayed the story to the play's star, Tony Randall, and its author, James Kirkwood, who would later pen *A Chorus Line*. The men thought it so amusing that Kirkwood decided to insert it into the script. In his review of the show, critic Martin Gottfried cited the line as an example of funny dialogue in an otherwise disappointing show: "You're rather tall for an actress—how many times have I told you to watch your height?"

This incident is just one example of how Mary's looks defined her work. Her career was shaped more by her physical features than by anything else, especially early in her career, when being tall carried a greater social liability for women. But Mary was never as large as people perceived, and this misperception rankled her. When a reporter wrote in 1973 that she was "over six feet tall," Mary quickly responded that she was only 5' 9¾". A costume-fitting document dating from when Mary was seventy-seven shows her height as 5' 10". It is possible that Mary was slightly taller before she began to age, but no doubt her overall presence left others thinking they were in the company of someone taller than she really was. This same costume document lists a 34" pants inseam, a size 11N shoe, 38" bust and hips, and a 23½" head size.

For decades, Mary withstood—as few others could—harsh public mockery regarding her appearance. Callous descriptions—"the wrinkle with lips" is how one character refers to her in a 1990s sitcom—became so routine that they limited Mary's career in ways she found hard to accept. "I don't know if she ever realized that she was such a homely woman," says actor and writer Peter Walker, one of Mary's favorite people. Though Mary was closer to him than to most, she never shared any feelings about her appearance, though surely it had a profound effect on the way she thought of herself and on the options she found in life. "But it was that homely thing obviously that got her the work. She knew that [her appearance and voice] was where her money was coming from, that she was never going to be the Claire Trevor or the pretty second leading lady. As a businesswoman she was very wise, and she kept her mother and herself very well," Walker says. Mary's appearance more than enhanced her career; in some ways, it allowed her to have one. Together, her height, her pronounced nose, her receding chin, and her attention-grabbing bark drew the notice of casting directors. Such was true from the very beginning. Not many young actresses got offers like this one, received by telegram in 1934: "What will you take for laughing out loud at dear Mrs. Post in subways and elevators. Stop. State lowest terms. Stop. Will pay carfare. Stop. Yours for publicity." Though money was tight at that point, there's no evidence Mary accepted this offer.

Perhaps the best example of how her appearance shaped her career was the 1961 Disney animated feature *One Hundred and One Dalmatians*. Because Mary is listed in the film's credits, many people believe she provided the voice of one of the film's beloved puppies. In fact, Mary's only contribution was her imposing figure: To bring the wicked Cruella De Vil to life, the studio asked Mary to pose for animators. So in January 1959, in black satin dress and costume wig (half black, half white), waving a cigarette extender with frightening élan, Mary preened and gestured on a bare stage to help Disney animator Marc Davis capture the woman who wanted to make fur coats out of cute puppies. But this was no quick day job; Mary was the model for a couple of weeks. "I thought, I'll just go out and they'll photograph me," she said. "The thing that's funny [is that] to me it was backwards. All the dialogue had been recorded. So I had to fit my movements to the dialogue. I would think it would be better the other way around." *Dalmatians* was the first and only time Mary took a job of this sort, but Davis says she did great work. "I used her suggestions and made them more so. If you looked at the footage of Mary and then the character, you would have a difficult time seeing the resemblance. It's suggestion you need," said Davis. The film was the last that Davis animated in a long career, "and I think I enjoyed working on Cruella more than any of the others. The broadest thing I ever had a chance to do was Cruella, and I enjoyed that aspect of her. She was just a nutty woman who probably went to the bathroom just like the rest of us. She had no realization whatsoever that she was cruel. That's just the way she was. She had no idea that the killing and butchering of these little puppies for a coat involved pain and suffering. She's pure evil, and that's what makes her interesting." The animated Cruella, voiced by Betty Lou Gerson, later inspired Glenn Close's live-action version in 1996. Even though Mary technically had no role in it, she still felt some investment in it. "She was very proud of *One Hundred and One Dalmatians*. She talked about it a lot, 'her' version, not the new one, like 'this one isn't as good as the one that I did' type-of-thing," says Emily Daniels.

One 1957 news article promoting *The Danny Thomas Show* reported that "Mary Wickes gets a special kick out of boasting that she's had no formal training in acting. What it boils down to is making the best of what you've got, such as a face like Mary's." Although the types of roles Mary was offered were limited, they frequently provided a given production's most memorable moments. Witness her brief part in 1953's *Half a Hero*, with Red Skelton. The movie, so plodding that it is almost painful to watch, comes alive only once, well into the film, when Mary appears for a few minutes as a prospective homebuyer who is clearly unimpressed by what she sees. When she asks Skelton incredulously, "You *bought* this rug?" she provides the film's only guaranteed laugh.

She excelled in these parts, which generated yet more offers, higher pay, and, ultimately, a stable career. But a close look at the roles she was offered—and the ones she was not—shows that her career suffered because of her appearance far more than it benefited. She was rejected many times for parts more challenging than the know-it-all nurses, nuns, and housekeepers that ultimately defined her. Certainly, she was passed over at every turn for romantic parts; her imposing physical presence and blustery demeanor meant her characters were almost always lonely, man-hungry spinsters. She throws herself at Buddy Ebsen on *The Beverly Hillbillies*; accosts the mailman and TV repairman in *Dennis the Menace*; chases Fred MacMurray aboard a cruise ship on *My Three Sons*; pines for the company of male townsfolk on *Bonanza*; laments her lack of a husband on *Make Room for Daddy*; and devotes herself to others' happiness as a professional matchmaker on *F-Troop*. She is a shrill, scheming biddy determined to marry off her "ugly as sin" daughters in a *Ford Startime* twist on Cinderella, and she is the Wicked Witch of the West in a stage production of *The Wizard of Oz*. Even when Mary is used only briefly, as when she provides a few lines of dialogue in an *I Spy* episode set in Mexico, her character jokes about not having married: "I never was a señora. She used to be," Mary says—pointing to the equally homely actress, Florence Halop—"but not me." Even as her characters aged, their hunger for men remained strong. As a wealthy matron in a *Murder, She Wrote* episode, performed when Mary is seventy-five, she tells a resort's roulette spinner, "Pierre, send in that boy in the tight pants. I need a glass of water." Her characters have spent so many years seeking men they have exhausted their patience with the notion of romance altogether, as when Mary cannot be bothered with a couple seeking to rekindle their honeymoon in her boardinghouse on a segment of *Inside U.S.A. with Chevrolet*. If one of Mary's characters finally entertained the prospect of marriage, things did not go well. In the TV series *Doc*, Mary's lonely Nurse Tully receives a marriage proposal, but the proposal is rescinded before she can prepare her answer. The few times any of Mary's characters were married, the marriage is beyond all convention, reassuring audiences that no ordinary man would desire her. *The Decision of Christopher Blake* is one such example: Mary appears as the happy wife of a thirteen-year-old boy in the boy's elaborate dream sequence.

But Mary had no illusions about any of this. A 1952 Warner Bros. press release for *The Will Rogers Story* opined, "Mary Wickes, the dour-faced comedienne, wants to know how a girl can expect to be sexy wearing a bun on the back of her neck. 'To paraphrase a line,' Miss Wickes said, 'you can't get a man with a bun, and apparently I'm doomed to wearing one for the rest of my screen life.' Like the clown who always wants to play Hamlet, the tall and angular Miss Wickes would like nothing better than to wear sleek satin and a poodle cut. 'But producers always see me as Miss Hatchet Face—the girl men run from,' she complained."

Mary's appearance often prevented her from being cast in even non-romantic roles. When John van Druten and Irene Selznick were preparing *Bell, Book and Candle* for its 1950 Broadway debut, Mary sought the part of Miss Holroyd, the eccentric aunt and witchcraft novice. Playwright and producer narrowed their choice to two actresses: Mary and Jean Adair, who had achieved fame as one of the sweet-but-murderous sisters in *Arsenic and Old Lace* on stage and in film. Mary did two readings for Selznick and van Druten, who ultimately chose Adair because of her softer, rounder features and because of her age. She and Mary shared the same birthday, but Mary, who had recently turned forty, was thirty-seven years younger. "We have talked it up and down and in and out from every angle—and on the whole we are a little bit afraid that just the matter of sheer actual physical height and youth might jeopardise a quality of fragility and tremulousness that we feel the part needs," van Druten wrote Mary in an especially gracious rejection. "God knows we may be all wrong and live to regret it bitterly—and we have been sorely tempted to stretch the point—but we have come to the conclusion that we do not dare go quite as far afield from our earlier conception of the part in a play which needs a pretty delicate balance of casting." (Always quick to return a kind gesture, Mary sent him a congratulatory wire on opening night.) For the 1958 film version, the aunt was played by Elsa Lanchester who, at about 5' 4", was both shorter and softer than Mary. More than thirty years later, Mary's height was still costing her roles. She was turned down for Gran in Hanna-Barbera's *Going Bananas* TV show about an orangutan with special powers after network executives decided a smaller actress would be more suitable for the animal. Marie Denn was given the role.

Casting legend Ethel Winant, who knew Mary for more than forty-five years, said casting fundamentals dictated that Mary could have been offered only the roles for which she became known. "Mary looked a certain way and was a certain kind of person. How else *could* she have been cast? What else could she have done?" Reminded of Mary's venturing into the lead in a 1968 production of *The Glass Menagerie*, Winant observes, "Amanda was a southern, gentle woman, a good product of the south, a product of generations of southern women who had fallen on hard times. She was filled with fantasy and total impracticality. Mary could not have done that in a million years. She didn't have any of the qualities. It's terrific that she did it [in this small production], but to cast her in it [in a commercial venue], you'd have to be insane." One of the first female executives in network television, Winant was a casting industry pioneer, having headed casting operations at both CBS and NBC during her long career. It was Winant who gave Mary the lead in "Mary Poppins" in 1949. If Winant could not see broader potential in Mary, could others be expected to?

Instead of trying to change her appearance, Mary sought professional avenues that would accommodate it. "She had a wonderful adjustment to her own personality and looks," says Betty Garrett, who recalls Mary being self-deprecating about her appearance, saying things like, "Any lady this tall," and "If you had a nose like mine." Many times, with a tone of I-told-you-so satisfaction, Mary told friends, "And they wanted me to get a nose job!" Joe Ross recalls Mary saying, "God gave me this, and I'm going to keep it. This is it. Hello, world, this is me,'" he says. "She always had that attitude—everything up, up, up." Maybe so, but she was always conscious of how others perceived her. On the back of a publicity photo for the 1972 *Here's Lucy* season opener, Mary scribbled in pencil to a photo editor, "In reproducing, can anything be done with that chin of mine?" She wrote an almost identical note on a publicity photo taken for the 1972 series premier of *The Don Rickles Show.* Jack O'Brien directed Mary in *You Can't Take It With You* on stage a year later. "I think she felt, maybe from the very beginning, that she had to work harder because she was so oblique, so isolated by her extraordinary looks and her height. She had to create a space, a necessity for herself. She gravitated to those writers who gave her the expression to do that," says the director, known more recently for his Broadway work on *Hairspray, The Full Monty,* and *The Coast of Utopia.*

One of the most astonishing examples of how Mary's looks shaped her career appears in a lengthy 1941 newspaper feature by Harold Heffernan, Hollywood-based editor of the *Detroit News*. The article, which also appeared in the *Milwaukee Journal* and the *St. Louis Post-Dispatch*, ran under headlines like "Homely Girls Doing Fine: Even if You are No Raving Beauty, You Can Make a Good Living in Pictures by Being Clever and Comical," and "Glamor-Gutted Hollywood Craves Homely Girls with Talent: Not Pretty, But Their Faces and Talents Pay Heavy Dividends in a Business Blanketed with Feminine Beauty." Discussing Mary together with Martha Raye, Patsy Kelly, Joan Davis, Judy Canova, Charlotte Greenwood, and Marie Blake, the article purported to laud the successful careers of sour-faced actresses who built lasting careers. Offensive by almost any measure, it would never be printed today. For instance: "One of the most important casting directors in town emphasized this swamping of the Hollywood beauty market to us and then added: 'For more than two hours today I have been trying to find a homely girl who can act. It seems impossible to get one. There's beauty, beauty everywhere, but not a homely gal in town. At least not one who can act.' We don't want to be responsible for a cross-country march on Hollywood by an army of ugly females but the cold, hard fact remains that while the town is surfeited with beauteous ladies, it is mighty shy of big nosed, long legged, gangly, clumsy and skinny girls—who are also good comediennes."

About Mary specifically, the article says, "[S]he'll never win any beauty cups. That doesn't bother her, either . . . Gangly and hawk nosed, she was soon known as the youngest character actress on the stage . . . Some of Woolley's sharper barbs [from *The Man Who Came to Dinner*] seem to have stuck to Mary. She has grown accustomed to people inquiring of her, 'Are you Miss Stomach Pump?' In fact, Mary loves it. 'If they want to call me 'Miss Stomach Pump' or the homeliest girl in the world, or both, it's quite okay by me,' said Mary. 'It shows I'm building a public. And I want to stay out in Hollywood and make a lot more pictures. I like the climate and the pay is swell."

Being identified with a small group of unattractive women meant occasionally being confused with other unusual-looking performers. Reviewing *You Can't Take It With You*, the *Davis (California) Enterprise* told readers that if Mary looked familiar, it was because they had seen her in *Bewitched* as the nosey neighbor, Gladys Kravitz. The paper confused Mary with Alice Pearce, a much shorter actress with a sharply receding chin who appeared in the first two seasons of that series. Similarly, the mostly reliable Internet Movie Database for many years put Mary in the cast of *The Jackie Robinson Story* (1951), and a film reference book puts Mary in *Andy Hardy's Private Secretary* (1941), but she appears in neither film. Small roles in these pictures were played by actresses whose sharp features merely resemble Mary's. Some sources list her in the credits of *High School Confidential* (1958), mistaking an uncredited Helen Kleeb for Mary.

If she was to get regular work, Mary knew she would have to resign herself to roles that exploited her looks. Why else would she accept, in *Dance With Me Henry* (1952), the role of a social worker other characters variously refer to as "that old dish-mop," "that sourpuss," "that female bloodhound," and a "flannel-eared floozie"? Even when her characters managed to marry, they were mocked for their appearance. Typical was a retort directed at Mary in *Anna Lucasta* (1949) by Broderick Crawford, playing her husband. Wistfully, she says, "For a hundred bucks, I could dress like a lady from Park Avenue." Without hesitation, he responds,

"It'd take more than a hundred bucks to overhaul you." In a 1967 episode of *The Red Skelton Hour*, Mary's character gets her long-unemployed
husband (Skelton) a job as a CBS page, but when she closes her eyes for
a kiss goodbye, Skelton slips $2 to another CBS page to substitute his lips
for Skelton's. In the TV series *Julia*, when Diahann Carroll's character
lands a job interview with actor Lloyd Nolan, who played Mary's husband, he tells Carroll: "Be here at nine. And make yourself as handsome
as you can manage. I'm tired of looking at ugly nurses. I married one."
Mary's *Julia* director, Hal Kanter, remembers Mary telling him that when
she was a young member of the Berkshire Playhouse company, she felt
self-conscious and awkward about her height until an older actor told
her it takes a tall board to make a good teeter-totter. "'And so from then
on, I stood up straight and I was a tall board,'" she told Kanter. "And she
remained a tall board. She held herself erectly and walked with dignity.
There was nothing of the clown about her. She was a believable, honest
character in everything she played for me."

By the time *Julia* surfaced, Mary was accustomed to ridicule about her
appearance. She had confronted it from the time of her very first films.
In *Who Done It?*, the 1942 Abbott and Costello mystery in which Mary
played a snappy secretary to a murder victim, her plain appearance was
exploited with dialogue such as:

COSTELLO: She ain't pretty.
ABBOTT: What's that got to do with it?
COSTELLO: It's got a lot to do with it.
ABBOTT: You're crazy.
COSTELLO: I've seen better heads on malted milks . . . She don' ap-
     peal to me.
ABBOTT: So what? You kiss her in the dark!

Dialogue that mocked her appearance was doubly damaging to Mary
because, once accepted, it permitted writers to pile on other unflattering
character traits. It was not enough, for instance, to make Mary a spinster;
writers made her an *unhappy* spinster (from *June Bride*: "I don't want to
miss Boo's wedding—I've missed so many of my own"). Even more often, she played a man-hungry spinster at that. Typical is this exchange
from *How's About It* between Mary, playing a secretary with the decidedly
unfeminine name "Mike," and her handsome boss, played by Robert
Paige. He enters the office and finds her at her desk, grumbling:

PAIGE, *cheery*: Good afternoon!

MARY: For some people.

PAIGE: Mike, it's great to be alive!

MARY: I'll have to take your word for it. It's been so long since anbody made a pass at me.

PAIGE: Better late than never! *He bends over her typewriter and gives her a peck on the forehead.*

MARY, *expectantly*: Your aim's a little high.

Paige changes the subject, and Mary's disappointment is never acknowledged. When he settles down at the end of the film with a gorgeous blond, Mary whispers to her, "Save me your old phone numbers—there's still hope." A desperate desire for men defined Mary's characters until the end. In an episode of *Trapper John, MD*, which Mary appeared in when she was seventy-one, Trapper (Gregory Harrison), asks her how old she is. "Too old for you, Gonzo," she says. "You got an older brother?"

This dynamic meant that even when Mary plays women of professional accomplishment, she cannot play to their strengths. In *The Petty Girl* (1950), a piece of romantic fluff, Mary is the very caricature of the dour headmistress, singularly bitter and unpleasant, drab in almost every way (serious gray suits, sensible shoes), and unrelenting in her efforts to protect her schoolgirls' virtue. In *Ma and Pa Kettle at Home* (1954), Mary is the town's helpful librarian, but she is quickly dismissed by Ma as "a maiden lady librarian who knows all about books but nothing about cooking." Ma's Christmas wish for Mary is that she has luck learning how to cook and finding the right man to marry.

Some of Mary's pictures, especially her early ones, made use of her size, forcing a physicality on Mary's comedy that she surely did not enjoy. In *Rhythm of the Islands* (1943), in which a wisecracking Mary leaves Brooklyn for the tropical island where she believes her boyfriend is cavorting with shapely native girls, Mary must flip the very heavy Andy Devine over her shoulder from behind, tossing him across a hammock and onto the ground. The scene is shot from behind, making it difficult to determine whether Mary did this pratfall herself or a double did it for her.

Cruel treatment on screen surfaced so frequently that some people felt safe treating Mary this way off screen as well. At the Muny theatre in St. Louis, publicist Jerry Berger was escorting Milton Berle around in 1971 when Berle stopped in front of a poster with a large publicity photo promoting an upcoming appearance by Mary. "She looks like a cunt with a torn pocket," Berle observed aloud, according to Berger. Berger was startled but ascribes no animosity to Berle's insult, preferring to believe "he tried to be funny and everyone was a target." Less cruel was a joke that surfaced after a 1974 fire at Goldwyn Studios. The fire started on the set of *Sigmund and the Sea Monsters,* a Saturday morning children's show, destroying this set and damaging the sets of other shows nearby, such as that of *Barnaby Jones. Sigmund* starred cute adolescent Johnny Whitaker and featured Mary, Margaret Hamilton, little person Billy Barty, and Sid Miller, a short, obscure actor who was Mickey Rooney's sidekick in a few *Andy Hardy* pictures. The day of the disaster, Mary had finished her work on the set at 3:00 p.m. and had been released. The fire began at 4:00 p.m. and spread quickly. Mary was unnerved for weeks, but as the joke goes, two old actors meet on Hollywood Boulevard as great clouds of smoke rise in the sky.

THE FIRST ACTOR: What's that in the sky over there?

THE SECOND ACTOR: Didn't you hear? That's a soundstage on the Goldwyn Lot. It just came over the radio, the whole stage is on fire. It's a four-alarm fire.

THE FIRST ACTOR: Oh, that's just awful. I work on the Goldwyn lot all the time. What were they shooting?

THE SECOND ACTOR: A show called *Sigmund and the Sea Monsters.*

THE FIRST ACTOR: *Sigmund and the Sea Monsters*? Who's on it?

THE SECOND ACTOR: Mary Wickes, Billy Barty, Sid Miller and Maggie Hamilton.

THE FIRST ACTOR: Oh. (Pause.) Well, you can only push God so far.

Mary sometimes took pains to remind others that she did, in fact, have some attractive features. She talked to Bob Wallsten about sitting in a dressing room beside stage star Margaret Sullavan during the Broadway run of *Stage Door.* "I remember her telling me *with glee* that she and Peggy Sullavan had sat side by side, looking at each other and at their reflections in the mirror. And she said, in a tone of artlessness, which was a little performance but was also part of Mary's nature, 'We decided our eyes were very similar.'" Mary was trying to point out that she was prettier than people gave her credit for, and Wallsten found a "charm and sweetness" in her desire to share this with him. Indeed, when reflecting years later on the visual impression Mary left, it is her eyes that people mention most. "Mary was not pretty, but had the most wonderful eyes," recalls Alfred Gellhorn, who performed with Mary in the St. Louis Little Theatre in the early 1930s, before building a distinguished medical career in New York. Actress Janet Fox, who was part of the Kaufman and Hart circle in which Mary socialized in the 1930s and 1940s, says, "I thought she had the most beautiful eyes I'd ever seen. I know that's a cliché, but it's true. Her eyes were like lamps, just beautiful. And she had beautiful hair. She wasn't ugly at all." Years later, Mary still may have felt the need to remind people that she had not always been unattractive. In Mary's Century City living room, Madelyn Pugh Davis always noticed a rather flattering photo of Mary as a young woman; Madelyn often wondered if Mary displayed it to make a point.

Certainly, Mary was invested in believing her looks were an asset that sustained her. "The older I get, the more valuable I get," she once said, noting that such wasn't the case for actresses who must depend on ingénue looks. "The great beauties are wonderful and I love to watch them, but I've never envied them. They can't always play character comedy, but I can get myself to look pretty jazzy, with makeup and clothes." Mary's statement about never envying beautiful women is doubtful; at times, she could not help but wish to be one of them. During the *Town House* run in 1948, a reporter wrote, "Mary says she used to feel like an insignificant little field mouse when she went to the various agents' offices in New York looking for jobs. 'I was enormously impressed when I went to the Louis Shurr office and saw all the beautiful show girls in their minks and silver foxes,' she remembers. 'I wore the good tweed suit and plain felt hat my mother said should be the correct things for young girls looking for work. But how I wished I looked the way those show girls did.'"

But rather than envy, Mary exhibited a disdain toward Hollywood's great beauties. Possibly as a protective, coping mechanism, she took on a smug, dismissive air, seemingly believing she was superior to them because she was not obsessed with her appearance. "The beauty queens never manage to forget they're gorgeous. Me, I never was . . . so I just tool along acting natural. And the men seem to like it. Anyway, I've always had plenty of 'em," she told the *Los Angeles Daily News* in 1951. She said glamorous actresses are "always working at 'how to get a man.' They spend all day being glamorous in front of the camera—and then go right on acting the same part at night . . . They're always 'on.' And after a while a guy gets tired of being an audience. Sooner or later, all that beauty's gonna go. And then where are you? Right down to the real you, that's where. That's what a man's gonna have to live with eventually. So why not start cultivating it from the beginning?" She spoke admiringly of women who "have other things on their minds besides worrying if their false eyelashes are on straight." Mary sometimes took pleasure in exposing the empty lifestyles she believed many beautiful women led. During the run of *Father Malachy's Miracle*, she came across a 1936 booklet, "55 Minutes to Beauty," by Elizabeth Arden. Mary sat down and wrote an uproarious parody of it, mocking the panoply of pomades, creams, and masks that women were expected to apply with glee during morning and bedtime ablutions ("You skip over to your dressing table . . .").

It was Mary's larger persona, not her appearance alone, that worked to her advantage as a comedienne. "You know how there are some people who still dress a certain way even though they shouldn't, but they're stuck in it? She was funny because she was stuck in that wonderful thing she was stuck in. But it wasn't a problem because it still worked for her," says Barbara Sharma, who worked with Mary both on stage and in TV, where Sharma was best known as the saucy window-dresser Myrna on *Rhoda*. If Mary's appearance and physicality affected her work, they also affected her off-screen relationships, making it difficult for others to extend any intimacy. "She wasn't a warm and cozy person. Her angularity put one off a little. If I'm going to give her a hug and I'm only five foot six, I'm only half-way up there," deadpans Anne Kaufman Schneider. Harriet Switzer, who escorted Mary during part of her 1998 visit to Washington University, remembers "this tall, gangly person who sort of '*swooped* around'" when she walked, bounding through groups of people. Jack O'Brien says, "You know how people project something? Some people are sex, some are sort of flirtation, and some people, even if they're very beautiful, hold you at a distance. Mary never pushed a button that asked for affection. I have no memory of holding her or hugging her. None, and I'm a touchy-feely, very embracing man. She didn't project any physical, any human complicity of any kind. She was extraordinary by dint of the fact that she didn't apologize for her singularity, she exploited it."

CHAPTER FIVE

Miss Bedpan

MARY WAS REHEARSING *SKYLARK* WITH GERTRUDE LAWRENCE AT THE Cape Playhouse in Dennis, Massachusetts, in August 1939 when she learned of the part that would cement her career. She received a letter from Irving Schneider of the Sam Harris production office, telling her about "a new farce-comedy" by Kaufman and Hart that would be "ideal for you." The play was called *Such Interesting People*, but shortly before previews it would be renamed *The Man Who Came to Dinner*.

In the play, a famous man of letters suffers a fall while traveling and is forced to recuperate in a stranger's home. Sheridan Whiteside becomes a houseguest of the worst sort—overbearing and condescending, barking orders right and left, upending the lives of the good-hearted people who extend care and kindness. Mary played Miss Preen, Whiteside's horrified private nurse, a well-meaning woman who tries her best to establish some order in the house, but who—humiliated by the verbal assault of names like "Miss Bedpan"—is ultimately pushed too far, exploding in a satisfying burst of resentment. Preen is memorable because the character always inspires applause: She gets to tell Whiteside exactly what she thinks of him, giving voice to the audience's own distaste for the lead character.

And she does so in a bonafide hit. The play was a smash success by any measure, playing for seven hundred and thirty-nine performances at the Music Box Theatre. Many predicted it was destined for the same success as Kaufman and Hart's *You Can't Take It With You*, which ran eight hundred and thirty-eight performances, and they were nearly right. *The Man Who Came to Dinner* was so popular that *Stage* magazine reprinted it in entirety in its November 1940 issue, accompanied by a photo of Mary as Preen telling off Whiteside, played with bluster by Monty Woolley. The show quickly became a staple of the regional, revival, and summer stock circuits. Whiteside is based on the effete critic and Algonquin

Roundtable wit Alexander Woollcott, and characters who come and go during his convalescence are none-too-subtle riffs on Gertrude Lawrence, Noel Coward, and Harpo Marx.

Mary, without an agent, signed a run-of-the-play contract on August 25, 1939, paying her $75 a week, 50 percent more than she made in *Skylark*. The show began a week of tryouts at the Bushnell Memorial Auditorium in Hartford, Connecticut, then proceeded to Boston's Plymouth Theatre for two weeks. The Boston try-out was extended a week to allow Kaufman and Hart to work on the third act, delaying the play's New York opening until October 16.

Both out of town and in New York, the reviews were sensational. "Preposterously, extravagantly, terrifically funny," exclaimed the *Boston Evening American*. The *New York Sun* enthused, "Those first-night howls must have been heard as far away as Mr. Woollcott's sacred island," referring to the critic's home on Neshobe Island, New Hampshire, where he entertained the literary crowd. Opening night brought out theatrical royalty: Edna Ferber, Oscar Hammerstein, Cole Porter, Lillian Hellman, Martin Beck, Bennett Cerf, and Dwight Deere Wiman were in the audience, as were Clifton Webb, Natalie Schafer, Norma Shearer, and Harpo Marx. Mary received opening night telegrams from major Broadway stars—Ethel Merman, Katherine Cornell, Gertrude Lawrence, Billy Miles, Margalo Gillmore, and Glenn Anders—as well as lyricist Dorothy Fields, Stockbridge's Billy Miles, and David Kent Orthwein, who, like Mary, left his St. Louis family to pursue a theatrical career (he had the year before appeared with Mary in *Father Malachy's Miracle*).

Mary adored working with Kaufman, who gave her great latitude, and she became his favorite comedienne. "There are lots of famous stories of his directing, where he was saying, 'Count to four, then do this.' He never did that with Mary, ever, because she heard it exactly the way he heard it when he and Moss were writing it down. He was absolutely uncanny on the rhythms and the hearing of things. He just knew exactly how she was going to sound," says Kaufman's daughter and Mary's friend, Anne Kaufman Schneider. One example is Preen's big exit, which may have been the only time Kaufman suggested Mary change the way she deliver a line. As Preen storms out, she bellows, "I am not only walking out on this case, Mr. Whiteside, but I am leaving the nursing profession. I became a nurse because all my life, ever since I was a little girl, I was filled with the idea of serving a suffering humanity. After one month with you, Mr. Whiteside, I am going to work in a munitions factory. From now on, anything that I can do to help exterminate the human race will fill me with the greatest of pleasure. If Florence Nightingale had ever nursed you, she would have married Jack the Ripper instead of founding the Red Cross." In rehearsals, Mary had been pausing twice in that long speech, once for a laugh at the end of "munitions factory," and once at the end of "pleasure," before starting into "If Florence." Kaufman asked her to skip that second pause—forgoing a second laugh—and instead go forthrightly into "If Florence . . ." "She told me that he said, if you will just carry it through to the end, without taking a break there, you will get an enormous laugh—and a hand. Whereas if it's broken up into two, she'd get three laughs, but it wouldn't be quite the same," says Anne Kaufman Schneider. "She did it and the audience fell about. She got an absolute roar every night—and a hand. I've seen *The Man Who Came to Dinner* a trillion times and every actress I've heard since then, no one can touch her. He had always told me—and Mary, too—that by *The Man Who Came to Dinner*, he never, ever gave her a reading. He never said to her, No, say it this way. He occasionally would say, If you would walk over to the chair, say the line and *then* sit down, you're going to get a bigger laugh, then she walked over to the chair, sat down and then said it. She always did exactly what he said."

When it was announced that a road company of *The Man Who Came to Dinner* would be mounted with Clifton Webb in the lead, the Sam Harris office received a petition from more than three hundred St. Louisans, asking that Mary be in the cast when the show reached St. Louis. The October 23, 1940, letter said, "Her many friends are going to be terribly disappointed if they do not see her in the St. Louis presentation of your comedy. Miss Wickes' work here with the St. Louis Little Theatre, the Municipal Opera, and the Casey Players at the Schubert is remembered by a large St. Louis public, who would be attracted to the American [Theatre] to see her performance. Could this be arranged?" It was the first time Harris had ever heard of a city petitioning management for an actress. Surprisingly, he obliged. Mary flew to St. Louis after her evening performance on Saturday, November 2, then began performing as Preen the next night for the second week of the St. Louis engagement at the American. Meanwhile, Ruth Sherrill of the road company took Mary's place at the Music Box theatre. "It was a swell arrangement, for New York was the other girl's home and it gave us both an opportunity to play our home towns for the first time," Mary said. When Mary arrived at Lambert-St. Louis Airport, she was greeted by newspaper photographers and presented with flowers by the Missouri Federation of Women's Clubs. She received this telegram from restaurateurs Vincent Sardi Jr.

and Sr.: "We are preparing a petition signed by two thousand five hundred to get you back." The experience was a sweet one for Mary, save for one unpleasant encounter: At some point, $50 was stolen from her belongings backstage. Mary complained to the touring company's management, prompting a written apology but no restitution. She pressed the matter further—$50 was no small amount in 1940—and ultimately was reimbursed by the Sam Harris organization. The incident was never made public.

A week later, Mary returned to New York, where she had played Preen for more than a year already. With no sign of the play losing momentum, producers asked Mary to renew for the 1940–41 season. She did, getting an increase in pay to $100 per week.

The show's success allowed Mary to penetrate a social set that would never have been available to her otherwise. Linda and Cole Porter invited her to a supper party at the Waldorf one night. Another night, she was invited to a cocktail party at the Ritz Carlton for the Porters, William Powell, and Leonard Hanna Jr., a wealthy philanthropist. She attended Gertrude Lawrence's surprise party at the Plaza Hotel for gossip columnist Radie Harris, and joined a late-night party for Monty Woolley at the Kaufmans' 94th Street apartment. When she played in a special production of *The Man Who Came to Dinner* at Bucks County Playhouse, she stayed with the Kaufmans at their nearby country estate, Barley Sheaf Farm.

During the show's run, she often spent Saturday nights and Sundays in New Hope, Pennsylvania, at Moss and Kitty Carlisle Hart's home. Hart frequently invited Edith Atwater and Mary to come down with his brother, Bernie, the show's stage manager. After the Saturday night show (in those days, plays were presented Mondays through Saturdays), "Bernie would get the car while we were getting out of our makeup and getting dressed in our street-clothes and he'd pull up to the stage entrance. Edie and I would come out and he'd stow our cases in the back of the car, we'd get in the car, and he said that was the last we said—that from the time we hit the car, we'd go right to sleep until ten minutes out of New Hope, when we'd begin to spruce up and fix ourselves up because we were arriving at Moss's." Moss and Bernie's father was often at the property. "They called him The Commodore, Old Mr. Hart. He was a great malaprop," said Mary. "One morning I came down to breakfast and there were some lovely halves of canned peaches at my place. I said, 'Oh, aren't these beautiful,' and he said, 'They're Vatican-packed' [meaning vacuum-packed]."

In June 1941, as the show neared the end of its more than eighteen-month run, Mary appeared in Kaufman and Hart's city-meets-country comedy, *George Washington Slept Here*, at Bucks County Playhouse. Hart came down to see it and again invited her to stay over at his country house. "The town is buzzing with your triumph. I really mean that, because you know how wonderful your notices were," he told her. Mary's affection for Hart was lifelong. When he spent a month in the hospital a year before his 1961 death, Mary sent a constant stream of cards and letters to him.

One of the people Mary most enjoyed during this period was Alexander Woollcott's secretary, Bill Chase. Mary and Chase had a playful relationship defined by a camp sensibility. They called each other "Igor" and "Maude." Chase wrote her once on White House stationery, no doubt lifted during one of Woollcott's many visits there, as Woollcott was a friend of Eleanor Roosevelt: "Mary, darling: I've telephoned you every day this week—and written and wired until I just don't know. Why haven't you answered? You're still the prettiest one, you know. Come and live with us forever. Ever fondly, Eleanor." On another occasion, a few days before they were to meet for dinner at Sardi's, Chase wrote: "Each time I call, you pretend to be the female operator. Credit me with a little sense—don't you know that your moustache grates on the transmitter and at my end it's just like having you in the room!" They were to attend a show after dinner, but he added, "I think it better—considering everything—that we do not speak to each other in the theatre at all. Let us try to give the impression to all those others that Dame Chance placed our seats side by side. You will of course wear 'Disguise 22X.' I shall be padded as usual."

When Woollcott briefly stepped into the Whiteside role himself in Philadelphia, Mary took the train down to see him in it, and Chase arranged for them to meet backstage before she and Chase had dinner. Mary, who was not usually impressed with celebrity, got a huge kick out of meeting Woollcott, and after he died in 1943, Chase presented Mary with an odd memento: Woollcott's Social Security card. During World War II, Chase served with the American Red Cross in France; he later moved to Tangier, Morocco, where he co-founded a nightspot called the Parade Bar that became a gathering place for the avant-garde, international expatriate community, and a favorite of Paul Bowles, William S. Burroughs, and Tennessee Williams. Mary kept up with Chase through at least 1958, but there is no record of contact after that.

Of all her stage roles, none brought Mary greater attention than Preen. Unlike some actresses who resent being typecast and become reluctant to reprise the same role, Mary relished opportunities to play Preen. Having genuinely identified with the character's sense of propriety and indignation, she considered Preen hers. Kaufman and Hart's comedy gave Mary the chance to don Preen's uniform in every medium: on Broadway (1939–41); in summer stock (at Bucks County Playhouse, in 1941, in a production in which Kaufman himself played Whiteside); on film (Warner Bros., 1942); on radio (a *Theatre Guild on the Air* presentation with Fred Allen in 1946); and on television (first a live *Ford Theatre Hour* version in 1949, then a *Hallmark Hall of Fame* special in 1972.)

Some of these productions were more satisfying than others. Take the *Hallmark* version, for instance. The series is known for high-quality story telling, but virtually everyone associated with this production—Mary included—left profoundly unhappy. Anne Kaufman Schneider minces no words: "It was perfectly revolting." But it didn't start out that way. With a cast led by Orson Welles, and with supporting players like Don Knotts and Joan Collins perfectly suited to their parts, Anne and Kitty Carlisle Hart (guardians of the Kaufman and Hart canon) were so optimistic that they flew to England to watch the filming, which was to take about five days. "I was beside myself at the idea of meeting Orson Welles. I was thrilled to meet him, but it was all very disappointing. It was a mess. He never learned it," Anne says. Hart was so dispirited at what she saw, she returned to London after the first day. "Kitty couldn't take the heat in the kitchen—she just saw the play going right down the tubes. She didn't leave in a huff, but she just didn't want to see the spectacle of Orson Welles making a fool of himself and the play," says Anne, who remained.

There had been at least one red flag in advance. A horrified Mary had phoned the two women to make sure they were aware the script was being updated with contemporary references. "She was the first person to tell us. We didn't know," Anne said. "She was a great believer in Kaufman and Hart, and was incensed. She said, 'They're talking about Jackie and Ari!'" Anne and Kitty convened a conference call with their agent, Irving Lazar. "We were very huffy and grand, saying, 'How dare they do this?' And Lazar, quite rightly, said, 'Do you want to give back the money that you've gotten?' I thought, give back the money? We're building an extension at our house at the beach. He said, 'Then you have to do what they're going to do.'"

Mary "was just rolling her eyes" during the production, Anne says. "We told her very early on that she was like the first wife. You can't sit around and say, 'Oh, that's not the way we did it before and what we did before was wonderful.'" But the problems weren't confined to changes in the script. By all accounts, Welles was unpleasant, drinking a lot, and generally not up to the role. Don Knotts remembers that when Welles became difficult, "Mary got very forthright with him." Knotts speculates that Welles's drinking stemmed from anxiety over not having carried such a big part in years and being unaccustomed to working in TV. Collins, who found Welles so overbearing that she referred to him disdainfully as "his Highness," is less charitable. She describes an angry man determined to overshadow others' performances to keep himself the center of the film. "Lee Remick and I sat in the transmission room watching a dress rehearsal on the monitor while Don [Knotts] had his best and funniest scene cut to ribbons by Welles. Welles insisted on restaging so that all of Don's best lines were shot on the back of his head," she said. When director Buzz Kulik suggested that "perhaps some of the other actors get a close-up occasionally," Welles boomed angrily that he was the star and this was not an ensemble piece. Later, Mary talked with Iggie Wolfington about the production. "She said it was pathetic to see Welles wheeling around the studio in the [golf carts], with the weight he put on. He got so huge. It must have been his disappointments, whatever. Because he *was* a genius. It was so depressing to see that he'd gone to pot like that. She wouldn't have put it as brutal as that, but that's what she meant." Welles, who had made Mary something of a protégé in the 1930s, now never even shared a meal with her during the production.

The show got a terrible review from critic John O'Connor in the *New York Times*. "Kitty said to me that morning, 'I'm going to call him, darling.' She was going to call him because everything he said was true—they massacred the play, Orson Welles appeared not to know his lines—and indeed, he was reading it all off cue cards. He was so fat that he didn't have enough breath to finish a sentence, and John O'Connor spelled it all out." As Kitty relayed it, whoever answered said he was busy. "She said, 'This is Mrs. Moss Hart and I want to talk to him.' He got on the phone and was sort of nervous and said, Is this about my review? And she said, It's not what you think—it's to tell you that you were right. He *was* reading. And it was a mess. It was horrible." The *Times* named the show one of the five worst TV shows of 1972, noting that "the production managed to transform a light comedy into heavy sledding."

Like many actresses who originate roles, Mary felt proprietary about Preen and was disappointed whenever productions were mounted without her. Among these was a presentation on *Best of Broadway*, a television series featuring theatrical hits in teleplay form. "The Man Who Came to Dinner" was broadcast live on October 13, 1954, with Monty Woolley in the lead, but with no others from the Broadway cast. "One of the few mandates I had from CBS was that every part had to be the biggest star I could get. I had to get Zasu Pitts for the nurse," says producer Martin Manulis. "Mary was really crushed. And so was I. It broke my heart. It was just terrible. Zasu was fine in it, but it was really Mary's part." The casting surely hurt more because of that particular replacement: Mary was often mistaken for Pitts and resented any perception that she resembled the mousey-looking actress. Besides Woolley and Pitts, the cast included Merle Oberon, Joan Bennett, Reginald Gardner, Bert Lahr, and Buster Keaton. The show eliminated some scenes and was paced quickly to suit its one-hour format. Keaton is clearly uncomfortable with his lines and at one point calls Whiteside "Mr. Whitehead." But Margaret Hamilton does delightful things with a small part as a maid, and an inside joke works well when Whiteside tells his assistant, who is nervously trying to reveal that she's in love, "Oh, stop acting like Zasu Pitts and explain yourself!"

When James Lipton adapted *The Man Who Came to Dinner* into a musical in 1967, Mary told the press she was to play Preen again. It's unclear why she thought so. This time, the part went to Janet Fox, who had toured as Preen years before. In the end, Mary was fortunate. The show, called *Sherry!*, hung on for two months, did not do well and has long been forgotten. Anne Kaufman Schneider dismisses it as "ghastly."

It was the film version that brought Mary the most long-term success. By this point, Mary had been in a few films, but they were either never seen (*Too Much Johnson*), gave her no dialogue (*Watch the Birdie*), or were short and forgettable (the nineteen-minute *Seeing Red*). But this was to be a proper, glorious Warner Bros. production. Mary had come to the film with surprising ease: Kaufman had promised her that if and when the show was adapted for film, he would ensure that she played Preen on film, and he stuck to his word. When Kaufman and Hart sold the story to Warners, Mary was the first performer signed. The actress who had never done a major film was not even required to take a screen test.

The story did not make it to the screen easily. Initial plans were for Kaufman and Hart to write the screenplay and receive a take from the gross of the picture. They also would produce the picture, which would be either directed by Kaufman or co-directed by Kaufman and Hart. Warners would receive 65 percent of the world gross, and Kaufman and Hart would share 35 percent. A subsequent plan envisioned Kaufman and Hart receiving nothing for providing the story and directing, but receiving 75 percent of profits after Warners recouped production and distribution costs. Late in the negotiations, Kaufman insisted that he and Hart have sole discretion over direction and cutting. Warners balked, considering this proposal a complete change from everything that had been discussed. A deal was reached in August 1940 for Warners to acquire the motion picture rights and employ the two men as producers. But Kaufman and Hart soon became disenchanted with the production process. Kaufman had objected to how many weeks he was expected onsite in Los Angeles, and to how much time during those weeks he was expected to devote to the project. They now sought distance from the project and, represented by agent Leland Hayward, decided to sell the story to Warners outright for $275,000 in November 1940. The screenplay was written by Julius and Philip Epstein (twin brothers who would later script *Casablanca*), but with several scenes prepared by Kaufman and Hart. It was directed by William Keighley.

Mary's agent of record was officially MCA, but Mary and Warners agreed privately to by-pass MCA. All her negotiations took place directly with Jake Wilk, the New York-based story editor who was Warners's longtime vice president in charge of eastern production. Wilk "thought she was one of the funniest women he ever knew. He was mad about her," says his son, writer Max Wilk. No doubt Mary reasoned that this job had come courtesy of Kaufman directly, so why should she relinquish 10 percent of her salary? (Ten percent, not today's customary fifteen, was standard.) What MCA knew of this arrangement is unclear because, almost comically, Mary was receiving two simultaneous series of telegrams, one from Wilk and the other from MCA's Edie Van Cleve, seeking to apprise her of the same developments. But working without an agent left Mary vulnerable. She was the only one of the nine key players, except Bette Davis, whose contract could be suspended without compensation.

Mary signed her contract with Warner Bros. on October 30, 1940. She would be paid $500 a week for a minimum four weeks, plus round-trip rail transportation between New York and Los Angeles. Filming was to begin no later than June 1, 1941, but it was delayed, first by a plagiarism suit—dismissed in favor of Kaufman and Hart—and then by the threat of a lawsuit from Woollcott himself. Though Woollcott had never objected to the play, the others now took his complaint seriously and decided to set aside $100,000 for any potential payment. They reduced this amount to $37,500 but then disagreed over whose money would fund it—Warners's or Kaufman and Hart's—and whose approval would be needed for any settlement. It's not clear any settlement was ever paid.

The biggest delay was due to a disagreement between Warners and Kaufman—and within the studio itself—over who should play Whiteside. John Barrymore and Robert Benchley were screen-tested for the part, and Charles Laughton wanted it badly, but the final candidates were Orson Welles and Cary Grant. Welles negotiated with Jack Warner personally at Warner's home in March 1941. In those conversations, it was agreed that Welles would be paid $150,000 if he both acted and directed and $100,000 if he only performed. In the end, Warners passed on Welles when George Schaefer, executive producer of *Citizen Kane*, refused to release him from that film. Grant, on the other hand, was to receive no compensation; instead, Warners would donate $125,000 to the British War Relief in the name of the U.K.-born star. Had the role gone to Grant, the film would have been directed by Howard Hawks. Though Woolley established himself squarely in the stage version, there wasn't a lot of enthusiasm for bringing him on board for the film version. Hal Wallis, Warners's head of production, felt Woolley's performance was mechanical, which he attributed to Woolley having played the same part on stage for two years. But Wallis was soon persuaded by budgetary pressure: Woolley was merely an actor developing a name for himself, not a star by any measure, and would come cheap.

For the female lead, Whiteside's devoted secretary, Barbara Stanwyck, Paulette Goddard, and Carole Lombard were all considered, and Edith Atwater's agent, Jane Broder, lobbied hard for Atwater to reprise her stage role. Broder unsuccessfully used the part as leverage for a broader studio contract for Atwater, which she believed Warners wanted; Atwater would sign a studio contract only if *The Man Who Came to Dinner* could be her first part. In the end, Warners gave the part to Bette Davis, who was already under studio contract.

The delays meant Mary suddenly found herself temporarily without income, since Sam Harris had released her from her stage contract in May. She managed to line up two weeklong performances in *George Washington Slept Here* almost back to back, first at Bucks County Playhouse opposite Charles Butterworth, and then at the Berkshire Playhouse opposite Whit Bissell. She did well. "Easily the most impressive performance of the evening," began the *New York Post* review, "was that given by Mary Wickes as the acidulous wife fed up with everything rural. Three days ago this reviewer would have pushed in the face anybody who dared to suggest that Jean Dixon could be improved upon in one of those bitter-cynic parts, but we are now obliged to report that Miss Wickes has accomplished the feat."

Mary boarded a train on July 18 for Los Angeles, stopping in St. Louis for a few days to visit her mother. Since she knew no one in Los Angeles at the time, Warners arranged for her to be met at the station in Pasadena on July 25. She checked into the Chateau Elysee at 5930 Franklin Avenue, a collection of short-term apartments popular with the theatre crowd, and reported to work in Burbank on July 30. The film had been shooting for two weeks, but her scenes were just beginning.

With a budget of $1.05 million, the film was a high-profile project at Warners. The largest chunk of salary money was absorbed by Davis, whom Warners budgeted at $66,667 for the whole picture. The other principal players received weekly salaries ranging from $7,500 for Jimmy Durante as Banjo, to $250 to Betty Roadman as Sarah, the maid. Woolley was paid $2,500 per week, Billie Burke $1,500 per week to play Mrs. Stanley, and George Barbier $1,250 per week to play Dr. Bradley. The reason Woolley, with the largest part, was paid so much less than Durante, whose part was modest, becomes clear only when one remembers how immensely popular Durante was in the early 1940s. In the end, Durante was required for only two weeks, while Woolley worked six, so each man earned $15,000. Mary's four weeks turned into six, so she earned $3,000 for the film. It was an introduction to a different kind of work: The studio had service trucks on every set, from which a uniformed attendant offered sandwiches and drinks. "I thought, gee, this is living. We don't get that in the theatre in New York," Mary said.

In August, Mary heard from a very pleased Jerry Wald, an associate producer on the film. "I just saw the rushes of your scene in which you tell Whiteside off," he wrote. "I'm sure the movie critics will go into word gymnastics with their typewriters as much as the dramatic critics did when you made your debut in the part." The story is presented in the film almost exactly as in the play, except for the opening scene where Whiteside is met at the train station and a later scene where Maggie ice skates. But the derisive Miss Bedpan sobriquet was removed at the request of Hayes Office censors, who feared it would offend moviegoers' sensibilities. It was replaced with "Miss Stomach Pump."

Filming itself was relatively smooth, though it was temporarily suspended in September when Davis suffered an unrelated nose injury that required her to recuperate at home for several weeks. Mary was impressed with Davis from the start and always spoke highly of her in later years. "She took me under her wing and made me feel so at ease on the Warner lot. I had never been on a sound stage before, and I will be forever grateful to her because she made my life so simple," Mary said.

Production concluded on October 18, sixteen days behind schedule. Mary had always planned to return to New York when shooting was complete but, after seeking work from Russel Crouse and others, the only specific job she was offered was as Nurse Pyngar in Alfred de Liagre's production of *The Walrus and the Carpenter*. Another theatrical run as a nurse so soon after *The Man Who Came to Dinner* held little attraction. She considered an offer from Max Gordon to replace Audrey Christie as Ruth, the sensible sister, in the Chicago company of *My Sister Eileen* (it was a role she had enjoyed in Stockbridge), but Lew Wasserman and Edie Van Cleve of MCA persuaded her that she would have more options if she remained in Los Angeles. Warners had real interest in her, they said, and was likely to give her good parts that would build to better ones. (This was a pre-mogul Wasserman, who had only recently come to Los Angeles from New York to head MCA's film division.) "Don't you think it better to give coast whirl first unless good New York part?" came a wise telegram from Van Cleve.

So Mary passed on *Walrus* in New York and *Eileen* in Chicago. Her choice proved prophetic: *Walrus* closed after nine performances, and Warners quickly hired Mary for another picture with Davis. The film was *Now, Voyager*, a sentimental story about a pathologically shy Bostonian (Charlotte Vale, played by Davis) who blossoms into a confident, stylish woman after finding love with a married man and his young daughter. Mary played Dora Pickford, the private nurse caring for Charlotte's manipulative, overbearing mother. The story was elegantly shot and accompanied by a hypnotic Max Steiner score. Mary played her part beautifully. Dora emerges as a lovable, no-nonsense nurse conspiring with Charlotte to handle the cranky elderly matriarch, played by Gladys Cooper. As soon as she saw the picture, Olive Higgins Prouty, on whose novel the film is based, told Mary she was "perfect" in the role. In later years Mary often said it was her favorite film role.

Mary next took a screen test at Universal Pictures for an Abbott and Costello murder mystery, *Who Done It?* At the time, Abbott and Costello virtually defined Universal, so this project sounded promising. The comedy duo would play soda jerks and amateur mystery writers who get caught up in a real murder. Mary would be the sarcastic secretary to a radio executive who gets killed. On a soundstage, "They put up a booth [that] was supposed to be at a country fair. I was behind the booth and Abbott and Costello came along to buy kisses. I said, 'Where's the script?' They said, 'There isn't any—this is an-lib test.' Abbott and Costello didn't always stick to the script, and they wanted to see if I could keep up with them. So for about ten minutes—honest to goodness—we ad-libbed the scene. Actually, it turned out pretty funny. It didn't have any relation to the picture." Mary won the role, and *Who Done It?* turned out to be a piece of capable, clever story telling that allowed her to shine. The three comedy pros work seamlessly together in a fast-paced tale.

But *Who Done It?* began the most peculiar stretch of Mary's long film career. As part of the deal, in April 1942, she was put under contract at Universal for six months. During this period, she completed three pictures, all forgettable and each only about an hour long: *Private Bucka-roo*, *How's About It*, and *Rhythm of the Islands*. Mary described this peri-od as "strange months" during which Universal put her in "three very strange scripts." *Buckaroo*, a wartime vehicle for the Andrews Sisters and bandleader Harry James, is weighed down by tiresomely long musical numbers. A romance between Mary's forceful character and Shemp Howard's passive one proves a thin excuse for moving the narrative from one uninspired military number to another, ending with planes spelling out "USA" in formation in the air. Twice, Mary punches Shemp in the gut, Three Stooges style. In *How's About It*, Mary is a grouchy secretary who laments the lack of men in her life; this picture again features the Andrews Sisters and Shemp Howard. In *Rhythm of the Islands*, Mary is a brash, wise-cracking woman who heads to the South Seas in search of her fiancé, Andy Devine, whom she fears is cavorting with beautiful island girls. Neither the shirtless, drum-beating natives nor some physi-cal comedy between Mary and Devine can pump this film up. While at Universal, Mary also performed in a short civil defense film. *Keeping Fit* appeals to the American public to stay in good physical condition to maintain workplace productivity during wartime. Robert Stack stars as a buff factory worker, seemingly the picture of fitness, who collapses at work because he is not caring for himself properly. Mary plays a woman who interrupts her housework to nag her overweight husband (Andy Devine) about exercising. The film is less than fifteen minutes long, but is more memorable than any of the three feature films Mary appeared in during this period.

Between each film, Mary returned to New York, starting a practice of frequent coast-to-coast travel with occasional stops in St. Louis. As more stage actors moved west for film work, Mary found she could rely upon her New York connections to help. For a trip to Los Angeles in 1942, ac-tress Edith Barrett sent her driver to collect Mary at the rail station. Mary had come to know Barrett in New York. The following year, Mary stayed with Barry Sullivan and his actress wife, Marie Brown, in their Belden

Drive home in Beachwood Canyon; the Sullivans had moved from New York to Hollywood in 1941.

As more offers came from Los Angeles, accepting the work was difficult because it often came with only days to prepare. Just one example: On July 4, 1950, while in New York, Mary was offered a role in the film version of *Born Yesterday*, but she would need to be in Los Angeles two days later to start shooting. The offer was $750 per week for two weeks, but producers would not pay travel from New York, surely a concern for Mary. And the notice was too short for Mary to get out of conflicting stage commitments. She was to perform in three plays with the Margaret Webster Company at the Woodstock Playhouse in New York that summer—and Mary had agreed to only $250 per week for those productions. It was time to move to the Coast.

CHAPTER SIX

Los Angeles, Mother in Tow

BETTY GARRETT WAS DRIVING DOWN SUNSET BOULEVARD ONE SPRING afternoon in 1951 when she caught sight of two pedestrians "dressed like ladies out of Edward Gorey," the illustrator of genteel but macabre gothic characters. In Southern California, "where nobody dresses formally at all," Garrett could not help but notice these women wearing long, high-waisted dresses and enormous elaborate hats. As she approached the corner of Sunset and Stanley, she realized the women standing before her were Mary and Isabella.

Garrett was thrilled, because she had not seen them since she left New York herself a few years earlier. "There was this huge stone bank with an iron gate and iron grill over the windows. I swung my car around and Isabelle, who had a wonderful way of talking [Garrett affects a clipped, imperious tone], said, 'We've just come in from New York and we're going to stay here for a while and we're shopping for a bank. You know, Father was a banker, and *we ... know ... banks*. And *this* looks like a substantial bank. I've decided we'll put our money here. All of these California banks, they look like they put the money in a shoebox and dump it in a backroom.'" Mary stood beside her mother, nodding in agreement the whole time.

Despite Mary's aversion to change, her decision to leave New York was natural. She was driven to avoid the financial predicament her parents faced during the Depression. She had, after all, left St. Louis to build a life in New York. She was quick to embrace the new medium called television, and she knew Los Angeles was where she should pursue it. "Live television is far more satisfactory than is film," she told the *Los Angeles Times* in May 1951, with an earnestness that suggested she hoped what she was saying was true. "Comedy requires spontaneity in order to come over to audiences. I know from experience that much of the humor and spontaneity is lost when that comedy material is faced with take after take for the cameras." Mary also felt that "every live TV show has the same excitement as the opening night of a Broadway show. This keys up performers and makes them spark. There's nothing so crushing to a comedienne as to play to a couple of cameras and a bored crew." What Mary might not have said, but which she surely felt, is that Los Angeles held the promise of more reliable paychecks. Her efforts to press for higher salaries in the New York theatre had not always ended well—a role in the 1945 national tour of *One Touch of Venus* starring Mary Martin is just one job she lost over salary—and it must have seemed as if the quickly growing TV industry had more to offer.

Job offers did come regularly in Los Angeles. Roles as nurses, nuns, and housekeepers kept her steadily employed in television, and gave her work in film and on stage as well. Although Mary wondered aloud at times whether she had given a theatrical career enough of a try, it is hard to imagine she could have worked as frequently—or had steady income—if she had relied on the New York stage for a career. But she would continue to confront salary struggles. In 1954, she turned down a gig on the *Kate Smith Hour*, an NBC daytime TV program, when producers refused to offer more than scale.

But Mary's life in Los Angeles was shaped more than anything else by the fact that she did not come alone. There was never any question that Isabella would go where Mary went; as all could see, these two lived life as one. They relied on each other in ordinary ways but to an extraordinary degree and were virtually inseparable. "If you had Mary, you had her mother. They were a duet," says Mary Grant Price, the costume and architectural designer who was married to Vincent Price for more than twenty years. It was a striking duet, to be sure, since Isabella always seemed "half the height of Mary."

Mary approached the move to Los Angeles with as much attention as anything else in her life, keeping detailed handwritten records of every aspect of the move. So we know that on March 26, 1951, the packers arrived at her New York apartment at 11:07 a.m. to wrap glass, china, and linens, and departed at 12:42 p.m. We know that, three days earlier, Mary sold her fur coat and hat for $10 to "Anna" on the seventeenth floor, since they would do Mary little good in Southern California. We can track the tips she gave "Arthur" for his help. And we know that Mary asked the ACLU to re-issue a paycheck for $49.96 that she misplaced in the move (she had performed for scale in a thirty-minute NBC radio special to promote the ACLU's "anti-communist, pro-democratic philosophy").

Mary and Isabella spent their first year in Los Angeles in temporary quarters at the Villa Carlotta, a 1920s Moorish-style hotel on Franklin Avenue at the foot of Beachwood Canyon. The Villa Carlotta had been home to numerous movie stars decades before and was still popular with actors traveling back and forth between the coasts. The pair stayed here partly because Isabella, who had come ahead of Mary, took sick in Los Angeles in March, just as Mary was closing down the Park Chambers apartment, and was therefore unable to scout out apartments. Isabella had disagreements with doctors at Hollywood Presbyterian Hospital over her care, prescriptions, and an unwelcome suggestion that she go to a nursing home until Mary could return. Nonetheless, she advised Mary not to rush back. Mary reassured a hospitalized Isabella: "I am so sorry I am not with you every minute, but you have nothing to worry about with me, at least. I am fine and eating and resting and Monday the Manhattan man comes and it *is all finished*—every bit. I don't want you to think about finances. We are being very economical in this move and you are to have *the best*! I love you dearly and cannot wait to get there. *Please* don't have anything on your mind but *getting well*!!! . . . You are the most wonderful person in the whole world and I love you dearly."

Isabella ultimately required surgery of some sort in early April 1951. This was at least her second operation, as she had previously undergone surgery in New York in 1948. The current operation was serious enough to prompt letters to Mary from friends like Vincent and Mary Price and Barbara Wolferman, who now worked at the Oscar Hammerstein organization. "This whole thing makes me so sick I can hardly stand it and I feel even worse, if that's possible, that I can't be out there with you—not that I could do anything but I'm a firm believer that the mere physical presence of someone who loves you both so much is a straw to grasp on to," Wolferman wrote. "I am there every other way but physically, and if . . . you feel the need to talk, please pick up the phone and call and reverse the charges. I'd call every day but I'm terrified of that being more a nuisance than anything else."

Isabella recovered and in April 1952 the two women settled into a more suitable apartment for the long haul. No doubt convenience was a big reason they chose the Voltaire, an elegant seven-story, French Regency-style complex at 1424 North Crescent Heights, just south of Sunset Boulevard and across from the more bohemian Garden of Allah apartments. If Mary needed to get to the Valley, she could drive straight over Laurel Canyon Boulevard, and if she needed to go to Beverly Hills, she would drive west on Sunset Boulevard. At the time, a major grocery store sat a block away and, for eating out, Mary and Isabella frequented Du-pars, the family diner at the Farmer's Market that has become a local institution. All of this meant driving, of course, and in New York Mary had never needed a car. She quickly acquired a new black Pontiac she described as "ritzy" and joked was sometimes mistaken for a Cadillac. Debt-averse Mary paid cash, of course. Isabella and Mary lived frugally at the Voltaire. In 1962, when they got new bedroom carpet and had the apartment painted, they had the old bedroom carpet put in their dinette area. No doubt, they never discussed such things. Intuitively, they both gravitated toward any option that would save money. Apartment 3-B was a comfortable two-bedroom unit with high ceilings. The antique furnishings from Isabella's McLean and Thomas ancestors followed them from New York, creating an old-fashioned feel for all who visited. But the Voltaire still had a bit of Hollywood cachet of its own. Many celebrities called it home: Marilyn Monroe would move in briefly two years later and, for a period, Ann Sothern occupied the apartment below Mary's.

Mary did indeed secure regular television and film work after the move, but she was never entirely comfortable stepping away from her theatre roots. Kaufman was still trying to find a part for her in one play or another, and he wrote her into every play he created as a placeholder character named Wickes. "I still hope to get you back here for a show— don't be surprised if it happens," he wrote from New York. "You are my favorite comedienne. Those are not just polite words, by the way." Kaufman tried many times to get Mary into one of his plays after her move, but a mix of scheduling, writing, and production difficulties conspired against them. In 1951, Mary agreed to appear in *The Small Dark Hours*, written by Kaufman and wife Leueen MacGrath. Unfortunately, delays in shooting *On Moonlight Bay* in Los Angeles forced Mary to pull out, because she now would be unable to arrive in New York for rehearsals. Mary was disappointed not to work with Kaufman again, but the play, a dated drama featuring a repressed gay man who turns to drugs to cope with others' hostility toward his homosexuality, closed after only twenty performances. Kaufman tried again unsuccessfully in 1955, a third time in 1957 (Mary was tempted by this one, *Apartment to Share*, a comedy he co-wrote with Helen Hunter about a glamorous woman sharing a flat with her non-glamorous friend, but the production never came together), and a fourth in 1959. The latter was *I Give It Six Months*, written with MacGrath; Mary's papers contain two versions of the script, which was never produced. Nonetheless, a missive from Kaufman in September must have been hard to take: "You can't keep on with that stuff out there. I saw *On Moonlight Bay* on the Ile de France, by the way—chained to my seat. Is there a law against giving you a funny line to speak? You are too good for that business—you can never get completely lost in it, the way most people do, because you are Wickes after all, but money you get that way doesn't do you any good, except for buying things. Come here and starve happily—everyone else is doing it, it's chic."

One major reason Mary sought a home in Los Angeles was to minimize travel. Living in New York required frequent travel to Los Angeles for filming, and, given the state of air travel in 1951, this meant long, cross-country train trips. By August 1954, Mary had made twenty-seven round trips between New York and Los Angeles, mostly by train, although stopping in St. Louis to visit made the trips easier. Mary expected a move to Los Angeles would mean both less travel, and that she would simply travel in the other direction when work arose in New York.

The 1953 half-hour sitcom *I, Bonino* is one example of how producers in the early days of television accommodated actors working on both coasts. The NBC series, directed by Gordon Duff and produced by Fred Coe, was intended to capitalize on the new fame of Ezio Pinza, the Italian tenor. In *I, Bonino*, Pinza played a widowed singer who decides to leave concert touring to care for his brood of children. Mary was hired to play Martha, the longtime family housekeeper, a much larger role than Mary's usual housekeeper character. Beginning in September 1953, *I, Bonino* was to be broadcast live from the old Hudson Theatre, just west of Times Square, but Mary had already committed to filming *White Christmas* at Paramount in Los Angeles and would therefore be unable to perform in all but the first few episodes. The show's sponsors, Philip Morris and Lady Esther cosmetics, wanted Mary for the role, so rather than simply look for another actress in New York who could commit to the show's entire schedule, they tried something novel. At NBC-TV in Los Angeles, they filmed several scenes of Mary by herself and inserted the resulting footage into the live broadcasts from New York, creating the appearance that Mary was part of the cast. The plot explained that Martha was traveling to Hawaii for a vacation with her sister, so Mary was shown interacting with the Bonino family via long-distance telephone calls in one scene and preparing to board a ship in another. Martha's vacation lasted until Mary finished filming *White Christmas* and could return to New York.

Living with Isabella allowed Mary to concentrate on her career with a devotion that other single actresses generally could not afford. Isabella cooked and cleaned and kept the household functioning tidily. She

prepared lunches for Mary to take to the set, and kept meticulous scrapbooks to document Mary's successes. In turn, Mary produced the income
to support them both, brought interesting people into Isabella's life, and
helped her mother forget she was alone. "Mary was a protector of her
mother, obviously. She was the breadwinner for the rest of her life. She
took care of her mother in whatever ways [Frank] would have done,"
observed Iggie Wolfington. It's entirely possible that, privately, Isabella
was pleased that Mary had not married, since in the absence of a son-
in-law, Isabella could remain the central focus of her daughter's life. The
"one-ness" of the life they continued building in Los Angeles left an impression on everyone. Decades after Isabella died, even people who had
only passing professional relationships with Mary remember Isabella vividly. Prolific TV director Gene Reynolds (*M*A*S*H*, *Lou Grant*) joked that,
at age seventy-six, he could not find his car keys, but he could remember
Mary Wickes's mother clearly, though he worked with Mary on only
three or four occasions. Likewise, producer Martin Manulis (*Days of Wine
and Roses*) immediately offers up Isabella's last name in an interview,
though he met her only once at a tea party in the mid-1950s. "*Wickenhauser* was a name that was hard to forget," he says. So, apparently, was
Isabella, who struck him as "a grand dame" and "very proper." As Mary
Jackson (Miss Emily Baldwin on *The Waltons*) put it, "She dominated
rooms."

By all accounts, Isabella was relaxed and comfortable in Mary's social circle. When Mary attended an elegant banquet at Ciro's in 1955,
she brought her mother, not a date. Mary occasionally hosted teas in
her mother's honor at their apartment, casting director Ethel Winant remembers. Doris Day recalls, "Being with Mary and her precious mother
was a double treat. They looked alike, acted alike and were inseparable
at times." Mary frequently hosted dinner parties, for which Isabella prepared many of the meals. "They entertained lavishly for the apartment's
size. They set up tables for twelve in their living room. It was beautifully
done, and Mother was a great cook," Peter Walker says. Mary entertained by categories, inviting from different lists of people. "She'd have
this group together, then she'd have *that* group together. And it was *her*
party. She was the prima donna. Isabella let her daughter do the whole
thing and sat there and beamed," Walker says. As to the guests, she was
less likely to befriend others in the business than people who worked
outside Hollywood. "There weren't many actors and actresses who she
included in her group. She wasn't close to them. It's very strange. Lucy,
yes. Vivian Vance, yes—they were great friends. But it was mainly writers

and people from the church, and very few actors and actresses who she worked with," says Max Showalter, Walker's life partner. Showalter and Walker became part of Mary's extended family in these years. Mary and Isabella spent many Christmas and Easter holidays with them, joined by actresses Signe Hasso and Dolores Quinton. "We were just sort of like a Hollywood family," Walker recalls fondly. "Once Isabella died, that whole family thing disintegrated. Signe went in her direction. I went off on tour [with *Hello, Dolly*]. The matriarch of the family was Isabella."

The friends Mary most cared for were those who respected the importance of her relationship with her mother. "I'm a very thoughtful person and I think it was that thoughtfulness—to her mother in particular—that Mary probably noticed more than anything. Mary loved anyone who liked her mother or who was thoughtful to her, and that's [one reason] she loved me," says Walker. "I'm the kind of person who always says, 'No wait a minute, if we're going out, we should get something special for Isabella.' Her antennae were out [for that sort of thing]." In fact, many of Mary's friends responded to Isabella with similar instincts. Invitations came not simply to Mary, but to "Mary and Isabella." When Lucille Ball sent correspondence during these years, she often addressed it to "The Wickenhausers" and opened with "Dear Girls." Thelma Ritter, corresponding with Mary in the 1950s and 1960s, wrote, "My love to both you girls," "Love to the Queen of Spain," and "How's the lady who shares the apartment with you?"

Once they came to know Isabella, many of Mary's friends quickly saw differences between them. "Isabella was nothing like Mary. Isabella was more open. A very gracious, uncomplicated person. Her mother was so easy to talk to," says Iggie Wolfington. Isabella was fond of simplistic inspirational tracts. From newspapers and church bulletins, she clipped scores of daily prayers, uplifting words and facile wisdom; it did not take much to capture her attention. Mostly, her attention was focused on Mary. When St. Louis friend Louis Westheimer visited Southern California in 1963 with his teenage son, they met Mary and Isabella for dinner at the Brown Derby. The conversation mostly revolved around Mary, and Isabella would jump in periodically with reminders like, "Well Mary, you're going to go there at four o'clock you know." Westheimer says, "Isabella was the power behind the throne. She was really on top of that gal. Everybody knew that Mrs. Wickenhauser was the force behind Mary."

Isabella continued to experience health problems, including an ultimately benign cervical cancer scare in 1953. She was diagnosed with a heart condition in 1961. After that, "she did lots of things she shouldn't have done, physically, but that was her pleasure—keeping house and entertaining our friends," Mary wrote Vincent Price. "She always said, 'I want to wear out, not rust out.'" Isabella wore out on February 1, 1965, at Hollywood Hospital at age eighty. She died in her sleep in the third day of her hospital stay, and Mary took comfort in knowing her mother had not suffered long. Officially, the cause of death was acute myocardial infarction and arterioschrotic heart disease. Isabella's death certificate has been altered by hand, cementing an inaccuracy. She was born in 1885, but someone has used dark ink to make it read 1895, evidently to suggest she was ten years younger than she really was. Though Mary's signature does not appear on this document, Mary likely had access to the version filed with Los Angeles County and altered it herself, just as she so often altered her own age on formal documents. None of four obituaries or death notices saved by Mary report Isabella's age.

Mary was filming *The Trouble with Angels* when her mother died and asked its producers, Bill Frye and Jim Wharton, to be among Isabella's pallbearers. "They have been my greatest source of strength. They have been so understanding and 'there' all the time," Mary wrote Vincent Price a few weeks after Isabella's death. Mary presented All Saints' Episcopal Church in Beverly Hills with a gift in Isabella's memory, a silver crucifix about fifteen inches tall that still sits in the church's presbytery. Isabella was buried in Shiloh [Illinois] Cemetery on May 22, 1965. Mary's cousin Elizabeth Dorsam, whom Isabella had helped raise, rode in the limousine with Mary. Elizabeth's son Bill, a cousin whose relationship with Mary was always tense, got lost driving to the burial site and never made it. Arrangements were made by Alexander & Sons, the same St. Louis firm that had handled arrangements for Frank's death in 1943. Isabella was buried near her grandparents, Captain John Randolph Thomas and Hester Thomas. Frank was buried in the same section, as was Isabella's sister, Hester Adkins (the vaudevillian "Aunt Hes"). Beside them is the section devoted to the descendants of Colonel John Randolph Thomas and Isabella Kinney Thomas, Isabella's great-grandparents.

Isabella's death affected Mary profoundly but, as was Mary's nature, she grieved privately. "Mary was a very strong, determined woman but, ultimately, without Isabella, would have been lost. Mary lived for that woman. The love was phenomenal. So often, women who never marry hold onto that. You know they're going to leave, and when they do, it's devastating," says Peter Walker. "She was a very lonely woman when Isabella died. And it was a long time before she allowed herself to be open again. She never allowed herself to be in vulnerable positions. This is where her tough guarded side would then somehow be terribly curt and rude and short." Indeed, Isabella's death left Mary increasingly closed to others. In 1968, while Mary was appearing in *The Glass Menagerie* in St. Louis, director Herb Metz was glad she chose to stay with Dorothy Haase, someone she knew well, because Mary seemed so lonely. Though she obviously felt at home in the university environment, she remained aloof during the production. "She was a very solitary person," Metz says. In the six weeks they worked together, she and her director never even shared a meal. "It would have been nice," he sighs with resignation, "but it wasn't necessary."

Isabella had been so central to Mary's life that Mary relied on her even after she died. "Mary would once in a while say, 'I can hear my mother saying, 'Now, Mary Isabelle!' Her mother was the one person in her life who would confront her and stand up to her and pull her back," says the Rev. Canon M. Gregory Richards, her pastor and trustee. "I would stand up to her at times, but that's what she was missing most in her life. She didn't have a husband, she didn't have a teenage kid, didn't have that kind of prophetic voice to kind of pull her back, so she had to imagine her mother talking to her and reeling her back in when she'd get on her high horse about something or get down about something or get in a real dilemma. Her mother was the anchor—and still was until Mary died. Her mother was the 'parent voice' that Mary would recapture, the voice of reason and balance and reality and love and relationships." Canon Richards and his family—wife Debbie and boys Michael and Matthew—were among Mary's closest friends from the time Richards took his post at All Saints' in 1973 and were by almost any measure her truest family.

When Isabella died, Mary consciously filled her schedule with social engagements, building a life where she would rarely be alone. She often went to the theatre with Walker, and she especially determined she would not be lonely at holidays. Holidays that were for so long hosted by Mary's mother were now spent with Lucille Ball or Vincent Price and their families. In fact, Mary was at the Price home for special occasions of all sorts. "We made a very big thing about Christmas, and it went on from early in the morning till late at night. And when our Christmas [family celebration] was over, Mary would come in for dinner and we would have Christmas dinner together. Sometimes it would be as late as 9:30 or 10:00 and she was an integral part of that," says Mary Grant Price, noting that Mary was usually the only guest outside the immediate family. Mary often attended the school plays of the Prices' young daughter Victoria at the Marlborough School. To Victoria, Mary was "Aunt Wicksie." Mary and Vincent often celebrated their birthdays together, since his was May 27 and hers June 13. (She and Vincent were less than a year apart and both grew up in St. Louis, leading many to assume they had been friends since their youth; in fact, they grew up in different parts of town, went to different schools, and did not meet until the 1930s in New York.)

But actually Mary did not have much social time to fill, because she was able to quickly throw herself into work to regain focus after her Isabella died. Even more than before, Mary's work now became her life. "Nobody worked more than Mary Wickes worked. If she wanted to, she could have worked every day of her life, and she worked *almost* every day of her life," says casting director Ethel Winant. Mary finished *Trouble*, which did well enough to prompt a sequel, *Where Angels Go, Trouble Follows*. The sequel took Mary to Philadelphia and Santa Fe, as well as other parts of California, giving her some welcome distractions. The two pictures remain among Mary's most popular today. She also took a stage role, playing Madame Arcati, the medium, in Noel Coward's *High Spirits* in Houston and Los Angeles.

At home, Mary found the television and radio a comfort, other voices to occupy the silence. "The minute you get home, turn on something— the TV or the radio—and just leave it on. Don't listen to it, just leave it on. It's wonderful. That's what I did when Mother died. It's the only way you'll get through it," Mary advised friend Stella Koetter Darrow when Darrow's mother died in 1968. It was in Mary's home life that she made the biggest change after Isabella died. Isabella had lived with Mary for almost fourteen years in Los Angeles and for seven in New York before that. Living at the Voltaire without her mother was hard. In 1967, two years after Isabella died, Mary left there and rented a small one-bedroom, one-bath apartment in Century Towers, much less space than she had shared with her mother. The Century Towers, twin twenty-seven-story residences that opened in 1965 in the Century City neighborhood of West Los Angeles, drew an upper-income Hollywood crowd from the start. Mary would occupy unit 503 North at 2160 Century Park East for the next twenty-eight years. Facing north, it was a dark unit with unremarkable views, but she liked the building's high-end services, including announcing visitors, which Mary felt was only proper.

Though the complex was modern, Mary's unit seemed of another era, filled as it was with as many Shannon family antiques as Mary could fit. Mary Grant Price remembers the apartment as "a tiny little Victorian box in the middle of this contemporary high-rise. The smallest space you ever saw, but she managed to get eight people in it for lunch. It was 'extremely Mary'—she was absolutely right in it." When the rental units were converted into condominiums in 1973, Mary agonized over whether to buy her unit or move to another rental. She had never owned property; in fact, mindful of her parents' financial reversals, Mary remarkably had no debt of any kind. The fact that she was faced with this decision during a writers' strike—which slowed job offers—made it even harder. She sought advice from many people, including Nanette Fabray, who had some real estate expertise, and Lucille Ball. "Lucy convinced her to buy the apartment and Mary always said that was the best thing she ever did," says Wanda Clark, Lucy's longtime secretary. Mary bought her unit in September 1973, meaning that at sixty-three—an age when most Americans hope to be out of debt and making retirement plans—Mary acquired her first mortgage. Now, with Isabella gone and Mary settled in Century City, the person who became most important to Mary was America's favorite redhead.

CHAPTER SEVEN

Lucille Ball's Best Friend

IN SEPTEMBER 1949, PRODUCER ARTHUR SCHWARTZ OFFERED MARY A regular role on *Inside U.S.A. with Chevrolet,* a half-hour, every-other-week TV variety show modeled after a successful Bea Lillie Broadway vehicle. At this point, Mary had made only a dozen appearances in the new television medium, including stints on a few game shows. A series meant regular work, and she took it. Broadcast live from New York by CBS, *Inside U.S.A.* starred husband-and-wife performers Mary Healy and Peter Lind Hayes and featured big guest stars of the day. Lucille Ball was to perform on the November 24 show, one of her first appearances on television. But because she was finishing a film in California, Lucy would be unable to arrive until shortly before the broadcast. Mary, who had never met Lucy, offered to stand in for her during rehearsals for the benefit of cast and crew. Lucy arrived during one of the last rehearsals and sat in bleachers beside the set as Mary performed Lucy's role. Watching Mary, Lucy said aloud, "She's clever!" A voice three rows behind her said, "Thanks. She's my daughter." The voice was Isabella's.

Mary and Lucy immediately hit it off and, from that meeting on, became especially close. "We were on the same wavelength, I guess because we enjoy all the same things," Mary would later say. "There were lots of people around her who wanted something—money, a job or whatever. But all I wanted was her friendship."

If Isabella was the dominant relationship in Mary's life, Lucille Ball was the defining one. Mary and Lucy would become each other's most intimate friend for some thirty years.

"Mary Wickes was my mom's best friend. That's not debatable," says Lucie Arnaz. "My mother had various 'best friends' vying for the space, who came and went—people who'd get right up along side Mary for good reason—and for one reason or another, my mother would get tired of those people and they'd kind of go away. Even Vanda [Barra]. Even Olavee [Martin]. We used to call these friends 'The Kids'—they replaced [Desi Jr. and me] when we left. Couples who would come into the house and be there every night for dinner and always when they ran a movie and always with backgammon. Then all of a sudden those kids would be gone and 'The New Kids' would be there. And the couples would last sometimes a year, sometimes three years. So there were people who got to be good friends for a while, but Mary was *always* there. She was like *forever*. They were like sisters." Certainly, they were closer than Lucy and Vivian Vance, with whom Lucy is so associated among the general public. "Vivian and she, through the years, had been estranged and on different coasts. They were more like girlfriends. Sometimes girlfriends can nit-pick at each other and have little fights and then they become best friends again. Mary and my mother were more like blood relatives, dependent on one another like family depends on one another," Lucie says, noting that Mary often spent Thanksgiving and Christmas with Lucy's family on Roxbury Drive in Beverly Hills, where for many years Jimmy Stewart lived on one side and Jack Benny on the other. "If there was some law where I could have made her an official family member, I definitely would have. I would have given her 'aunt' status because she was closer to me in many ways than some of my actual blood relatives were. She was there so much more often."

In many respects, Mary's place in Lucy's life recalls that of Ebba Sedgwick, the widow of director Ed Sedgwick, who worked with Buster Keaton and the Keystone Cops. He had seen great talent in a young Lucille Ball and provided pivotal advice early in her career. Forever grateful, Lucy was generous to his widow for many years, serving as caregiver of sorts. "Ebba was a brilliant woman. Intellectual. Knew words. Read everything ever written. In her later years, she got frail and my mother saw to it that Ebba was always taken care of," says Lucie. "Ebba and Mary were like Tweedle-Dee and Tweedle-Dum. They were there together, and I think they had their moments where one was on the outs with the other one, and yet Mary helped my mother take care of Ebba. Mary would do whatever—that was the marvelous thing about her. If Mary sensed that something needed to be done, she would be the one doing it. She'd hear through the grapevine that DeDe [Lucy's mother] was looking for something she needed, and she'd just put it away in the back of her head. She'd be out somewhere and say, I'm going to get that for DeDe because she needs it. She'd get it, take it over and hook it up or whatever."

Wanda Clark, Lucy's longtime personal secretary, says Sedgwick was "more or less always at Lucy's house," even though she maintained her own residence near Roxbury and Pico. "Ebba was always there for holidays and special occasions, included like a member of the family. Mary was with Lucy a lot when Lucy took Ebba places." Lucy intervened on Ebba's behalf to secure a place in the Motion Picture and Television Fund retirement complex, which had a long waiting list. Ebba died there in 1982, almost thirty years after her husband passed away.

"Mary and Ebba were the people who would tell her when she was full of shit and not be afraid of her. She wasn't Lucille Ball to them. She was Lucy," says Arnaz. "They'd known her enough years and both had the types of personality that were not impressed by celebrity. Those are the kind of people my mother really, really liked to be around."

"I can tell you what Mary said about why they were friends," offers actor Laurence Guittard, who befriended Mary during the 1979–80 revival of *Oklahoma!* "She said, 'Because I knew her before she was famous.' They go way, way, way back, well before Lucille Ball was *Lucille Ball*, so she trusted her. I'm sure that's appealing to somebody who can't trust what anyone around them says. Mary did not mince words. Tact was not her middle name." Adds Mary Grant Price, "Actresses are surrounded by phonies. When you come up against one who has integrity and who doesn't try to get something from you or from the friendship but is just *there* for you, then that's important. Mary wasn't a hanger-on. She and Lucy were important to each other and they shared a lot of the same values."

Indeed, their similar view of work and family was one of their bonds. "We both adored our mothers and we had the same approach to our work. We didn't fool around . . . Work always came first, and we were always giving our best right from the first read-through," Mary once said. Their work ethic was a significant piece of common ground; neither of them ever took employment for granted. "That was one of my virtues from the very beginning," Lucy said at a 1984 Museum of Broadcasting tribute to her in New York. "I have been happy to be a part of the business and I never complained. I never thought it was better if I said [affecting haughty tone], '*I* won't do that, that's beneath me' or 'Why should I do that? Give me one good reason why I should do that. I've already done *that* sort of thing.' I never had that attitude. I knew it was important to do the best that I could . . . I just wanted to be in there and learning."

But the two women had much more in common. Both were strong-willed and direct. Both were unusually thrifty and valued simplicity over excess. Lucy, who did not attend college, admired those who did, and much of Mary's life was enveloped in her college experience. Neither had any real interest in politics or world affairs. Like Mary, Lucy was resistant to change; when she died in 1989, she was still using rotary dial telephones in her home. Born only fourteen months apart (Mary was older), they could reminisce about industry beginnings: Lucy appeared in the film version of *Stage Door*, while Mary appeared in the original Broadway production—for which Lucy had unsuccessfully auditioned. And they survived, building long careers that evaded many young actresses who began in the industry with them. "They were two ladies who'd been through it," says Guittard. He escorted Mary to the taping of the 1986 premiere of *Life with Lucy*, Ball's last series, and accompanied both women to the Ahmanson Theatre for the opening night performance of *Social Security*, a comedy starring Lucie Arnaz and husband Laurence Luckinbill. He remembers Mary and Lucy being completely comfortable with each other. "Lucy was impressive. Like Mary, she had this kind of straight-from-the-hip, direct, no-bullshit personality. But they were so different that they weren't competitive. Mary was not pretty, so that enabled Lucy to not be a 'woman-competitor' with Mary. They were not trying for the same jobs or the same anything," he says.

Another characteristic the two women shared was their inclination to view people as more than their professional status. Both had close friends who had nothing to do with Hollywood, and both often found pleasure in new people who entered their lives. Mary's relationship with Lucy's secretary Wanda Clark was relatively independent of Mary's relationship with Lucy, for instance. Mary and Clark visited each other's homes, went out together, often had tea at Neiman-Marcus—all without Lucy. Sometimes they were joined by Clark's husband, Peter, tall, warm, and delightful company. And they remained friends long after Lucy died; Clark joined Mary at her apartment just a few weeks before Mary died. Clearly, Mary viewed Clark as a friend, not just as Lucy's secretary. "But I think Mary treated most people like that," Clark says. "And Lucy felt that way about people—she didn't necessarily think of them as their position. She liked them, had fun with them, enjoyed being around them."

Lucie believes her mother was drawn to Mary for "her honesty, her responsibility, qualities my mother always tried to create in herself. Her genuine 'can-do' quality . . . 'Ask Mary, she'll be able to do it.' Or if it was taking care of somebody in a hospital. That's *the* trust, isn't it? You trust people with your life and if you're lucky, maybe you can count on one hand the people you can say that about and [about whom] you think, no matter what happens, 'I know I can trust that person on all these various levels.' My mother trusted Mary with her life." Whenever Mary arrived at the home Lucy shared with husband Gary Morton, "she never came in quietly, she just came in the back door. Always. She wouldn't even have to ring the doorbell if my mother knew she was coming over. [Lucie mimics Mary bounding in the house, booming, "Well, where is she?!"] My mother adored Mary. She was just great to be around—she'd go anywhere, do anything, she'd play games, she was funny. My mother never had to worry about Mary [because] she'd take care of herself. She was gung-ho to do, to go and to see."

The two women were so close that those who wondered if Mary ever spoke honestly about her feelings—disappointment at losing a role, grief over the death of a friend, the pain of loneliness—again and again said the same thing: "Maybe only with Lucy." "She probably told my mother a lot," Lucie says. "They had a very deep, close relationship. My mother would tell her things, I'm certain, and I'm sure that she relied on [Mary's] advice, her sensibility. Whether Mary reciprocated and told her about her problems, I don't know. But I never got the sense from Mary that she was gonna complain to anybody." Iggie Wolfington, a friend of Mary's who also knew and performed with Lucy, offers that "Mary was a very direct person, and I could see how she and Lucy would hit it off. Lucy liked me and we had a good rapport, but she was rather intimidating. Mary would not be intimidated by Lucy, and therefore Lucy would have great regard for her. She'd talk that straight language with Mary, though Mary wasn't [used to it]. Lucy had a pretty fiery tongue and Mary didn't," he says. Both women were born entertainers and could be extraordinarily funny. "Mary had a wonderful sense of humor and could always make Lucy laugh. I don't think there were a lot of people who could make Lucy laugh, and she *loved* to laugh," Clark says.

But that day in 1949 may have inspired more than a friendship: Seeing the husband and wife stars of *Inside U.S.A. with Chevrolet* work together happily may have fueled Lucy's own television aspirations. In the collaborative spirit of the early days of television, there wasn't much separation between celebrity guest stars and the regular cast, so sharing dressing rooms was common. Sheila Bond, who was then the series's eighteen-year-old featured dancer, shared a dressing room with Lucy and Healy. "My hair had to be put up, because I had very straight hair. At that time, you didn't have rollers, so you had to do 'spit curls.' Lucy was so cute—she used to spit on it and make pin curls while I was getting notes. I remember sitting there while she was doing my hair one day, and she said to Mary Healy [about the domestic comedy setup], 'This is the kind of thing I'd love to do with Desi. If I can only get something with Desi so I could *be* with him. If only we could get a show together.' She wanted to do something with Desi so that she wouldn't have to follow him around to see if he was dating anybody. She got so tired of him running around. She thought it was such a great idea that [husband and wife] Peter and Mary were working together. That's really how the germ of the idea started." Lucy and Desi Arnaz had been married about nine years at this point. Six months later, at the Chicago Paramount Theater, they began a twelve-week vaudeville tour to promote the act that would, a year later, become *I Love Lucy*. "When they got the show, I thought, 'She's trying to do what [Hayes and Healy] did!'" Bond says.

Mary surfaced a second time in the context of developing *I Love Lucy*. She was among those considered for the part of Ethel, the character ultimately made famous by Vivian Vance. *The Lucy Book* author Geoffrey Fidelman writes that Mary turned down the role partly because she knew that Lucy's perfectionism might hurt their friendship, and partly because she believed she could make more money in film and other TV projects. But others say Mary was rejected for the role and was forever disappointed. "Mary never quite understood why Vivian was hired. [In later years] she mentioned to me several times that she expected to have that role, and I gathered that Lucy had said so," says Emily Daniels, who was camera coordinator in the first season, and whose husband, Marc, had been the series's original director. "I don't know whether Marc had anything to do with that, because Marc was the one who brought Vivian in. Marc knew Vivian was playing down in La Jolla and took Desi and Jess [Oppenheimer] down there to see her. They liked her so much that they just hired her immediately, so Mary must have been eliminated before then, but maybe they just didn't tell her." Mary mentioned her disappointment to Emily "two or three different times" in the late 1980s and early 1990s. That Mary would still feel regret forty years later makes the friendship she extended to Lucy even more remarkable. Daniels can't speculate as to why Mary didn't let the incident come between her and Lucy. "But of course she was so close to Lucy. She was really Lucy's best friend." Nor did it hurt Mary's relationship with Vivian Vance. They, too, were friends for many years.

Although Mary was not chosen to play Ethel, she was hired to perform in "The Ballet," a first-season episode that remains one of the series's most memorable. She plays Madame Lamond, a severe, humorless ballet instructor who tries to help a clumsy Lucy Ricardo dance well enough to perform in one of Ricky's shows. Mary modeled the instructor on Albertina Rasch, the Austrian-born dancer and choreographer known for carrying a baton. The episode features an inspired bit of physical comedy in which Lucy, in a tutu, attempts to continue the lesson after her right leg improbably gets caught in the barre. The resulting chaos as she tries to untangle herself is comedy at its best. During rehearsal, Mary recalled years later, "I started to ad-lib. I said, '*A bas!*'—my faulty French, meaning, down. And Lucy said, 'What's that mean?' I said, 'It means down.' Lucy said, 'Oh.' The next thing you know, I said, '*A bas,*' and Lucy said, '*A bas, a bas, a bas.*' It was such fun." In a cover article celebrating the series's fiftieth anniversary in 2001, *TV Guide* chose the ballet as the tenth funniest moment of the series. When *Entertainment Weekly* issued a glossy collector's edition in 1998 to celebrate "The 100 Greatest Shows of All Time," editors selected a photo of Mary and Lucy from this episode to represent the series. This scene was also featured in an ABC primetime special in 1995, "Fifty Years of Funny Females."

The episode has caused some confusion among TV historians. Years later, Lucy claimed her foot got caught unexpectedly during filming, forcing her to ad-lib the resulting schtick. But this wasn't the case. "Oh God, no. Lucy rehearsed absolutely everything. Everything was tight and set when she did it. The fact that she was such a good actress made it look as though she just thought of it, but no, she *insisted* that everything be absolutely set. I remember them [in rehearsals] working out where Lucy got her leg caught up there. I think Lucy kind of invented most of that," says Emily Daniels.

This was Mary's only appearance on *I Love Lucy* (1951–57), and it is probably the best remembered of any of their performances together. Mary and Lucy worked together twenty-one other times: the *Inside U.S.A.* episode; a 1950 episode of *Star Spangled Revue*, in which Lucy was a mayor and Mary her maid; nine episodes of *The Lucy Show* (1962–68); nine episodes of *Here's Lucy* (1968–74); and a *Lucille Ball Special* (1977). Mary played various comic characters, including nurses, maids, and overbearing relatives. On one show, she played a courtroom witness with the tongue-in-cheek name "Mrs. Wickenhauser."

If Mary didn't play Ethel on screen, it sometimes seemed that she did so in real life. Mary and Lucy shared some adventures worthy of being filmed, like the time in 1967 when they went shopping with a baby chimpanzee. "Lucy called me up and said, 'What are you doing this afternoon? Bullocks is having a white sale and I want to get some sheets and pillowcases and stuff.' She picked me up and we tooled on out. And we drove up to a house. We knocked at the door and it was the trainer of some chimpanzees [the Marquis Chimps] who had been on *The Lucy Show*. One of them was a grizzled white-faced elderly chimp who was very lame; he'd been mistreated [but] then these people had adopted him and he was doing fine. There was also a baby chimp that Lucy had fallen in love with. It hadn't worked on the show, but it had been *around* the show—a little baby chimp, just able to kind of sit up, open its eyes and look around. The man greeted us at the door and said, 'Oh, come in.' He said to Lucy, 'Just sit down, my wife is getting the baby ready.' So we sat there and pretty soon the woman came out with the baby chimp in ruffled panties and a bonnet. I kind of looked at Lucy and she said, 'It's OK.' So she said [to the owners], 'Now, we'll be back in about an hour, an hour and a half, is that alright?' Off we went with the baby chimp [and] Lucy carried it around through Bullocks." Lucy still managed to spend $600 on linens that day. Lucie Arnaz, who has heard this story before, finds it ironic, because while she grew up, her mother sometimes refused to take her out in public for fear of people swarming around them. "She wouldn't take me to the market, but she'd take a chimpanzee and a six-foot-tall woman in a long plaid skirt because God forbid she should draw any attention to herself!"

Another outing involved the Rolls-Royce of gossip columnists, Hedda Hopper. Hopper lived around the corner from Lucy and on many mornings stopped in at Lucy's for coffee while out walking her dog. After Hopper died in 1966, Lucy bought her Rolls-Royce at auction. Shortly thereafter, she asked Mary to accompany her on a Sunday afternoon to visit Lucy's longtime maid, Harriet McCain, in a nursing home on Washington Boulevard. Lucy brought along some flowers and caramel corn, a favorite of Harriet's. It was the first time Lucy had driven the luxury automobile. "We had a nice visit with Harriet—we laughed and scratched and by the time we got back in the car, it was dusk. Lucy said, 'How do you turn on the lights?' I took a good look at the dashboard and it was a forest of knobs and buttons and dials. I said, 'Pull over, under that street-lamp there, Lucy, and let's see.' So we got out the beautiful leather-bound owner's manual and it said [things like] 'Where to Have the Tires Changed in Bangkok,' but nothing that tells us how to turn the lights on. I got out in front and Lucy pulled knobs. We kept pulling things and finally found the right one and we started for home." On the way, Lucy wanted to stop for gas. "There used to be a Standard station at the corner of Camden and Little Santa Monica. We pulled in there. A young boy came to the window and Lucy said, 'Fill it up, please.' He disappeared and we went on chatting. Pretty soon he came back and said, '*Where?*' She said, '*I* don't know.' She looks at me, and I said, 'I don't know.' He came back with the owner and we could hear a lot of muttering but together they found the place to put the gasoline.'"

But outings with chimps and luxury automobiles were not typical. In truth, Lucille Ball off-screen, with or without Mary, bore little resemblance to Lucy Ricardo. Most of what the two women did together was rather ordinary. They visited friends together. They laughed together. They sometimes traveled together. Very often, they played games together. "Lucy called me up one afternoon and said, 'I'm cleaning out my closet, so come on over.' I went upstairs to the bedroom and she was limping. I said, 'What's the matter with you?' She said, 'Oh, I think I broke my toe. I rounded the corner of the bed when the phone rang and hit it and, oh, boy, it hurts.'" This had happened the day before, but Lucy hadn't phoned the doctor or had the toe X-rayed. "I said, 'Don't you think you should, if it's hurting that much, Lucy?' So she went to the phone. Now their doctor at the time was a Dr. Probert. Wonderful little guy, very peppery. And I heard her say, 'Hello, this is Lucy. May I speak to Dr. Probert?' There's a pause. Then she says, 'Dr. Probert, I think I broke my little toe. I . . .' and then there was a looooong pause. And she said, 'Oh. Thank you, Doctor,' and she hung up. I said [concerned voice], "Well, what did he say, Lucy?!" Lucy told Mary that the doctor said, "You broke your toe? You know what to do for that! I've got a cold—nobody can help me! And, *boing!* He hung up!" (When Lucy's mother DeDe died in 1977, Mary rode in the limousine to DeDe's services with Dr. Probert, a man she always thought was "awful funny.")

Elizabeth Wilson, who acted with Mary in the TV series *Doc* in the 1970s, says, "Mary used to go there a lot and play cards. I remember she said she had to park the car in sort of a careful place. Lucille Ball sounded like a lonely woman, and I think Mary was kind of lonesome too, so maybe they shared that. I always tried to imagine what it was like, these two dry wits."

"I met Lucy through Mary, and Mary would often play games," says Mary's friend Peter Walker, an actor and writer who was especially close to Mary in the 1960s and '70s. "You know Dictionary? Mary loved it. Gary [Morton] and Lucy and Mary and Vivian Vance and a bunch of us would go up there and play Dictionary at Mary's place." Dictionary is a parlor game in which players try to fool each other with faux definitions of real words. In the early 1970s, when Washington University professor Richard Palmer told Mary he would be in Los Angeles for a convention, she invited him to join a small group for a buffet dinner and Dictionary. Palmer and his wife, Becky, arrived to find themselves standing in Mary's living room with Lucille Ball. Also present were Charlie Henry, a retired advertising executive who was a frequent companion of Mary's, and one or two others Palmer cannot recall. But, thirty years later, he remembers two things about that evening clearly: Lucy stumping the others with the word *lammergeier*, a large vulture, and him putting aside any doubts he had about Mary's closeness with Lucy. "You always wondered with Mary, but her credibility was beyond question from that point on," he laughs. "It was clear they had a very warm, longstanding relationship."

But it was not all laughs. The women relied on each other in serious moments, such as when Vivian Vance was dying of bone cancer. It was Mary who accompanied Lucy for a final good-bye to Vance in the summer of 1979. Lucy flew to San Francisco, where Mary was performing in *Oklahoma!*, and the women rented a limousine for the ride to nearby Belvedere, where Vance was bed-ridden at home. "I told the nurse when she came to the door, 'Now, you give us the high sign so we don't stay too long. We don't want to wear Vivian out,' Mary said. 'Well, we were there for two hours and laughed. I sort of stayed in the corner, because Lucy and Viv had so much to talk about. Finally, I said, 'I think we'd better go, we're gonna wear Viv out,' and she said, 'Oh, no!' Vivian loved it. We left and cried all the way back."

If Mary was Lucy's sidekick, she was also Lucy's protector. Emily Daniels recalls attending Christmas parties at the Bel Air home of Madelyn Pugh Davis, who scripted much of Lucy's TV work, and her husband, surgeon Dick Davis. "Mary would sort of 'guard' Lucy from everybody who wanted to come up and sit down and chat with Lucy. Lucy would pass them quickly onto Mary, and Mary would take them on and get them away. Lucy just didn't want to get 'stuck' with anybody, I guess. She did that with almost everybody. I remember because I was [once] shoved aside almost immediately and I thought, 'God-dammit, I *know* you. I've known you well, and I don't like being shoved off like this.'" This was the sort of thing Lucy sometimes did at restaurants, too. In the 1970s, Lucy bought tickets to entire tables at charity events and invited the same people to every event so they could create a protective wall against strangers who wanted to speak with her.

Just as Mary looked out for Lucy, Lucy looked out for Mary, as when Gordon and Sheila MacRae struggled to produce a 1959 TV pilot, *There's No Place Like Home*, loosely based on their own Toluca Lake family life. Gordon played a TV cowboy star, and Sheila played his put-upon wife.

Also cast were Chill Wills, Walter Brennan, Phil Silvers, and Ellen Corby, who played the housekeeper. The production was going poorly and had gone through many revisions. Having been conceived as a sixty-minute comedy/drama with occasional singing, it now looked more like a thirty-minute sitcom. Lucy, a friend of Sheila's at the time, advised them that "someone taller, like Mary" would be funnier as the maid than the much shorter Corby, Sheila recalls. The MacRaes fired Corby and replaced her with Mary. But director Bill Asher remained so dissatisfied with the final product that he re-shot the entire show, paying the cast and crew a second time. Even then, Gordon and his agents so disliked the show—which was designed to revive his sagging career—that it never aired.

The gifts that Mary and Lucy exchanged over the years offer additional insight into the nature of their friendship. Mary often sought out gifts that would be unusual in some way. But what, after all, does one give a national icon? After Lucy sold Desilu to Gulf+Western, Mary presented her with one share of Gulf+Western stock that she purchased in Lucy's name as a novelty. But exasperated Gulf+Western finance people kept asking where this one share came from. "It just screwed up the bookkeeping, because Lucy got paid in a certain amount of stock for Desilu. I don't remember all the implications, but it didn't do what Mary wanted it to do," laughs Clark. But most of Mary's gifts were remarkably simple—and sensible. She gave Lucy the same candles and mail-order cheese baskets that she sent to a dozen other close friends. She regularly gave Lucy subscriptions to the *New Yorker* and *Smithsonian* and, over the years, gave her a potted plant ice bucket, a traveling jewelry case, an address book, key rings, a scarf, and (after a stay at Lucy's Snowmass condo) a tablecloth. Lucy's gifts to Mary were sometimes on a grander scale, including air tickets to visit her in Snowmass, and offers of free weekends at Lucy's hotel investment in Indian Wells, California, near Palm Springs, which was managed by her brother Fred.

But, reflecting their shared appreciation for frugal living, Lucy's gifts to Mary could also leave something to be desired. Seeking a Christmas present for Mary one year, Lucy carelessly picked something up from her own bedroom and wrapped it, completely forgetting she had received it from Mary. A hurt Mary asked Clark about the gift, but Clark is not certain Mary ever told Lucy directly. "Lucy was pretty bad about wrapping things up and giving them back. She did that a lot, but she only did it once to Mary," says Clark, who cannot recall the item.

Lucy also sometimes gave Mary the same item more than once: a large tote bag, for example. "Mary, the second year she got it, would say [to Clark, sounding puzzled], 'She gave me this last year!' I said, 'But Mary, couldn't you use more than one?' And Mary kind of said [annoyed, but persistent], 'But don't you remember, she gave me this last year?' If Lucy liked something, she'd give it to you [again and again]. I've got about twelve clocks here that Lucy gave us. She'd always write [on the card], 'I always have time for you.' Mary got a few clocks, I'm sure."

Lucy's frugality sometimes had greater implications. According to contracts from ten episodes of *The Lucy Show* and *Here's Lucy*, Mary was paid from $750 to $1,750 for four days of work each time. Most payments are in the $850 to $1,250 range—surprisingly low for a performer of Mary's stature and experience at the time. For instance, for four days' work in November 1973 on the "Lucy, the Sheriff" episode of *Here's Lucy*, Mary received $850. To put that amount in context, this is the exact amount Mary's friend Bill Swan received for his first television job eighteen years earlier, an appearance on *Navy Log* for which he worked three days. Swan says it's "distressing" to learn Mary was paid so little in the late 1960s and early 1970s. Like others, he assumed the Lucy programs had been "very lucrative" for Mary—in the range of $3,000 to $5,000 per episode—especially given that Lucy was so fond of her. But this wasn't the case. "Mary Wickes was hired for one episode I directed," recalls Herbert Kenwith. "I used to do the salary lists. I said to Lucy, 'Is there a mistake here? You gave Mary Wickes only *six hundred dollars* for a full week?' It was her *best* friend." Lucy confirmed the amount was accurate.

Mary traveled to Hawaii with Lucy and the Arnaz family in 1957. She enjoyed herself tremendously. Perhaps not coincidentally, it was one of the few times that Mary vacationed without Isabella. The trip was first suggested by Vivian Vance, who was relaxing there with third husband Phil Ober, an actor who had just appeared in *North by Northwest* and *Love is a Many Splendored Thing*. Mary was completing *Don't Go Near the Water* at MGM when Vivian invited her to join them. Mary had never been to Hawaii, so she agreed to meet Vance and Ober in Honolulu.

The night before she was to leave, Mary's phone rang. It was Lucy. "She said, 'When are you leaving?' I said, 'Tomorrow night, it's a midnight plane.' She said, 'Desi and I have decided to go and take the two children and Harriet, the maid, and Willie Mae, our nurse.'" Thoughts of being on the islands with a large crowd gave Mary pause. "I thought, *Holy Moly*, I don't know that I want to go. Mother said, 'Yes, now, you'll have a good time.'" Years later, Mary recalled the trip fondly, even the flight on a small inter-island plane from Honolulu to Kalua on the Kona Coast, where they would spend most of the trip. "I had introduced Lucy to Irish coffee the night before at the Queen's Surf," Mary said, laughing mischievously. "We got hysterical. I don't know why. Everything struck us as terribly funny. She had never had Irish coffee before. We weren't tight, we were just giggly [and] had a ball." The next day, having boarded the small plane, everyone in their party was "kind of quiet because we'd had a few the night before, just enough so that getting up was a little troublesome." On board were Vivian and Phil, Lucy and Desi, Mary, Lucie, Desi Jr., Willie Mae, and Harriet. But no one else. "When the stewardess came through, I said, 'Excuse me, how come there are no other passengers?' She said, 'Because you have so much luggage, all of you.' It turned out the Arnaz group had forty or fifty pieces of luggage!"

One afternoon during the trip, the men had gone fishing and Vivian was out, leaving Lucy and Mary sitting at the hotel, admiring the ocean. "We had gotten some of what they call passion fruit. I said, 'Have you ever tried this before?' She said no. I said, 'I haven't either.' So we bit into it. Well, of course, passion fruit has tons of seeds in it. You have to keep spitting seeds. Again, we got hysterical—it struck us as so funny. All these tacky seeds!"

Mary's affection for Lucy extended to Lucy's children as well. When Lucie turned eighteen in 1969, she moved into her own apartment, which happened to be in the same two-tower Century City complex where Mary lived. Lucie lived in the building at 2170 Century Park East, while Mary lived at 2160. Mary, then fifty-nine, showed great respect for Lucie's independence. "She was right across the way but it was almost like she was not there. She never bothered me or checked up on me," Lucie says. That same fondness for Lucie resurfaced when Lucie married Phil Vandervort two years later. Mary gave Lucie the first of three wedding showers. (The other two were hosted by Wanda Clark and Marge Durante, wife of performer Jimmy Durante.) Mary invited Clark and several other women from *Here's Lucy*, such as Vanda Barra. Her little apartment was crowded but, for Lucie, the event was delightful. "As far as I know, she made everything—great salads and tea cakes and things. We all dressed in long summery bridal-type '70s clothing. It was very special, and I thought it was amazing for her to do such a thing. Isn't that what your contemporaries are supposed to do for you, your girlfriends? Well, Mary Wickes and Wanda Clark [both considerably older than Lucie] *were* my contemporaries. I didn't have a girlfriend. My matron of honor was Wanda Clark, because for the previous two years, I had been at the studio all day long, every day and Wanda became one of my best buddies. It just felt wrong to suddenly go back to my high school friends and say, 'Who wants to be my maid of honor?' I sort of lost my connection with them."

Some twenty-five years later, when Mary and Lucie (now living in New York) no longer saw each other regularly, Mary still honored their relationship. In the spring of 1995, Lucie found herself in Los Angeles, staying at the Century Plaza Hotel. "I called her and said, 'I'm right across the street practically, and I want to come see you.' We made a plan to have tea the next day." Mary sprang into action and invited Clark, Madelyn Pugh Davis, and Mary Jane Croft (who played Betty Ramsey in the Connecticut episodes of *I Love Lucy*). "We had 'the Little Ladies Luncheon Tea.' She threw this thing together for me in three seconds, and I had so much fun. I was almost in tears when I was there, remembering how much I loved these people and what great friends they all were to me." It was also the last time Lucie saw Mary alive. "I *adored* her. Because I knew I could play around with her. I could always tell her exactly what was going on. I didn't have to mince my words with Mary, and she never minced her words with me." Lucie in her youth especially liked Mary because "Mary didn't talk different to kids, and kids love that. Grown-ups who don't baby talk to you, they just talk to you like regular people: 'Hello there! Come over here and sit down. What do you want to eat?' DeDe, my grandmother, was like that, and they were very close because they were very similar. That's probably why my mother got along with Mary well—she reminded her a little bit of DeDe's strength and character."

It is worth noting that while Mary stubbornly rejected unkind or bullying behavior in colleagues, she seemingly overlooked it when it came from Lucy. Those who worked with Lucille Ball often found her domineering and belittling. In her work, Lucy was sometimes so unkind that stories about her reducing the likes of Joan Crawford and Jack Benny to frightened milquetoast when they appeared on her shows are legion. Mary was certainly present to observe her share of all this treatment. Did she look the other way because she never found herself personally on the receiving end of Lucy's sting? Did she decide, guided by her strong faith, that everyone has faults and Lucy's was simply sometimes unbearable behavior? Or was she more calculating, reasoning that enduring this behavior was a small price to pay for the friendship of America's favorite comedienne? The answer is not clear, but Mary was able to rationalize Lucy's behavior in a way that allowed Mary not to challenge it.

"Sometimes she was abrupt, but it was usually because of time," Mary once said of Lucy. "She knew what was right for her. And there was no quarreling with her. I had great respect for her, but I think she scared some people."

Having the top comedienne in Hollywood as her closest friend undoubtedly helped Mary feel good about herself. It was important to Mary that others know how close they were. "If any of us are guilty of dropping names, she was guilty of dropping Lucy's name," says Bill Swan. "She talked about Lucy all the time. Hollywood is so inbred and if you've been out there long enough, everybody does at times say [something like], 'My good friend Bob, Bob *Redford*,' to impress people. Not that Mary was trying to impress me, but she certainly let it be known that Lucy was very dear to her and that she went down to Palm Springs with Lucy and the kids and so forth. If I said to her, 'Next week, do you want to go to a movie or something?' she'd say, 'No, no, I can't, Lucy's going to be in town.' Lucy was very important to her."

One afternoon in the mid-1980s, Jack Pirozzi and a colleague were visiting Mary at her apartment (Pirozzi was the Washington University development officer who helped Mary plan her estate). Mary was serving tea when her phone rang. She excused herself, answered it and said into the receiver, "Can't talk to you now. I've got some people here. I'll call you back." Mary hung up, returned to her guests and casually said, "That was Lucy. She's my pal," and the conversation returned to other topics. To Pirozzi, it was clear that Mary was making him aware of her relationship with Lucy, "but at the same time was so offhand about it that [it seemed] Bette Davis might be calling next. She didn't say, 'Do you know who that was?! That was Lucille Ball! We've been friends for years!'"

Mary did not exploit the relationship. Though she often talked about Lucy, she did not often tell stories about Lucy and *her*. Mostly, she repeated stories Lucy had told about herself, such as one about the girls in the beauty shop of Rome's Hotel Excelsior who were startled when Lucy walked in with her own henna rinse, saying she would color her hair by herself. Or the one about how Lucy received a surprise delivery of fifty pounds of Egyptian henna from a Saudi Arabian sheik after she had remarked to a journalist years before that she feared a shortage of the product, as it had been hard to find during the war. These were the sort of stories Mary had planned to tell Jay Leno during a *Tonight Show* appearance in 1992, but "dreary Tom Brokaw took up more time than he was supposed to, so we had to cut some," she said.

People who knew of Mary's closeness to Lucy occasionally sought to tap into it, some with greater success than others. Wolfington, who helped establish a West Coast office for the Actors Fund in 1969, found himself the following Christmas trying to help a fledgling actor who had driven cross country in his station wagon, family in tow, to find work in Hollywood. Wolfington told Mary, "He's got these kids who just arrived from out of town, they're trying to get settled and for Christmas they're really going to have a terrible time. I can get them a little bit of money through this source or that, but I'm sure Lucy gets all *kinds* of presents and then has to figure what to do with most of them." Mary agreed to call Lucy, who said, "Oh, God, that's the answer to my prayers! Tell Iggie to have the fellow come out Christmas Eve with his station wagon and come to my house." Wolfington gave the man careful directions to Lucy's, then helped him load his car "with all sorts of things for his family" from Lucy.

Other times when Mary was asked to impose upon her friendship with Lucy, things did not go as well, such as the time dancer Ann Miller was badly injured in St. Louis. Miller, whose career dated to RKO studio days when she and Lucy appeared together in *Stage Door, Room Service*, and *Too Many Girls*, was touring in a revival of Cole Porter's *Anything Goes* in 1972. On opening night at the Muny, as Miller made her entrance, the theatre's "steel curtains" closed off cue and she got caught. Two performers ran out to help her, and dragging her back in the dark, somehow injured her further. Miller lay in Deaconess Hospital, "holding press conferences and hiring and firing doctors left and right," Muny press agent Jerry Berger remembers. To ingratiate himself with the actress and because Muny feared a lawsuit, he found himself bringing Miller fresh peaches every day from an Illinois orchard. Berger turned to Mary for help. She was in town rehearsing for *Student Prince*, which was to replace Miller's show the following week. Because Berger knew Mary was close to Lucy, he pleaded, "Mary, please, please for the Muny, you've got to call Lucy and have her call Ann and convince her not to sue." Berger says Mary slapped her knee with her hand and said, "I'll be happy to!" "A few days later, I traipsed back up to Ann's room with a basket of something and she's all a-titter," he says. The conversation went something like this:

"Ann, how are you?"

"I feel much better."

"Oh, that's good."

"Yes. You know, I just got off the phone with Lucy. She called me out of the clear blue sky."

"Oh, really? Lucille Ball? What did she have to say?"

"She recommended a great lawyer."

Miller did, in fact, sue. The case dragged on for years, but in the end, Berger says, she was awarded only workers' compensation benefits of about $7,500. Berger suspects that instead of helping to dissuade Miller from suing, Mary may have encouraged her. Given Mary's strong identity with working actors, that's entirely likely.

The clearest insights into Mary's friendship with Lucy may come from Lucy herself. Mary's papers contain about fifty-seven pieces of correspondence, spanning more than twenty years, from the comedienne. Most are personal letters that Lucy typed when at home and wrote in longhand when traveling. There are also five postcards, five telegrams, and a handful of greeting cards. Together, they document a relationship cemented by great humor and deep affection. They reveal both the mundane (Lucy's distaste for the false eyelashes she was expected to wear during a 1968 European publicity tour) and the poignant (Lucy's presenting Mary with a possession of DeDe's as a memento after her mother's death). In one missive, Lucy playfully calls Mary "Snookey," her childhood nickname. The correspondence was sent from Beverly Hills, London, Paris, Monte Carlo, Capri, New York, Las Vegas, Aspen, Hawaii, Sun Valley, Idaho, and a French cruise ship. The earliest appears to be a May 8, 1957, postcard from Honolulu. The most recent is a June 12, 1980, mailgram sent on Mary's seventieth birthday during her long New York run in *Oklahoma!*. "Still miss you like crazy," wrote Lucy.

Mary undoubtedly discarded many more of Lucy's letters. Lucie guesses her mother wrote Mary about ten times a year over the course of their friendship, even though the two lived just over a mile apart. Discarding letters from Lucy might be the best evidence of Mary's refusal to exploit their friendship. It is precisely this kind of loyalty that enabled Lucy to trust her, sharing matters both personal and professional. Though the most revealing letters might not have been preserved, those that remain offer insight into the friendship these two women shared.

And many letters offer previously unknown insights into how Lucy perceived her own career. In 1973, during production of Lucy's ill-fated motion picture *Mame*, the star seems to have had little idea how badly the film would be received. "Everything going remarkably on *Mame*. Little annoying episodes raise their ugly heads almost daily, but I have managed to keep a civil tongue and treat each case as it comes up with what I hope is a modicum of propriety. They seem to be delighted with the few rushes that we have seen, and that means a lot. It means we are on the right track at least and my interpretation of *Mame* is coming through and approved," Lucy wrote Mary. A film version of the 1966 Broadway musical that starred Angela Lansbury (itself based on the play that starred Rosalind Russell), this *Mame* quickly joined the annals of especially bad adaptations.

In 1960, Lucy temporarily relocated to New York to star in *Wildcat*, a Broadway musical about a female wildcatter in the Texas oilfields. It was a professional gamble, to be sure. On August 22 she wrote Mary about rehearsals for the show, which, like *Mame*, would flop with critics. "[I] am happy and strangely enough feel quite at peace with everything and everyone—and not panicky at all the way I expected. I have taken things so unbelievably quiet [that] since I arrived, I don't even recognize myself. A great calmness has descended. I don't know whether it is because I'm really terrified at my move and my nerve to tackle anything like this or that I really have learned to let each day take care of itself and gather all the strength I need from my years of experience in my 'chosen profession.' Whatever it is I'm grateful for the way I feel . . . I flipped over the score because it's fun! And I can do it without worry, voice or no voice. The shenanigans are all in the musical end of the show and, well, no, that's not true. There are plenty of other shenanigans throughout, enough to make everyone happy if they came to see 'Lucy.' On top of all else, I do think I've surrounded myself with some really great people that know what they're doing, and that *always* appeals to me." But by December 23, just a week after the show's New York opening, Lucy confides to Mary, "This is the toughest work I have ever done and I am sorry to find myself asking 'What do I need with it?' I am looking forward to a vacation about four years long."

In March 1968, Lucy wrote Mary from Las Vegas, where she was preparing to appear on the *Ed Sullivan Show*, about plans for the debut of *Here's Lucy*. This would be her third series and her first since Desilu was sold to Gulf+Western and transformed into Paramount Television. (Lucy had been Desilu's majority shareholder.) In *Here's Lucy*, which would be made under the auspices of Lucy's own production company, Lucy cast Lucie and Desi Jr. as Lucy Carter's children. "We are up to our neck reorganizing and setting everything up. I'm glad I'm staying at Desilu and don't have to move offices and people and stages n'everything. The first script from Milt [Josefsberg] and [Ray] Singer is good and I'm grateful. They have written good stuff for both kids. They really have good lines and good action and it's a typical Lucy show—and a damned good first show to set up the new format. And *so* similar to the other format. There will hardly be a noticeable difference . . . I'm using the next two or three years to train the kids. I've nothing to prove—so I know I'm doing the right thing—for them. Hurry home."

When Lucy married Gary Morton in November 1961 in New York after *Wildcat* closed, she writes Mary, "I got myself a real doll!" and signed off as Lucy Morton. But about Desi Arnaz, her letters (at least those Mary saved) remain silent. During a lengthy 1959 European cruise ostensibly designed to revive the Arnaz marriage, Lucy uncharacteristically avoids addressing anything of substance. "The weather so far is divine. The accommodations are the greatest. The food superb. The trip, boring. I'd rather be having a ball in Paree. But we *are* getting a much-needed rest, and Oklahoma City seems far, far away," she writes, referring to a public bruising she took the week before when, after learning that only two thousand of fifteen thousand seats had been sold, Lucy apparently left a Kiwanis Club youth rally where she had agreed to appear. "We are having fun but getting tired of traveling."

Occasionally Lucy muses on events of the times, such as during a 1968 visit to London with Morton. She writes that other than some cashmere items and some coats for Lucie and Desi Jr., all she has purchased on her trip is perfume. That's about all that makes sense in London, she tells Mary, "unless you are buying for the mad, mad, mod group. You should *see* some of the *unbelievable* 'getups' on some of these 'birds' over here. Skirts either up to the upper thighs or down midcalf with goucho boots and Spanish Don hats—and ratty, *real* ratty furs and you just *don't* believe it!! London is disastrous for young people these days. They are falling on their faces, after all the adulation they have had as forerunners of fashion these last three years, and now they don't know what to do next because they are losing ground and, too, the drug situation has depleted them—their energy is sapped. The suicide rate is way up and disease rate is too terrible and homosexuals, now legal, are finding it hard going—they made it legal but damned uncomfortable. And why the hell am I telling *you* all this??"

Some letters reveal Lucy's thoughts about celebrities of the day, such as when she writes about the former Grace Kelly, whom she found charming during a 1968 stay in Monaco. "Princess Grace is gossip-hungry, so we got along fine," Lucy writes. "We've gotten palsy-walsy. She's a doll—a bored doll, but a doll. A bored *Catholic* doll so she's stuck!" And the letters reflect humor. "By golly we better get together," Lucy writes in a 1958 invitation to an open house. "If you don't want to come yourself, Mary, take pity on poor Isabelle and let her get drunk once in a while. You're much too hard on her. I understand you have ruined her sex life." Surely no one but Lucy dared joke this way about Isabella, who almost certainly had no sexual experiences after Frank's death in 1943. A 1973 letter written while Mary is away says, "Your plants are thriving, but they ask for you and wonder why you don't drop by. I think one of them is pregnant if you have any instructions concerning same." From shipboard on the *Liberté* during the 1959 vacation with Desi and the children, she writes about her pre-trip vaccination. "Holy Cow, as they say in India. My left wing is the size of the smokestack on ye Liberté. And as you know my left toe is busted. And as you may or may not know, my left kidney is in severe straits. So all-in-all I'm one hellofa mess—leftwise that is. The right side I get all dandied up each eve and sally forth and pretend to be enchante with ever so many whom are just too old, too tired—and too fat. I smile until they grab my sore arm for an autograph and then I wander away." From Hawaii in 1970, Lucy writes, "I'm scribbling cuz I'm in a hurry trying to get downstairs to the beauty parlor. My hair, as usual, looks like an unmade bed constantly—I'm thinking of shaving my head."

She opens a 1971 letter "Dearest Queen Isabella" and closes it, "Love to your Highness. Your Obedient Servant, Lucie Arnaz's mother." She closes a 1973 letter with, "My health is improving daily. My singing voice is nil. My husband is handsome and wonderful. My Mom is thriving in Snowmass. My dogs are still guarding Lexington. My future in pictures is questionable. My love for you goes on."

Lucy's letters are sometimes those of a loving mother, warmly chronicling the lives of her children and fretting about their futures. On at least one occasion, Lucy wrote in the voices of her young children. In the first days of 1959, when Lucie was seven and Desi Jr. almost six, Mary received this letter: "We loved our little stockings, and Mommie tried to fool us into thinking they were from Santa Claus . . . and thereby hangs a tale. She sure got herself in a lot of hot water trying to sneak into our rooms at 2:00 AM with the cute little things, and she damn near loused up the whole tale. If you want more details on the tale, see you after January 5. Love, Lucie and Desi IV." Mary was such a part of the family that Lucy could playfully sign a 1968 telegram "Desiree's Daughter and Desiree's Mother," knowing Mary would understand. (Lucie's middle name is Desiree, in honor of her maternal grandmother.) In 1968 Lucy thanks Mary for a Steinbeck novel, which she says she will make sure Lucie and Desi Jr. read, too. This thought prompts her to reflect about arranging proper tutors for her children. "Good tutors for languages and readin', writin' and arithmetic are hard to find, I know," she writes. "Those little ol' lay teachers are not as equipped as I prefer, so this takes real thought and canvassing. I want [Lucie and Desi] to have a better idea of some subjects than they have had in school. Neither school has ever given them a love of learning—a wish to do more than has been a daily requirement—and I'm hoping to find someone or perhaps *two* teachers that will really push them through the paces."

She also confesses concern about her children as they mature, date, and become young adults. She wrote Mary, for instance, about Desi Jr. living in Malibu with Liza Minnelli (they "seem to be playing house very successfully"), and about Lucie's dating illusionist Jim Bailey and Phil Vandervort, whom she would marry in 1971. In February 1970, Lucy wrote Mary after a three-week vacation at Snowmass: "The kids made me very happy by coming up and really enjoying themselves. Desi and Steve March [son of family friend Hal March] had five glorious days and I cooked and washed sweaters and socks in cold water and Woolite until my hands almost froze off. But I loved it. Even withstood the alcoholic teacher they had to bring with them. Then Lucie and Phil came up and admired the view and said, Very beautiful, Mom. But what do we do after two days if we don't ski? I produced our ski instructor instantly and you don't *believe* the way the two of them are flying down the slopes. I do wish you could have come up but I know your college work was important and too you wouldn't dig the little plane into Aspen from Denver so . . . I'll try you again and bring you in by oxcart or dog sled."

While on a 1970 family vacation to Hawaii, Lucy writes, "Everyone satisfied with the rooms and suites but everyone anxious to get the hell outta Honolulu—Waikiki in particular. It is a screaming pounding hippy madhouse. Even Desi can't wait to get to the other island where peace and quiet is promised. We have all voiced our disapproval of this area—and never plan to waste time here again. You really can't believe it unless you see it—it is *so* changed [from when Mary was with them thirteen years before]. Will have lots to tell you when we return."

Lucy genuinely missed Mary's company while the two were apart. "Think of you constantly!" Lucy writes from Monte Carlo, where she was a grudging member of the jury at the seventh annual international Festival de Television. "The musical comedy being enacted is really too much for me to take alone. I need you for *roaring*. I can just hear you," she says. Seemingly glued to seventeen TV sets, using ear-phones for translation, she deemed the whole thing a lot of dreary nonsense, "a challenge to wake-up pills." She calls her fellow members of the jury—on which she was impaneled for two weeks—"a sober and sobering group—the whole pack about as much fun as a trip through United Nations just as war was declared." In a telegram sent August 5, 1968, the day Mary opened in *Show Boat* in St. Louis, Lucy says, "I haven't forgiven you for leaving during the month of August but if you mind your manners [this is a favorite phrase of Mary's] I may allow you to participate in some RSVP action upon your return and I still have some leftover Christmas presents as prizes." (RSVP was a popular word game, and word games were a favorite of Lucy's.) While Mary was in San Francisco for an extended period in 1973 with the American Conservatory Theater, Lucy writes her, "I do wish you would find time to come down over a weekend. It ain't such a big trip, you know—nor is it expensive. And, Miss Wickenhauser, I would appreciate at least one call a week from you. You could always reverse the charges if you are visiting a friend or whatever. Wouldn't matter to me just so I hear from you. I really mean that."

These and other passages reveal deep affection. "I hate to think that you'll be gone when we return. Please *please* write to me," Lucy writes from Monaco in 1968. "You are real special in my life." A week later, while in London to promote the film *Yours, Mine and Ours*, Lucy opens an eleven-page letter with "I don't know what the hell you're doing there in St. Louis today, but I cannot get you off my mind—and I've tried. God knows I've tried!" She attaches two small notes, saying, "Wonder what Mary Isabella's doing today??" and "Keep thinking about Mary—miss her very much." She closes with, "I'm *so* anxious to hear from your ruby lips the details re: your teaching seminar [or] whatever. Hurry home." The following month, again writing to Mary in St. Louis, Lucy says, "Alright now Mary Isabella, hear this! Called you today [and] your maid said you'd left for rehearsal or something. Miss you like crazy! Getting home without you bopping in was no good. And you're so darned far away. Got your letter written on the train but that isn't enough." In February 1971, Lucy writes, "Just talked to you a short time ago but have a feeling I might not run into your beautiful body before I take off again . . . Hope you get your sexy body out of bed before I leave." She signs off, "At any rate, I love you."

On their face, expressions of this sort between any other two women could suggest a lesbian relationship. Even Lucie was puzzled by the nature of Lucy's letters when shown them in 1999. Looking at them, she describes her mother's strong expressions of affection variously as "odd," "weird," and "strange." "There definitely was a very special nature to their relationship, but I don't think it was that. I'm racking my brain

[for] another reason for why these would be so intimate. There's got to be another reason. I would find [a lesbian relationship] hard to believe, only because there's never been another instance of it anywhere certainly in my mother's life. And yet, when you said that to me, as soon as you showed [the "beautiful body" letter] to me, the first thing I thought was, 'Oh, my God, is *that* who she was? Was *that* their relationship? Is *that* why they were there all the time?' It's real interesting, the wording and everything, but I don't think so."

Lucie agreed to read copies of some of the letters privately, and to reflect on the exchanges between her mother and Mary. (Mary often wrote Lucy when Mary was away from home, Clark says, but Lucie has not found these letters in her mother's effects.) Lucie decided to share her mother's letters to Mary with Gary Morton, Lucy's husband for twenty-seven years. After she read several passages to him, he laughed out loud and told her this was simply the way Lucy and Mary spoke to each other. Mary might stand, point critically at her own tall, gangly figure and complain to Lucy, "I look like a tree," while Lucy, across the room, would dismiss Mary's self-deprecating remarks with a wave of the hand and say, "Oh, stop it and get your sexy body over here."

Lucie speculates that her mother's statements about being unable to get Mary off her mind might refer to a problem that Mary had confided in her that caused Lucy concern for Mary. Lucy was a chronic worrier, so much so that Lucie was often reluctant to tell her of her own troubles. Clark, who worked for Lucy for twenty-seven years, says, "Lucy talked that way to the people who were important to her, not her casual friends. She wanted to know about them and what they were doing, if their life was OK. She talked this way to Ebba. She talked this way to me, in funny little ways."

Dolly Reed Wageman happened to be at Mary's apartment shortly after Mary received word of Lucy's death on April 26, 1989. Lucy died from surgical complications at Cedars-Sinai Medical Center in West Hollywood. Mary was broken up, but characteristically, as Wageman said, "you'd never know it." "Stiff upper lip." Mary no longer drove, so when she said she would like to be at Lucy's that day, Wageman offered to drive her. Wageman dropped her in front of the home on Roxbury, which all morning had been a chaotic swirl of activity and cameras. Gary Morton phoned Clark at home very early that morning and asked her to join him, Lucie, and Desi Jr. at the house to help them control the crush of attention. Fans had started gathering out front, where they would stay for days. Clark was at the house from six thirty in the morning until about eleven o'clock that evening, answering an endless stream of condolence phone calls. Also present that morning was Ray Katz, a family friend and producer who was Lucie's manager for many years.

"Gary had posted somebody at the door to send everybody away. Celebrity people came and friends came, but Gary [had them] turned away. He didn't want to see anyone. That was his way of handling grief and I couldn't argue with that. As the morning went on and the word got out, Mary was one of the first people to come," Clark says. Lucie happened to be near the front of the home when she heard Mary's voice. She went to the door, grabbed Mary by the arm, and pulled her in from the crowd. "I will never forget that," says Clark. "Otherwise, Mary would have been turned away." Mary did not stay long. "Where Mary came from, and where I come from too [Oklahoma], when somebody dies, you go there and you take food," Clark says. "Maybe you don't stay or have a party, but you go there and let somebody *see* you and know that you're paying your respects. It's just what you do, and it would never occur to her not to do that.

Talking about Mary's response to her mother's death forces Lucie to choke back tears. "It was horrible for all of us. I could see that she had been crying for a long, long time. But she came over like I would have expected her to: 'What do you need me to do?' She was just there, always. And she wasn't going to be the one to fall apart. *Everybody* else did." The over-the-top reactions to Lucy's death from some fans and friends forced Lucie to yell at one of her mother's longtime friends, a bawling, inconsolable woman who was seemingly turning to Lucie for support: "How bad could this be for *you*? She was my mother!"

Two weeks later, on Mother's Day, Lucie arranged a memorial for close friends. She rented a vacant home in Mandeville Canyon and threw a picnic on the grounds, something Lucy always loved. She provided Lucy's favorite family-style foods on a large buffet table. Friends ate and drank and reminisced. Mary was offered a ride to the picnic by Emily Daniels, who preferred not to go alone, and who suspected Mary was no longer driving. Daniels's husband, Marc, who directed many of Lucy's television programs, died on April 23, three days before Lucy. Losing within days the most important people in each of their lives brought Mary and Daniels very close; in fact, these events initiated one of the closest friendships of Mary's last years.

Mary and Daniels sat most of the time with Madelyn and Dick Davis. "Mary was rather quiet. She didn't move around and talk to other people," Daniels says. Daniels occasionally got up and visited with people, as did Madelyn Davis. Ordinarily Mary would mingle, too, but on this day she did not seem very social. "I don't know whether she was uncomfortable, but she knew everybody there," says Daniels. Indeed, Mary had known many of these people for decades. "I'm sure she was affected [by Lucy's death], but she would be able to handle anything—so she did. I don't remember her ever getting really emotional about it where she allowed it to show. She would talk about it, but it was not what some women would do, go off into sobbing." Talk, indeed. When asked about his experience with Mary just a few years later on the *Sister Act* pictures, make-up artist Michael Germain offered this out of the blue as his first recollection: "She talked a lot about Lucille Ball, talked about her quite a bit."

When Lucie set out to chronicle her parents' lives in *Lucy-Desi: A Home Movie*, a television documentary that would earn her an Emmy in 1993, she invited those who were important in her parents' lives to share recollections on camera. Many immediately signed on, including Mary Jane Croft and Madelyn Pugh Davis. But to Lucie's surprise, Mary, who participated in a 1991 tribute to Lucy at the Academy of Television Arts & Sciences, chose not to appear. "She didn't actually turn me down. She just made it too difficult to get her on tape. She was strangely more trouble [professionally] than she had ever been," Lucie says. For one thing, Mary was particularly concerned about the way she looked. When the director and producer tried to schedule an interview with Mary, she insisted she needed to have a hair person, then a make-up person. She raised concerns about lighting. "She needed to have a 'this' and a 'that,'" Lucie says. When the producers responded with a date that hair and make-up people could be present, Mary could not make herself available. Lucie told her, "'OK, I'm going to be back in L.A. to do some more work, so I'll come to you, wherever you are.' But somehow, it just wasn't going to work out." Another obstacle was money—specifically, AFTRA residuals that would be paid if the program were eventually sold to a TV network. "She was the only one who raised those issues. As she got older, she got a little more testy. Everybody wanted her for nothing, so she wanted to be paid. She wasn't really bitter, but she had turned into a person who wasn't going to let anyone screw around with her," Lucie says.

Lucie believes Mary did not feel safe talking about Lucy publicly, "even with me, as much as she loved me. I was disappointed, but not angry. I loved her so much that I just tried to accept her for whatever she was, even if I don't understand all of it. I really was telling the producers, 'OK, lay off. If she decides she wants to do it, fine, and if not, fine.' It won't be complete without Mary's thoughts, as far as I'm concerned, but she means as much to me as my mother does, so I'm not going to pester her. It'll be what it'll be without her input." In all likelihood, this was a decision Mary agonized over. Lucy had been the most important person in her life since Isabella's death, maybe the only person in whom she truly confided. This wouldn't be a cavalier chat on the couch opposite Jay Leno. Could Mary talk about her feelings for Lucy in a serious setting where she might have to let her guard down? Mary decided she could not. But knowing that Lucie would be disappointed, neither could Mary bring herself to tell Lucie of her decision—just as, twenty-five years earlier, she could not tell Bill Frye she skipped the swimming lessons he arranged. Instead, consciously or not, Mary sabotaged her participation.

That Lucie never got Mary on tape for this program is one reason Lucy's friendship with Mary is not widely known. But Lucie is not bitter. "I have no bones to pick with Mary Wickes. She was extremely good to me, always. A divine human being. I didn't push it because I respect her and maybe she just didn't feel comfortable about this." After viewing a version-in-progress on tape, Mary wrote Lucie, "I was surprised to find how hard it was to see the empty house and the grounds. I have not seen either since the day I went to the house the day your mother left us. Oh me."

CHAPTER EIGHT

Cookies and Milk with Mother

BILL SWAN MET MARY IN STOCKBRIDGE, MASSACHUSETTS, IN THE SUM-
mer of 1957, when he was performing in *Bus Stop* and she was rehearsing
The Great Sebastians. After they both returned to Los Angeles, Mary sug-
gested they get together, so Swan picked her up for a night at the Holly-
wood Bowl. At the end of the evening, when he drove Mary back to the
Voltaire, she invited him in. "If you'd like to come up, we can have some
cookies and milk and you can meet Mother. She'll be waiting up for me,"
Mary said. So, at a time when scotch and soda was the typical offering,
Swan went upstairs and had milk and homemade cookies with Mary and
Isabella around their kitchen table. Mary was forty-seven.

This homespun approach to life defined Mary her entire life. She
seemed an anachronism to virtually everyone she met, living as she did
with the values and tastes and manner and clothes and furniture and
habits of someone from a bygone era. The roles she picked, the people
she befriended, the ways she spent her time off camera, the expressions she chose—they all spoke of another time. Again and again, when
friends are asked to describe her, the word *Victorian* surfaces quickly.
"She didn't change—I'd say she didn't even adjust. And that's what carried her through. She was really one of the most principled persons I
have ever known. She had a very special, enormous faith in her God
and in her beliefs and, dammit, nobody was going to change them. And
nobody did," says Dolly Reed Wageman.

Principled is also one of the first words Mary Grant Price associates
with Mary. "She just maintained her own standards. The fact that she
was Victorian was a matter of choice, but her essential character was that
she was very, very principled. She just had a large feeling about right and
wrong and was happy to tell you it." To Lucie Arnaz, Mary's old-school
nature could be summed up as character: "In the old days, people who
had character didn't change it with every person they met. They didn't

change to fit the style or the clothes or to fit the mood, to be hip or what-ever. They were who they were. Mary had her own character. She had it all her life."

Mary's attachment to propriety extended to the way she referred to herself, always "Miss," never "Ms." It affected the way she dressed: almost never in slacks, usually in matronly blouses, blazers, and long, heavy plaid skirts ("like a big Madeline doll," one friend jokes). Even in the 1990s, she often donned a hat and gloves to visit her agent's of-fices. She liked to shop at Talbot's, known for its conservative women's clothing.

Her fondness for tradition was especially evident in the way she spoke. Mary peppered her conversation with dated expressions like "Glory to Betsy." If she thought someone was too taken with himself, she frequent-ly cracked, "He's heady with his own perfume," an expression Betty Gar-rett has used herself ever since she first heard it from Mary. If Mary was really impressed with someone, she might offer an enthusiastic, "He's all wool except the buttons!" Encountering someone who wasn't very bright, she might say, "He has a glass eye at the key-hole." Someone was never merely dead; they were always "dead as a mackerel." "Push-face" was something Mary often called people, sometimes endearingly and sometimes not. She frequently ended phone calls and letters with an admonishment a schoolmarm might yell at young children: "Mind your manners!" No doubt, this was something Isabella drummed into Mary in childhood. Mary's phrasing reflected a formality that she simply considered proper. Anne Kaufman Schneider remembers being struck the first time Mary introduced her to Madelyn and Dick Davis at dinner. "She always called him 'Doctor.' She would say, 'Doctor, do you want your tea black or with sugar?' She never said 'Dick.' And they were very close friends." Mary's language, as much as anything else, shaped the way others responded to her. "There were surges in Mary of being very prim and proper," says Jerry Berger. "To Merman, I'd say, 'Oh, fuck it all, Ethel.' But you would never dream of saying that with Mary. There was something prohibitive about her. Never a *damn*, a *hell* or an *Oh, shit*. But I wouldn't call her unpleasant. We had a few laughs, if you could laugh with your Sunday school teacher."

This was Mary's way even at the start of her career. Janet Fox, an actress who worked with Mary in *Stage Door* in 1934, remembers, "She had a wider 'moral path.' People watched it in the four-letter-word de-partment around Mary. If somebody told a dirty story, she would not laugh, even if it was funny. That was something she really had distaste for. I don't remember her even being faintly salacious. And she had a very strong ethical streak. She knew that so-and-so slept with so-and-so, but she wasn't a gossip at all." Anna Crouse, who roomed with Mary on the road during Broadway tryouts in 1939, remembers, "She had a little routine about going to bed and about getting up, and it was almost a little old-fashioned. She was very disciplined about her health. And very neat." Her penchant for orderliness was such that "Mary would come in like Joan Crawford and scrub down her dressing room," recalls Warner Shook, who worked with Mary in the 1970s at American Conservatory Theater in San Francisco.

But it was manners that mattered most. When guests arrived at Mary's small apartment, she insisted on interrupting whatever conversation was already taking place among earlier arrivals to introduce the newcomer properly. When she received a gift of any sort, she was quick to respond with a hand-written thank-you note. If friends' parents visited from out of town, she made a point to invite them over or take them to lunch; Dick Davis, Rita Pico, Peter Walker, and Warner Shook are among those who experienced this courtesy. Walker was so appreciative of Mary having invited his mother to an Easter meal at her apartment that when his mother died, he gave Mary her sapphire earrings, one of the few good pieces of jewelry Mary ever owned.

For Mary, these standards worked, even if others found them off-putting, as they were often accompanied by a rigid, judgmental streak. As longtime casting director Ethel Winant puts it, "Mary had a lot of principles and lived by them—and demanded others live by them as well." In the early 1940s, Mary found herself at the Barbary Room—an elegant bar at the Berkshire Hotel on East 52nd Street that was popular among actors—when Ann Corio entered. Corio had been a stripper almost as well known as Gypsy Rose Lee. She performed in burlesque all over the country, had an enormous following, and produced her share of headlines, fueled by provocative shows like *The Sultan's Daughter*. By 1936 she was the highest-paid stripper in the United States. But in the summer of 1940, she gave up stripping to pursue a legitimate acting career. Although she was well-liked by many in the theatre, she found offers limited to films like *Sarong Girl*, in which she wore little more than she did in burlesque. "A little group of us were sitting around having a drink in the Barbary Room and [actor] Boyd Crawford came in with Ann Corio. She was very sweet. But she was a stripper. And Mary Wickes got up and left. It was like, 'I don't mix with strippers.' She did it in a nice way—she said, 'Oh, I have to go,' but it was fairly obvious why. This just didn't interest her," said someone in Mary's group who asked not to be identified in print.

But Mary rarely voiced judgment about others' behavior. Take, for instance, George S. Kaufman, who had a long romance with Natalie Schafer, decades before Schafer achieved fame as Mrs. Howell on *Gilligan's Island*. "Mary probably thought it was awful that my father was having an affair while married to my mother. But maybe, like a lot of us, she wasn't judgmental about people who she really cared about—and she really loved and admired my father," says Anne Kaufman Schneider.

There was nothing abstract about the contrast between Mary's Old World ways and her Hollywood life. Mary's puritanical sensibilities were at least as evident in her professional life as in her personal life. "What is acceptable today as humor or as what you can say in public was not acceptable to her," says friend Jane Sutter. "She was quite prissy. She was raised in a genteel family—that's an old-fashioned word and it always sounds funny. But the way she was raised is no longer understood today." To anyone who would listen, Mary groused about the dialogue she encountered in film and TV projects. "Mary could be a little holier than thou," says Max Showalter. Says Emily Daniels: "They'd send her a script and if it had anything even slightly distasteful or prurient, she wouldn't do it. She'd read the line and say [gruffly], 'I'm not gonna do *that*!'" "She found almost everything offensive. She turned down a lot—she didn't like it or the script or thought it wasn't proper," says Ethel Winant. Mary turned down the part of Molly Ringwald's grandmother in the comedy *Sixteen Candles*. Mary dismissed it as "the dirtiest script I've ever read. How dare they send me a script like that!" The film was wildly successful and quickly became a touchstone of sorts for 1980s adolescents. Mary's role was taken by Billie Bird, whose character, ironically, yells to another, "Watch your language, Mr. Dirty Mouth."

For similar reasons, Mary passed on a role in *Mrs. Doubtfire*. Initially, she accepted the part, but when she received the final script, the dialogue offended her. "She hated all the curse words. The thing that upset her the most wasn't what she had to say but the language the kids were using. She actually went to some trouble to get out of it," says Bill Givens. After Mary backed out, "they cut the part immensely. It ended up being next to nothing, but in the original script it was a big role. She talked about this one a lot because she really wanted to do the movie. She liked Robin Williams, and she had some real qualms about backing out." Mary might have regretted her decision, since the film turned out to be rather sweet—and a smashing success. "She wouldn't do blue material, ever.

She'd say, 'I don't want to do a movie that I wouldn't want my friends to see,'" says Madelyn Pugh Davis. Mary phoned her in 1991 to ask for advice about a sitcom pilot she had been offered. Mary read Madelyn one of the jokes in the original script that offended her, a line that didn't even belong to Mary's character. She told Madelyn, "They promised that when we get going, we won't do that sort of thing." "I said, 'Don't believe that, Mary. You'll be real unhappy.' I knew enough to know that if it's raunchy going in, it's going to be like that, and you don't want to do that unless the mortgage is due." Mary turned it down and the pilot, which Madelyn declines to identify, proceeded without her. It did not sell.

Mary never felt the need to apologize for decisions of this sort. In 1969, she told the *Toronto Telegram*: "Today, they're making a lot of films that I don't want to touch with a ten-foot pole. I was offered a part with a group, a very good group with whom I very much wanted to appear. But it was a script that offended my tastes. It broke my heart to turn that down. I was so upset that I talked to my minister about it. I've been with too many good people and done too many good things and I don't intend to stoop to it. I don't like dirt for dirt's sake. I don't use four-letter words, and I don't care for them very much around me. I just wasn't raised that way." Five years later, she told *St. Louisan* magazine that the TV sensation called *All in the Family* held no interest for her. "That whole trend of comedy goes against everything I am. I don't object to it, but I simply wouldn't want to do anything like that myself." In fact, she wrote a poem about it. In a chatty 1975 letter to George Seaton after he directed her on stage in *Juno and the Paycock* in Los Angeles, she wrote:

> *This is what Mother warned me:*
> *"Life won't be worth two hoots*
> *If you throw good taste to the doggies*
> *And betray your standards and roots."*

It would have pleased her that some of her St. Louis contemporaries noticed. Without even being asked, college classmate Helen Margaret Aff-Drum observed that "she never took any parts that were mean and nasty like so many do now. If you went to see her, you didn't have to be embarrassed."

If Mary's attitude caused her to miss out on some great successes like *Mrs. Doubtfire*, it also caused no end of conflict with jobs she accepted. In the 1975–76 TV season, Mary grew disappointed with the language spoken on the sitcom *Doc*. Emboldened by a feeling of success in the air—*Doc* was a product of MTM Productions, the powerhouse behind popular programs like the *Mary Tyler Moore Show*, *St. Elsewhere*, and *Newhart*—Mary did the unexpected. She insisted on the right to demand changes in any dialogue she found distasteful, even dialogue assigned to others. Producer Grant Tinker refused and fired Mary instead—the only time Mary was fired in her long career. It was an embarrassing moment, and Mary led others to believe she left willingly. It was an incident she felt keenly, because she had developed genuine fondness for the show and for her character, Nurse Tully—so much so that Mary and Canon Richards registered a story idea about Tully with the Writers Guild. Co-star Elizabeth Wilson, whose character had just been written off the show, does not understand why Mary pressed this. "The scripts were wildly innocent. There was nothing abrasive. We were very middle of the road," she says. Barnard Hughes, the show's star, says, "I always thought she [regretted] that she went as far as she did with it. Objecting to anything on *Doc*, you had to go looking for it, really. I don't know what set her on the quest for script approval, but whatever she was looking for didn't work out. Grant Tinker said, 'Mary, we can't allow you to have that position,' and he was absolutely right." Publicly, Tinker said Mary requested a release from the show because its format was changing, and she "expressed discomfort with the harder comedy."

Mary no doubt felt comfortable requesting dialogue approval because she had experienced success with a similar gambit once before, on the TV pilot *Ma and Pa* the previous year. Before signing her contract, Mary submitted two demands: that she not be required to speak, gesture, or appear in any manner or situation that she considered offensive, and that no other cast member would be instructed to use any language or gestures that Mary found offensive—even if she was not in the scene. Warner Bros. Television, which produced the program, rejected the second demand but, remarkably, agreed to the first.

Even in inconsequential professional settings, Mary's approach seemed out of step. On a segment of the 1970s quiz show *Match Game*, Mary was a guest panelist when the phrase was "*Barbara* _____." The strategy, as Mary surely understood, was to propose names that would resonate widely with a studio audience. Joyce Bulifant offered "Streisand" and Gary Crosby offered "Stanwyck," both to loud applause. "Walters" and "Eden" were suggested by others. By contrast, Mary proposed "Fritchie," an obscure Civil War heroine whose name was met with awkward silence from the audience and a puzzled look from host

Gene Rayburn. In another segment, when asked to complete the phrase, "My husband thinks he's a fireman. When he comes to bed, he brings a ____," Mary was the only guest who did not say "hose." She offered up "ladder." As Mary Jackson put it, "She lived by her Campfire Girl rules." This old-fashioned approach to life was sometimes corny. She collected Snoopy items from the Peanuts comic strip. Her favorite television programs were of squeaky-clean family fare; late in life, she especially liked *Home Improvement*, and, at one point, she and Canon Richards considered collaborating on a script for this show, too.

So pronounced was Mary's Victorian ethic that others in her life responded to it on a purely intuitive level. Pioneering TV personality Johnny Stearns and his wife Mary Kay (their *Mary Kay and Johnny Show* on the Dumont Network was one of the earliest TV sitcoms, premiering in 1947) were chatting with Mary at a party at Alan Handley's in the 1960s, when conversation turned to women driving alone at night. Mary did not live far—Handley's Frank Lloyd Wright-designed home was at the top of Mulholland Drive, just above the Hollywood Bowl—and Mary had driven there frequently. Nonetheless, when the evening ended, the Stearnses surreptitiously followed Mary all the way home, directly into her underground garage, before letting themselves be known. "We said, 'We just wanted to be sure you made it home,'" Stearns recalls. "She couldn't have been more surprised"—nor, undoubtedly, more pleased. Mary's attitude about such things was, "If you went out in the evening, two ladies alone, you have to be cautious because you never knew if there were gentlemen out there who would not treat you too well," says Rita Pico. "It was turn-of-the-century, almost. We would valet park because women have to be very 'proper.'"

This attitude often affected her relationship with other actors. Mary's rapport with the 1972 company of the American Conservatory Theater in San Francisco was typical: Though she was in the ACT company, she was not really *of* it. Mary had known William Ball, ACT's founder and general director, since 1950. She found him self-important, but she liked him. He set a mood for the company that season that made it hard for her to feel comfortable. "Bill loved communal experience. More than he wanted to be a director, he wanted to be seen as a pater familias kind of guru, a great father figure. He wanted his 'children' to be loved and loving," says Jack O'Brien, a guest director that season. "This was San Francisco at its halcyon, hedonistic best. *Hair* was playing and we were hanging out with those kids. There was a lot of free sex and dope and everybody loving everybody. And a cactus like Mary in a rose garden is bound to feel a little bit isolated. But she liked it when it was hard. It validated her Yankee raw-wood finish that 'we're not kidding around here. Comedy's hard work.' That was her area of expertise, so she wanted other people to feel that but, honest to God, they weren't into it. They were into having a great time. There were lots of parties, lots of picnics out on Mount Tamalpais. And although Mary came, she never stayed long."

Even her gift giving reflected old-fashioned tastes. She often made candied grapefruit peels for Christmas presents. When Anna and Russel Crouse's son Timothy was born in 1947, Mary sent the new parents a framed sampler on which she embroidered "Now I Lay Me Down to Sleep." "There aren't too many busy young actresses who would sit down and do that. So much heart had obviously gone into this little cross-stitch sampler," says Anna Crouse. Mary also crafted a needlepoint of the Lord's Prayer that she gave Barry and Marie Sullivan when their daughter Jenny was born in 1946. It hung in Jenny's bedroom throughout the years she was growing up. Mary gave those she was fondest of the same inexpensive, unremarkable gifts year after year: a candle, a calendar, jars of jelly, or mail-order cheese. Bill Givens smiles when he remembers Mary coming to a black-tie dinner in Beverly Hills in honor of his fiftieth birthday, bringing a little candle for his bathroom. Meticulous with everything she did, Mary kept careful notes to remind her of what she gave to whom, what she might have received in return, and when she thanked them. Her notes reveal that—at least with regard to gifts—Mary treated her friends in same-sex relationships the same as her friends in heterosexual relationships. At Christmas in 1965, Mary gave blocks of cheese to "Viv and John" (Vivian Vance and husband John Dodds) and "Thelma and Joe" (Thelma Ritter and husband Joe Moran), and also to "Bob and George" (Bob Thomsen and George Bradshaw) and "Bill and Jim" (Bill Frye and Jim Wharton). That Mary's gift to Frye and Wharton was larger than the others was her way of expressing appreciation for their support after Isabella's recent death.

Bill Dorsam, her cousin Elizabeth's son, says Mary was sometimes thoughtful in remembering his mother. In the early 1990s, when Elizabeth's osteoporosis meant her standard-size wheelchair had become uncomfortably large, Mary, without being asked, sent Bill a check to acquire a special smaller one. When Medicare ultimately paid for the chair, Bill returned the money. But he believes many of the gifts Mary sent his mother "were hand-me-downs that she couldn't use that she tried to pass off as new. Stuff that she had around that she couldn't use—and neither could my mother."

Occasionally, Mary's gifts were both clever and generous. She gave Moss and Kitty Carlisle Hart a small silver toothbrush upon the birth of their son Christopher in 1948, gave Danny Thomas an antique cigar knife in 1961, and gave Mary Grant Price a sterling silver cross for the top of a Christmas tree. She reserved her most personal gifts for Peter Walker. On one occasion, she gave him a traveling jewelry case with his name embossed in gold. On another, she gave him a monogrammed leather pill case. And on a third, she embroidered his initials on a cook's apron, which he still has.

That Mary generally spent so little on gifts reflects one of the most pronounced aspects of her old world nature: her frugality. No doubt rooted in Frank and Isabella's financial struggles, Mary's concern about money was almost neurotic. Once, late in Mary's life, someone told her she was cheap. Mary had never perceived herself this way, and was so wounded by the comment she was almost brought to tears. "She called me and was very upset. Very hurt. She asked me if I thought she was too frugal or penny-pinching," says Rita Pico. "I said, 'No, I don't, not at all,' because I understood where she was coming from. Maybe she was, but that was her business." Not incidentally, this was one of the few times Mary allowed herself to reveal genuine emotion. "When Mary was not working, she told me, 'You don't know when your next job is going to be there, so it's like the squirrel, you must put your things away for the winter. Be cognizant that this may be your last job.' When she wasn't working, we'd go to Hamburger Hamlet or Jerry's Deli. But when she was working, she took me out to dinner for my birthday to a place where she could spend some money," Pico says. "I don't know why she felt that way, because she was in demand." Given that she was rarely out of work, if Mary had invested in the stock market, she might have become a truly rich woman. But she managed her money as conservatively as she managed her life, keeping her assets mostly in certificates of deposit and treasury bills, not stocks or mutual funds.

But it is difficult to believe that Mary did not understand that others perceived her as cheap. Her thrift had been notorious for years. "We always said she was very near with the buck," says Bill Herz, Mary's friend since the days of the Mercury Theatre Company in the 1930s. Mary stocked her freezer with large quantities of meat from out-of-the-way butchers. She clipped coupons for bran cereal and decaffeinated coffee. She resisted paying for cabs when she could no longer drive. She re-used whatever she could. Ten years after moving to Century City, she was still using stationery that bore her old address at the Voltaire;

she simply crossed out the Crescent Heights address and wrote in the new one. The decorative touches that she affixed to clothes—little bows and buttons—were often intended to hide flaws. "An elegant-looking sweater was practically held together with safety pins," marvels Debbie Richards, who sorted Mary's clothes after her death. And Mary could not let go of the belief that long-distance phone calls were a costly extravagance. When Mary was on location in Denver filming the first season of *Father Dowling*, the late 1980s series in which she played a rectory housekeeper, Pico often phoned so Mary would not feel lonely, but they never chatted long because Mary wanted Pico to avoid the expense of long-distance calls. And in 1994, when the two women were in different hospitals—Pico at UCLA with a pulmonary embolism, and Mary at the Motion Picture Home with cellulitis—Mary often initiated their regular phone calls because she did not want Pico to incur the expense of even an intrastate phone call.

Seeking bargains wherever they could be found, she frequented Pick-N-Save, a discount market popular with working class families. "She had all these shopping places she liked to go out in Santa Monica, where they had really reduced-rate clothes. How she found them, I don't know," marvels Emily Daniels, who, with some amusement, accompanied Mary on some of these outings. Daniels recalls that Mary would pick up a really cheap garment and exclaim enthusiastically, "That's a good bargain—only $17 for a whole dress, I'll buy that!' Then she'd wrap them up and send them off as Christmas presents." She shopped for herself, too. She liked a cut-rate shoe store where she would special-order shoes, either because of her size 11 feet or because the store offered the plain styles she preferred. Sometimes, when the shoes arrived, Mary would find something wrong with them and not accept them, but the staff was not flustered. "They didn't care—they loved her. She was so funny in dealing with the help that they would just laugh along with her. There wasn't any rancor there at all," Daniels says.

When out with friends, Mary did not hesitate to confront money issues. "She was very adamant about each actor getting their own check when you ate," says Harve Presnell, who performed with Mary on the road several times. "She would say things like, 'Everybody's working for a living here and we all pay our own,' so seven people would have seven separate checks. I'm sure the waitress went nuts, but that was her thing and she didn't make any apologies." One might think, then, that Mary would welcome occasions when someone else offered to pay for dinner at the end of a meal. But such was not the case. "That was a *big* deal, boy," says Presnell. "I was going to take Mary to dinner once. I said, 'Now, it's understood—my wife and I are going to take you out to dinner.' And she started in, 'I pay my own way!' I said, 'Not in this case you don't, because I invited you and you'll have the good grace not to bring it up again or I'll never invite you again.' She was very uncomfortable, and I never figured out why. She wasn't gracious about that; in fact, she was almost rude where that was concerned. It was unlike her."

This characteristic was something Mary had in common with Lucy, Presnell theorizes. "There was a great disappointment in both their lives some place, and there was a rapport there, a great understanding of a shared experience in their background. It was never talked about, and it was probably over men: Don't trust them. It had to do with being snookered, hoodwinked or tricked more than the financial thing. I never knew the details, except there was an almost adversarial relationship on Lucy's part especially after Desi's fall from grace," he says. While performing in a play with Lucie Arnaz in the 1980s, Presnell spent a lot of time at Lucy and Gary Morton's home until he could arrange for a house where his wife and family could join him. One night, Lucie invited him to have dinner with her and her father. "Lucie was anxious for me to visit with him because we had had some running horses. Desi was a terrible gambler, just awful. He was living in Del Mar. We were going to a restaurant, and on departing the house, Lucille was yelling at her to make sure her father paid, not to let him snow her into paying the bill. Jesus, it was very uncomfortable. She thought all men were going to take you to the cleaners because they have no standards when it comes to finances." Presnell, a generation younger than Mary, has found this suspicion common among older character actors. "All those people who came out of that same era, even [fellow comic character actor] Eddie Horton, had a great distrust of anybody on the production side of anything. They didn't trust the bookkeepers, the double set of books, and I guess it was from experience. 'Make sure you got it in writing.' 'Don't owe anybody anything in this business because they'll get you.' Showgirls in the early days were abused and taken advantage of at $200 a week. That was a big thing with Lucy."

Mary's tightness with money stopped when it came to entertaining at home. Be it lunch, dinner, or the afternoon teas she liked to arrange, she was a lavish, generous host who offered liquor and hearty amounts of food, most of which she prepared herself. She served with family crystal and silver, and she went out of her way to make guests comfortable. The food she served was distinctly midwestern. No matter how famous the guest, Mary's meals were likely to include chicken salad or chili, home-made brownies, and Jell-O. She liked to prepare an appetizer that she called actor's pâté made of liverwurst, cream cheese, chives, Worcester-shire sauce and dry mustard.

And Mary showed in other ways that she was not always cheap. In 1991, Edith Meiser (Mrs. Littleton on *I Love Lucy*) threw a party for Bill Herz's seventy-fifth birthday at Sardi's. Herz never thought Mary would part with the money to fly from Los Angeles to New York. But at eighty-one, Mary sought opportunities to spend time with people she knew in her youth. "It was a shock to me when she decided to splurge and come to New York. When she said she was coming, Anne Schneider said, 'I don't believe it!' but she did. We were stunned." Sometimes Mary could be spontaneously generous. In the 1970s, playing in *Wonderful Town* in San Francisco, Mary mentioned to Lee Roy Reams that it was her birth-day. "I said, 'For goodness sake, Mary, happy birthday! We didn't know.' 'Aw, well, that's alright,' she said. 'But what I'd really like is to go over to the Curtain Call restaurant [a little bar across the street from the the-atre], and I'd like you to sing all my favorite songs tonight.' I said, 'Mary, you got it.' So we went over to the bar with some of the kids from the show, and we started drinking Irish coffee and of course we had a fabu-lous time. God knows, I barely made it home that night. The next day Mary said [playfully], 'I had a whole thing of traveler's checks last night and when I got home, all my travelers' checks were gone. Guess who bought the drinks for my own birthday party!'"

Only on rare occasions did Mary treat herself to something nice, like the cruise she took around the Virgin Islands in 1977. The $2,900 pas-sage represented the single extravagance of her life, the only time she spent any real money on herself, so making that payment was not easy. She toyed with the idea of offering herself to Princess Cruises as on-ship entertainment—performing a one-woman show, for instance—in exchange for her passage, but in the end decided against it. She invited college friend Amy Jane Ax to join her; when Ax declined, Mary sailed alone.

CHAPTER NINE

She Kept It to Herself

IGGIE WOLFINGTON OFTEN VISITED RESIDENTS OF THE MOTION PIC-ture and Television Fund's nursing home, part of an industry-supported retirement community in Woodland Hills, California. One day in the early 1970s, he arrived while Mary was visiting as well. "She was being very thoughtful with an old, cantankerous character actor," a well-known, second-tier performer of about eighty whom Wolfington prefers not to name. Because Mary had been gracious to this actor, "the next time I was out there, I said, making conversation, 'Have you seen Mary Wickes lately?'" Wolfington was startled when the man responded gruffly that he found Mary's visits tedious and bothersome and her company more annoying than pleasant. "I thought that was the most ungracious thing I ever heard. She was giving of herself so freely, and he was being such an old bastard," Wolfington says. He felt obligated to tell Mary, so when he saw her next, he said, gently, "'Mary, you know that actor you've been so gracious to?' And she said [cheerily], 'Oh yes!' I said, 'He's not grateful at all, he said so-and-so-and-so.' And there was a big pause." She was clearly hurt. "Mary said to me [slowly and softly]: 'Why did you tell me that, Iggie?'" He was flabbergasted by Mary's reaction. "How could I have *not* told her? If it had been me, I would have said, 'Well, thanks a lot for telling me—that's the last good will I show *that* person!' But I had hurt her terribly by being very frank about this man, and I've never forgotten that. You just didn't do that with Mary." He perceived Mary as saying, "Why did you crack that shell of the egg of my life and let me know that somebody is not grateful for something I enjoy doing for them?"

"Mary was so self-confident and so 'specific' a person. That was something that she'd built up in the business and the roles she played. And also as a wall of protection, more or less," says Wolfington. "Where there came to be so very strong a wall [in Mary], I'll never understand. She kind of locked things away with a key."

146

In many ways, Mary lived behind walls; not merely walls against unpleasantness—like that displayed by the old actor who disparaged her visits—but also walls of secrecy about her health; walls of fear about her political leanings being discovered; walls of lies about her age; walls, certainly, against physical intimacy. These were walls of privacy so great that when friends wrote her apartment number on mail addressed to her, she was angered, fearing others might learn the precise location of her apartment. Most notably, she erected walls against any emotional closeness. Mary joked and laughed and told stories, but never really opened up—not even with her closest friends. In virtually every context, Mary placed limits on the warmth she would extend, so much so that emotional reticence is one of the first qualities friends mention when asked about her. "Mary never really lifted the whole veil. I had a good time with her and we always enjoyed each other's company, but it was a little on the performance level as far as her private life," Wolfington says. "She used 'the distance thing' so much in her work that it may have taken over her life," he says, observing that even Mary's small holiday parties were "always a performance." Nanette Fabray, who worked with Mary in two stage productions, calls it "a don't-get-too-close attitude," but says Mary was more complicated than that. "She didn't come across as having an emotional outside," Fabray says. "She was a darling person, but she never presented any of her personal life at all. She would express caring about you, but you didn't know anything about her."

Until she moved to Los Angeles in 1951, Dr. Lester Coleman was part of Mary's inner circle in New York. A surgeon who also specialized in "psychological medicine," he theorizes Mary was like many other unattractive people who "find solace in secrecy. They build an encapsulating wall around their own microcosm and protect themselves from the invasion of curiosity, from being hurt. She had a kind of personality that didn't allow invasiveness. She was aware that she was ungainly and unattractive, but she was so charming and warm that you loved her," he says. "She had what we called *shtoltzkeit*, an inner glow of self-preservation."

Mary and Elizabeth Wilson (Dustin Hoffman's mother in *The Graduate*, Ralph Fiennes's mother in *Quiz Show*) met in 1975 when they co-starred in the sitcom *Doc*, and they remained friends for many years. "I liked her enormously, but I never really *knew* her. You never really got that close to her. Part of my attraction to Mary is that she seemed sad to me. She put on a happy face—she loved to play and put on this voice—but I never thought of her as content," Wilson says. "I don't know what happened. She hadn't resolved some things somehow, something inside was [unsatisfied]. She couldn't really give herself or open up to people. We talked about everything under the sun, yet there was something about her [that projected] 'Don't get too close.' She put on a kind of gruffness. She was an enigma."

But it was not just private thoughts that Mary kept to herself; she chose not to share even professional aspirations with fellow actors. "She would never allow herself to share them [because] if they don't come true, then she's in a vulnerable position of having failed," says longtime friend Peter Walker. What about professional disappointments, such as roles lost out on? Again, Walker says no. "She never talked about frustration like that because she would never allow you to peek into the real her. It was always *Ha, ha, ha, ha*. It wasn't a phony *Ha, ha, ha*—it was just [along the lines of] 'Hail fellow, well met.' She was always covering, in case you would find her situation sad or vulnerable. She wouldn't allow you to come near that area."

Mary's reluctance to open up often extended even to those who knew her best. When Bob Thomsen died in 1983 (his was a painful death from prostate cancer that had metastasized to his throat and lungs), Mary wrote Bob Wallsten a letter that he found flippant. He has not kept it, but he remembers its glib message: "I'm not able to absorb the fact that Bobby is no more. Oh, well, I'll just pretend he hasn't died!" Given all that Thomsen meant to Mary for almost fifty years, Wallsten expected her to display greater regret at his passing. This disappointment led to the only harshness that surfaced during their six-decade friendship. Wallsten wrote Mary "a rather stiff little letter," saying that "people who were fond of him were more affected than you seem to be." Mary did not respond—doing so, after all, would have meant sharing feelings—and for some years, they had no communication, even when she was in New York visiting their mutual friend Whitfield Cook just four blocks from Wallsten. They did eventually see each other several times at Cook's apartment, and Wallsten no longer believes Mary "meant it quite as flip or callous" as her response had seemed, but their relationship "never got to the point where it had been," he says. Mary never mentioned his letter.

Max Showalter, one of Mary's closest friends, thinks that even with Lucille Ball, Mary never genuinely opened up. "No. I don't think so. The only person she really opened to completely was her mother. Isabelle knew all the secrets." Were there secrets? "I think so. I hope there were, because then her life wouldn't have been so un-fulfilled if there were secrets of unrequited love or whatever it was, something that gives your life fulfillment, rather than working all the time, because that isn't enough." Lucie Arnaz says, "Part of the reason we loved her is that she was complicated. A complicated individual with lots of secrets, maybe, and she was interesting because of that."

Even if Mary were to have entered a romance, she kept others at such an emotional distance that building a relationship would have been impossible. "She never allowed herself to be in a vulnerable position where she would be open to a possible disappointment. She was always very guarded with herself," says Walker. "Who knows if she missed romance," wonders actor Joe Ross, another friend. "Many times, I wanted to say, 'How's your love life?' but I didn't. You just don't ask questions like that of certain people. We never really got into [discussing] the bedroom scene—you talked lightly all the time. Iggie Wolfington says, "Even if the idea came to me, I would never have broached it." Elliot Reid, who met Mary in the late 1930s and remained a friend for many decades, explains, "We were old-time people who didn't intrude on the other's privacy. You conclude certain things from knowing people you know well and still not talk about it. I come from a different generation. Everything is out on the table now. I don't know if she had 'a very close friend,' something that had nothing to do with sex but where the chemistry was right and they enjoyed each other. I never ventured into those waters with her. Nor she with me."

The reserve she so treasured did not affect Mary's casual relationships as much as it did her close ones. Mary often left a strong impression—almost always a good one—on those she encountered for a single, specific purpose. Perhaps she found it easier—or simply expedient—to summon gracious behavior for situations that required no ongoing commitment. Stuntwoman Bonnie Happy, for instance, doubled for Mary only once (an episode of *Trapper John, MD* in which Mary's character takes a fall), but Mary's warmth and approachability were unforgettable, leaving Happy "totally in awe." Richard Baratz, the artist who has drawn the caricatures that have graced the walls of Sardi's restaurant since 1974, becomes absolutely effusive when asked to describe his experience preparing Mary's caricature in 1977. Of the almost seven hundred celebrities he drew over twenty-five years, Mary stands out vividly. "She was the most warm, lovable woman I've ever met. It's hard to describe that kind of charisma. Her personality was such that you could hug her and kiss her. It was like being with everybody's grandmother. On a personal level, I meet a lot of big stars, but a lot of them are not nice people.

The rarity of her is that you love her the minute you see her. She projected such warmth and caring," he says. Baratz saw Mary only once or twice, but says, "Of all the people who have touched my heart—and I can count them on one hand—she's one of them."

Mary's disinterest in forging close long-term relationships extended to the children in her life. Certainly, she was affectionate with some children; by all accounts, she was a doting godmother to Michael Richards, the oldest son of her pastor and close friend, Canon Greg Richards, and his wife, Debbie. And she reached out to her young costars in *Sigmund and the Sea Monsters*, Johnny Whitaker and Scott Kolden, even attending their weddings years later. But these were exceptions. Those who knew her best laugh quickly at her general discomfort around children. During the years that Mary and Isabella spent holidays with Max Showalter— mostly during the 1950s and 1960s—Showalter's sister and her children often were present. "Isabelle was the one who related to my sister's children. Isabelle would [bend down and] say, 'Oh, come here!' And Mary loved that thing of her mother and the child. But for Mary to sit and hold the child? It would never have happened. She wasn't really *giving* to a child." Amy Jane Ax, Mary's closest friend in St. Louis, says, "She wasn't particularly fond of children. She was very nice to my daughter Janie, but she wasn't maternal." It's not that Mary was openly hostile to children, Ax says, but "it was things that she didn't say and do. She just sort of ignored them. Absence is often much louder than what you do." Jerry Berger worked with Mary during a production of *The Wizard of Oz* in St. Louis in 1987, one of the Muny's occasional "kiddie shows," for which the theatre held open auditions to select thirty to forty youths for the chorus. Mary would recoil during these productions: "*Eeeeek!*' She used to hate kids," he says.

But Mary kept nothing so private as her health. Over the years, she endured a mastectomy, placement of a pacemaker, encroaching blindness, decreased mobility, debilitating arthritis, shoulder surgery, and vertigo, among other things. She went to great extremes to keep her medical troubles secret from the public, from friends, and, most of all, from potential employers, who she feared would not risk production money on someone not hale and hardy. Her reaction to learning in about 1990 that she needed a pacemaker to correct a heart arrhythmia was typical. She was apprehensive and sought advice from Wendy Borcherdt LeRoy, a friend who had herself received a pacemaker a few years earlier. "Mary was afraid she'd be 'damaged goods' and wouldn't be hired again. We probably had four or five lengthy conversations about it. Not once, but *each time*, she'd say, 'Now Wendy, you're not going to tell anybody about this, are you?'" These conversations took place by phone because, while they saw each other at church services, Mary would not discuss this with LeRoy there for fear that other church members might overhear. Richard Davis, the surgeon who was an unofficial advisor to Mary on all things medical, introduced her to the cardiologist who performed the operation. As with other hospitalizations, Mary insisted on being admitted as Mary Shannon, the name of her maternal grandmother. "She said, 'Now, I don't want you coming to see me.' She just wanted to slip in and out," says LeRoy. After the surgery, Davis says, "the cardiac problems never bothered her in any way or shape. It was all taken care of, and she never missed a day's work."

Breast cancer presented Mary with her most profound health challenge. In the summer of 1963, having just turned fifty-three, Mary was advised to have a breast removed. She had never undergone major surgery, and given the stigma surrounding cancer in those years and the drastic nature of the surgery itself, Mary experienced the greatest fear she had known. Ordinarily, in a time of stress, Isabella would have been a source of support. But Isabella herself was seriously ill with the cardiac condition that would soon kill her. Mother and daughter were hospitalized at the same time in the same hospital with very different conditions.

The mastectomies of the early 1960s are not the mastectomies of today. They were harsher procedures that damaged more tissue and left many women at least as scarred emotionally as physically. Certainly no speculation about the role of romance in Mary's life can occur without considering how she was affected psychologically by her mastectomy. For a woman already insecure about the body she would present to a lover, this surgery undoubtedly heightened those anxieties. Mary underwent a Halstead radical mastectomy of her left breast. The practice was to remove the entire breast, the chest muscles and all the lymph nodes in the armpit. "They don't do this any more but in those days that's how it was done," explains Richard Davis. Davis was a longtime surgeon at UCLA who retired in 1990, but because he and Mary were friends—his wife was Madelyn Pugh Davis, the *I Love Lucy* writer—Mary came to trust his opinion, and he became familiar with her medical conditions. Davis calls Mary's surgeon, Robert J. McKenna, who was her doctor for years, "a wonderful guy who was president of the American Cancer Society and all sorts of things, from USC, a professor, but clinical. When you do that extensive surgery sometimes, you can mess up the lymphatics in your arm. It used to happen all the time. She had that complication."

Mary consequently had difficulty with lymphatic drainage. For the rest of her life, she covered her left arm with an elastic sleeve, purchased over-the-counter, to control the swelling. She almost never wore short-sleeve clothing again. Few people knew about the elastic wrap or had reason to suspect she wore a prosthetic breast. Even close friends had no idea. At the time of the mastectomy, for those few people who required an explanation, Mary said she was having surgery on her shoulder.

Dolly Reed Wageman remembers a conversation between Mary, Emily Daniels, and herself when the subject turned to cancer. This was at Daniels's house in Valley Village, California, about 1993, by which time Wageman had known Mary for more than twenty years. "That's when she said, 'Oh, yeah, I had breast cancer and had a mastectomy.' At the time she talked about it, it was no big deal any more. But when it happened it was a big deal." Wageman was surprised because there were "absolutely no visible [signs of it]. She never talked about having special bras made or anything like that. But she's not the kind of person who would."

Mary did tell Lee Roy Reams about her cancer, but she didn't dwell on it. "It wasn't a big dramatic moment. She mentioned it so that I would know. She said, 'I'm dealing with it. You just do the best that you can with what God gives you and you get on with life.' She was like a pioneer lady. She knew I would not discuss it with other people, because I was too sensitive to how things like that get around. You say, 'Oh, you know Mary's dealing with cancer,' and two weeks later [the gossip has her] dying in a hospital someplace and nobody calls to hire her." Likewise, she discretely disclosed some of her health troubles to actor Larry Guittard. "But she told me, 'Don't tell anybody,' and I never mentioned it to a soul. She was very, very secret about stuff like that because she feared she wouldn't work if anybody heard." Some might dismiss Mary's fears as exaggerated, but "all of that is very real," says Elizabeth Wilson. "Mary was very wise to keep all that hidden. She wasn't being paranoid about it. I've had so much surgery and so much trouble with my eyes and on and on and on, and I know that when producers and directors hear little hints, it becomes blown up. Producers today, particularly in films, want everybody who's working for them to be physically and psychologically in good shape." Some of her closest friends—including Amy Jane Ax, Max Showalter, and Peter Walker—had no idea Mary had had a mastectomy until they were interviewed for this book, even though they were important in her life when she had it. Except for Reams, Guittard, Wageman, Daniels, and a few others, those whom Mary told were not friends, but people who needed to know for work reasons. Mary's first concern, after all, was her work, never her emotional well-being.

When Mary began rehearsals for *You Can't Take It With You* at ACT, she presented the director with an odd demand: Her costumes must have long sleeves. "In summer [when the story took place], women don't wear long sleeves, but she *had* to have long sleeves. That was her only condition in everything I was going to do," says Jack O'Brien. "She said she was wearing a support sleeve under her arm for medical reasons. I thought it had to do with the veins in her arms." Another reason Mary requested sleeves in this particular production is that she would be required to handle kittens and wanted to avoid having her support bandage scratched by them. Clinton Atkinson, who directed Mary in a 1977 production of *Meet Me in St. Louis*, had a similar encounter. While trying on costumes in front of him in the dressing room, Mary revealed the elastic wrap on her arm, and explained that surgeons had removed a breast due to cancer. "She wasn't looking for sympathy or saying, 'Take it easy on me.' She simply told me what it was," Atkinson says. Anne Kaufman Schneider says, "She didn't talk about it much, and only as a fact." But when filming a TV version of *The Man Who Came to Dinner* in England with an obese Orson Welles, Mary complained, "I have to push this tub of lard around all the time in the wheelchair and it's very hard on my arm."

Mary's experience with breast cancer fueled her interest in patient advocacy. Already a longtime hospital volunteer, she now committed herself even more to improving the experience of cancer patients. Sometimes she offered help quietly. After friend Bill Givens mentioned in passing in February 1993 that his sister Janie Miller had been diagnosed with breast cancer, Mary finally confided in Bill that she, too, had experienced the disease. Then she asked for Janie's phone number in Tennessee.

The call came while Miller was home recovering from a modified radical mastectomy. At first, Miller didn't understand: an actress calling from Los Angeles to offer encouragement to a forty-three-year-old, part-time University of Memphis employee she had never met? The call was extraordinarily meaningful to Miller. Mary offered moral support, empathy for the soreness Miller felt, and advice about exercises she could do at home to restore affected upper-arm muscles. She also offered these cautionary words: "Don't tell people you've had a mastectomy, because all they'll do is look at your chest. Just don't tell them at all. All they're going to be thinking about is that you've had something cut off." "She was like a friend to me without even seeing my face," Miller says. "The way she talked, she just made me feel so comfortable. It was as if my mother had called me, like we'd known each other forever. She had a strong, funny, raspy voice, but she was so upbeat. She couldn't talk about [her own mastectomy] like now, when we can share with other survivors. She just had to keep it in. She said, 'If I had told anybody, I couldn't have gotten work.'"

A few friends who later developed breast cancer also benefitted from Mary's support. In about 1970, when Dorothy Hempleman Haase, a fixture in St. Louis society circles, was anxious about how a pending mastectomy would affect her looks, Mary said, "Oh, Hemp, all you do is get the false bosom and put it in. It's nothing—nothing!" Mary sometimes spoke before groups of people with cancer. Occasionally, she allowed her remarks to lapse into the first person, sharing with strangers what she chose not to tell friends. At a 1988 National Cancer Survivors Day event at St. Vincent's Hospital in Los Angeles, she talked about the important contributions that former cancer patients can make as hospital volunteers. "Because we have survived we know the questions and the fears when a cancer diagnosis is heard and we can help, sometimes just listening or showing we care. We have a perspective on the situation and that helps," she told those assembled.

A Republican in an industry dominated by liberal Democrats, Mary wasn't about to share her politics, either. Her attraction to Republican philosophy is rooted in her larger resistance to change. Throughout her life, if Mary liked something—an institution, a professional relationship, a friendship, an approach to life—she didn't want to see it transformed. "She was a die-hard Republican. She was *terribly* conservative," says Peter Walker. "She followed those conservative dictums of the Republican Party, which are rather obvious. She wasn't a racist. But she was a snob, and she was a little intolerant."

Because she feared losing friends and jobs, Mary made a conscious decision to avoid political discussions. If the Hollywood Blacklist had forced some to pay a price for one kind of political belief, surely, she thought, a price could just as easily be exacted for another. Other performers of her generation shared her concerns, then and now. Marjorie Lord, for one, avoided discussing her own Republican politics for the same reasons. "I learned early on, keep your darned mouth shut. Just go in the poll and vote the way you want to vote," says Lord, who co-starred with Mary in *The Danny Thomas Show*. She recalls once participating in a promotional tour with George Murphy, the actor and political conservative who later served California in the U.S. Senate. "One of our sponsors gave me Holy Hell. I gave it back to him! I said, 'I thought this was a free country. You talk about being liberal and I respect you, that's your opinion. I can have an opinion,'" she said. She describes herself as "a middle-roader, not extremely conservative." Mary and Lord did not talk politics much. "I just knew that she was [conservative] and she knew that I was. She and Hans Conreid and I were quiet about it. You don't talk much about it unless you're one of those activists."

Perhaps the only person Mary spoke candidly with about politics was Wendy Borcherdt LeRoy. A political consultant and former White House staffer in the Reagan administration, LeRoy spoke with Mary about much more than pacemakers. "I'm a self-described traditional, conservative Republican, and Mary and I would discuss politics and end up in agreement most of the time. She was very much for individual rights. She was a woman who had succeeded in her field. She was very much a traditionalist. She was a great admirer of Ronald Reagan, not only politically, but for his stand with the Screen Actors' Guild when he was president and took on the left wing of movie wing," LeRoy says. "She had great affection for the people in her industry, but at times she said she was working in a very liberal industry and, 'I have to watch what I say. I can't talk to them like I talk to you.' Because LeRoy worked in the political arena, Mary trusted that LeRoy would not cause her harm by disclosing their conversations.

Mary's reluctance to disclose her political leanings was not simply a fear of professional consequences. Every facet of her upbringing conditioned her to believe that this was the proper, even lady-like path. She deferred to the old maxim about not discussing politics, religion, or sex in social settings to avoid rancor with others. "Mary very much followed that old rule—you didn't get caught up in politics because you can lose a friend that you're fond of. If you mixed them all together in a pot, some people are going to walk away and be very angry that you have a different opinion," says Iggie Wolfington. Consciously or not, Mary's friends obliged, choosing avoidance over discussion. "My policy is don't ask because sometimes you like people a lot and if they don't have your politics, it can get sticky," says Madelyn Pugh Davis. She considered her relationship with Mary special, but it was rooted in a love of theatre, show biz, and their shared experience as women who had worked all their lives—not in any shared view of world issues. Davis and her husband are Democrats, "but it isn't so much the party, it's an attitude. There's another couple we see and I know they're conservative, so we never bring anything up, because I like them, so let's not get into that." Dolly Reed Wageman often took this approach with Mary, even though Wageman, too, is Republican. She found Mary to the right of her on many issues. "I held my tongue most of the time, because I was considerably more progressive than her."

But it was easier for Mary to conceal her political views than her health problems, because politics held so little interest for her. She was not the sort to be swept up in any movement. For one thing, she had little patience for hidden agendas, false faces, and hypocrisy—and where would politics be without these things? "She didn't suffer fools graciously. That goes double for politics," says director Jack O'Brien. Mary never attended political events, endorsed candidates, or lent her name to lists of supporters for a political cause. Upon her death, Canon Richards, Mary's trustee, discovered not one item of a political nature in Mary's belongings, nothing that even vaguely suggested an interest in current events. In the scores of boxes of Mary's papers—including her personal library and collection of videotapes—the only item that even hints at political interest is a single letter from Vice President Richard Nixon thanking her for her help with his 1960 campaign for the presidency, which he lost to Senator John Kennedy. The letter, which is dated January 19, 1961, the day before his term ended, and appears to have been signed personally, does not specify what Mary did on his behalf. But for all of her efforts, Mary did not succeed at keeping her Republican leanings as secret as she kept her medical issues. Based on her behavior in other areas, many people in Mary's life simply presumed she was politically conservative. Actress Janet Fox puts it this way: "There was something quite virginal about Mary, and her politics were virginal, too."

At a dinner party once, Canon Richards remembers someone being introduced to Mary and complimenting her on a role from years before, innocently offering up, "That was a long time ago." Mary, who went to great lengths to hide her true age, took offense. She lied about her age often, and resented anyone inferring she was older than she wished the world to believe.

None of this was vanity. It was, again, merely Mary's attempt to preserve her ability to market herself to producers for as long as possible. Many actresses of her generation shaved years off their official ages, but in Mary's case, the steps she took to mask her true age bordered on the absurd.

Mary's papers are a case study in obfuscation. She obliterated the date of birth printed on her official college transcript. With a pair of scissors, she excised the text that stated her graduation year in the caption of her fiftieth college class reunion photo. On the 1972 work permit that enabled her to be in the U.K. to tape *The Man Who Came to Dinner*, she clumsily stapled a small strip of white index card over the date of birth that was typed beneath it. On a 1980s passport, she glued a tiny piece of white paper over the last two digits of her birth year. And in her own copy of *Who's Who in the Theatre* (eleventh edition), she hid the year of her birth, first by fountain pen, and then—fearing the numbers could still be seen beneath the ink—by scratching them out, and this was in a book that already reported her birth as six years later than it really was. She was so angry that this reference book stated her birth year that she wrote the publishers, forcing longtime editor John Parker to delete her birth year from subsequent printings. Several years later, when Mary provided data for the debut issue of the biographical dictionary *Who's Who of American Women* (1958), she omitted her year of birth and pushed up her college graduation by eight years, to 1938; only when that edition came out did Mary feel safe boasting that she was included. In June 1980, when she took two days off from the Broadway production of *Oklahoma!* to attend her fiftieth college reunion, she told no one in the production the reason, saying only that she had business in St. Louis. "She was afraid that they'd [perceive] her as an old lady and she wouldn't have parts any more—that they'd think, 'Oh, *fiftieth!* She must be seventy-one or seventy-two," says Elizabeth Danforth, who spent time with Mary during that visit. Each time she returned to Washington University, she pled with her alma mater to keep her graduation year out of promotional materials.

These were not just the acts of an aging woman trying to forestall the advances of time. Mary was still a young woman when she began shaving years off her age. A *St. Louis Daily Globe-Democrat* profile of her in 1938, featuring her success playing an old woman in *Father Malachy's Miracle*, reports she graduated from college in 1931 at age 18. In fact, she was almost twenty when she graduated in 1930. Subtraction was a practice she continued for the rest of her life. Six years was the most she apparently believed she could get away with safely, so 1916 was the year she used most often when asked. But sometimes the discrepancy became greater. While promoting her work on *Make Room for Daddy*, forty-six-year-old Mary told a reporter she was "still in her thirties." The *Los Angeles Mirror*, in a feature about Mary's frequent roles as older women, described her as "in her early thirties" two weeks before her forty-seventh birthday. In one of the many career chronologies that Mary prepared herself, she wrote in 1964 that she played in the Theatre Guild production on Broadway of *Father Malachy's Miracle* "before she was out of her teens," when actually she was twenty-seven. These things can take on lives of their own; this same misinformation would be repeated often.

But it is also true that Mary thought of herself as a young person—and, despite her many ailments, often *felt* like a young person—and simply disliked being perceived as old. Alone at sixty-seven, she took a cruise around the Virgin Islands, and she was disappointed to find herself touring with a group of white-haired senior citizens from San Luis Obispo, California. As a coping mechanism, Mary adopted a certain smugness toward them, seemingly oblivious to the fact that she was their contemporary. "There were more loud Hawaiian shirts than there were male bodies, and I know now where the Marcel wave [hairstyle] went. It went to San Luis Obispo County," she wrote in her travel journal. While waiting in a slow line to check in for her flight, Mary overheard snatches of conversation unlike those she usually heard at airports: "I've got to get a package of Polident," "When we went to Hawaii last year, I took my arch supports in my white tennis shoes," and "You take your graham cracker crust and . . ." "The people on this cruise under forty, you can count on the fingers of one hand!" she wrote. "Dinner turned up more over-carbohydrate bodies than I have seen in one place for a long time—short of a fat farm. Polyester blouses and double-knit trousers that fit too tight across the fanny are 'in.'" Happening upon a cha-cha dance class, Mary shook her head. "Really the human hope burns eternally. Bless their hearts! Everyone tried so hard. 'Step, step and cha-cha-cha. Step, step and cha-cha-cha.' The cha-cha-cha's were really more like stomps."

CHAPTER TEN

Mary's Secret Cousin

MARY WOULD HAVE LIKED JERARD BROOKS ADKINS. BORN TWO YEARS after Mary, he lived by many of the same values she did. Driven by a strong midwestern work ethic, he assembled Buick steering wheels at a Dayton, Ohio, factory before beginning a forty-year sales career at Central Ohio Paper Company. Brooks, as he was known, had gone to church

At Forest Park in St. Louis, July 1920. Rear: Grandma Shannon, Isabella, and Frank. Front: Elizabeth. Miller (Aunt Hes's child with Ed Miller), Jerard Brooks Adkins (Aunt Hes's child with John J. Adkins), and Mary. Courtesy Mary Wickes Papers, Special Collections, Washington University Libraries

regularly since he was five years old, always at Dayton's Christ Episcopal Church. He married, bought a home, raised a son, put him through college, and became a grandfather. He liked big band music, especially his Russ Morgan record collection. When his wife died, he married a retired social worker and wonderful cook whom he had known for years through church. At age eighty-seven, tall and trim, with thick white hair and large, dark-rimmed glasses, he would have reminded Mary immediately of Lew Wasserman, the Hollywood mogul who was one of her earliest agents. Brooks was Mary's first cousin. Mary knew this, but Brooks knew nothing of Mary Wickes.

Throughout her life, Mary professed great devotion to family. She spoke with near-reverence of the importance of family history, and she claimed special pride in her ancestry. But her actions tell a different story. Mary always maintained that besides her mother, she had only one surviving relative, a first cousin of whom she was very fond. This was Elizabeth Dorsam, the daughter of Isabella's sister Hester Margaret Shannon. In fact, Mary's "Aunt Hes" had a second child, who was seven when his mother died in 1920. This child was Brooks.

Brooks learned for the first time that Mary Wickes was his cousin—and also that, in Elizabeth, he had a half-sister—when contacted for this book in 1999, after both women had passed away. At this point in his life, a stroke had transformed Brooks's speech into a coarse, barely-audible whisper. But he was so startled to learn of these relationships that he agreed to an interview at his Dayton house, just a short walk from where the Wright Brothers had lived. In his cozy home, the lower level of a two-story brick duplex, he struggled to come up with explanations for such a break in the family. He was earnest in considering the possibilities. After reflecting on his family history for almost five hours, he concluded softly, "There was something not right with this family. Nobody that successful in their life would ignore the rest of the family or part of the family except for some reason. Somewhere, somebody didn't like somebody."

In the months after that meeting, Brooks sought out films that featured Mary, delighting in this new connection, though he could only wonder what knowing her might have been like. He and his wife watched *White Christmas* and *The Trouble with Angels* and looked for Mary on TV.

Whatever the true reason for Mary's lifelong rejection of Brooks, this was no mere falling out among relatives. Mary and Isabella made a conscious decision to live as if the only son of Isabella's only sibling did not exist, a decision that had crueler consequences than simply preventing cousins from getting to know each other. This decision denied Brooks access to important personal papers that remained in Mary's possession, like those surrounding his guardianship when he was a child. Most troubling, it prevented Brooks from discovering the piece of information that would mean the most: His entire adult life, Brooks longed to know where his mother was buried, but he learned it only during this interview. Aging and ill, he died two years later at eighty-nine, never able to visit her grave. Mary, meanwhile, made many visits to Hes's plot in Shiloh, Illinois, a place Brooks could never have known about.

Brooks's story is in many ways Mary's story. And like many family stories, it is complicated. This one begins a generation earlier.

Aunt Hes was markedly different from the rest of the family. First, in a tradition-bound family, she turned from the family's religious heritage (the Thomases and McLeans had been mostly Episcopalians and Methodists) to become a Christian Scientist. Second, at a time when proper young women didn't venture out alone, and certainly didn't work in the theatre, she moved from the St. Louis area at a young age to pursue a career as a singer and actress. Along the way, she married a Californian named Edward Miller. When Hes and "Ed" had a child in 1903 in Kansas (or Missouri; records are unclear), they named her Hester Elizabeth Miller and would call her Elizabeth. Around 1909, Hes and Ed separated or divorced, further setting Hes apart from her family. So that she could continue performing, Hes sent little Elizabeth to St. Louis to be raised by Hes and Isabella's mother, Mollie Thomas Shannon. Ed apparently agreed that Elizabeth would fare better in St. Louis, where she had more family. Frank and Isabella were living in St. Louis, where Frank had a good job at the Mercantile Trust.

Shortly afterward, Hes became seriously ill and underwent surgery in Ohio. Mollie left St. Louis to care for Hes, knowing she would be unable to return by the time Isabella was scheduled to give birth in June 1910. Mollie took little Elizabeth with her and wrote Isabella from Ohio, "I cannot say yet when I'll be home as Hes is still in bed and has to be lifted from one bed to the other bed . . . and the Dr. is still coming to the house. But she is not any worse, just weak, very weak." When Hes recovered, she began a relationship with John Jerard Adkins, a musician who, like her, saw the theatre as an escape from the strict upbringing of small towns. Together, they traveled the vaudeville circuit as "Adkins and Shannon," returning to Dayton between engagements. John played the violin, Hes sang, and together they performed in skits, often in theatrical costumes. They promoted themselves in advertisements as "The Singer and the Violinist: High Class Musical Entertainers," and were sometimes billed as "the contralto and violinist." They never made it big. As one reviewer succinctly put it, "He plays a solo while she changes to evening gown and she sings a solo while he changes to evening dress. She sings fairly well and he plays all right, but they are not performers."

Hes became pregnant again in 1911. She and John were performing in New Orleans as delivery neared. To be near family for the birth, they traveled in advance to Wilmington, North Carolina, where John's mother lived. It is unclear why they chose to be near John's family rather than Hes's family—especially since Mollie and Isabella were about a hundred and fifty miles closer in St. Louis—but Brooks was born in Wilmington on March 10, 1912.

John's mother was a widow, Alice London Williams Adkins. Three months after Brooks's birth, Alice married Henry Bucher of Ohio. Hes and John now asked the Buchers to raise baby Brooks for them so they could continue performing at vaudeville houses. The Buchers agreed and moved to Hamilton, Ohio, so Henry could work at the Herring-Hall-Marvin Safe Co. In 1913, they moved to Dayton, where Henry worked for NCR. This is how they lived for the next seven years. Hes continued performing around the country while her first child (Mary's cousin Elizabeth, fathered by Ed Miller) was raised in St. Louis by her maternal grandparents, and her second child (Mary's cousin Brooks, fathered by John Adkins) was raised in Dayton by his paternal grandmother and step-grandfather. Brooks grew up calling Mrs. Bucher "Mama," though no one mistook her for his biological mother. Often, he lay awake at night wondering where his mother and father were. "Did you ever hear a train whistle? *Whooooooooo.* I would cry when I heard that whistle. My grandmother would say, 'What's the matter?' I'd say, 'I want to know where my daddy is, and my mother.'" His parents were performing all over the country. Theatre listings from 1910s newspapers show they appeared in Montgomery, Alabama, Aurora, Illinois, Manhattan, Kansas, and Waco, Texas, as well as big cities like Chicago, New Orleans, and New York.

In 1920, Brooks was informed that his parents were getting a divorce. One sticking point was determining what faith Brooks would be raised in, since neither his father nor his grandmother shared his mother's Christian Science beliefs. He was instructed to see a local judge, who told him his mother would like him to begin attending Scientist Sunday school. Brooks had attended Episcopal Sunday school since age five and told the judge he did not want to go to Scientist Sunday school. "He said, 'You go there one Sunday and go to the Episcopal Church another Sunday and after you do that two times, come back and tell me where you want to go.' So I did. I came back and said, 'I want to go to the Episcopal one.' He said, 'Why?' I said, "Because at the Science Sunday school, they make me sit on the floor and at the Episcopal church, they have little chairs for you.'" The judge determined Brooks should be raised in the Episcopal Church, and Brooks never went to any other.

So extensive was Hes's touring that Brooks had seen his mother only four or five times since he was an infant. While Hes was separated from John, arrangements were made for Brooks to see his mother more often on Sundays. She was living in a rooming house on South Robert Boulevard and working as a saleswoman at the Rike Kumler Co. (Rike's was a prominent department store that changed hands and later became known as Lazarus.) "The second time I went, the woman at the house said, 'Your mother is in bed, she's sick.'" Brooks walked up to her second-floor room on this cold winter day to find Hes with the window open, her long red hair blowing in the bitter January wind. "She was sitting up in bed, shouting to me, 'I'm not sick! I'm not sick!' I went home and told my grandmother and they sent a doctor down for her." Hes was taken to the Buchers' home at the Churchill Apartments, a ten-story rooming house. She was diagnosed with a severe respiratory infection, but she rejected medical help because of her religious beliefs. She died the next day, January 26, 1920, from pneumonia, probably aged thirty-seven. Brooks was not yet eight years old.

John evidently acceded to Isabella and Mollie's preferences—which would have been strong—that Hes be buried with the Thomas family in the Methodist cemetery in Shiloh, Illinois. The divorce proceedings, though never finalized, probably left him without strong preferences about Hes's interment. Her body was shipped to St. Louis, where Isabella, Frank, and Mollie took charge. They arranged for a private funeral on January 29 at Kron Chapel, after which the body was driven to Shiloh for burial. A St. Louis newspaper obituary identified the Shannons and Isabella as survivors, but strangely made no mention of Hes's two children or of her previous marriage to Ed. (Both this obituary and the death certificate identify her as Margaret Adkins. Margaret was her middle name.) Her true age remains unclear. A family gravestone marked Hester M. Adkins declares her to have been born in 1883, her death certificate says she was born in August 1884, and the 1920 U.S. census, taken just twelve days before she died, suggests she was born in 1885. Probably she was born in 1884. It is unlikely she was born in 1883, because her parents Mollie and James were not married until October 1883, and 1985 is unlikely because that is the year Mollie gave birth to Isabella.

A few months later, Mrs. Bucher and Isabella had an exchange of letters that discussed a possible St. Louis visit by Brooks. Mrs. Bucher pushed to make that visit happen, Brooks says. "She made me write letters. I said things in letters to get them to think I was a nice kid and all that sort of thing," so that they would welcome him. Brooks rode the train by himself from Dayton to St. Louis, his name pinned to his clothes in case he got lost. For that very hot summer, Brooks stayed with Isabella, Frank, and Mary at the Wickenhauser home on Harris Avenue near O'Fallon Park. Like everyone else in Mary's life at that time, he called Mary "Mary Isabelle." But Brooks knew only that these were people he had been asked to visit. He was never told that Isabella was his aunt, Elizabeth his half-sister, and Mary his first cousin—and his mother's name was not mentioned once the entire summer.

By his recollection, it was an idyllic trip. He played baseball in the park with neighborhood boys, using a broomstick for a bat. He went to church with the Wickenhausers and accompanied the family on visits to "Aunt Belle" in Belleville, Illinois (Belle Rentchler was Mollie Shannon's sister, and therefore great aunt to Brooks and Mary). Each afternoon, Isabella, whom Brooks that summer called "Aba," insisted that he and Mary come inside, strip to their underclothes in the heat and take a nap, a recollection that amuses him eight decades later. Brooks remembers distinctly that Mary "was the apple of her mother's eye." He recalls Frank merely as "nice." Since Frank worked during the day, "he wasn't home often enough to pay any attention to," Brooks says. But Frank did once take Brooks to a Browns baseball game.

Only one activity that summer appears to have been recorded. Isabella and Frank took Mary and Brooks to the St. Louis Zoo in Forest Park. It was July 15, 1920, a Thursday. They were joined by Mollie and Elizabeth, and the day had all the trappings of a special outing. For a group photograph, presumably taken by Mary's grandfather (Mollie's husband, James T. Shannon), Mary and Elizabeth each held a straw hat in front of their crisp summer dresses. Brooks stood between them in a beanie. This is one of the few existing photos of Frank, who has his arm around his daughter. Frank and Isabella look serious, and Mollie, partially obscured, looks positively severe. Brooks was eight, Mary had just turned ten, and Elizabeth was seventeen. For seventy-five years, copies of this photo sat in boxes in three homes in three states, but no one wanted to explore what the photo meant. Brooks kept a copy in Dayton. He produced it for this book, but he did not understand who any of the others in the photo were or how he came to have it. Elizabeth kept a copy in St. Louis. Upon her death in 1994, it was among the possessions that passed to her son Bill, who had little interest in examining long-buried family secrets but who also produced it for this book. And Mary, for decades the only person living who knew the identities of everyone pictured, kept a copy in Los Angeles in a scrapbook that had been started by Isabella. Isabella's caption beneath the photo declared hesitantly: "The Whole _____ ? Family."

Brooks could not have known at the time, but the 1920 visit was a test of sorts, to see if Frank and Isabella would be comfortable having Brooks live with them. No doubt they reasoned their home would be a warm, loving place for their motherless nephew. He would be near his half-sister Elizabeth and would have a playmate in his cousin Mary; in their company, maybe he would miss his mother less. Certainly, such a move would put him in a calmer household than he had in Dayton with Mrs. Bucher, whom Brooks describes as mean-spirited and difficult. The Buchers ran rooming houses and moved whenever Mrs. Bucher identified an opportunity to make more money. But after he returned to Dayton at the end of that summer, Brooks never saw Mary, Isabella, or Frank again. The Wickenhausers did not once attempt to communicate with him, though his contact information was always in their possession. Instead, they behaved as if he did not exist.

Brooks had only two additional connections with the family, each of them peculiar. First, in July 1926, Aunt Belle Rentchler was briefly named guardian of fourteen-year-old Brooks and in that capacity received $1,800 from the estate of Mollie Shannon, who died in 1924. Brooks was never told about these funds, but clearly the money was a sign that he was recognized as family. In September 1926, guardianship and the $1,710 that remained were transferred to Mrs. Bucher. Separately, when Aunt Belle herself died six years later, her estate was divided equally among the offspring of Isabella and Hes. The Depression and complex negotiations with creditors delayed disbursements, but in 1936 it was determined that Mary would receive $920, and Brooks and Elizabeth would each receive $460. Mary and Elizabeth received their funds immediately, but Brooks did not receive his until 1943, when Isabella, responding to a frustrated trust officer at Belleville Savings Bank, finally provided Brooks's address. Second, in 1927, when he was fifteen, Brooks received an unexpected visit from Elizabeth, who apparently traveled alone from St. Louis specifically to see him. By this time, Mollie had died, and Elizabeth, twenty-four, had been living with Frank, Isabella, and Mary. Brooks does not recall the stated purpose of Elizabeth's visit, but he says emphatically he did not know she was his sister. They spent a pleasant day together, during which a pal of Brooks took Elizabeth for a recreational ride in a small plane. The Dayton area was home to pioneering aviation activities in those days, including research at Wright Field, the aviation-testing site.

Brooks and Elizabeth never communicated again. Elizabeth's son Bill Dorsam says the name Brooks Adkins vaguely "rings a bell," but his mother spoke very little about her youth or family history, and Dorsam is the sort of man for whom family stories do not matter much. He suspected his mother had been married once before marrying his father, auto parts dealer Waldo Dorsam, but he never asked her about it. "Everybody back then was tight-lipped. It isn't like it is today. They didn't tell kids anything back in the forties or early fifties, and I never asked my mom anything later on. I never took an interest in it, and it really burned Mary that I wasn't interested in the family tree," Dorsam says. "Mary would tell my mom, 'You need to tell the kids [family history], so they'll know,' but my mom wouldn't volunteer anything. I guess if we had asked her, she'd have told us." The irony, of course, is that even if Dorsam had asked Mary about family history, she would not have mentioned Brooks. Dorsam says Mary once prepared a family tree for him, which he now cannot find. No matter. The family trees Mary prepared, which remained with her until she died, do not include Brooks.

Mary's rejection of Brooks seems especially odd in light of how closely her own life came to resemble Hes's life. Mary's long Broadway run in *Oklahoma!* was at the Palace Theatre, where Hes performed in the 1910s when the Palace was the country's premier vaudeville house. It is possible they even used the same dressing room. And Hes's constant battles with theatre owners and managers would certainly have resonated with Mary. "At every theatre they were in, she wanted top billing, she wanted more money, she wanted this, that and the other thing," Brooks was told. He unknowingly described Mary's own tenacious approach to the business. His father told Brooks, "She was terrible. I just couldn't get along with her and she couldn't get along with the theatre owners." Brooks assumes these differences are what caused them to seek a divorce.

"There are some big holes in my life that I'd like to know about," he says. Indeed, Brooks's life was in many ways shaped by unanswered questions. Why did his father, John Adkins, not ensure that Brooks knew he had a half-sister? (John lived another forty-three years after Hes died, during which he remarried and for a time ran a violin school in Springfield, Ohio.) If he tried, were his efforts rebuffed by Mollie and Isabella? Why did Hes send loving postcards from the road to her niece Mary, opening her eyes to places outside St. Louis, but apparently not to her own son, who has nothing written in her hand? If she did write Brooks, why were her letters never shared with him? Why didn't Elizabeth reach out to her half-brother, since—nine years his senior—she no doubt understood the true nature of their relationship? Why did Mary and Isabella cut off all ties with Brooks, when they publicly professed such dedication to maintaining close family relations? Embarrassment over a close family member turning away from the particular brand of Christianity that was so central in the family is an unlikely explanation, even for a family driven by convention. If living as if Brooks did not exist had originally been Isabella's decision, why did Mary continue ignoring Brooks after Isabella died? Why does Hes's obituary report no children?

Brooks sometimes suspected he was born out of wedlock, which might provide the answer. If he were illegitimate, Mary's puritanical streak would certainly force her to favor the child of a legal marriage (Elizabeth) over one born out of wedlock (Brooks). A woman having two children with different men, marrying only one of them, leaving the children to be raised separately by other families while the parents traveled—"that kind of situation in that environment, seventy years ago, could have been considered an absolute scandal. They just would not have been able to talk about that. Just knowing the times, what could seem like an everyday event now, might have been scandalous at the time. St. Louis was really a Southern town in that sense. It's hard to imagine how much things have changed in fifty or sixty years," theorizes Bill Carson, a family friend of the Wickenhausers who left St. Louis in 1960 and ultimately settled in Santa Fe, New Mexico. Another possible explanation, offered up by Brooks, is that Mrs. Bucher kept the Wickenhausers at a distance out of fear that they would want Brooks to live with them. She had experienced the pain of losing two daughters in childbirth and did not want to lose him, too. "She put all her affection onto me. I was this thing for her to put her love into . . . and she didn't want to let me go." But this rationale would not explain why Mary and Isabella continued to ignore Brooks after Mrs. Bucher died in 1943, by which time Brooks was an adult. He was reachable at the same address and phone number for forty-nine years. If Mrs. Bucher asked Isabella and Frank to let her raise Brooks, it's possible that Isabella and Frank gave in, deciding it might be selfish for them to pursue custody of Brooks, since they already had one child, while the Buchers had lost two. They may have wished not to deprive Mrs. Bucher of the experience of raising a child.

When Brooks turned fifty, he determined he would attempt to understand his family history. He traveled to North Carolina with his wife Mary and son Jerard Brooks Adkins Jr. Among other things, he sought his birth certificate, which he hoped would provide some answers. "I thought many times that people should share with their children [information about] some relationships—whoever, what it is. But the average family doesn't do that, even today," he said. They visited Wilmington and Southport, found at least one cousin and learned Brooks's grandfather's name was not what he had thought it was. His grandfather was James Brooks Adkins but, until then, Brooks had always believed him to be Jerard Brooks Adkins. Brooks returned with no documentation and concluded his birth had not been properly registered.

Mary's father, Frank August Wickenhauser (1880–1943), about 1908. Photo by Dilks, St. Louis, courtesy Mary Wickes Papers, Special Collections, Washington University Libraries

Mary's mother, Mary Isabella Wickenhauser (1885–1965), about 1908. Photo by Dilks, St. Louis, courtesy Mary Wickes Papers, Special Collections, Washington University Libraries

Mary at age four. Photo by Murillo Studio, St. Louis, courtesy Mary Wickes Papers, Special Collections, Washington University Libraries

Mary and her father walking to a Fourth of July picnic, 1917. Courtesy Mary Wickes Papers, Special Collections, Washington University Libraries

Hester Margaret Shannon, Mary's Aunt Hes (1883–1920), the vaudevillian who performed as part of Adkins & Shannon. Photo by C. F. Gairing & Co., Chicago, courtesy Mary Wickes Papers, Special Collections, Washington University Libraries

Mary in her teen years. Photo by Dieckman Studio, St. Louis, courtesy Mary Wickes Papers, Special Collections, Washington University Libraries

Mary preparing to leave St. Louis to join the Berkshire Playhouse company in Stockbridge, Massachusetts, June 1934. Photo by Jules Pierlow, courtesy Mary Wickes Papers, Special Collections, Washington University Libraries

In her first season at the Berkshire Playhouse, Mary appeared in *Biography* with Ina Claire, a popular actress who gave producers an emphatic endorsement of Mary for the coming Broadway season. Courtesy Mary Wickes Papers, Special Collections, Washington University Libraries

Barbara Wolferman (r), an heir to the Wolferman baked goods concern, was one of Mary's favorite people from their first meeting in the 1930s. This 1940s image is notable because Mary almost never wore pants, believing skirts were more "lady-like." Courtesy Peter A. D'Auria Jr.

Mary's first Broadway hit was *Stage Door* in 1936, an ensemble piece with (l–r) Janet Fox, Margaret Sullavan, Sylvia Lupas, Juliet Forbes, and Beatrice Blinn. Photo by Vandamm Studio, copyright Billy Rose Theatre Division, New York Public Library for the Performing Arts

The Mercury Theatre Company's *Too Much Johnson* in August 1938 was the biggest flop of Mary's career. Mary is standing behind Orson Welles, with Virginia Nicholson, his wife, seated on his lap. To the right of the poster (l–r): Bill Herz, Erskine Sanford, Eustace Wyatt, and a soon-to-be-discovered Joseph Cotten. The man at far left is unidentified. Photo originally appeared in *The Theatre of Orson Welles* by Richard France, published by Bucknell University Press/Associated University Presses, 1977

Mary (with back to camera) sits in a carriage with actress Ruth Ford and Marc Blitzstein while shooting the film segment of the play *Too Much Johnson* in 1938. Photo from *Stage*, September 1938

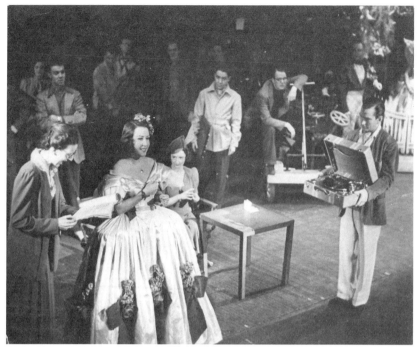

Mary with Ethel Merman during the Boston try-out of *Stars in Your Eyes*, 1939. Photo by Richard Tucker, Boston, copyright Billy Rose Theatre Division, New York Public Library for the Performing Arts

Mary in 1939 as Miss Preen in *The Man Who Came to Dinner*, the role that cemented her career, with (l–r) Grant Mitchell, Billie Burke, George Barbier, Monty Woolley, Elisabeth Fraser. Photo by Bert Six for Warner Bros.

Mary liked working with Bette Davis, who confided her marital troubles in her. In 1942's *Now, Voyager*, she tells Mary, "I suspect you're a treasure." Photo copyright Vitagraph

With Lou Costello and Bud Abbott, the comedy duo of the 1940s, in *Who Done It?* in 1942. Photo copyright Universal Pictures

Mary appeared with Frank Sinatra in his first leading film role in *Higher and Higher* in 1943. (l–r:) Mary, Sinatra, Michele Morgan, Jack Haley. Photo copyright RKO Radio Pictures

Out with girlfriends in New York in front of Mary's *Higher and Higher* poster, just before *Jackpot* opened on Broadway in 1944. (l–r:) Betty Garrett, Edith Atwater, Mary, Frances Robinson, Nanette Fabray. (Robinson was Fabray's understudy in *Jackpot*.) Photo by Metropolitan Photo Service, New York

The high society comedy *Park Avenue* in 1946 gave Mary a rare chance to show she could look glamorous in couture. Photo by Lucas-Pritchard of New York, copyright Museum of the City of New York

By 1946, Mary had established herself as a standout in comic roles, so her first lead dramatic role was a gamble. When the Berkshire Playhouse re-opened after the war, Mary played the title character in *Elizabeth the Queen*. Photo by Talbot of New York

As part of the publicity effort for *June Bride*, this photo from the set, with Robert Montgomery, appeared in the *Seattle Times* and the *Chicago Daily News* in December 1948. Mary stopped smoking in the 1960s.

Mary as the director Mrs. Pampinelli in the backstage comedy *The Torch-Bearers* at Bucks County Playhouse, 1949. At left is a young Grace Kelly in her professional stage debut. Also pictured are Carl White and Jerry Reed. Courtesy Mary Wickes Papers, Special Collections, Washington University Libraries

Mary with Gloria Swanson in 1948 on *The Gloria Swanson Hour*, an early live talk show on the DuMont television network. Photo by Maurey Garber, courtesy of Michelle Amon, Gloria Swanson Inc., and the Harry Ransom Center at the University of Texas at Austin

For the *Studio One* television anthology (1949), Mary brought the Mary Poppins character to life for the first time anywhere. Photo by Kumin-Olenick Agency, Beverly Hills, courtesy Mary Wickes Papers, Special Collections, Washington University Libraries

During the live "Mary Poppins" in 1949, Mary is lowered dramatically onto a CBS soundstage by a hook-and-pulley contraption that created the appearance she was flying through the air. Photo by Bernard Hoffman, Time & Life Pictures, Getty Images

Mary with Dorrit Kelton, Tommy Rettig, Iris Mann, and Valerie Cossart during "Mary Poppins." Photo by William Leftwich, New York

In 1925, Mary was the harsh dance instructor Madame Lamond in "The Ballet," one of the best-remembered episodes of *I Love Lucy*. Photo by Loomis Dean, Time & Life Pictures, Getty Images

In *By the Light of the Silvery Moon* in 1953, Mary skates on ice with Doris Day, Leon Ames, and Rosemary DeCamp. Courtesy Mary Wickes Papers, Special Collections, Washington University Libraries

Emma in 1954's *White Christmas,* with Bing Crosby, became one of Mary's most enduring roles. Photo by Paramount Pictures Corp.

After costume tests with Edith Head at Paramount for *White Christmas*, Mary wore each of these outfits (and others). Photos from author's collection

Perhaps the only photo of the two premier comic character actresses of the twentieth century: Mary and Thelma Ritter during a break from filming an episode of *Alfred Hitchcock Presents* in 1956. Courtesy Mary Wickes Papers, Special Collections, Washington University Libraries

On the town in the 1950s: Mary with Bill Raiser, the industrial designer, and Humphrey Doulens, a Columbia Artists Management agent, at the Stork Club. Courtesy Mary Wickes Papers, Special Collections, Washington University Libraries

It Happened to Jane in 1959 was Mary's fourth picture with Doris Day. Here, with Dick Crockett, Mary plays a blowsy, beer- guzzling switchboard operator with aspirations of being a newspaper columnist. Photo by Cronenweth for Columbia Pictures

Mary preened on a bare sound stage with Barbara Luddy to give Disney animators inspiration for the villainous Cruella De Vil in *One Hundred and One Dalmatians* in 1961. Photo copyright Disney

This was Mary's family for important gatherings in the early 1960s: Dolores Quinton, Mary, Isabella, Max Showalter and Signe Hasso, in Showalter's home, Christmas 1964. Courtesy of Mary Wickes Papers, Special Collections, Washington University Libraries

During *The Trouble with Angels* in 1966, after learning Mary failed to take the swimming lessons Columbia arranged, producers hastily arranged for crewmembers to stand in the water off camera to "walk" Mary in and out of the pool. Courtesy Mary Wickes Papers, Special Collections, Washington University Libraries

For the sequel *Where Angels Go, Trouble Follows* in 1968, Mary did take lessons, learning to drive a double clutch on a bus without a synchronized manual transmission. Photo copyright Columbia Pictures

Mary as Amanda in *The Glass Menagerie* at Washington University, 1968. Courtesy Mary Wickes Papers, Special Collections, Washington University Libraries

Mary backstage at *The Glass Menagerie* in 1968. Courtesy Mary Wickes Papers, Special Collections, Washington University Libraries

Mary as an upscale maid in "The Diamond Cutter" on *Here's Lucy* in 1970 with Lucille Ball and Gail Gordon. Courtesy estate of Lucille Ball/Desilu, too LLC

This photo was used to promote the 1972 *Here's Lucy* season opener, "Lucy's Big Break." Mary asked photo editors on the reverse, "In reproducing, can anything be done with that chin of mine?" Courtesy estate of Lucille Ball/Desilu, too LLC

Lucille Ball, Harriet Nelson, Eve Arden, and Mary at a holiday gathering in the 1970s, believed to be at Mary Jane Croft's apartment in Century City. Courtesy Mary Wickes Papers, Special Collections, Washington University Libraries

Helen Hayes thanking Mary for her help on a 1971 tribute that raised funds to establish the Actors Fund on the West Coast. Courtesy Mary Wickes Papers, Special Collections, Washington University Libraries

While playing in *Wonderful Town* in San Francisco in 1975, Mary visited Reno with co-stars Lee Roy Reams and Joe Ross to see Carol Channing's nightclub act. Courtesy Mary Wickes Papers, Special Collections, Washington University Libraries

During the *Wonderful Town* run in Los Angeles in 1975, Lee Roy Reams and Mary are joined by Leonard Bernstein, the show's composer, and Max Showalter. Courtesy Mary Wickes Papers, Special Collections, Washington University Libraries

Mary with producer and director Alan Handley, a frequent escort in the 1970s. Courtesy Mary Wickes Papers, Special Collections, Washington University Libraries

To The Sardi Salute! Mary Wickes

Mary's portrait joined the famous wall of caricatures at Sardi's restaurant, an institution in New York's theatre district, in 1977. Illustration courtesy of Sardi's, with the permission of artist Richard Baratz

Mary wasn't taking any chances at missing the bridal bouquet at the wedding of Beatrice Colen and Patrick Cronin in Los Angeles in 1977. Egging Mary on at left is Natalie Schafer, about ten years after her *Gilligan's Island* series ended. Courtesy Anne Kaufman Schneider

Oklahoma! brought Mary back to Broadway in 1979 in a nine-month run that received strong notices. She was the frontierswoman Aunt Eller opposite Laurence Guittard as Curly. Photo by Fred Nathan Co., courtesy Mary Wickes Papers, Special Collections, Washington University Libraries

Mary as Marie, the rectory housekeeper in *Father Dowling Mysteries*, 1989–91. Photo copyright American Broadcasting Companies Inc.

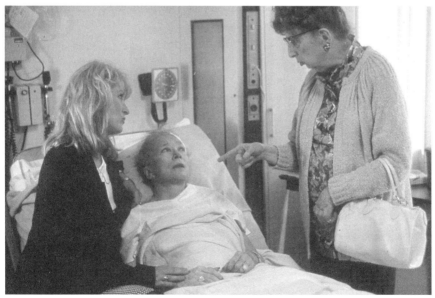

After so many disappointments, Mary was flattered that Mike Nichols hired her for 1990's *Postcards from the Edge* without asking her to read for the part, the grandmother of Meryl Streep and mother of Shirley MacLaine. Photo by David James, copyright 1990 Columbia Pictures Industries, all rights reserved

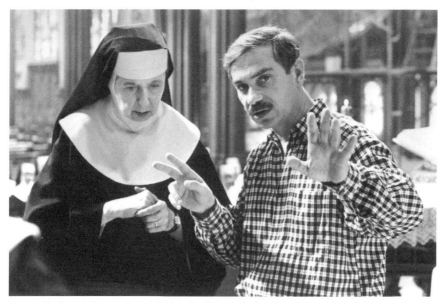

Director Emile Ardolino confers with Mary in 1992 while shooting *Sister Act*, one of the most popular films of Mary's career. Photo by Suzanne Hanover, copyright Touchstone Pictures, all rights reserved

At 84, Mary found *Little Women* difficult because of location shooting in Canada, but she enjoyed being in a story she had loved since childhood. Photo copyright 1994 Columbia Pictures Industries, all rights reserved

CHAPTER ELEVEN

"Not an Ounce" of Romance

MARY JACKSON, THE CHARACTER ACTRESS BEST KNOWN AS MISS EMily Baldwin from *The Waltons*, invited Mary to a small dinner party at her Hollywood Hills home in the early 1970s. The actor Kendall Clark, who lived a few doors away on Whitley Terrace, phoned Jackson to explain he would be running late. Because Clark had earlier offered to pick Mary up, Jackson now phoned Mary to suggest that she come over by herself, as it seemed unlikely Clark would have time to go from Hollywood to Century City and back during rush hour. "I expected her to say, 'Well, I'll be by early and help you make the sauce' or something. But instead she suddenly got all 'proper' on me. She said she wouldn't come unless Kendall picked her up. She could have driven so easily, but she said, 'Mary, it's only proper that we have an escort after dark. It's time we taught these boys a lesson. A lady should not be seen outside of her house alone.' Not because she was afraid of anything—because she wasn't—but just because it was 'proper.' And Kendall, who'd been working all day, had to leave here, go all the way to pick her up in Century City and back 'to teach the boys a lesson.' It was bossy," Jackson says.

But Jackson was not really angered by Mary's cranky response. "It was done with such integrity. And from the standpoint of Victorian propriety, she was right, of course."

Victorian propriety, indeed. Mary led her life according to a rigid set of standards that often frustrated—and sometimes amused—those around her. And her Victorian approach to life was never more evident than in her attitude toward romance. Mary's insistence that Clark pick her up may seem reasonable if one understands that she perceived him to be her date. They had spent much time in each other's company since their days at the Berkshire Playhouse in the 1930s, and he was clearly a favorite of Mary's. Jackson always suspected Mary was romantically interested in Clark, though Mary never told her so.

Never courted by men who were interested in her sexually, Mary nonetheless spent most of her time in the company of male friends. Most of these men were gay, a significant fact Mary did not realize. From the very beginning of Mary's career, those who showed greatest interest in her company—including Clark, Bill Roerick, Max Showalter, and Bob Thomsen—were gay men. Given her limited experience dating, Mary thought of some of them as suitors far longer than a young woman might today. "Oh, I think that's very true. She was a very, very Victorian-like woman who thought of men as possible beaus or gentleman callers or whatever. All of those men were the hope of possible marriage. Kendall and Bill would never have revealed their orientation or talk[ed] about anything like that—people just did not talk about it in those years," says actor Bill Swan, a friend of all three. "I know she loved Kendall very much. When I say she *loved* him, I mean he was one of her best friends: 'Mary and I are doing this,' 'Mary and I are going to the premiere to-morrow night.' I think she really thought one day he would ask her to marry him." Mary and Clark, a former World War II Army captain, once co-wrote a teleplay about a strong-willed girl who tries to save a home for under-privileged boys from closure. It did not sell.

Whether it was with Clark or someone else, Mary did think about marriage on occasion, such as the time she was sitting on a beach in Los Angeles with New York-based writer John Patrick. In the 1950s, Patrick came to the West Coast frequently during the filming of his screenplays, such as *Three Coins in the Fountain*, *High Society*, and *Love is a Many Splendored Thing*. During a conversation one day, out of the blue, Mary turned to him and said, "Pat, I think I'm going to get married." Caught off guard by this declaration, Patrick asked her if she was engaged or going with anyone at the time, to which she replied, "No, I just think it's time." To Patrick, "she seemed quite matter-of-fact about it," as if it was simply a task that needed tending.

Anne Kaufman Schneider, one of Mary's closest friends, went to Stockbridge in 1946 to see *Elizabeth the Queen*, a period drama that gave Mary one of her few non-comedy lead roles. Anne was twenty-one, and this was the theatre's first season after World War II. She met Mary's closest friends in the company, several of whom were gay men. "I have a feeling that in those days she *didn't* know," Schneider says. She is quick to add that, in the 1940s, this purblindness reflects the times as much as naiveté on Mary's part. "Nobody knew anything in those days. I was a little dense in that department—I think I thought they were all kind of boyfriends of hers, which they weren't. It was almost at the beginning of knowing [about gay identity]."

There was no intent to deceive Mary. At the time, these men were motivated by a strong desire to keep secret something they had good reason to believe would hurt them professionally, just as Mary concealed her age and medical conditions. Swan—whose long career includes a co-starring role on TV's *Dr. Kildare*, more than two hundred prime time guest star parts, and the role of Olivia de Havilland's son in *Lady in a Cage*—sums up carefully the context in which Mary formed relation- ships with men who were gay. "We were all anxious to work and in those years if that got around, my God, you'd be tarred and feathered. I never hung out with a gay crowd or went to gay bars—*never*—for fear that it would somehow infringe on my work, that my agent would find out, that I'd turn out to be the Fatty Arbuckle of my season, that I'd be drummed out of the business. None of us were out in the open about that kind of thing in those years," Swan declared when interviewed in his seventies. "I don't think Mary knew [about me] because I've never come out and declared it from the rooftops. If somebody asks me now, I'm quite forthcoming. But you don't get hired to play fathers and uncles and everything if you're thought of as gay. I don't talk about myself in that regard because most of the men that I play at this time in my life are daddies or granddaddies."

Longstanding fear among gays in the industry that their sexual orien- tation will overshadow their talents is not without merit. As he sat down for an interview for this book, the respected television director Hal Kant- er asked about others being interviewed. When the author mentioned having just come from the Motion Picture Home seeking an interview with director Irving Rapper, Kanter's quick response—virtually the first words he shared in the interview—were, "He's gay, you know." It was a passing remark said with no trace of judgment. But the fact that Rapper, a talented director of pictures like *Now, Voyager*, could be so immediately defined by his sexual orientation—by someone who understands the in- dustry as well as Kanter does, no less—may help explain the reluctance of some of the men in Mary's life to be identified as gay.

Three of the most important people in Mary's life—gay men, all— were singer Clifford Newdahl, writer Bob Thomsen, and designer Bill Raiser. Their lives offer a window into the kind of people to whom Mary was most drawn. Seven years Mary's senior, Clifford Newdahl was a dap- per, slightly balding, somewhat stocky young man with deep eyes, round cheeks, slender lips, and a friendly smile. He grew up in Seattle and Leavenworth, Washington, where he discovered he had a strong voice. As a young man, he traveled around China performing with an American jazz band before establishing himself in New York. In the 1930s, he performed around the country for the Shubert organization, and frequently had engagements at the St. Louis Muny. It was during one of these Muny engagements in the early 1930s that he met Frank and Isabella and, through them, Mary. In 1933, Mary performed with Newdahl at the Fox Theatre in St. Louis in a production of *Queen High*, a comedy that had been on Broadway for two years. Newdahl sang tenor in various municipal opera companies, including the short-lived American Opera Company in the 1930s, but a need for more regular income pushed him into a nightclub career. He performed often at New York's Hotel St. Moritz and at the Number One bar at the Hotel One Fifth Avenue, where he accompanied himself on piano. Mary and Cliff shared a love of musical theatre, a devotion to their mothers (he often closed letters to Mary by sending his love "from Mother and me"), and an appreciation of small-town values. He was bright and fun, the type of fellow who frequently sang at parties. Newdahl visited Mary at Stockbridge and became a constant companion during her early years in New York, but nothing more.

"This was a totally asexual alliance," says Lester Coleman, the physician who was part of Mary's adopted family in New York in the late 1930s and early 1940s. Mary frequently brought Newdahl to the Colemans' home for dinner. "It was a sweet, loving, caring relationship. They went out together but I never had the feeling that they had a romance. I never saw them in any vaguely suggestive physical association." As World War II approached, Newdahl found himself in the Anti-aircraft Artillery Command. Since he was one of Mary's few theatre friends who also knew her father, Cliff was a source of emotional support when Frank passed away in 1943. Cliff wrote her immediately upon receiving the news at Camp Pendleton, an example of the kind of loyalty Mary valued. "My dear Mary, what you and that darling mother of yours must have been going through. It just does not seem possible. How I wish I could have been there to help in some way," he wrote. "And as for you going back to work, it's the only thing to do. I can hear your Mother tell you so—she is a lady of great character and strength! It has been a tremendous blow but you just watch Isabella—she knows the answers! . . . To be with you and your interesting work and friends will be the only solution. It may sound hard-hearted . . . but you must both get away from St. Louis for the time being. It helps no one to brood. You won't have to worry about

Dear Isabella now—she has so much to do—her quality will bring her through—but when she comes to you, then you will be strong and patient and that is when Isabella will need you most."

Newdahl returned safely but, like so many soldiers, not to the career he had before the war. He returned to Washington State, where he grew up as Clifford Newdall, and taught music. He died only a few years later in his early forties. "Mary was absolutely bereft when he died," recalls Bob Wallsten, who often accompanied Mary and Isabella to Newdahl's appearances at the Number One. Upon Newdahl's death, a tribute in the *Leavenworth Echo* told readers that "Cliff did not care much for sports, as a participant. He could cook a meal; he could even do fancy work, but he was never labeled a 'sissy' by his fellows. He was equally at home with small youngsters, with a gathering of ladies at a tea, or with a group of young men."

For the rest of her life, Mary treasured one life-long memento from Newdahl. Newdahl had been friends with another Shubert player, Archie Leach, who secured a film contract and left for Hollywood directly from a performance in St. Louis. Thinking his future would now be in films and not in touring stage shows, Leach passed his Herkert & Meisel wardrobe trunk on to Newdahl. When he later went into the Army, Newdahl asked Isabella if she would keep it for him. It sat in the Wickenhausers' basement on Pershing Street until after the war, when Newdahl returned to Washington State and no longer needed it. So the trunk became Mary's . . . and Leach, of course, became Cary Grant. "The Cary Grant trunk is lovely. It has a place for a high silk hat; I always thought that was rather chic. You could drop it from a twentieth floor window and it would be fine—it's one of those sturdy ones, not meant for beauty, but for sturdiness," Mary said. It's strictly a man's trunk, with hanging space for about eight things on one side and drawers on the others, but it suited Mary's needs perfectly. "And besides, it was Cary Grant's, and that made it even more wonderful." Later, when performing on tour, she regularly used this H&M trunk for her theatre things and her own H&M trunk for her personal things at her hotel.

If Mary valued Newdahl for his sweetness and thoughtfulness, it was something more exciting that drew her to Bob Thomsen. Mary met Thomsen shortly after arriving in New York and was immediately drawn to the 6' 1", well-built redhead with freckles who was three years her junior. Sometimes mistaken for Danny Kaye, Thomsen was attentive and charming. "When you were with him and talking with him, you were the only person who existed—his intensity was like that," recalls his niece, Nancy Thomsen Brown. Unlike Mary, Thomsen had formal theatre training, having graduated from the American Academy of Dramatic Arts. He performed in summer stock and on Broadway, where he had been the only white cast member in *Mamba's Daughters* with Ethel Waters. In the 1930s, Thomsen became one of Mary's intimates, a circle that included writer Bob Wallston, Bill Herz of the Mercury Theatre company, and Garson Kanin, the playwright and director who directed Mary on Broadway in 1937 in *Hitch Your Wagon*, his first production independent of George Abbott. Four decades later, Kanin would reminisce to Mary, "I remember vividly the hours at Bob Thomsen's apartment and how we plotted to change the theatre and the world. Come to think of it, we did not entirely fail in this, did we?" Mary and Thomsen worked together at least twice: In *Stage Door*, Thomsen played Hastings, the gentlemen caller from Texas, and in *The Man Who Came to Dinner*, he replaced Theodore Newton as Bert Jefferson, the young reporter.

Of all the significant people in Mary's life, Thomsen, a civil libertarian who was raised a Quaker in Baltimore, was probably most driven by politics. When a heart murmur kept him out of the military during World War II, he enlisted in the British Eighth Army unit, driving an ambulance in North Africa assigned by the American Friends Service Committee. Militantly anti-McCarthy, Thomsen was blacklisted after taking part in a benefit performance for the Spanish Civil War and was constantly investigated. Because his longtime New York apartment was around the corner from the Russian Embassy, Thomsen sent Christmas cards each year to its staff, something "the FBI looked dimly on," his niece says. As a young actor, Thomsen was intent on becoming a writer, and he eventually became one. He published short stories in the *Saturday Evening Post, Colliers, Ladies Home Journal, Woman's Home Companion, American*, and *This Week*. He wrote several plays, including *Carriage Trade*, about an elegant whorehouse on the edge of Gettysburg during the Civil War. The play had been on George Abbott's production list for almost a year, expected to feature Gene Tierney, when Abbott relinquished his option on it. It was then given a weeklong run at the Stamford (Connecticut) Community Playhouse in August 1940 with Zachary Scott as a lead. Thomsen wrote a part specifically for Mary—a stuttering, Bible-quoting prostitute—but her contract for *The Man Who Came to Dinner* prevented her from appearing. Thomsen also ghostwrote for Chester Bowles, the diplomat who served as President Kennedy's advisor on foreign affairs. Thomsen moved to Los Angeles in 1950, about the same time Mary did, to write screenplays for MGM producer Edwin Knopf. There, he often wrote for television, including the *Topper* series. Much of his writing was done in collaboration with George Bradshaw, whom Mary also knew from her early days in New York and of whom she was quite fond.

And therein lies a tale. In the late 1930s, Mary considered both Thomsen and Bradshaw "beaus," enjoying their company separately for various social outings. It's not surprising she liked Bradshaw, an elegant, debonair Princeton grad who spoke fluent French and loved cruise ships, as a child having sailed on the maiden voyage of the *Queen Elizabeth*. Nor is it surprising that Thomsen also liked Bradshaw. In short order, the two men became lovers and remained a couple until Bradshaw's death in 1973. Nancy Thomsen Brown, Thomsen's niece who knew them both well, says their gay identity "was never discussed in the family. All that was unsaid and unspoken—but very well-understood." Wallsten does not recall Mary "ever saying anything that indicated that she knew anyone was gay [but] she must have known. I think she did what a lot of women do—ignore it. That was the thing to do at the time."

She certainly knew many years later. In the late 1980s, Mary was able to joke knowingly with Anna Crouse: "I introduced the two of them— and never saw either of them again." Mary's quip was a good-natured way of deflecting disappointment that two men who interested her chose each other instead. But her recollection may not be accurate: Wallsten distinctly recalls meeting Bradshaw at a party in New York thrown by actress Patricia Collinge and introducing him that night to Thomsen, since Thomsen was going to Washington (to depart for wartime service) and Bradshaw was already there. "They met, and the rest is history," he says. In reality, neither account may be true. It's quite likely that the men met in 1935 during the run of *It's You I Want*, Bradshaw's adaptation of a Maurice Braddell farce at the Cort Theatre. Thomsen was in the cast.

Nonetheless, Mary remained Thomsen's close confidante. During the war, he wrote her about a particularly frightening episode: "Did I tell you that when I thought death was knocking at my door (and don't think you'll ever hear the end of that) I wanted very badly to call the padre and tell him to arrange for all my remaining money ($56.28) to be transferred to you. You were to give a lovely evening for Bradshaw. I think it was to be just you two . . . a real old soiree de gala! But sometime during the evening you were both to promise me that you would 'stand still and remember.' That was the phrase. Stand still and remember and it was with me for days, over and over on the hospital train coming back the wheels kept saying it. I didn't call the padre but once several months ago you were almost fifty-six dollars richer."

Mary arranged for Thomsen to meet her parents during a trip he took through St. Louis. Just weeks after Mary's father died, Thomsen sent her these touching words: "I thought if I put a sheet of paper into the typewriter this afternoon instead of V-mail blanks I'd somehow feel less limited, somehow free-er to talk to you. But I couldn't have been more wrong. The limitations are all with me. You see, I don't want to write you a letter at all this afternoon. I know exactly what I do want to do. I want a car, a fine one with a top that goes back and a chance to ride way out into the country somewhere with you. We wouldn't have to talk, we could just ride and then we'd stop for a drink (you'd know the very right place). Then I'd like to be able to start and tell you a story. I wonder if it would surprise you . . . 'cause you see it would all be about your father.

"Sometimes it is awful to have outsiders talk about our families. They can't ever know the whole story, not the way we do, and their silly little half impressions don't sound at all the way it was.

"But I'd take a chance this afternoon if you'd let me. I don't think you'd mind listening to my story about the time I was in St. Louis. It is all just as clear as this morning. I wouldn't make any pretense of knowing the whole story . . . but I wish I were around somewhere to tell you the reflection of it I got one night when he took me to dinner and oh Lordy, so vividly when he got up at six in the morning to come down to the station and see me off in that black day coach. That, Mary Isabel, is one of the nicest things that ever happened to me (and I mean it and I've had a long time over here to remember the nice things). It was so terribly cold that morning and the train seemed never to get going, but he never seemed to mind, it all seemed to be fun for him. I'm very glad I met your father. I'll always feel 'good' remembering him."

For his part, Bradshaw published about a hundred and fifty short stories. One was the basis for the film *How to Steal a Million* with Audrey Hepburn, while another became *The Bad and the Beautiful* with Lana Turner and Kirk Douglas. He also wrote five cookbooks. Though New York was his home, he lived for a time at Zuma Beach in California, where a visiting James Dean once accidentally set fire to one of Bradshaw's favorite armchairs. In theatre circles, Bradshaw is perhaps remembered best for his death. After a lovely, formal evening at the theatre in November 1973 with actress and frequent escort Dorothy Stickney (of *Life with Father* fame), he suffered a sudden heart attack as the taxi pulled up in front of the home he and Thomsen shared at 68 East 86th Street in New York. Thomsen ran out and frantically administered CPR to his tuxedo-clad partner, but Bradshaw could not be revived. In Los Angeles, Mary soon heard from Patricia Collinge: "I expect by now you have heard of George Bradshaw's sudden death. It was a shock to all of us. Bobbie Thomsen is holding up, but you can imagine what a wrench it has been for him. And what loneliness is ahead."

Thomsen found solace in a writing project. Having overcome an alcohol addiction some years before, he now worked beside Bill Wilson, the founder of Alcoholics Anonymous, and in 1975 published Wilson's biography, *Bill W*, still available today. Later in life, he became especially close to Jean Dixon, the salty actress best known for playing the maid opposite William Powell's butler in *My Man Godfrey*. When she died in 1981, Thomsen inherited most of her estate. Thomsen died in 1983 in New York after a long battle with cancer. Reading of Thomsen's death in the Authors League Bulletin, a stunned Garson Kanin wrote Mary, "Is this indeed our Bob? If so, I am grieved beyond words."

It was Thomsen who introduced Mary to Bill Raiser. He did so by V-mail (known formally as Victory Mail), the long defunct system of wartime correspondence shipped out on microfilm and reproduced in miniature for the recipient service member. "I have a friend," he wrote in July 1943, when Mary was in California for film work. "I saw a lot of him right after you left New York and well, he got drafted and . . . now is commissioned and is doing something in Jo Mielziner's line of work at your March Field. [Mielziner is the set designer; March Field the air base in California.] He is lonely and has heard so much about 'Mary.' Could he look you up? Hell, it's for the Cause and he is tall and very decorative so if he comes calling you'll understand." Raiser was an aesthete who traveled with the smart set. The first things mentioned today by those who remember him are his looks and his wardrobe. Tall and handsome, Raiser was featured by name in 1950s magazine ads for silk suits. He lived in a stylish apartment in Beekman Place, a sought-after address that overlooks New York's East River. He was likeable and, by all accounts, sweet natured. Mary enjoyed his company immensely, and went with him often to dinner, nightclubs, the theatre, and social gatherings.

Raiser was perhaps the only man in Mary's life at this time who was not of the theatre. Trained at the Parsons School of Design, he was an industrial designer who specialized in architectural interiors. Before the war, he worked for Raymond Loewy Associates, the design firm that created such American icons as the Coca-Cola bottle, the Lucky Strike cigarette logo, the design of Air Force One, and the streamlined Greyhound Bus. Working for Loewy, Raiser designed interior fixtures for Lord & Taylor in Manhasset, Long Island, but when Mary met him, Raiser was known for having created the refrigerator that shaped America's kitchens for decades. Raymond Loewy had convinced the Frigidaire people in Ohio that his firm could design a better appliance. "So he turned the project over to Bill. Bill on his lunch hour went out and bought a lot of silver and blue paper and came back and took an old refrigerator and dolled it up with trays inside in blue and silver and a new handle and some various open grids and so forth and converted this old thing into something that was real snazzy," recalls Stewart Williams, a colleague who would later receive acclaim for his Palm Springs architectural work. "About nine months later, I saw a manufactured new model of Frigidaire and opened the door and saw those blue and silver things now in enamel. Just the way it was designed by Raiser." Today, the model is sought after by collectors of mid-century Americana.

Raiser remained affiliated with the Loewy firm in one way or another for almost thirty years. He became especially close to Loewy's wife, Viola, whom he escorted to events in New York when Loewy was unavailable or uninterested. "My mother made a comment to me that he was becoming well known as her partner in these social gatherings. And there were rumors about them, which amused her, given that he was gay," says Loewy's daughter, Laurence. "I remember most his sense of humor, which made him delightful to be around. He was very uplifting—a generally outgoing, compassionate, very kind person." In the late 1960s, while vacationing on St. Kitts, Raiser met Arthur Elrod, an interior designer, and fell in love. About a year later, Raiser moved to Palm Springs to join forces with Elrod personally and professionally. He moved into Elrod's home, a spectacular property called Southridge that was designed by noted architect John Lautner, and joined Elrod's residential interior design firm. They created a commercial division, Raiser/Elrod, and worked throughout the United States and Europe. Raiser also designed high-end carpets for Eddie Fields and took on projects for the Dayton Hudson stores.

Mary remained an important part of Raiser's life once he moved to the West Coast. "I think he was closer to Mary than he was to almost anybody else," Wallsten says, although Raiser had many other friends from the theatre. Natalie Schafer, who will forever be remembered as Mrs. Howell on *Gilligan's Island*, was a frequent weekend visitor in Palm Springs and a frequent date in New York. He escorted her to the 1956 premiere of *Anastasia*, in which she appears.

On a Monday morning in 1974, Raiser and Elrod were driving to their office in Raiser's Renault when a teenage driver ran a light and hit their sports car broadside at a busy intersection. "They were supposed to be [flying out] to Chicago. They had said goodbye to me the night before and for some reason changed their mind and decided to come to work," says Hal Broderick, their business partner. Both men were killed. Raiser was fifty-eight.

When Mary came to understand the true nature of gay men in her life, by most indications she accepted it, for example, sending gifts and invitations to Thomsen and Bradshaw at their home in both their names, and regularly visiting Bill Roerick at the home he shared with his partner, actor Tom Coley. But in general she remained in the dark about the gay men around her—or she pretended to be. Actor and cabaret performer Lee Roy Reams became friends with Mary when they performed together in *Wonderful Town* in 1975. When the company prepared to try out in San Francisco before a Los Angeles opening, Mary suggested she and Reams fly up in advance of the others. "Let's go up a day earlier on a different flight, just you and me on our own. That way we can take our time, we don't have to be ordered around like cattle, everybody in little groups," she told him. Reams, who by now had lunched with Mary almost every day of rehearsals, happily obliged. On the flight up, "Mary said, 'When we get to San Francisco, I have a friend I want you meet.' I said, 'Oh, how sweet, Mary.' She said, 'She's a wonderful girl and I think you two would really hit it off.' I said, 'Are you joking with me, Mary?' She said, 'No!' I said, 'I'm homosexual, Mary.' She paused and looked at me with that look of hers and said, 'Well, then I guess we *won't* be fixing you up!' We laughed and howled. I was amused by her innocence and her naiveté, because we had spent so much time together in rehearsal and I'm a pretty 'out there' kind of guy who's never allowed [being gay] to interfere with my life." By this point in her life, in her sixties, Mary had surrounded herself with so many gay men that ignoring their sexual identity could only have been intentional, not naive.

In 1969, she said, "If you play comedy, and you're not married, people are inclined to say, 'Pour soul.' But I have a lot of male escorts, and I'm very choosy. My friends are always saying, 'Oh, you can't go on waiting for somebody absolutely perfect.' And I say, 'The hell I can't—I'm havin' a ball.' For a tall skinny dame, I haven't done bad." In 1982, Mary wrote, "I have always had many men friends. I love them and they say they love me and I believe them. I've just always had too much fun to narrow down to one gentleman, and ladies in groups make me rather nervous. I have really good friends in both sexes and in that I am fortunate because my family consists of one cousin. I think men are dandy, bless

'em!" Sometimes Mary approached her solitariness with humor. At the
1977 wedding reception for George S. Kaufman's granddaughter Beatrice Colen, Mary extended her skirt out in front of her, shaping it into
a net of sorts to better catch the traditional bridal bouquet. With Natalie
Schafer egging her on, laughing out loud, Mary did in fact catch the
bouquet. When actor pal Joe Ross married, "She'd say, 'I can't believe
you— you're so normal and married and everything else!' When she met
my wife Loretta [a home economics major], she said, 'My God—*Jenny
Basic*. Where'd you find her, in the convent?' She just loved families. She
loved coming over here, my God!"

In December 1971, Lucille Ball wrote her, "Have a happy New Year,
but, if you don't use that ticket I gave you [a plane ticket to visit Lucy in
Snowmass, Colorado], I'll wrap you around Alan Handley, which Gary
[Morton] thinks you might like." Handley, an Emmy-winning TV director who produced Dinah Shore's twice-weekly TV show from 1951 to
1957 and later directed several Academy Awards telecasts, was a frequent escort of Mary's in the 1960s, '70s and '80s. He had great wit
and style, and was good company for Mary, who enjoyed relaxing at his
home. He lived above the Hollywood Bowl in a Mulholland Drive house
designed by Frank Lloyd Wright for Huntington Hartford, the A&P su-
permarket heir. But Handley (who died in 1990) was an unlikely suitor:
Although he had been married earlier, Handley was also gay.

Even with the straight men in her life, Mary sometimes operated on
unwitting assumptions, seemingly unable to distinguish between dating and friendship. Her relationship with Iggie Wolfington is a good example. Mary met Wolfington in 1947 when they performed on stage
in *Heyday* with John Craven and Robert Keith Jr. (who would become
better known as Brian Keith). The show closed out of town before arriving on Broadway but, for several years, whenever Mary saw Wolfington,
she greeted him with a loud, friendly call to his character, "Hiya, Pinky!"
Years later, both living in Los Angeles, they became close, and it's easy to
understand why. Wolfington was a warm, gracious, down-to-earth actor
with a strong commitment to charity work, having helped establish the
Actors Fund on the West Coast. He shared Mary's awe of the theatre legends of the twentieth century, speaking reverentially of Helen Hayes and
in almost hushed tones of Fanny Brice. And, like Mary, he loved musical
theatre, originating one role in *The Music Man* on Broadway (Marcel-
lus) and playing another (Mayor Shinn) in a Broadway revival more
than twenty years later. Mary and Wolfington spent considerable time
together over many years. Wolfington says firmly that there was never

any romance, but Mary, who had little experience with men and the nu-ances of relationships, naively assumed that what she and Iggie enjoyed constituted dating. There is no other reasonable explanation for Mary having led others to believe that the time she spent with Wolfington was the stuff of romance. Lee Roy Reams remembers two occasions, both after Wolfington married, when Mary specifically implied having had a romantic relationship with Wolfington. "Not that it was anything sexual [but] more than a platonic friendship," he says. "Maybe it was in Mary's mind. But I do remember those two occasions in which she implied to me that she and Iggie had dated. I think that's the term she used."

In a February 4, 1971, letter to Mary, who was home alone suffer-ing with the flu, Lucy writes, "I still say you should have married Iggie and these things wouldn't happen to you." When this passage was read to him twenty-eight years later, Wolfington was baffled that Mary may have viewed their relationship so differently from the way he viewed it. "Lucy had seen me with Mary a great number of times, and they were very close. I can see why people think it's likely that we had an interest. We saw lots of each other at a time in our life, doing a lot of different things together, just the two of us. But I wouldn't call it dating. There was never anything romantic. She's not anyone you'd ever think of making a pass at." "When you've lived to be the age Mary was when she was settled on the Coast, after she lost her mother, I think she was so set in her ways that she wouldn't be able to let anyone into her life, any more than I did for years," says Wolfington, who did not marry until his early 50s.

Iggie is not the only person Mary led others to think she had a re-lationship with. The cast of *Dennis the Menace*, in which Mary appeared from 1959 to 1961 as Miss Cathcart, was given the peculiar impression that Mary was married to character actor Elliott Reid. Paul Barselou, who played Maurice, the TV repairman, remembers most of the cast hav-ing lunch together one day at a restaurant near Columbia Studios when Reid stopped by to chat with Mary. Mary introduced Reid to the group and Barselou says with confidence that they all understood Mary and Reid were married. When pressed, he says some may have believed that they were only living together.

Occasionally, newspapers published short items about Mary in gossip or theatre columns that alluded to romances that likely did not exist. This was common practice years ago, especially to deflect gossip about gay actors. Typical were reports in several papers based on this February 12, 1951, press release from Warner Bros.: "A most understanding girl is Mary Wickes. Her boyfriend, Bob Shaw, New York business executive, phoned to ask her for an autographed photo—but not of herself. He wanted one of Doris Day, with whom Mary is acting in *On Moonlight Bay*, the Technicolor musical at Warner Bros. Studios. When Mary recovered from the shock she sent the picture." No one in Mary's life then remembers today a "Bob Shaw" who was special to her, and there is no reference of any kind to him in her papers or correspondence.

Max Showalter, one of Mary's closest friends for more than thirty years, has thought much about the emotional distance Mary put between herself and others. "I've always wondered if there was someone she loved and gave herself totally to who hurt her and [made her] afraid of ever letting that warmth and that love out to a full extent again, protecting herself, especially without Isabelle," says Showalter, who played the earnest honeymooner transfixed by Marilyn Monroe in *Niagara*. "At times I feel terribly sorry for Mary because I feel it was a life unfulfilled of love, that she just wasn't capable of opening up, really and totally." Most of Mary's friends believe she was satisfied with a rich career, her hospital volunteerism, and her church. This is certainly the perception she nurtured. Joe Ross says, "She was happy with her world, 'happy with her own divan.' As she said many times, 'Look, I got this new divan, and I got this wonderful furniture—who else do I need?'" In 1976, she talked with UPI reporter Vernon Scott about never having had a family of her own. "It just didn't work out that way. But I'm a cheerful, happy woman and I love my work."

Occasionally, she let slip that she wanted more. In 1977, Mary was at home watching the *Mike Douglas Show* when Douglas began singing "Happy Anniversary" to guests Ruth Gordon and Garson Kanin, the long-married actress and screenwriter. Tears welled in Mary's eyes as she sat alone in her living room reflecting on these remarkable people, whom she first met when all three were young and unattached. She immediately grabbed pen and paper. "I feel so close to you both and you haven't the faintest idea that I do," she wrote them. "And I am absolutely kelly-green with envy over your thirty-six years of companionship and love. I've always had a fine time and am still having it, but I don't *belong* to anyone. Lots and lots and lots of good friends and I wish it would not sound like bragging to tell you of some of my accomplishments, but it would."

Malcolm Goldstein met Mary in 1975 while researching a biography of George S. Kaufman, and he saw her numerous times when he visited Los Angeles from New York. In 1990, after spending a day together at the Getty Museum in Malibu, he was driving them back to Mary's apartment. It was late in the afternoon and the sun was going down when Mary said something revealing. "I always thought she was perfectly happy never to have married and that her career and her church were really the important things in her life. But she told me that she always felt a little sad about going home because there would be nobody there for her to be with." Goldstein was "astonished" by Mary's sudden frankness. "And I felt sorry for her. It isn't exactly as if she had to be lonely—she had lots of friends, lots of people in her life," he said. "I really didn't know what to say. I think I tried to move the conversation into something else."

Harriet Switzer had a similar encounter. A former nun who works as secretary to the board of Washington University, Switzer was asked in 1988 to escort Mary to the auditorium where Mary would give the inaugural Adele Starbird Lecture. Mary was chosen in part because she had been a personal friend of Starbird, the university's long-serving dean of women. Switzer picked Mary up at the Chancellor's Home, a campus residence for special guests. "I remember her coming down the steps from the second floor and greeting me. I told her a little bit about my life. She wanted to know if I was married," Switzer said. Switzer, who was dating at the time, said she would like to marry some day (four years later, she married David Cronin). As they spoke in the front hall of the residence, Mary told Switzer, "I've always regretted a little the fact that I never got married. It's a lonely life." Switzer says, although Mary expressed only *some* regret, "I could tell that her feeling level was deeper. She had a wonderful career, but at times it was lonely." Mary had not met Switzer before, but Switzer says women frequently open up after learning she was once a nun. Maybe Mary opened up because, having a great respect for those in religious life, she trusted Switzer. Or perhaps Mary had engaged in a lot of reflection while staying in a retreat-like campus setting. "I felt she had shared a bit of intimacy with me that she probably didn't share with a whole lot of people. I felt a bond with her somehow," Switzer says. About this time, a reporter asked Mary if she had ever married. "I used to date a lot, but I was always too busy, too deeply involved in this or that show. In some ways I wish I had," she said.

Sometimes the absence of intimacy in Mary's life surfaced in her performances. Herb Metz, who directed Mary as Amanda in the *Glass Menagerie* in 1968, says the production made him wonder if Mary ever experienced romance. During the play's jonquil speech, when Amanda talks wistfully of the many gentleman callers she has had, he believes

Mary conveyed a pathos that struck a personal chord, a sadness that "this never happened to me." Jack O'Brien observed something similar when he directed Mary in *You Can't Take It With You* in 1972. When Kerrie Prescott, playing Mary's husband, went to put his arms around Mary and cuddle her, "that was slightly foreign territory for her. She was better by herself in the kitchen than she was in the sort of familial warmth of the Thanksgiving table."

Lucie Arnaz offers these observations, putting Mary's life in context: "This was a woman who lived alone except when she was with her mother. She had her great friends, like Iggie Wolfington and those people she hung out with, but she had sort of martyred herself to her work and her mom and her volunteerism, and that was the way it was. I didn't get any long face, sad-soap about it from her. You just gotta assume that it takes a certain kind of person to live alone. She fought her whole life against [seeming like the archetypal spinster] by this magnificent bravado that she had about life in general. And she stayed busy and she had other things to do. For some people, it isn't about having a romance and getting married and raising a family—and that doesn't make their life less important or less valuable. I think she had a great life, and I think *she* felt she had a great life. But I have a gut feeling that she *was* lonely, especially after her mother died."

Virtually all of Mary's closest friends voice certainty that she never experienced sexual contact; in fact, many raised this issue in interviews themselves. Showalter's comments were typical. "I always wondered if she died a virgin. Mary was almost asexual. There was nothing really sexual about her. I never saw an *ounce* of romance in her life," he says. Says Coleman, the physician, "I think she lived in a world of deprivation, physically, with contact with men. There were 'great buddies' of hers, but I don't remember any time that she had any kind of romance going." Harve Presnell, who performed with Mary in *Show Boat* in 1964 and toured with her in *Oklahoma!* in 1979, believed Mary was totally asexual and that the absence of sexuality led to some neurotic behavior. "Everything was preparing for the next eight thirty curtain because the only reality [for her] was when the curtain went up and she was on stage. That's very sad," he says. At a Midwest stop in *Oklahoma!*, cast members were invited to a nearby farm for a barbecue, a welcome diversion from restaurant fare. "Mary was intrigued by the growing of the crops and the way they prepared things and they way they did this and the way they did that, and I thought, 'My God, she's a poor, lonely lady.'" He remembers her as the "quintessential" small-town schoolmarm. Anne

Kaufman Schneider speculates that Mary lived without sexual experiences by choice. "I would have thought she was a certified virgin, and there are not many of those around. I don't know when you make a decision like that. Maybe you *don't* make a decision like that and [sexual relationships] just go past you." Anne believes that for Mary sexual intimacy "would have been something unnatural, although I hate to use that word. But for Wicksie, unnatural."

In fact, Mary had at least one sexual encounter. Bob Wallsten knew Mary from the 1930s summer stock circuit. An actor turned writer and playwright, he had been a Stockbridge player from 1931 to 1933. They performed together once, in a production of *Spring Meeting* starring Gladys Cooper at the Cape Playhouse in Dennis, Massachusetts, in July 1939. But they were more than just co-stars, and they were more than just friends in the Thomsen and Bradshaw circle: They dated briefly. It was during *Spring Meeting* that Mary and Wallsten had sex, something Wallsten is not entirely comfortable speaking about. Ultimately, he says only that the two had "an understated, not very serious, romantic relationship." He says Mary was a virgin when they met, and about this, he says he is certain. "We were a couple of kids fumbling around, not what you'd call a sexual relationship," says Wallsten. In fact, sixty years later, he does not recall whether it was actually consummated.

But G. Whitfield Cook III does. Cook, a popular stage manager in the 1930s, who would later write most of the *Life with Father* television series and the screenplay for Alfred Hitchcock's *Strangers on a Train*, was so close to Wallsten that for years the two referred to each other playfully as "Uncle Whit" and "Uncle Bob." Cook was also one of Mary's dearest lifelong friends. Cook told Wallsten that *he* knew about Wallsten's sexual relationship with Mary, first-hand. As the Cape Playhouse's stage manager during the *Spring Meeting* run, Cook stayed in the same boarding house as Wallsten. From the window of Cook's upstairs room, he could see directly into Wallsten's room on the first floor below. Cook told Wallsten he watched Mary and him make love one night.

Wallsten acknowledges that Cook has no reason to mislead him about witnessing Wallsten's sexual encounter with Mary, conceding that he simply "cannot remember whether we went all that distance or not—that's how unimportant it was. It certainly wasn't very important to me, and I don't think it was to her. We were friends much longer than we were romantically inclined toward each other." Wallsten and Mary remained close for most of the rest of Mary's life. He went on to write short stories for *Esquire* and *McCall's* and TV scripts for *Alfred Hitchcock*

Presents, DuPont Show of the Month, Alcoa Hour, Lux Video Theatre, Cavalcade of America, and *General Electric Theater.* Wallsten, who describes himself as bisexual, later married the actress Cynthia Rogers. She died in 1971, and he died in 2005, after sitting for two interviews for this book.

Cook declined several requests to be interviewed, explaining that he was reserving his stories about Mary for his own memoir, which was in progress. Cook led a rich, interesting life, filled with many names from the theatrical and film worlds. He became a close friend of the Alfred Hitchcock family, actress Anne Baxter, and Elaine Steinbeck (widow of John), among others. He published two novels and more than sixty short stories and sold scores of television scripts to *Studio One, Playhouse 90, Suspense, Climax, Front Row Center, You Are There,* and others. After his wife of twenty years died in 1974, Cook spent many years in the company of Sumner Locke Elliott, the Australian novelist and prolific dramatist of American live television. The openly gay Locke Elliott took an apartment adjacent to Cook's; knocking down a common wall allowed the men to have separate homes with a large shared living space. They traveled together annually to Anguilla until Locke Elliott died in 1991. Mary frequently visited them in New York and at Cook's second home in Jefferson, New Hampshire. Cook died in 2003, never having published his memoir.

Even when there was genuine romantic interest in Mary—as with Wallsten briefly in the 1930s—Mary didn't have an easy time of it. Wallsten remembers being invited to a party at the Beekman Place home of Patricia Collinge, who played Birdie in the original *Little Foxes* with Tallulah Bankhead and, later, Teresa Wright's mother in the film *Shadow of a Doubt.* "[Collinge] said, 'If you'd like to bring a girl, please feel free.' I said, 'All right, I'll bring Mary Wickes.' She got very cold and said [disdainfully], 'Well, I don't mean *that* girl.'" Respecting his host's wishes, Wallsten did not invite Mary to the party. It's not clear why Collinge did not like Mary. Collinge had been helpful to Mary in her early days in New York, giving Mary encouragement when she was hired by Marc Connelly for *Farmer Takes a Wife.* "She could have been jealous of Mary, even though she wasn't beautiful, because Mary was younger. Or she might have wearied of Mary's parlor behavior, which could be very eccentric. Mary was often the life of the party," Wallsten says. Either way, he believes Mary was unaware Collinge disliked her because "Pat was two-faced" in general, a trait Wallsten did not fully understand until he examined Collinge's papers, which he received from her husband after her death in 1974.

Wallsten recalls one incident during his brief dalliance with Mary that suggests Mary found pleasure in the mechanics of courtship. During the run of *Spring Meeting*, Wallsten's parents came to visit. They knew Wallsten and Mary were "seeing each other in a romantic context," but they also knew he was interested in the film actress Karen Morley, who had appeared in George Cukor's film *Dinner at Eight*. Wallsten brought Mary to meet his parents at a restaurant in Brewster, Massachusetts. "We were seated on a porch having dinner at a glass table. My father started talking about Karen Morley, and he was hard to stop when he got talking. He mentioned something about her with the kind of knowing chuckle that older people do about young people's affections, and my mother put out her hand and [rested it on his knee under the table] and did that wifely kind of, 'Go easy, dear' gesture. And Mary sitting there saw it happening through the glass-top table." But rather than react with hurt at a dinner discussion that had turned to another of her date's love interests, Mary was "touched and amused" that Wallsten's mother was trying to shield her from hearing the story, he says.

Mary's only other romantic attachments appear to have been even more fleeting than her relationship with Wallsten and, like that one, to have occurred only in her youth. Janet Fox, an actress of Mary's generation who played similar character parts, knew Mary from their early days in New York. A niece of playwright Edna Ferber, Fox had helped Mary get her role in *Stage Door* in 1936, and a grateful Mary introduced Fox to Berkshire Playhouse Director Billy Miles, who hired Fox for several productions. Fox remembers Mary developing a crush around this time. She no longer remembers the man's name, but she recalls that he was married: "She got kind of dewey-eyed when she talked about him, somebody perfectly safe for her to be dewey-eyed about because he was taken. She could get kind of romantic about a man, almost like a schoolgirl crush. But the people she [was interested in] were unavailable. It was almost a cliché. I have no idea if they were consummated. I kept wishing she'd fall in love with some plain [unattached] man. I think Mary would have enjoyed a great romping romance."

One other man for whom Mary expressed romantic interest was Glenn Anders. Anders was a character actor and leading man on the stage in the 1920s and 1930s, known for originating roles in three Pulitzer Prize-winning plays: Hatcher Hughes's *Hell-Bent for Heaven* (1924), Sidney Howard's *They Knew What They Wanted* (1924), and Eugene O'Neill's *Strange Interlude* (1928). His leading ladies included Tallulah Bankhead, Helen Hayes, Claudette Colbert, Judith Anderson, Gladys Cooper, and

Ruth Gordon, and he was especially close to Alfred Lunt and Lynn Fontanne. He was a major stage star, but today is probably best remembered for a film role in Orson Welles's *Lady from Shanghai* (1948). Twenty-one years older than Mary, Anders was fun and appealing, "a great wit and full of laughter," as Hayes recalled in 1977. In the early 1940s, Mary raved so much about Anders that her friend Louis Westheimer became convinced she was in love with him. He cannot be certain that she used those exact words, but "She told me enough for me to know. She was crazy about the guy," says Westheimer, an important part of Mary's life in St. Louis. "One time, they went down to Cape Cod. It was daring in those days for a woman to travel with a guy." As it happened, Mary and Anders performed together in Cape Cod. At the Cape Playhouse in Dennis, Massachusetts, in August 1939, they appeared in *Skylark*, a comedy starring Gertrude Lawrence. Mary remained close with Anders for a time. In 1942, she included him in a dinner she gave at her temporary Los Angeles apartment for Isabella, who was visiting from St. Louis. At dinner parties, Mary was known to sometimes offer the toast "Here's to crime!" the toast Anders makes to Welles in *Lady from Shanghai*.

Elliott Reid was in Los Angeles in the early 1940s for some film work. He recalls driving west on Franklin Avenue in Hollywood one sunny afternoon, when someone called to him loudly. Reid, known to friends as Ted, turned to see Mary and Anders together, leaning out of a ground floor window of the Villa Carlotta, a residential hotel that was home to many actors and where Mary often stayed during that period. "They yelled, *Ted!* It was joyful to see people I knew from New York who were friends. Mary had this lovely smile. I'll always remember how she looked. I wanted to park my car and get out and beat on the door!"

"I knew she was in love with this guy," Westheimer says. But the relationship was unlikely to advance since Anders, too, was gay. Mary may not have known, but certainly it was obvious to some. Anders once even described himself as "the most effete young man that ever existed." Reid, who decades later visited Anders several times at the Actors Fund Home in Englewood, New Jersey, where Anders spent his last years, says, "Mary would have loved him and he would have loved her, but it was one of those theatre friendships, nothing more than great pals. I'm sure she understood the scene." He remembers Anders as "a wonderful man, entertaining and so funny—the most amazing raconteur I've ever known. And he was a very good person. He told me he put four or five young men through college. He said, 'I've got one thing I'm proud of—I got them all through college.'" Anders died in 1981 at ninety-two.

This relationship was not meaningful to Mary beyond the 1940s, although in 1951 Anders came to see her at the La Jolla Playhouse where she was playing in *Ring Around the Moon*. Mary remained sufficiently fond of Anders that shortly before she died, recording notes for a possible autobiography, she included a story he liked to tell about working with Bankhead in *They Knew What They Wanted* in London. "Every time Miss Bankhead went out the stage door of the theatre, there were always fans lined up. She'd wave and sometimes stop and sign an autograph. One matinee, she'd had a hard night the night before. She thought, Oh, she'd have to run the gamut of these fans down the stage door alley, so she put on her hat, pulled it down, turned up her coat collar because she knew she looked pretty peculiar, and went out the stage door alley to her waiting car, quite quickly waving her hands and saying [to fans], 'Bless you, darling, bless you, thank you so much, bless you, bless you.' Got in the car, slammed the door, turned around—and there hadn't been a soul there."

Though in many ways Mary's manner practically defined a camp sensibility, she did not revel in the gay identity of the men in her company—simply because most never came out to her. In fact, Mary sometimes felt safe speaking snidely of gay men and lesbians in their company. Larry Guittard says, "I can remember her making anti-gay cracks of a minor nature, smart sentences that I think of as George Kaufman-isms. Absolutely, she could be judgmental for people who didn't meet her standards. And they were very high. But Mary's standards were mainly for herself. If she liked you, she didn't worry about stuff like that. Like everybody, these things are flexible. With her, I never felt that—but we never talked about it." He does not know if she knew he was gay. "She certainly never used the word faggot. She would just say droll things about people, suggesting she didn't think it was the very best idea in the world. But I don't think she was prejudiced *in fact*. It didn't change [the way she treated me]. Either she trusted you or she didn't. And she trusted me."

Malcolm Goldstein had lunch at the Polo Lounge in Beverly Hills with Mary and Anne and Irving Schneider in the 1980s. During the meal, Mary described someone as "queer as an eight-dollar bill." "One of us said, 'The phrase, Mary, is 'queer as a *three*-dollar bill,'" to which Mary quickly retorted, "Haven't you heard of inflation?" Goldstein thinks Mary's punch line was spontaneous, that she was familiar with the phrase but simply misspoke, and that she did not intend to be mean-spirited. "I don't think she thought of [gay people] as any different from anybody else. I really don't think that was a big deal with her. She wasn't hostile to gay people at all." Likewise, Mary Jackson did not perceive Mary as judgmental of gay people. She suspects Mary simply felt sorry for herself that so many of the men who interested her were gay.

Jerry Berger is less charitable in his recollections. A longtime columnist for the *St. Louis Post-Dispatch*, Berger is well known in Mary's hometown, where he also managed media relations for the Muny from 1968 to 1978. "Mary was very homophobic. She always talked about 'pansies.' She'd start to say the word fag but it would trail off; she wouldn't quite finish the word. The way she did it was very derogatory, almost contemptuous. Like, 'Oh, isn't he one of *those!?* Isn't she one of *those?'* Maybe it was fashionable among some straight people in those days to be homophobic, but a lot of [what Mary said] was unacceptable even in that era," says Berger. ("Pansy" certainly was part of the vernacular in Mary's world when she was younger; in a 1948 letter to her, George Kaufman uses it to describe the producer Arnold Saint Subber.) Because of his role as press agent, Berger, who is gay, did not challenge Mary. "You want to make the client or performer as comfortable as possible. You'd never do anything to challenge them, because you're worried about the next interview or the next favor you might ask." How could Mary reconcile hostility toward gay people with the great number of gay men she surrounded herself with? In this regard, Berger likens her to Ethel Merman, who had a substantial gay following. "And yet she stood on the rehearsal platform and yelled to me, '*Jeh-errrrrr*—have you ever seen so many faggots in your life?' *In front of them.* I was humiliated." In Mary's case, "She didn't want to know. She swept things like that [away]."

Many people who knew Mary wondered over the years if she was lesbian. Numerous people raised the possibility in interviews even before they were asked for any thoughts on her sexuality. As Berger puts it, "Being very masculine, having absolutely no interest in the opposite sex, *abhorring* children, probably the butchest actress I've ever seen next to Patsy Kelly, maybe she was closeted all along." Iggie Wolfington thinks that those who wondered if Mary was lesbian did so because she never married, "but also because she became so staunch. After a while, the parts you play affect your life. They do. I can see how [some came to think this]." It is possible that Mary was lesbian and that, given the time and place in which she grew up, she could not allow herself to express or explore that part of her identity. Like many women of her generation, Mary may have associated any romantic feelings for women with such shame that she could not permit them to surface. Lesbian or not, had Mary been born forty or fifty years later, she would surely have lived a life of less sexual repression. "One or two people sort of asked me [whether Mary was lesbian] much later, but in the days when we were young, that really never came up," says Anne Kaufman Schneider. "That would be like saying, 'Are you going out with Kendall Clarke? He's gay.' It's not even that people were closet-y, they were just *private*. So we would never, ever have discussed that." But her guess is that Mary was not lesbian. "To me, she was so uptight—repressed, even—that, if she couldn't get it together with men, the whole idea [of sex with women] would have been anathema to her."

Lucie believes that Mary, sexually, simply "was neither here nor there. Maybe because of her religion and the era she was born in, it was just taboo and she wasn't happy with either one of the options. Certain people just [say], 'I'm not happy with the options. I can't go against my morals, so I'll just deal with it.' I don't think she had romances with men. Maybe she had a great relationship in her life that I don't know about. I hope so. But it was very private if she did." To Larry Guittard, Mary "never opened up in terms of her 'personal-personal' life and never talked about relationships. Never," he says, laughing at the thought. He vaguely remembers her referring to a romance from her past, "one man somewhere along the line," but he can't recall exactly when she said it took place. "We talked honestly about stuff, but we never talked about sex or boyfriends or about what her sexuality was or wasn't or any of that." He observes that, even professionally—and even early in her profession—"Mary was sort of a non-sexual personage. But if you put certain thoughts together, you could say, yes, definitely, gay tendencies there. It was certainly possible that she was a suppressed gay person. On the other hand, I have no reason to know that or not know that."

Even Emily Daniels, one of her closest friends in Mary's last years, does not know what role romance or intimacy played in Mary's life. "I think she just accepted that she was just not going to meet somebody and dealt with it. I never heard her mention anything about men or love affairs or anything like that. She went out a lot and I don't know who they all were, but I know some of them were gay." During their friendship of more than sixty years, Amy Jane Ax says Mary never voiced regret at not having married. But, amazingly, Ax never asked her about it— purposely. "Mary just did not appeal to men in that way," Ax says. "I felt that she would like to marry, and if she couldn't, then I didn't want to make her feel bad."

Today, if Mary is widely presumed to have been lesbian it is less because of anything observed while she was alive than because of something published after she died. In about 2002, Mary's entry in Wikipedia,
the Internet-based reference database, was changed to describe her as
"lesbian" and "the longtime companion of playwright Abby Conrad."
Neither statement was true. Certainly, no person by the name Abby Conrad was ever part of Mary's life. There is no reliable record that any
playwright by this name even exists. Wikipedia users who monitor content for accuracy have removed this line numerous times, only to see it
reappear. Wikipedia's platform, which permits most entries to be edited
by anyone, has made it difficult to identify the user who continues to
post this misinformation, so the motive for perpetuating this fiction is
unclear. The website has often been criticized for allowing misinformation to be promulgated as fact; enabling this report about "Abby Conrad"
to appear regularly over the course of ten years is a good example of this
flaw.

CHAPTER TWELVE

Nurses, Nuns, and Housekeepers

Nuns in Hollywood movies are nicer, braver, wittier, tougher and sometimes even sexier than other women, with the implication that nuns are fun. Actresses playing nuns are probably only marginally better than the other way around.

—RONALD BERGAN, "The Nosy Nun Next Door," Mary's obituary in the *Guardian*

IT'S ONE OF THE MOST MEMORABLE SCENES OF HER CAREER, BUT nothing about it was as it seemed. In *The Trouble with Angels*, Mary plays Sister Clarissa, an earnest but unconventional nun at a Catholic girls' school that is turned upside down by two mischievous students. Sister Clarissa is the school's physical education instructor, and when the two girls begin flailing during a swimming lesson, the script called for Mary to jump into the pool in full, flowing nun habit to rescue them.

Unfortunately, Mary had never learned how to swim. When she confided this information in advance to producer Bill Frye, he arranged for her to take lessons at a local YMCA to prepare for the shoot. The scene was to be filmed at the Westlake School for Girls in the Holmby Hills section of Los Angeles (today, the co-educational Harvard-Westlake School). The day of the shoot, Mary was standing by in her habit, director Ida Lupino was providing the set-up, and the two girls were positioned in swim suits on the diving board for their next move, when Frye got a phone call from the set. It was about Mary. "I got myself there very fast. Ida said, 'Darling, this silly little bitch can't even jump in the pool.' I said, she'll *have* to jump in the pool. But she just couldn't do it. She was absolutely petrified. Now here you think, Tough Old Mary. But she said, 'I'm scared to death of water. I'm afraid I'll sink.'"

Frye was angry, but salvaging the scene was a higher priority than extracting explanations from Mary. The fastest solution was to hire a stunt double. "Naturally, we didn't have a [stunt]man her height standing by to put into the habit and all of that. I had to call Screen Extras Guild. It held us up and everybody was very, *very* upset with her. Why wouldn't they be? It cost us thousands of dollars, for chrissakes. You'd be upset if you were the producer. I had to go back to the studio and they said, I thought you gave her lessons. What do you think Frankovich [Mike Frankovich, head of production at Columbia Pictures] was saying? 'What the hell are you hiring another stunt person for?'" The stuntman donned a habit and jumped in the pool, photographed from behind so that filmgoers would believe he was Mary. Off-camera, two crewmembers walked Mary gingerly into the shallow end of the pool, each holding one of her arms. There, she stood in about three and a half feet of water and crouched down until the water came up to her neck, creating the impression she was in the pool's deep end, as the story required. Lupino restricted the shot to the desired close-up of Mary's flustered expression, careful not to capture the men standing beside Mary in the water. When Lupino had the shot, the men then walked Mary out of the pool.

The scene now had to be re-classified as a stunt for union purposes, further increasing costs. "One thing escalated to another. She was on my shit list for some time," said Frye. He was flummoxed. Having worked with Mary on the TV show *Halls of Ivy*, he knew she took her assignments seriously, so what happened? "I gave her all these lessons. Of course, I never went to see that she was actually taking them. I'd say, 'How you coming?' She'd say, 'Oh, wonderful, it's helping me so much' and so forth. I'd promised Ida Lupino that all was well in preparing for that scene and it never entered my mind that Mary wouldn't be able to do it."

It was, in fact, fear that prevented Mary from learning to swim, as she said. But it was not fear of sinking; instead, it was fear of others learning about the mastectomy she had undergone only three years before. Swim lessons would require exposing her swollen left arm, which she still kept wrapped in an elastic bandage to control swelling from lymph fluids, and she could not risk questions or gossip. So great was Mary's desire to hide her mastectomy that, even though she was now cancer free, this consummate professional made a conscious decision to let her co-workers down rather than reveal her condition. Once she decided to mislead her colleagues about learning to swim, she was compelled to maintain the charade publicly. Soon after, she told a reporter that she learned to swim for this film, something that she had simply never had the time or opportunity to learn before, and bragged that she was a "card-carrying member of the YMCA" because of it.

The Trouble with Angels is notable in Mary's life beyond this incident. Sister Clarissa is one in a long sequence of nurses, nuns, and housekeepers that ensured Mary employment in her sixty-year career. Mary played these roles more than any other types, followed only by landladies and spinsters. They defined her professionally—hers was a career spent wearing mostly black or white—and Mary, in turn, defined the genre: the put-upon but lovable housekeeper; the no-nonsense nurse; the rigid nun; the officious landlady; the spinster aunt; the man-hungry neighbor; the haughty society matron; the nagging wife. Her nurse and housekeeper roles were not only limiting by type, but within the type, too. It sometimes was not enough to cast Mary as merely the housekeeper; often, she had to be the spinster housekeeper, or the eavesdropping housekeeper. Screenplays called on her to eavesdrop in *Fate is the Hunter*, *I'll See You in My Dreams*, *The Sins of Rachel Cade*, and *White Christmas*, among others. Television scripts called for her to eavesdrop in *Studio One*'s "Mrs. Hargreaves," *Mrs. G. Goes to College*, and (often) *Father Dowling Mysteries*. One of the reasons nurse, nun, and housekeeper roles were important to Mary is that she was so often rejected for other parts. The occasions in which she was able to play something other than a nurse or housekeeper are so few that they come to mind quickly: an eccentric, kleptomaniac cousin on *The Waltons*; a welfare case worker in *Dance with Me, Henry*; a lab technician on *Kolchak: Night Stalker*; a secretary drunk on champagne in *How to Murder Your Wife*; an operator of a roadside diner in *Willa*; a machine-gun toting secret agent on *Matt Houston*.

Privately, Mary revealed resentment throughout her career about how narrowly the industry viewed her range. In 1973, turning down an offer to join San Francisco's American Conservatory Theater company for a second season, Mary reminded director Bill Ball of the diverse summer stock parts she had been playing when they first met in the 1950s. "There's a wide spectrum and I like that feeling. I am not ready to be pigeon-holed as your friendly neighborhood character actress who is so dear with the students. My manner is sometimes my worst enemy because as a person I have no 'side,' and it is sometimes assumed that I am exactly what I look like and that is all," she wrote him. "But I also make up to look like a million in sophisticated roles or musicals. I have chic and style and the gift of being able to wear clothes."

Nonetheless, it's no surprise that in the films Mary cited most often as her own favorites—*Now, Voyager*, *The Trouble with Angels*, and *White Christmas*—she is a nurse, nun, and housekeeper, respectively. Of the three characters, it was the housekeeper's apron that she donned most often. Mary played a maid or housekeeper in scores of film, TV, and stage productions. So closely was she associated with this role that even when her character need not be a housekeeper, such as her semi-regular role in the *Temple Houston* series, she was made a former housekeeper. Mary even played housekeepers on radio, suggesting it was not merely her appearance that prompted casting directors to think of her in this role, but her larger persona. She was Louise, the Archer family maid, in the 1943 CBS radio series *Meet Corliss Archer*, and Malena, the maid, in a 1950 radio version of *Alice Adams* starring Judy Garland. Certainly the maid can occasionally be a central character; after all, Judith Anderson will forever be remembered as the maid in Hitchcock's *Rebecca*, a role that earned her an Oscar nomination. And in *Christopher Bean*, about a painter whose family has little interest in him until he is declared an artistic genius in the wake of his death, Mary's Abby is central to the story, the only person truly devoted to the painter. But most of Mary's housekeepers were peripheral, used for comic relief or to give voice to the folly of a plot point.

Mary found the comedy in housekeeping roles very early in her career. In her first season at the Berkshire Playhouse in 1934, she was cast in eight plays. In four of those, Mary was a maid, in a fifth she was a nurse, and in a sixth a landlady. When *Spring Dance*, a comedy set at a women's college, opened at New York's Empire Theatre on August 25, 1936, one critic observed that "Mary Wickes as the long-suffering maid found no difficulty in raising a laugh merely by walking across the stage." The frequency of Mary's housekeeper roles did not escape notice. A TV critic reviewing a *Shower of Stars* episode in 1955 observed, "Mary Wickes played the maid. She's a good actress, too, and when she writes her memoirs I suspect the title will be 'I Played Maids.' Surely she rates better roles by now."

Mary certainly wanted more, especially early in her career. Happy to be cast in her first TV series, *Inside U.S.A. with Chevrolet*, in 1949, she did not always like her roles in that short-lived variety series. "She'd say, 'Do I have to be a maid *again*?' She got kind of bored with that. She felt she was getting locked into something," says Mary Healy, who starred in the show with husband Peter Lind Hayes. A year later, the couple hired Mary for their next series, *The Peter Lind Hayes Show with Mary Healy*. Theirs was among a small group of pioneering television programs that essentially opened the door for successes like *The Adventures of Ozzie & Harriet* and *I Love Lucy*, which entered right behind. "Every time we got a new show, we tried to find work for Mary. We regarded her with much talent," Healy says. But in this show, too, Mary was the maid, and she did not enjoy the role, Healy says.

Over time, Mary came to accept these seemingly limited roles and even see their value for her. "I just happen to have been given a face which could play an age and any period, and it never bothered me not to have been the romantic leading lady. It has always been my ambition to be the best supporting actress in the business," she told a reporter in 1976. She even approached the situation with some humor. Doing press for the *Father Dowling Mysteries*, in which she played a rectory housekeeper, she joked that the role gave her "some great sweaters to wear." After she played housekeeper to Doris Day in *On Moonlight Bay* and *I'll See You in My Dreams*, Mary joked on Day's radio show, "One more housekeeper and . . . total strangers will stop me on the street and instead of asking for an autograph, they'll hand me a mop and tell me I can have every other Thursday off." And she sometimes took roles that allowed her to poke fun at her persona, such as an episode of *Sanford and Son*, in which she played a maid who was laughably incompetent, or a segment of *The Love Boat* in which she played an imperious woman of wealth who recoils when she learns she has been mistaken for her maid. She had clearly decided to make the most of what is generally a thankless part. "She was always looking for whatever she could do with a refrigerator. Or a vacuum. Or answering the front door. Or carrying some ungodly thing. Whatever little trick. She was always busy thinking of Mary Wickes," says producer Bill Frye. He is not critical when he says she tried to expand these parts; in fact, he points out that any successful actress (he names Bette Davis and Tallulah Bankhead) would do the same thing. "Mary had plenty of ideas. The director used to say, 'Jesus!' I'd say, Oh, well, go along with it."

But even when she was content to play domestics, the going was not always easy. Mary was fond of her role as housekeeper to the Hall family in *Halls of Ivy*, a rather highbrow 1954-55 series featuring former silent film star Ronald Colman and his wife, Benita, as the distinguished president of Ivy College and his wife. It was an erudite show based on a radio series of the same name, in which the maid was played by Elizabeth Patterson. In fact, many of the show's stories were taken directly from the original radio scripts, which were adapted into teleplays. But as TV casting began, in real life "the Colmans were living in a magnificent English Tudor house with a cook, a governess, a butler, a chauffeur and a maid and were not quite living down to reality about playing a part, because

Benita said [haughtily], 'But dear, isn't she a rather *unattractive* house-keeper for us? For *the Colmans*?' I said, it's not the Colmans, for Chris-sakes, Benita. It's the Halls," says Frye. "I don't even think we ever put Mary in a uniform—she was always in a housedress like a housekeeper would be, with an apron, and kind of sloppy. Well, of course, that wasn't Benita's idea of how they should live."

Mary's first prominent housekeeping role in film was in *The Decision of Christopher Blake*, based on a play by Moss Hart. Mary's role, which does not appear in the play, was written specifically for her. She was house-keeper to a divorcing couple in a dispute over custody of their thirteen-year-old boy, and she has some nice scenes. In one, when young Chris-topher asks Mary nonchalantly if she is married, Mary responds, "No," with a tone and inflection that conveys in one word both disappoint-ment and puzzlement, as if she cannot figure out why. Later, her matter-of-fact character endears the audience to her when she tells the boy's mother, "I've never been divorced, Mrs. Blake, on account of I never was married. But if anybody asks my opinion, I usually give it to them, come what may. That boy's been moping around here all morning, and if you don't tell him soon what's going on, I will." The film is distinguished by the boy's elaborate dream sequences; in one, Mary appears as his wife, all frills and bows and bobby socks.

The picture was directed by Peter Godfrey, whom Warners assigned after suspending Irving Rapper, the intended director, over casting dis-agreements. "He wanted Gary Cooper and Norma Shearer. And the stu-dio said, 'You'll do it with Robert Douglas and Alexis Smith.' So he came back with an alternate—Joel McRae and Barbara Stanwyck. And they said, 'No, you'll do it with Robert Douglas and Alexis Smith.' And he re-fused. Rapper felt this was a very serious piece, an important piece, and I believe he felt he wouldn't get that with Alexis," says Ted Donaldson, who played the boy. "It definitely would have been a different film had he done it. Peter [Godfrey] was a nice, nice man, but we were rather left on our own so far as the character and interpretation went. His forte was placement, positioning, a good visual sense, and good business sense. We kind of had to work things out by ourselves. Rapper would have had an intense and much more serious approach to it. He would have been very hands-on and right 'in there.'"

In Hart's original play, called simply *Christopher Blake*, the boy ulti-mately decides to live with his father. But in a cowardly nod to the times and to the repressive Production Code, the film is given a contrived and saccharine ending: The divorcing parents reunite for the sake of their son. This was not the only concession to censors. A scene in which the boy engages in horseplay with Mary's character by wrapping her dishtowel around his neck is eliminated to avoid offending the public by alluding to teen suicide.

One of Mary's most enduring housekeeper roles is Emma, who keeps order at a small Vermont inn in *White Christmas* in 1954. The picture promised to be special from the start. It was the first film shot in VistaVision, the widescreen high-resolution technology that Paramount developed to help Hollywood's film studios compete with television. It was directed by Michael Curtiz, whose successes included *Casablanca* and *Mildred Pierce*. It brought together some of the biggest names of the day: Bing Crosby, Danny Kaye, Rosemary Clooney, Vera-Ellen, and Dean Jagger. (The Danny Kaye role was intended for Donald O'Connor, who was forced to withdraw because of illness.) Songwriter Irving Berlin would occasionally be on the set. And *White Christmas* was a reworking of an earlier film that was already popular, *Holiday Inn*, which about twelve years before had featured Crosby and Fred Astaire. The *White Christmas* cast expected the picture to do well, but none of them realized it would become a part of American pop culture decades later, Clooney says. The sentimental story about a small group of entertainers who secretly bring Army veterans to a small New England inn to cheer their retired general at Christmas has touched a chord with American moviegoers in the generations since.

Except for scenes at a train station, the picture was filmed entirely on the Paramount lot, falling snow and all. Clooney remembers a businesslike set with little time for socializing. Instead of having lunch at the studio commissary, each day Mary brought her lunch, a sandwich made by Isabella. For her part, as soon as she completed her scenes, Clooney was shuffled off to a rehearsal hall for other work. The same pace held true for young Anne Whitfield, who played Susan, the general's granddaughter. "I was fifteen at the time, constantly going back and forth between my teacher and the set, and I just didn't get to know anybody very well," she says. Whitfield had not wished to pursue an acting career; she was an obedient child who sought to please a stage mother. As Annie Phillips, she later became an environmental educator for Washington State, specializing in clean water issues.

The picture was really Crosby's. "Everybody sort of took, not orders, but the tone of behavior, from Bing. That applied to Danny, certainly," Clooney says. "Mary was outrageous, but she was just one of the boys— she would give as good as she got. She was wonderful with Bing and would break him up constantly. It was really a wonderful thing to be around. Everybody kind of gathered around when they had a scene together because they were hysterical." But having Crosby drive the film meant the production was subject to his moods, and he was not in his best humor during this picture. Whitfield remembers Kaye as "terrific," Clooney and Vera-Ellen "pre-occupied with their personal lives," and Crosby as "a grouch." "He had a lot of back trouble and a lot of pain, and he also had a lot of personal stuff," Whitefield says. Indeed, shooting had been postponed from January 1953 to mid-August because of the November 1952 death of Crosby's wife Dixie, and it was on the set of *White Christmas* that Crosby met Kathryn Grandstaff, who would become his second wife. Early in the production, Whitfield approached Crosby because "I really liked a movie he had made called *Little Boy Lost* that had no music in it, a very quiet kind of human story. I thought he had done a great job and wanted to compliment him, but he just shoved away my comments and said [annoyed], 'Oh, Jesus Christ, I didn't do one god-damned thing [on that]' and looked away. I never wanted to approach him again after that, and didn't really have any opportunity, even though we were in the same scenes. He just wasn't really talking to anybody."

Whitfield had performed in many live radio shows before this, but *White Christmas* was her first film. "I didn't really enjoy it a lot. I didn't know why my character was there. I didn't seem to be adding anything to the plot. I was very much a side-liner, kind of a watcher," she says. She also did not care for Curtiz. The only direction he gave her during the whole production was to her and Mary together in advance of an emotional moment in the story: In his thick Hungarian accent, he told them, "Two girl have small tear."

For Mary, the picture was a pleasant experience. Curtiz had worked with her at least twice before this—he directed *The Story of Will Rogers* and *I'll See You in My Dreams*—and Clooney says, "I know that Mike had nothing but respect for Mary. I think he was more respectful of her work than anyone else's in the picture." One of Mary's most memorable scenes was not scripted. "There was a scene where Danny, Mary and Bing are in the lobby of the inn, and suddenly they have the information they need for something—I forgot what it was, in such a convoluted script—and Danny gave her a kiss and started away. Then Bing gave her a kiss and said, 'Wait a minute!' and went back for another kiss, which was hysterical. That was in the picture, but it was not in the script," Clooney says.

The picture completed shooting in late 1953 and premiered at Radio City Music Hall in 1954. It was shown in VistaVision then and at other special events, but because the technology required complicated projection equipment, most viewers since have seen it only in a conventional format. Mary herself enjoyed the film so much that as late as 1992, she still occasionally popped in a videotape of it, and complained that TV showings were insufficiently promoted.

For Mary, *White Christmas* came on the heels of two other strong housekeeper roles. In *On Moonlight Bay* (1951) and its sequel, *By the Light of the Silvery Moon* (1953), Mary played Stella, the wisecracking housekeeper to an early twentieth-century homespun Indiana family. The nostalgic films, musicals based on Booth Tarkington's Penrod stories, featured Doris Day, Gordon MacRae, Leon Ames, and Rosemary DeCamp. *Moonlight Bay* began production in January 1951. Mary arrived in early January from New York, where in preparation for the big move west she had begun closing the apartment she shared with Isabella. This would be the first picture she would complete as a California resident, and she is visible throughout it. She has some interesting scenes, like giving Doris Day's tomboy character a cold alcohol rub after a leg injury, but she is mostly relegated to approaching the kitchen's swinging door with a tray of china or dessert at the moment someone else happens to push through from the other side. She was paid $750 a week for three weeks. By comparison, DeCamp received $1,000 per week and Ames $1,500 a week, each of them for five weeks.

The folksy *Moonlight Bay* was so popular that it inspired a sequel with the same cast, *By the Light of the Silvery Moon* (or, as DeCamp referred to it, "Moonlight Bay Strikes Back"). Mary's bits are more interesting this time. She has the film's opening lines, introducing the story as a narrator of sorts. She dances with MacRae in the kitchen, sings a little bit, and has some pratfalls on an ice-rink. She wrestles in the kitchen with a live turkey, the intended Thanksgiving meal. "I managed to pick up the bird safely and do the exit. It isn't easy because turkeys have claws on the backs of their ankles with which they can scratch you pretty good. The next day when the scene was seen by Mr. Warner in the rushes, he liked it so much he wanted the director to take some closer shots of me and the turkey. Fine. The prop man brought in the turkey, we did the dialogue, I picked up the turkey and exited," Mary said. "The director said, 'Cut! We have to do it again.' The turkey's wattles were not red enough to match the long shot of the day before."

One of the more unusual cleaning persons Mary played was a character in a 1984 stage production of *Detective Story*, the drama by Pulitzer Prize winner Sidney Kingsley about a cruel, unforgiving police officer who discovers his wife has secretly had an abortion. The original cleaning person was a male janitor named Willy. For this production, the role was enlarged and changed to Willie, a cleaning woman, mostly by assigning her lines from characters that had been eliminated, as well as ad-libs suggested by Mary herself during rehearsals. "It just sort of happened naturally," she said, noting that a writer was not hired to adapt the part. "For about two weeks of rehearsals, I just sat and watched the show, watched everybody else, and I'd make notes about where I thought, still keeping faith with the author's intention, the character could be used. She doesn't have much to say to them but you can tell that her sympathy is a bit with the underdog. We had set a deadline whereby, if by that deadline it wasn't coming to fruition, I would be free to leave, no hurt feelings, it just didn't work. But it's worked beautifully, I must say." The show, starring Charlton Heston and Mariette Hartley, played first in Los Angeles and then in Denver and was well received. One critic noted that the changes in the play's structure "give us a chance to watch the wonderful movie actress Mary Wickes steal some limelight in a cameo role with a minimum of lines. She is a pro who proves there are no small roles."

The most cherished character in Mary's retinue of domestics was not a housekeeper per se, but a governess by the name of Mary Poppins. Today's audiences know the character best from the 1964 film that introduced Julie Andrews as a whimsical, relentlessly cheery governess to the Banks family of Cherry-Tree Lane. But it was Mary who introduced the British nanny to the American public in a live one-hour television drama fifteen years earlier.

Mary had already appeared in several live television dramas when she was offered the lead role in this *Studio One* presentation in December 1949 (in fact, she had appeared in *Studio One*'s debut episode the year before). But this character resonated with her, so she prepared especially earnestly. She referred to an illustrated hardback of *Mary Poppins*, the children's story by Pamela Travers on which the teleplay was based, carefully noting references to Poppins's appearance, such as this bit on page six: "Jane and Michael could see that the newcomer had shiny black hair—'Rather like a wooden doll,' whispered Jane. And that she was thin, with large feet and hands and small, rather peering blue eyes." And she noted this reference on page sixteen that would be useful in costuming: "So Mary Poppins put on her white gloves and tucked her umbrella under her arm—not because it was raining but because it had such a beautiful handle that she couldn't possibly leave it at home. How could you leave your umbrella behind if it had a parrot's head for a handle? Besides, Mary Poppins was very vain and liked to look her best." Mary's appearance and temperament were ideally suited to Poppins. As the teleplay opens, an obviously windblown Mary arrives to care for the Banks children dressed in a straw hat decorated with flowers, long woolen scarf and gloves, hair in bun, umbrella in hand, high-ankle black shoes, dark overcoat, and carpet bag. Mary's Poppins is terse, stern, and matter of fact—almost severe—yet she clearly has the children's interests at heart and will be an advocate for them. Sliding up the banister is the first sign that something is amiss, but only the children seem to notice.

Mary was paid $500 for the performance, including a week of rehearsals. The show featured E. G. Marshall and Valerie Cossart as Mr. and Mrs. Banks, and child actors Iris Mann and Tommy Rettig as Jane and Michael, the Banks children. It featured several moves that were tricky for a live production, such as affixing Mary to a large hook that would transport her in the air across the soundstage.

The show was broadcast from CBS Studio 42 above Grand Central Station. It aired December 19, 1949, and was a resounding success. "I liked the script to begin with, but I really wasn't expecting much of a show out of it when it started," says Paul Nickell, who directed this and about a hundred and forty other *Studio One* episodes. "But it grew and grew and grew and in the end, I just loved it. I was very pleased with it and I can't say that about all of them." The show drew what CBS said at the time was the greatest amount of fan mail it had received for any program in this burgeoning medium. Sherman Marks, who was directing Mary in *Inside U.S.A.* at the time, telegrammed her immediately after the show: "Congratulations. I know 'Mary Poppins' has made radio and movies a thing of the past." Indeed, Marks himself would soon find a prolific directing career in television.

Mary took great pride in Poppins and prominently displayed in her apartment a large photo of herself in costume. "God, was she proud of that," says Max Showalter. "'*I* was the original Mary Poppins—nobody did it before me!'" She wanted to repeat the performance, and tried for years to interest producers. Because the original was broadcast on CBS, when TV viewing increased dramatically, it was CBS Television that Mary pursued first about mounting another production. In 1955, she wrote Hubbell Robinson Jr., vice president in charge of national programs, who confirmed that another teleplay was in the making and assured her that CBS would give her every consideration when the production finally came together. Nothing came of that effort, so two years later, she approached CBS again, this time sending the original script and photos of her as Poppins to producer Martin Manulis. The reply came from Dominick Dunne, who told Mary that the story was unavailable to Manulis's group because producer Paul Gregory had the rights and intended to produce it as a CBS special the following season. Mary must have continued pressing, because a year later Manulis sent Mary good luck wishes on Poppins, saying, "I'd give you a double A for effort."

She even talked with Walt Disney himself about producing the story as a film. The first time, in 1958, while filming several episodes of the TV series *Zorro* on the Disney lot, Mary was having lunch in the studio commissary when Walt Disney came in. "I kind of smiled at him and he said, 'May I join you?' I said, 'Oh, please.' He sat down and we chatted and he was talking about looking for properties." She pushed *Mary Poppins* so enthusiastically that she came to believe it was she who got him to proceed with the project, although she acknowledged at least once that someone else had already mentioned it to him. In fact, he first learned of the book when he found it on the nightstand of his young daughter Diane.

It was not until 1960 that Pamela Travers finally agreed to work with Walt Disney Studios, after several meetings with Walt and his brother Roy in both the United States and the United Kingdom. The studio, of course, turned the story into a full-length musical film starring Julie Andrews, who was twenty-five years younger than Mary, and Dick Van Dyke. This production brought Andrews wide success and—in her first film appearance—an Academy Award as Best Actress. "It broke my heart when it was finally made and I didn't have a part in it," said Mary, who forever felt that her own contribution had been overlooked. Again and again, she reminded others that it was she who originated the role; that she helped persuade Walt Disney to make the film; that she should have been featured in it; and, especially, that the final version was an inappropriately saccharine rendering of the character. "She wasn't bitter, but she was disappointed when Mary Poppins turned out in the movie to be fluff. Mary Poppins, the real character, is not a nice lady, and Mary made her nicer than the books. Mary didn't like that the original story was changed that much," says Judy Sutter Hinrichs, a friend from St. Louis.

In this, Mary was not alone. "I just can't understand the Julie Andrews casting at all. It's completely beyond me why Mary wasn't even considered for it, as far as I know," says Nickell. "She really understood it. It just struck me as Julie Andrews being wrong. It seems to me Julie Andrews would have to be a much more sophisticated kind of character that I don't think Mary Poppins was." Literary purists, too, were upset with the Disney approach. After a conservative educator and politician wrote a syndicated column extolling Disney's efforts to promote clean entertainment, a leading critic of Disney's "debasement" of traditional children's literature replied that Disney "shows scant respect for the integrity of the original creations of authors, manipulating and vulgarizing everything to his own ends . . . The acerbity of Mary Poppins, unpredictable, full of wonder and mystery, becomes, with Mr. Disney's treatment, one great, marshmallow-covered cream-puff." While it is doubtful that Disney ever considered Mary for the leading role, Disney did consider Bette Davis, who would certainly have brought a sterner edge to Poppins—but this was before deciding the film would emphasize singing.

When Mary was not keeping house, it seems she was caring for the sick. She played almost as many nurses as maids. When she was not playing a character engaged in nursing per se, writers still found reason to make her character a nurse. In *Trapper John, MD* ("Hate is Enough"), she is a hospital patient whom viewers learn happens to be the hospital's former chief nurse. She played so many nurses that when writer Malcolm Goldstein arrived at Mary's apartment in the 1970s to interview her for his biography of George S. Kaufman and found her wearing hospital whites, he thought, "Is she dressing for this interview, playing the part?" In fact, she had just returned from a hospital volunteer shift.

The nurse Mary is best remembered for is also the one she most enjoyed playing. In *Now, Voyager*, Mary is an assertive private nurse—"My name's Pickford—Dora, not Mary"—called to a Boston mansion by Charlotte Vale (Bette Davis) to care for Charlotte's cruel mother (Gladys Cooper) and help keep the aging Mrs. Vale's melodramatics at bay. Mrs. Vale has dismissed Mary already, but Mary does not take being fired seriously and remains on duty. "I suspect you're a treasure," Davis's character tells her. With her mother occupied, the shy, neurotic Charlotte is free to blossom into a lovely, confident young woman, giving the film its powerful story of a woman's self-discovery. (The film initially emphasized this transformation even more: One scene that was cut featured Davis lying on a settee in a beauty shop smock, getting a salon make-over while a cosmetician hovers.)

"She had fond memories of *Now, Voyager*—I remember her making a point about that. She said that was her happiest experience—the subject content, the working and the people. She held it very close to her heart," says Mary Kay Stearns, echoing what others say Mary told them. And it's no wonder. Mary was surrounded by star performers (Davis, Paul Henreid, Claude Rains) and famous names of the day (Ilka Chase), she earned $500 per week for the role, and the story was advanced by a hauntingly beautiful Max Steiner score. Seventy years later, at least two elements of the film remain pop culture touchstones: Its last line ("Don't let's ask for the moon—we have the stars"), and the sensual lighting of a cigarette. Intended to show the growing intimacy between Davis's and Henreid's characters, the scene initially called for Henreid to offer Davis a cigarette, take one himself, light his, then take her cigarette out of her mouth, give her his and put hers between her lips. "The idea of a shared cigarette was right, but the procedure was too long, too clumsy," Henreid recalled. When he and his wife, Lisl, wanted to smoke while driving, one would often light two cigarettes and put one into the other's mouth, a trick Henreid proposed to Davis before rehearsals. "She immediately recognized the significance and allowed her hand to touch mine. It was just right." But director Rapper—whom Henreid strongly disliked—resisted. Davis phoned producer Hal Wallis and asked him to visit the set to see both versions. Wallis loved the adaptation, which quickly became cinematic shorthand for sexual foreplay.

At one point, J. L. Warner raised concerns about how long the picture was taking to complete. Rapper replied: "I've always brought my productions in on schedule. Unfortunately, on this script I was given a week less time even though I have twenty-five pages more than my last script. Most of our scenes are comparatively short sequences which necessitate numerous production problems of major camera, wardrobe and make-up changes. And above all, Miss Davis is a very slow and analytical lady whose behavior has to be treated with directorial care and delicacy. Believe me, that in itself is a full day's work . . . and I am trying so hard to bring an even finer quality to what I think is the best picture I've made." Davis wore thirty costumes, all designed by Orry-Kelly, more than she had worn in any previous picture. The film was so popular it even inspired a stage spoof decades later. In *How, Now, Voyager*, all the characters except the domineering mother are gay, and Mary's character becomes "Donald 'not Mary' Wickes." But the film meant more to some than others. *Now, Voyager* does not even warrant a mention in the autobiography of John Loder, the British actor who played Elliot Livingston (and who married Hedy Lamarr after Davis introduced them).

At least one nursing role was written specifically for Mary. In a 1975 episode of *M*A*S*H*, Mary is Rachel Reese, the army's most decorated nurse in the Korean War, a force-of-nature colonel so desirous of male affection that she will violate almost any military rule to get it. Reese combines two of the characters Mary often played: the nurse and the man-hungry, unattached woman. Like so many others Mary played, Reese is entirely self-sufficient. She lusts openly for men and makes a play for a main character, Major Frank Burns. When the emotionally needy Burns comes looking for his paramour, Nurse Houlihan, and instead finds Mary in a flowing kimono, Mary calls to him, "Sit down, doll. Come on, hon—you tell the colonel all about it." She eases Frank onto her cot, where she massages his neck, compliments him on his masculine cologne, plies him with brandy, and forces a kiss. When he says, "I wish you wouldn't do that. I hardly know you," she replies, "What's to know? You're a man, I'm a woman, trapped together in the ravages of war." When he continues to resist her clumsy attempts at a kiss, she tells him she can do things for him, like get him a hospital position stateside caring for top military officers. "Come on, pucker up," she commands.

This episode came from longtime writing partners Jim Fritzell and Everett Greenbaum, who knew Mary and had written the work on *Mrs. G Goes to College* that earned her an Emmy nomination. "They said, 'We've got a part and we have to use Mary Wickes.' They wrote the part for her," says producer Gene Reynolds. Mary said she found it "hysterical—she really was a funny, funny character." But this is also one of the few regrettable moments in Mary's career, even if it's not certain Mary ever saw it that way. The episode presents a surprisingly cavalier attitude about sexual violence against women. When Houlihan walks in on Burns and Mary kissing, Mary bolts up and screams, "Rape!" to avoid being detected as the real seducer. Exposing part of a black bra, she tells the gathering crowd, "the man is a savage!" The story boldly reinforces the notion that women often claim rape when it does not happen, but it does not stop there. The episode offers cringe-worthy attempts at comic dialogue, like "I've never been to a rape before" (from the surgeon Trapper John), and "Maybe for your next birthday" (the reply from the surgeon Hawkeye, the show's star), as if watching a rape would be a treat.

But mostly, Mary took her nursing roles seriously. Over the years, she developed great respect for the nursing profession, partly through the many nurses who came to meet her when she performed in *The Man Who Came to Dinner*. She sometimes asked producers if her characters could wear the proper uniform, including cap, to confer that respect. "Of course, I play for laughs, but I refuse to do anything to detract from the dignity of the nurse, who I feel is too often unappreciated. I won't give an inch on that," Mary told one reporter. "I'm no Florence Nightingale, but I couldn't bear to offend the sensitivities of people I admire."

Mary took this desire for authenticity even more seriously with nuns than with nurses. "She would say, 'A nun wouldn't say that' or 'A nun wouldn't do that,' and they would change it," says Madelyn Pugh Davis. Mary played nuns on film, TV, and stage, and excelled at doing so, partly because, off-screen, she often had a nun's manner and disposition. "She reminded me of somebody who might have been a nun. If she hadn't been an actress or if she had been Catholic, she might have been a nun," speculates Harriet Switzer, who came to know Mary through Washington University affairs and is a former nun herself. "She lived at a level of faith that almost maybe had something to do with her being single," she says, suggesting that Mary put so much energy into her relationship with God—and into her career—that she had little left for intimacy with another person

Mary has the opening line in *The Trouble with Angels*, and both this picture and its sequel give her memorable scenes. Sister Clarissa is not just the physical education instructor, but also the school's bus driver. When the bus stalls on train tracks during a cross-country drive with a bus full of girls, Sister Clarissa frantically tries to maneuver the bus out of harm's way, and, in the process, reveals unexpected high-top sneakers under her habit. This instantly establishes her character's practical personality. The sneakers were Mary's idea. "She was driving one day in leather shoes and she said they were slippery. So the next thing I know, she has [the high-tops]. See, this is Mary's thinking, always planning a little something *for Mary*. I saw them, and she said, 'Don't worry—they won't show! They won't show!' I said, 'They'd better not,'" says Frye, the producer. "But when we were shooting it and had to get some brake shots, the cameraman or the director said, 'You know, she's got on those shoes, but it doesn't look bad.' I said, 'Oh, it'll make her happy. Let her have them. I don't care.' It was a nice little touch." For those scenes, Mary had to learn to drive a bus—and this time she took the lessons she said she would. "That means double-clutching, if you know what that means. It means leg and foot cramps of the worst kind!" she said.

But even when she was able to make these characters colorful, a career built on three archetypes meant Mary's range would never be broad. In *The Trouble with Angels*, she was playing a nun from the old school, set in her ways, who does not cope well with either change or strong personalities. Twenty-five years later, in *Sister Act*, she plays virtually the same character—minus the high-tops. The *Trouble* films were box office successes and have remained popular for more than four decades. By 1999, Frye himself had received more than $250,000 in residuals over the years from his 18 percent ownership in the first picture alone. But the films were never received well critically. "The sisters, performed by such old troupers as Mary Wickes, Marge Redmond and Binnie Barnes, seem either deliberate comics or a little weak in the mind. It is not necessary to be foolish in order to humanize a nun. There is so much that is icky in this picture, so much that is redundant and in poor taste, that one can be grateful to be able to enjoy the impudence of Miss Mills," the *New York Times* declared about the first film. Critically, the sequel fared worse. *Variety* dismissed it as "fluff reigns supreme" with "essentially cardboard characters in unreal situations," a film whose "creatures are from another planet."

It was on the *Trouble* pictures that Mary learned to appreciate the habit, partly from Rosalind Russell, who starred as the Mother Superior. (Frye chose Russell after a transatlantic courtship of the reclusive Greta Garbo, his friend, failed to persuade her to return to the screen.) On both productions, Russell, a devout Roman Catholic, instructed everyone in the precise etiquette required to play nuns. "She knew her faith and her religion backward and forward. Some of the things I learned from her, I was able to bring into [the *Sister Act* pictures]," Mary said later. "For instance, that long panel, that's part of the habit, that hangs front and back—you never sit on that. You lift it aside when you sit down. It's important to be correct. I get letters from religious people who notice these things." For the most part, Mary thoroughly enjoyed these roles. "There is a romance about it. There is a tradition," she observed about the sisterhood in general. "I loved playing a nun. I loved being in a habit. It gives you a certain serenity," she once told a reporter. Certainly, she was conscious of how the nun's habit affected those around her. "It's amazing, when you are in the habit you get quieter as far as your gestures are concerned. You find yourself quite relaxed and reposed, which is new for me." At times, she enjoyed it because "you don't have to worry about getting [to the set] early and getting your hair done."

Feeling comfortable in the habit was made easier because Frye commissioned original outfits from one of the most famous fashion designers
of the day, Sybil Connolly, whom he brought over from Dublin. Connolly, perhaps Ireland's top fashion designer, was known for chic linen
gowns (including one worn by Jacqueline Kennedy in a White House
portrait), but she had also created modern habits for religious orders in
Ireland and the United States. For Frye, it was important that the production look good off-camera, too. He had a special wardrobe created for Ida
Lupino to wear on the set. "I had her always in black or white. I bought
four fur coats for her, so that she could wear black or white fur coats and
then black or white pants. It kept everything in black and white, because
the nuns were in black and white. That's the way I like to do things. I
didn't want her coming out in red one day and green print the next and
a brown coat the next." For all the actresses playing the principal nuns,
like Mary, he had special umbrellas designed with black and white polka
dots to keep the sun away. "Who wants just a black umbrella? Big deal,
they cost $35 each, so what? I couldn't have [just Ida] walking around
with it, they'd say, 'Geez, she's the star, how come we don't get one?' So
I gave them all umbrellas."

The attention to costume detail was striking. During breaks between
scenes on location in Santa Fe for *Where Angels Go*, Mary and Barnes
strolled around visiting shops selling Native American jewelry, but often
found crowds looking at them. "People would motion us to the front and
say, 'Go right ahead, Sister,'" she said. While shooting in Philadelphia,
Mary needed dental care. She found a dentist, but not knowing how
long she would be detained, arrived for the appointment in costume. She
got funny looks when people saw a cigarette in her hand (she would stop
smoking for good a few years later), but she also benefitted from acts
of courtesy, such as others letting her on the elevator first. "The dentist
wouldn't believe I wasn't a real nun," she said.

The films did not start so smoothly, especially with regard to the relationship between the star and the director. This was one of Lupino's
few directing assignments in film; most of her directing work had been
in television. Producer Bill Frye recalled: "Roz called me about the fifth
day of shooting and said, 'I think we're going to have to get rid of Ida.
I cannot work with her in the afternoon. She's having these drinks at
lunch.' Now, Roz liked her booze as much as anybody, but Roz never
touched it until she got home. So I had to talk to Ida, who was drinking heavily in those days. She said, 'Who the fuck does she think she
is, that goddamn bag?' and so forth. I said, 'Ida, I'm just telling you,

sweetheart, I'll close production or whatever I have to do until I replace you. I don't *want* to replace you. I had a woman write the story, I had a woman write the script, I had a woman director, I had thirty-five or forty women in it, I had a woman editor, I wanted everything woman.' She came around . . . but there was never a relationship again between Roz and Ida. They wouldn't go to dailies together." When the sequel was made, most of the original cast was invited back, but James Neilson was brought on to direct.

In the sequel, too, Russell exerted a star's power. The story called for the nun played by Dolores Sutton to ride into town on a donkey. In the script, the scene looked like it would work well—too well for Sutton, it turns out. In rehearsals, "It was very funny and everybody laughed when I did it. The next thing I know, it's been cut from me, and Miss Russell had the scene." But the sequel left Mary with some memorable scenes. When the bus runs out of gas in the desert with the vehicle full of schoolgirls, an incredulous Mother Superior (Russell) has this exchange with Mary's Sister Clarissa:

> RUSSELL: But if the gas gauge read empty, why didn't you fill up in the last town, Sister?
> MARY: When it read empty in the old bus, there was still five gallons in the tank. I understood the old bus.
> RUSSELL, *deadpan*: I'd appreciate it if you established a similar rapport with the new bus.

Mary engaged in considerable publicity for these films, both in advance of production and after their release. As a promotion for *Where Angels Go*, Mary toured the country with Binnie Barnes and associate producer Jim Wharton, holding contests to select attractive young women who would appear in minor parts as Catholic schoolgirls. Together, Mary, Barnes, and Wharton flew to seven cities in seven days in July 1967, selecting one winner each in Chicago, Cleveland, Dallas, Indianapolis, Oklahoma City, Philadelphia, and St. Louis. They made appearances on TV and radio and drew attention from local newspapers along the way.

The Trouble with Angels had its global premiere at the grand Fox Theatre in St. Louis. In fact, everything about the opening was grand, with klieg lights in the sky, lots of press, local dignitaries, a formal welcome at the airport for the stars' arrival, and Mayor A. J. Cervantes presenting Russell with a ceremonial key to the city. Lieutenant Governor Thomas Eagleton served as master of ceremonies. At the time, Mary led others to believe St. Louis was chosen because of her influence in Hollywood. "When they were looking around for a site to open this movie, they were considering several different cities and she convinced them to do it in St. Louis," Jack Pirozzi, director of development for Washington University's School of Arts and Sciences, said, echoing Mary. She told him she had told producers, "I'm from St. Louis and St. Louis is a very Catholic city, so there'll be a great deal of interest in a new religious-themed movie, and there are so many girls schools here that I think it would be a great hit." As she wrote studio executive Frankovich, "My home is St. Louis and . . . I'm box office there with a capital 'B.' I'll be glad to do anything I can to help publicize the picture."

But that's not exactly how it happened. Russell had gone to school years before with a woman who was now head of Marymount Academy, a private Catholic girls' school in nearby Florissant (which closed shortly after this event). As a nun, the school head reached out to ask Russell if the film could open in St. Louis as a benefit for the school. Frye had no agenda with regard to where the film opened and was as happy to have it in St. Louis as anywhere. "Mary would have no pull for having the premiere there. But Mary was in seventh heaven," he says. "Well, *my god*, she went back to her home town and the police force was out— gloved guys!" Frye, Russell, and Mary flew together from Los Angeles for the event and, deplaning at the St. Louis airport, "Oh it was funny. Roz got off in a sable coat, naturally, a Galanos dress, red roses. Mary looked very nice behind her. And up comes this sister. *Jesus!* Roz said, 'Jesus Christ, she looks a hundred—they're going to think I'm a hundred years old!' Roz kept her age way back, you see," Frye says.

During both films, Mary spent most of her down time with Binnie Barnes. They got on "like a house-afire," Mary said. Mary did not get to know other cast members, like Marge Redmond, another principal nun in the first film. "I don't know why, really. She went about her business and I went about mine," says Redmond, remembering a busy set without a lot of socializing. Mary did establish a rapport with Russell and, although the two women never became intimates, Mary played a significant role in Russell's life a few years later. Russell suffered from serious health problems, and had both breasts removed due to cancer. Like Mary, she suffered her breast cancer in silence, not wanting the public to know. But when Russell subsequently also developed rheumatoid arthritis, which started to affect her ability to perform in the 1971 film *Mrs. Pollifax, Spy*, she debated going public with her condition to raise awareness. Now she turned to Mary for advice. "Mary told me about conversations she'd had with Roz. She said that she and Roz had some very heart-to-heart talks about this," says Pirozzi, who had been a close friend of Russell since 1968 through channels unrelated to Mary or Washington University. "Roz had a real soul-search: Should I go public with this, because if I do, it may effectively mean the end of my career—which it did. From what Mary said, she encouraged Roz [along the lines of], 'Look beyond yourself and see what kind of greater good you can do for society.' I can just see her giving a pep talk like, 'C'mon on kid, what's gonna have a bigger impact on people's lives, these movies or what you're really trying to do?' Roz was going through a difficult time. She developed a rapport with Mary, and they were friends, and she thought she could turn to her and talk with her. I think Roz had already made up her mind that she was going to do this, but maybe needed support to do it."

Russell did go public, becoming one of the first Hollywood stars to disclose a serious, debilitating condition directly. She raised funds for what became the Rosalind Russell Medical Research Center for Arthritis at the University of California at San Francisco in 1978, two years after her death at sixty-nine. Going public meant attracting significant contributions from high-wattage friends like Frank Sinatra, Gregory Peck, and Jimmy Stewart. By encouraging Russell, "I really think Mary was instrumental in helping to establish this wonderful center that treats rheumatoidal arthritis," Pirozzi says. One of several notes from Russell to Mary offers, in an unsteady hand, "gratitude and love" to "Nurse Mary Nightingale" from "Mother Inferior."

The irony, of course, is that Mary would not speak publicly about her own serious medical conditions. But Mary knew that any disclosures she might make could never have the impact that Russell's would. Mary had less to gain and more at risk than Russell. Among other things, she had to support herself, whereas Russell, married to theatrical producer Freddy Brisson, was not the sole wage earner in her family. "Mary saw that [Roz] is somebody who *could* make a difference, whereas if this wonderful character actress went public and said, 'I have had breast cancer and other kinds of problems,' people would say, 'Oh, that's too bad,' and go onto the next thing," Pirozzi says.

If nurses, nuns, and housekeepers kept Mary working most of the time, landladies filled her dance card completely. It was a landlady who brought Mary her only Emmy nomination. In 1962, she was nominated for Outstanding Performance in a Supporting Role, Actress (this was before the award was bestowed separately for comedy and drama) for playing Winona Maxfield on *Mrs. G Goes to College*, later renamed the *Gertrude Berg Show*. "Maxie" runs the Maxfield Apartments, where she befriends Sarah Green (Gertrude Berg), a widowed grandmother who decides to become a college freshman after twelve years of night school. Maxie is cheerful, neighborly, likes betting on horses, and is happy to get involved in her tenants' problems. She, too, is widowed. She is also lonely and full of advice. For Mary, Maxie was a nice-sized part that allowed her more than a series of sarcastic quips. The show was meaningful for Mary, but it did not last long. It was first broadcast in October 1961 and ended in April 1962, when the cast was told on a Tuesday that Thursday's shooting would be their last. "I'm truly disappointed because I thought we were several cuts above those bum ones that are renewed over and over and over. The bright side is that it did me a great deal of good personally and I am now a nationally known television personality and there I am out of a job," she said at the time.

The awards were presented on May 22, 1962. Mary brought Peter Walker as her escort. They sat close to the podium at a table with June Allyson, Dick Powell, and Rod Serling. Mary was competing against Colleen Dewhurst (for a program called *Focus*), Pamela Brown (*Hallmark Hall of Fame*'s "Victoria Regina"), and Joan Hackett and Jeanne Cooper (both for *Ben Casey*). Though the evening had gone smoothly so far, when actor Walter Brennan announced the nominees, he clumsily introduced her as Mary "Wick-ess." Brown won for her role as the Duchess of Kent. Berg herself was nominated for the equivalent of today's Best Actress in a Comedy Series, but lost to Shirley Booth for the sitcom *Hazel*.

For Mary, getting cast as characters other than nurses, nuns, or housekeepers was not easy. In 1949, she wrote a pilot script for a weekly TV series in which she would star with Hiram Sherman. *Rehearsal for Breakfast* was to follow a weekly show-within-a-show format and feature TV show hosts rehearsing on a soundstage the night before their show's early morning live broadcast—with all sorts of complications ensuing while they put the show together. It went nowhere. In the 1950s, Mary tried unsuccessfully to attract interest in a film that would pair her with James Gleason in a Hildegarde Withers mystery. Withers, a fictional schoolmarm turned amateur detective, had been played by Zasu Pitts and Edna May Oliver in a series of films in the 1930s and 1940s. Mary wanted to star in "The Riddle of the Green Ice," in which Withers tries to solve an emerald heist, but she failed to generate interest. In 1954, she took matters into her own hands and, inspired by a high-end personal shopping service at the Plaza Hotel in New York, wrote a concept for a television show that she called *Mary Go Round*. Mary would star as the proprietor of The Wickes-Works, run from a small office in a deluxe hotel. Each episode would find Mary mixed up with a hotel guest who has sought her help with an odd task. Supporting players would be the bellman, the house detective, the hotel manager, elevator operators, and, of course, housekeepers. She dusted the concept off in the 1970s, renamed it *Donna Quixote* and registered it with the Writers Guild, but neither treatment moved forward.

When Mary did get a role other than nurse, nun, or housekeeper, she usually did well. When the Berkshire Playhouse re-opened in 1946, after the war ended, she was offered the title role in Maxwell Anderson's *Elizabeth the Queen*. The play, first produced by the Theatre Guild with husband-and-wife performers Lynn Fontanne and Alfred Lunt, features the love affair and political battle of wills between England's Queen Elizabeth I and Lord Essex. Not only would Mary be the lead, but it was a dramatic role and the sort of high-profile part for which director Billy Miles normally brought in a star. Stockbridge regular Kendall Clark played Essex opposite Mary, who wore Fontanne's original costumes from Eve's Costumes in New York.

By now, audiences had seen Mary in prominent film roles, but nothing like this. "I was terrified. Audiences have been laughing at me every week in comic roles—I was so afraid they'd laugh at me when I came out dressed as Queen Elizabeth," Mary said. Lenka Peterson, a member of the Playhouse company that summer, says *Elizabeth the Queen* was "about the only time I can remember sensing that she was pretty anxious. There was some tension in rehearsals. She would sort of stop and say, wait a minute, wait a minute, let me go back. She was especially careful, and I think she was very concerned. Other times, she always seemed so loose to me." The show went well, but not perfectly. Mary recalled: "We had a very trying opening nite when an awful lot of things went wrong technically, as well as some of the actors blowing lines. And I remember being really [frustrated] and wishing to heck [in] the middle of the week the critics would come because by then we were giving a show that was really great and I was so proud of. But when you get into something like that, and with a week's rehearsal, and all the costumes and wardrobe changes and set changes and technical things, it's remarkable that things got on as well as they did."

The reviews were kind but restrained. "Because the Berkshires have taken Mary Wickes to their collective heart, with considerable reason, her intriguing and courageous experiment with a highly exacting dramatic role has a tendency to overshadow the production as a whole. This is too bad because Mr. Miles' *Elizabeth the Queen* is an exceptionally fine effort when viewed as a play rather than as a vehicle for Miss Wickes. I have an idea that there was too much build-up, both from an audience standpoint and from that of Miss Wickes," said the *Berkshire Eagle*. The review continued: "Her Elizabeth was always competent and frequently excellent. Judged entirely from last night's performance, she lacked two elements I should say are vital to the best possible performance of the role: the light timbre of her voice weakened the authoritative power of many of the lines, and her stage personality, which has both charm and dignity, did not have the domineering, sometimes ruthless quality it seems to me is necessary to filling in the portrait of a queen who was a queen first and a woman second, though she yearned to have it otherwise. Trying to find out whether reactions spring from intelligence or hope; whether many years of watching an actress in one type of role blinds one to what she can do with quite another type; whether an unusually tense first night is a fair criterion for deciding whether or not somebody should play a role; all these questions tie the mind up in painful knots."

Elizabeth the Queen was memorable, but many times when Mary was not a nurse, nun, or housekeeper, she was under-used and left kind of flailing in the production. *The Actress* is perhaps the best example, since the film gives her not even one line of dialogue. At first blush, Mary's decision to be part of the film appears perplexing, even with a stellar cast that included Spencer Tracy and with director George Cukor at the helm. The story is based on the youth of actress Ruth Gordon, who wanted a career in the theatre, but whose father wanted her to follow in the steps of her gym teacher. During Mary's single scene as an early twentieth-century athletic instructor—a peculiar bit in which, circus-like, she performs a fitness demonstration with Indian clubs—she appears for maybe thirty seconds, smiles broadly but does not speak. Mary spent three weeks on an MGM sound stage practicing twirling the clubs, which are like bowling pins, with a German man who had been a champion in this sport decades earlier. With blisters developing on her hands, she went several times to Cukor and said she felt she could stop. He insisted she rehearse more. "But it was all worth it because Tracy thought it was hysterical—he didn't see any rehearsals, so when we did it for the first time on the set, he fell on the floor," Mary said. Her character, Emma Glavey, was based on Gordon's real life gymnasium teacher, Gertrude Glavin. The chance to work with Cukor, Theresa Wright, and Spencer

Tracy (whom Mary sometimes referred to as the "dream actor of the world") was certainly attractive, as was the promise of prominent billing.

But why would Mary accept a role with no lines at this point in her career? In truth, she did not. Mary filmed a scene of about six pages of dialogue in the restaurant of Boston's Hotel Touraine with Tracy, Wright, and Jean Simmons. The scene took place after the gym exhibition, but it was cut from the final film. "I was always sorry that Mr. Cukor over-shot the film," Mary said. MGM had already asked Gordon to halve her original script, so that the picture would come in at about the same length as her screenplay for *Pat and Mike* (about ninety minutes), but more needed to go. The scene was amusing, as Tracy desperately tries to push his daughter into an athletic career. Mary puts her sherbet spoon down, pushes her chair back from the table in a very business-like manner, and, right there in the restaurant, gives her accidental protégé an unwelcome critique of her posture, before inviting her to enroll in a nearby school to train in physical culture.

The only other films in which Mary had so little to do are the mawkish, plodding *Good Morning, Miss Dove* (1955), and the truly touching *Dear Heart* (1964). In the former, Mary is a small town schoolteacher with hardly a line at all, yet she inexplicably is featured prominently in the film's lobby cards and other promotions. In the latter, Mary is a sour, complaining postmistress, one of three fastidious spinsters attending a convention together. She has only about six lines, but this cranky trio provides an important contrast to Geraldine Page's whimsical, sweet-natured Evie Jackson. *Dear Heart* stands out as one of the superior films of Mary's career. Written by Tad Mosel, directed by Delbert Mann, and produced by Martin Manulis, it holds up beautifully decades later. Mary was paid $3,000 for her small part; the other two spinsters, Alice Pearce and Ruth McDevitt, received $3,000 and $4,500, respectively. (By contrast, Angela Lansbury received $16,000, Page received $100,000, and Glenn Ford received $250,000.)

Mary's part was small, but the production was eventful. This was the last film to shoot in the ornate, regal Pennsylvania Station. Penn station was razed immediately after filming and replaced with today's soulless station of the same name. Much of the production was occupied with hiding Page's pregnancy, which came as a shock to both producer and director the day she showed up for filming. Careful use of camera angles, strategically placed pocketbooks and an assortment of scarves, coats, and flowing dresses hid her soon-to-be twins from filmgoers. Then, during the very last moments of shooting in November 1963, word reached the set that President John Kennedy had been shot. Page had been close to Kennedy, who was expected to name her and husband Rip Torn to head a new national theatre organization, and director Mann knew that once she heard the news, she would be unable to perform the final scene, a dramatic, emotional one. "We had only an hour's work to do, so I decided to try to get the film in the can, to not tell her until the scene was completed," Mann recalled. The crew was instructed to say nothing to her, allowing her to perform as expected, full of the tears and anger required of the scene. Take after take, Page performed spectacularly, until Mann called "Cut. Print. Wrap!" At that moment, she broke into convulsive sobs, having known about the assassination all along, but having decided to suppress her personal pain long enough to finish the film. "It was an incredible exhibition of courage and control," Mann said.

The one type of role that Mary almost never handled well was mothers. Mary may have played the greatest number of childless women in American performing arts history. Even the stern, severe Marjorie Main was given a brood to raise in the *Ma and Pa Kettle* series. But Mary simply did not conjure up any motherly feelings in audiences, so casting directors rarely gave her the chance—and, for the most part, their instincts were right. When Mary did play mothers, she was often ineffective.

For instance, in *Bloodhounds of Broadway*, a 1952 musical comedy about racketeers, Mary is unconvincing as a frazzled working-class mother trying to persuade Bo-Peep Didy Service to take her family's laundry. The shop is a front for gambling operations in the back room, so the counterman tries to tell her that another cleaner nearby would do a better job, but she doesn't understand. Even with a baby carriage behind her and a toddler with sticky hands tugging at her sweater, she suggests nothing maternal. In an exaggerated bowery accent, Mary says, "You ever used that soyvice? Shreds—they send everythin' back in shreds. Don't tell me about 'em. I used them for little Alexander, and what they did!" But that same year, filmgoers saw Mary in one of her few successful roles as a mother. In the little-remembered *Young Man with Ideas*, an overbearing Ruth Roman persuades passive husband Glenn Ford to move their family from Montana to California in hopes that he can become a more successful attorney. Mary is their Los Angeles neighbor, Mrs. Gilpin, a pushy stage mother. She is loud and lively and full of energy—and completely believable as the force behind her little boy, Willis. She ultimately moves her own brood to New York, declaring grandly, "Willis belongs in the legitimate theatre!"

One mother Mary dearly wanted to play was Amanda Wingfield, the fragile Southern matron in Tennessee Williams's semi-autobiographical

The Glass Menagerie. Immersed as she was in the New York theatre community of the 1940s, Mary without doubt saw the show during its now-mythical 1945–46 Broadway run, probably accompanied by Isabella. The obvious, perhaps painful, parallels between Amanda and Isabella, both St. Louis mothers with strong influence over their families, surely did not escape Mary. Laurette Taylor's moving performance in that show has become the stuff of theatre legend; no doubt it stuck with Mary for years.

When Irving Rapper began casting for the film version he would direct in 1949, Mary sought the role. She felt she had a chance, since she had done good work for him in *Now, Voyager* and *Anna Lucasta.* He wrote Mary in early May that he hoped Bette Davis would accept the role, but that she had reservations about playing someone of Amanda's "maturity." But Mary remained sufficiently confident she would get the role that, during visit to St. Louis later that month, she told the *Globe-Democrat* she would start filming it in October. Rapper liked Mary but didn't seriously consider her for the part. Davis accepted *All About Eve,* and Amanda went instead to Gertrude Lawrence, a much bigger star than Mary. (The glamorous Lawrence, perhaps an equally unlikely choice for Amanda, two years later would create the role of Anna in *The King and I* on stage with Yul Brynner.) Just three days before shooting was to begin on *Menagerie,* Lawrence wrote Mary: "Do go after Irving Rapper. He seems very nice." Since the major roles had been cast by this point, it's likely she was encouraging Mary to pursue Rapper romantically. Of course Rapper, like so many in Mary's orbit, was gay.

Mary never forgot the Amanda character, one of the most richly drawn women in American drama, and, eighteen years after this film's release, she finally tackled it. In 1968, she became Washington University's first artist in residence, a short-term position built around a production of *Menagerie,* in which she would star. The suggestion came from Richard Palmer, an English and theatre instructor who had been tasked by the university with bringing Mary back into its good graces. Mary had been nursing resentment toward the university, and "there was some concern on the part of the college as to where it stood in her gift-giving plans. She was always threatening to add Washington University to her will or take it out of her will," Palmer says. "Mary wanted to be wanted. Her disenchantment with the college was initially because she felt they weren't paying as much attention to her they should. She was happy to have the attention." Mary immediately understood that part of his role was to "re-ally" her with the school, he says.

Amanda is most often depicted as something of a villainess, but in Mary's hands, Amanda's humor came out. "She was wonderful and discovered the comedy in the role, which so often is lost," says Palmer, pointing out that Laurette Taylor herself had been known as a comedienne. "I felt that role was perfect for a comedian to do. I think the subsequent productions of it have lost sight of it. Mary and I talked about it in those terms, and she agreed with me. She saw a lot of comedy and potential comedy in the character. She was very pleased with the way it turned out." The show, presented for four performances, was staged in Brown Hall, an aging space that the university replaced with a proper theatre in 1972. In this setting, it must have seemed especially odd when the playwright's mother and brother, Edwina and Dakin Williams, arrived to see the performance. Palmer says they were impressed. Because some believe Mrs. Williams had never accepted the fact that Amanda was based on her, "I think she enjoyed the light touch Mary gave her," Palmer says. Mary's papers contain an undated black-and-white photo of Mary and Tennessee Williams chatting, but Palmer is certain she did not confer with him before these performances.

For Mary, the working experience was generally positive. "The students deferred to her, as they should, and she deferred to the director [the university's Herb Metz], in the sense that she recognized he had the final authority, though she was quite willing to express her opinion about what should be done," Palmer says. Nonetheless, if offering her a chance at Amanda was the university's attempt to bring her back into the fold, it did not entirely succeed, though through no fault of Metz. "The disenchantment went back before that, it was really pre-sixties. Whatever happened was really from the [former chancellor Thomas] Eliot era," says Pirozzi. "For the most part, Herb deferred to her and there were no great problems. A certain amount of friendly grousing behind one another's backs, but they got along OK."

Regardless of type of character she played, Mary was grateful to be employed, never forgetting how much her family's finances suffered during the Depression. In January 1975, she shared this sentiment with George Seaton, director of films ranging from *Miracle on 34th Street* to *Airport*. "Because I know your sleep has been affected by not knowing the play-by-play account of Mary Wickes vs. television pilots, let me say the script never came up to scratch, so the option money was paid. Since then, George, three more pilots have been offered me. I'm not bragging. I'm stunned and consider myself lucky with all of the actors out of work."

CHAPTER THIRTEEN

When Acting Is Everything . . .

SOMETIMES, ESPECIALLY AFTER ISABELLA DIED, IT WAS AS IF MARY PUR-
posely arranged a grueling schedule to avoid being alone. Consider this
eight-week period in a seemingly ordinary summer in 1971. On May
24, she began a four-day assignment on *Here's Lucy*, taping "Lucy and
Her All-Nun Band." While taping, she signed a contract to perform the
following week in an episode of *The Jimmy Stewart Show*, beginning June
2. That job behind her, she flew to Oregon to shoot scenes with Michael
Douglas for Disney's *Napoleon and Samantha* film. She returned to Los
Angeles in late June in advance of her next job, which would begin July
19. But resting in the interim was not an option for Mary. Instead, she
began organizing a bridal shower for Lucie Arnaz, which took place July
17. The following afternoon, Mary boarded a TWA flight to St. Louis,
where she appeared on stage for a week in *The Music Man* with Peter
Marshall.

Singularly devoted to her craft, Mary was happiest when at work.
When not working, she was consumed with lining up her next project.
She did not take jobs for granted. Indeed, Mary's professional drive is
one of first things people mention when asked about her. "She was an
actress from the bottom of her toes to the top of her head. She *loved* doing it, loved everything about being on the set. She especially took a kind
of pride that I admire enormously in being incredibly professional in her
behavior and in what she delivered in the performance," says television
director Joan Darling, whose credits include the iconic "Chuckles Bites
the Dust" episode of the *Mary Tyler Moore Show*. After directing Mary in
an episode of *Doc*, Darling hired Mary for the film *Willa*. "She was the
absolute consummate professional in every possible way. She was an
on-time, prepared, wonderful comedienne who always knew where the
laugh was."

Mary found such joy in her work that, entering rehearsal rooms, she sometimes grandly—and playfully—proclaimed, "It's Mary Wickes, grand old lady of stage, screen and shortwave radio!" As Joe Ross says, "She made up her mind, I am an actress and that was it, full-blast." Tying her identity so closely to professional success produced some peculiar behavior. Mary's pursuit of work was obsessive. She was represented by a succession of agents, but she hounded casting directors and producers herself, at every stage of her career reminding them of her accomplishments with a relentlessness that would embarrass other actresses of her stature. Also, professional slights took on greater significance than they might have for performers with more satisfying personal lives. Mary was quick to see a slight, even when none was there—and even quicker to go to the mat over it. And living for the theatre meant living *with* the theatre, so creating family-like relationships with colleagues became essential. This was not always easy for someone with Mary's strong personality.

When pursuing work, Mary wrote to every leading theatrical and film producer, director, and casting agent of the day, capitalizing any way she could on prior relationships. Her uncommonly aggressive pursuit was something she adopted at the very beginning of her career. For instance, while staying at the AWA Clubhouse in Manhattan in March 1935, her biggest role so far having been as understudy to Margaret Hamilton, she wrote theatrical producer Crosby Gaige for an interview. He didn't bite, but a year later he did cast her in *Larger than Life*, a comedy about a domineering woman who pushes her timid son into marriage. Disappointing tryouts in Springfield, Massachusetts, kept the show from Broadway but paired Mary with Thelma Ritter for the first time. Mary and Ritter, the two premier comic character actresses of the twentieth century, would work together twice more, in a radio version of "Rip Van Winkle" in 1948 and an *Alfred Hitchcock Presents* television show in 1956.

By 1949, since she had already turned in memorable performances for Moss Hart in three stage productions and one film, Mary should have felt no need to remind this leading playwright of her work. But she wrote even him whenever it appeared he might be casting something interesting, such as when he began assembling the musical comedy *Miss Liberty* early in 1949. "I have just about put my toes into the water," he replied. "As soon as we get down to it, which should be in about a week or two, I'll be glad to throw my weight around for you." Three years later, responding to yet another overture from Mary: "Unfortunately, there is nothing in this play, but by God, before you or I die we will do one together."

Clearly, Mary's persistence annoyed some directors. When she wrote Michael Curtiz in 1949 reminding him of her credits, the director of *Casablanca* and *Mildred Pierce* told her, "There is no need to trouble yourself to come in on an interview. I know your work well. I have put your letter in my desk file, and if anything turns up, I will certainly call you." He would, in fact—twice. Curtiz later used her in *White Christmas* and *I'll See You in My Dreams*. Typical of Mary's pursuit was this exchange with producer Josh Logan. Logan, who had directed Mary on stage in *Stars in Your Eyes* in 1939, received this request in 1963: "Please consider me for the wise-cracking secretary in *Ensign Pulver*. I really am a darned good actress and I would so like to work with you again. I've been digging in the Diamond Mines out here lately . . . most recently the film of *The Music Man* and the Gertrude Berg series on television, for which I was nominated as one of the five best supporting actresses, and the play *Antigone* with the Theatre Group at UCLA. I also just did a guest appearance on *The Lucy Show* and one with Stanley Holloway on his show," referring to *Our Man Higgins*. When Logan replied a few weeks later that the film had no wisecracking secretary and that producers had already offered the part of "head nurse" to another actress, Mary pressed once more. "RATS!!! Tell that other actress that Mary Wickes is warming up in the alley! P.S. I could save you a lot of money, too, because I have several nurses' uniforms, shoes, et cetera at Warners from *The Man Who Came to Dinner*!!!" The role went to Kay Medford, who would soon receive an Oscar nomination for playing Fanny Brice's mother in *Funny Girl*. Three years later, when the Music Theater of Lincoln Center was mounting a revival of *Show Boat*, Mary appealed directly to Richard Rodgers, the theatre's president, for the role of Parthy Ann. He was encouraging and said he would recommend her to those making the hiring decisions, but the job went to Margaret Hamilton.

Mary was still pounding the pavement some twenty years later, when she asked writer and director Garson Kanin to consider her for the play *Peccadillo*, which he was casting in 1984. "I understand that you have a new comedy for production soon. Please keep me in mind!" she wrote Kanin, whom she had known since the 1930s. She offered up a list of accomplishments, then added, "I have excellent character references, and keep a bag packed for just such emergencies as trekking east to read for a friend/producer/director/writer." The show premiered in Florida a few months later without Mary, but did not make it to Broadway.

In all likelihood, Mary was propelled by some experience early in her career that taught her she could not rely on others to advocate for her.

She may have missed certain parts because she had not been submitted properly, or had not been submitted at all. Agents may have overlooked her, not thinking to submit her for something that she felt she could do. She wrote Sam Behrman, Jerry Chodorov, Alfred de Liagre, Maurice Evans, Ellis Rabb, Samson Raphaelson, George Schaefer, and others. She even found herself appealing to Eva Gabor when it appeared Gabor would mount a production of *Blithe Spirit* in 1978. Rejection seemed to fuel even greater pursuit. She was turned down for roles in every medium, including: the carousel owner, Mrs. Mullin, in the original production of *Carousel* (lost to Jean Casto): Ruby the maid in TV's *The Mary Tyler Moore Hour* (lost to Dody Goodman); and Amanda Wingfield, the troubled matriarch in the 1950 film *The Glass Menagerie* (given to Gertrude Lawrence). She was passed over even in radio. In 1947, nine years after Mary appeared with Jimmy Durante in *Stars in Your Eyes*, she asked him for work on his popular radio show. Durante replied that the show had been looking for a male singer and a female foil, but then decided to seek a woman who could do both. They hired the popular singer Peggy Lee, "so now we can't use another girl on the show. I'm awfully sorry, Mary, but those are the conditions that prevail," he told her.

Because she worked so hard to remain part of her profession, Mary expected to receive support from friends in the industry. She kept copious notes about which friends offered congratulations for which performances, methodically typing them up. So we know, for instance, that she received twenty-eight phone calls after her *Ma and Pa* pilot was broadcast in 1974, from new friends (like actor John Schuck), longtime friends (Lucy, Iggie Wolfington, Kendall Clark, Billy Miles, Peter Walker, Mary Grant Price, Mary Jane Croft), members of Lucy's circle (Ebba Sedgwick, Olavee Martin), church members, and her agents. That same need to be valued by the industry meant, when she felt wronged by it, she was unable to let the insult go. This resentment surfaced in ways small—resentful at being overlooked by organizers of a 1988 *Danny Thomas Show* reunion, she wrote Thomas an angry letter—and large, such as fights over billing. Watching *The Trouble with Angels* for the first time at its premiere at a Westwood movie house in 1966, Mary was furious to see herself introduced in the opening credits together with seven other actresses under the collective heading "The Nuns." That her name appeared first was no consolation. Having understood she would receive "special feature" billing, she protested directly to Columbia Pictures executive Mike Frankovich, but to no avail. Mary, unwisely, had signed a contract that did not specify billing. She said she had done so because

Columbia, pressing her to sign the billing clause in the fourth week of shooting, assured her that special feature billing would be worked out. In the 1968 sequel, the actresses playing the three main nuns received greater prominence in the credits, but billing was equal among them (after Rosalind Russell, the star). Binnie Barnes, who was married to Frankovich, appeared first, followed by Mary and Dolores Sutton.

Billing issues often bothered Mary. A couple of years later, she complained about billing disagreements to Bill Vaughan, an editor of the *Kansas City Star*, at the time one of the country's most prestigious dailies. Vaughan, a college classmate of Mary's, had talked with her while she was in town to perform in *Damn Yankees* with Vincent Price. "What interested me was that she was infuriated about her billing. It wasn't a matter of pride. It was just that this is her livelihood and she has to protect it," Vaughan wrote in a 1968 column. A decade later, when she believed print ads during her 1979 *Oklahoma!* tour did not promote her sufficiently, Mary turned to Actors' Equity Association. The union concluded no claim was possible because Mary's contracts left billing up to management's discretion unless any actor was billed, in which case all billing would become an issue. The ads that Mary objected to had named Rodgers, Hammerstein, and DeMille, but no actors. But Mary found a way to increase her billing opportunities. Soon after, when producers agreed to amend her contract to accommodate a four-week leave (so she could film *Touched by Love* in Canada), she secured a rider requiring that "in the event anyone connected with the production is billed in any media under direct control of manager with sole exception of Rodgers and Hammerstein and Agnes De Mille," Mary also would be billed on houseboards and the title page of theatre programs. She was more successful in a dispute in 1987 when she was backed by agent Don Wolff. She challenged the way she was billed in advertisements for a stage production of the *Wizard of Oz* in St. Louis. As a result, her name and photo were made more prominent in the subsequent print ads, comparable to those of Cathy Rigby, the star. Remarkably, the revised ads even stated, "The Muny apologizes for the incorrect billing of Mary Wickes in previous ads."

So great was Mary's need to feel connected to others—to feel herself a part of the extended Hollywood family—that much like an adoring fan, she methodically saved correspondence she received from well-known people. She did this even if the correspondence was mundane and even if she did not know the sender well. Her papers contain notes, cards, and letters from the likes of studio mogul Jack Warner; producers Theron Bamberger, Max Gordon, Jed Harris, Sam Harris, and Jerry Wald;

musical theatre legends Irving Berlin, Russel Crouse, Dorothy Fields, Mary Martin, and Richard Rodgers; stage stars Katherine Cornell, Lynn Fontanne, Helen Hayes, Ruth Gordon, Angela Lansbury, Walter Huston, Ethel Merman, and Margaret Webster; playwrights Edna Ferber and John Patrick; actors Fred Astaire, Ronald Colman, Joseph Cotten, Jose Ferrer, Van Johnson, Ricardo Montalban, Vincent Price, and Edward G. Robinson; actresses Kaye Ballard, Anne Baxter, Carol Burnett, Cloris Leachman, Thelma Ritter, Rosalind Russell, Mary Tyler Moore, and Vivian Vance; directors Jim Bridges, Hal Prince, and William Hammerstein; TV pioneers Arthur Godfrey, Worthington Miner, Frank Schaffner, and Ed Sullivan; and even furniture designer Charles Eames who, like Mary, landed in Los Angeles after a youth in St. Louis.

Because some of these people knew Mary for many years, their words offer interesting insights. Van Johnson, for instance, affectionately calls her "Mary Bones" in a 1971 letter and reminds her of the day they met at RKO years before, very early in both of their careers. But a careful reading of these letters, and follow-up interviews with many of the authors, reveals that many of these relationships were fleeting, limited to passing professional encounters. Few of these people shared any meaningful friendship with Mary. Though she keeps two hand-written notes from Patrick McGoohan, for instance, his only encounter with her was at a Los Angeles dinner party given by Max Showalter. He is surprised she even kept his notes, one of which was simply to decline a dinner invitation. Similarly, Mary kept two letters from the early 1980s written by Jim Dale, who won a Tony Award for Best Actor in *Barnum*. But Dale has no recollection of ever having met Mary, let alone of what prompted his letters. Mary saved a 1978 Christmas card from Shirley Booth, but why? Although they performed together in 1945 in *Hollywood Pinafore*, and spent a weekend together at the Connecticut home of the vaudevillians William and Madeline Gaxton during the show's run, nothing suggests they were important to each other afterward. In all likelihood, Mary reasoned that if, while she was alive, the public did not fully appreciate the extent to which she mixed with the great names of film and theatre, surely they would see it after she was gone. She had long intended to leave her papers for use by performing arts scholars, although she did not select a repository until shortly before her death.

Preserving correspondence wasn't the only way Mary tried to strengthen her ties to fame. She sometimes led people to believe she was closer with well-known people than was the case. Mary led both Dolly Reed Wageman and Madelyn Pugh Davis to believe she was very close to Bill and Elizabeth Danforth, prominent St. Louis figures. But in fact, separate interviews with the Danforths make clear that the couple and Mary were simply acquaintances who respected each other. More substantive correspondence exists from Anne Baxter, Bette Davis, Doris Day, Moss Hart, George S. Kaufman, and, of course, Lucille Ball. After Lucy, Doris Day is the only other female star with whom Mary grew genuinely close. Stars, especially beautiful women like Day and powerful women like Davis, could let their guard down around Mary, as she posed no threat to them. Mary lived her life sufficiently under the radar that they came to trust her and occasionally confide in her.

Mary worked with Doris Day six times (in *I'll See You in My Dreams*, *It Happened to Jane*, the two Moonlight films, one episode of the *Doris Day Show* on television and another on radio) and saved twenty-seven pieces of correspondence from her. These span forty-one years, ranging from a May 1953 postcard from Marrakech, where Day was filming *The Man Who Knew Too Much*, to a thank-you card written in 1994, the year before Mary's death. The letters are brief, chatty and friendly. Mostly typed, they speak of vacations, film assignments, and family. At least one came with snapshots. Again and again, Day asks Mary to call her—chastises her for *not* calling, it sometimes seems—so they can spend time together. Day writes with a humor that Mary surely appreciated. In the midst of renovations on her Beverly Hills home in 1971, Day writes, "I'm fine and my mother is fine and my dogs are fine. My house is fine, too, even though you didn't ask, but I'm remodeling my kitchen and it's a bit hectic . . . My mother is cooking in the bathroom, which is different, you must admit. Let me tell you, she can whip up some good dinners in that bathroom. In fact, I think she cooks better in there than she does in the kitchen." Day often thanks Mary for holiday gifts of cheese and candles, and in 1975 she thanked Mary for enlisting All Saints' Episcopal Church in Beverly Hills in finding homes for unwanted pets. (Mary imposed upon Day to be a surprise guest at the church's Blessing of the Animals in the early 1970s, just as she did with Betty White and Earl Holliman, other animal rights advocates.) Day praises Mary's work in *Mrs. G. Goes to College* as "marvelous as always." In 1977, after Mary shared a recollection of Day's mother, Alma, Day responded, "Can't believe she's been gone a year this last October. I know how you feel and you know how I feel, and there isn't much more that we can say. We were blessed, both of us, to have sweet moms, and for a long time."

In later years, Day often asked Mary to visit, even inviting her to spend Christmas with her in Carmel in the 1980s by reminding Mary that the flight is only "40 min from L.A. and I meet you in Monterey." In the late 1980s, Mary was staying with friends Janet and Pete Lewis in Pebble Beach, California, when Day invited Mary to her Carmel Valley home nearby. Janet Lewis accompanied Mary—Mary needed someone to drive, of course—and observed Mary and Day reminisce "like the best of friends," Lewis recalls. Day showed them around her property and introduced them to her animals, many of which were named after TV characters. Mary and Lewis marveled at Day's home on a cliff overlooking the Quail Lodge golf resort, and Lewis was impressed that Day covered furniture in public areas of the home with bed sheets that matched the upholstery so that pet odor could easily be washed away. After about four hours, "It was getting onto the cocktail hour, so I said, 'Mary, I think we'd better say our goodbyes,'" Lewis says. "And Doris said, 'Oh, won't you stay and have a drink?' I'd read where Doris Day only liked ice cream sodas, so I said, 'Thank you kindly, but we'll make it another day.' She said, 'Well, I'm sorry [you can't stay], but I'm going to have a vodka on the rocks.' I said, 'Well, I guess we can stay.'" This was the last time Mary and Day saw each other.

To Lewis, it seemed Day "adored" Mary. In fact, by all accounts, their relationship was an easy, comfortable one. "The two of them hit it off, and Mary was very fond of her," Madelyn Pugh Davis says. For this book, Day agreed to answer questions about Mary, but then changed her mind. But she allowed correspondence Mary saved to be excerpted and offered a brief statement, which reads in part: "Working with Mary was totally wonderful . . . Mary was a real friend in the movies—and in life."

Mary's relationship with Bette Davis was more complicated. Mary worked with Davis in three films (*The Man Who Came to Dinner*, *Now, Voyager*, and *June Bride*, all in the 1940s), as well as a 1960s television pilot that failed to sell (*The Decorator*). Mary spoke admiringly of Davis, who once advised her, "You have got to stop wanting everybody to like you." From that, Mary said, "I learned that people only respect you if you respect yourself." Mary saved eleven pieces of correspondence from Davis over the years. Together, they suggest that Davis treated Mary as a trusted confidante, sharing news of her life with unusual candor—at least during certain periods. In the fall of 1948, resting at her New Hampshire home, called Butternut, with husband William Grant Sherry, Davis wrote Mary in a maternal tone: "We are loving it here. Sherry is painting every day, B.D. [their young daughter] is running up and down our hills—and I am running after her!!" The following April, Davis invited Mary to join her and Sherry for a midnight supper at the Dakota, the

Manhattan apartment house where Davis was staying. When her marriage to Sherry came apart in 1950, Davis wrote Mary of her troubles.
"My mind has not been free to think of anything but lawyers, protecting
B.D. and getting *free*. These past nine months, no pregnant woman could
have had more hell giving birth to a child—and the last month was *truly*
a succession of labor pains. But, as we say, the curtain has to come down,
and it has, and on to the next performance. His last gesture of taking our
nursemaid to be his future wife made it necessary for me to whisk B.D.
out of California which we did on three days notice," she wrote. "I drive
to El Paso and on Friday cross into Mexico to marry Gary Merrill . . . This
is what I should have waited for. The reverse financial situation makes
a horror of the nicest man. [As a result of the divorce,] Sherry is *really*
well off—alimony and all—plus the fact my money supports Sherry and
nurse girl for four years!! I hope I never meet her in a dark alley! . . .
Wanted you to know my news. Wish me luck. It has to happen sooner
or later."

A few months later, married to Merrill and living in Southern California, Davis shared her relief at Merrill's apparent gift with children. Davis
is pleased B. D. has taken to her new adoptive father, but the actress
still resents Sherry's having left her for governess Marion Richards. "I go
home to a most awkward situation—how to explain to a three-year-old
that her father just up and married her nurse-girl has me a bit baffled.
I have trouble enough trying to explain it to myself. What a shock that
was. I must say in a long list of blows over a period of months, this was
the best . . . No script that is sent me would seem very exciting in com-
parison to my true life drama of this past year. Come out soon and make
a picture," she wrote Mary, who was still living in New York. "We can lie
on the beach at Malibu and settle the world. It gets tougher all the time
to figure it all out but if anyone can, we can."

It is possible that Davis's warmth toward Mary faded later. In the
memoir of his fifteen-year friendship with Davis, which began in 1958,
Roy Moseley concludes a description of Mary by noting, "Miss Wickes
was a close friend of Lucille Ball. Bette decided not to like her." If that
statement is true—and it's hard to identify a reason it would be—it certainly wasn't always the case. Nonetheless, Peter Walker remembers being surprised at Mary's demeanor when he escorted her to an American
Film Institute tribute to Davis in 1977. Because Mary liked Davis very
much, Walker expected her to greet Davis warmly. But rather than an
"Oh, darling" embrace, Mary extended a respectful, professional hand-
shake, with a courteous, "Congratulations, Miss Davis." Most likely, this

simply reflected the distance that had grown with time, and the fact that Mary understood her place in the celebrity pecking order.

Just as Davis confided in Mary, so did others. When Ethel Merman's daughter died in 1967 of a drug overdose, Merman wrote Mary that the family crisis had been "a nightmare" that she could not believe, and asked Mary to contact her at the Beverly Hills Hotel. Vivian Vance wrote Mary of the "horrendous" emergency appendectomy she needed after a curtain call in Florida. When CBS canceled its daytime version of *Match Game* in spring 1979, host Gene Rayburn wrote Mary: "We are all in a state of shock. Remember the Peter Principle: 'Mediocrity rises to the top'—and they're running the network."

Mary's penchant for corresponding with celebrities was almost as compulsive as her pursuit of work. Her letter writing was lifelong and constant. She wrote actors, writers, and directors, congratulating them on a performance, applauding a film, or wishing them luck on an upcoming production. She was extending a kindness, to be sure —"minding her manners," Isabella might say—but it was more than that. Her notes helped keep her name in mind. They helped her feel connected to others. And, because the hand-written gesture seemed reminiscent of another era, they were often received with genuine affection.

After Mary complimented his Broadway show *Tea House of the August Moon*, writer John Patrick wrote: "Thank you, thank you, thank you. You don't or can't realize how much it means to have the play liked, because it is a kind of vindication. I had to fight [producer Maurice] Evans from the first to keep this from being a British Music Hall farce—he even wanted dragons belching smoke to come out of the jeep—and also the author of the original book so loathed my dramatization he wrote an eight-page blast and announced to the *New York Times* he would do his own dramatizations after this. So you see, nice things said now mean more to me than you think." After Mary offered kind words to Maureen O'Sullivan in 1992, the actress wrote, "What a lovely thing for you to do—sit down and tell me you enjoyed a performance! So often I mean to do just that and seldom do. After Nancy Marchand left the show [*Morning's at Seven*], I was so hoping you would be able to take her role as Ida, but you were busy. I hope someday we work together as I always felt I would like to know you better."

One of the most unusual signs of her brushes with celebrity is an assortment of audiotapes from Rosemary Clooney. In the late 1980s and early 1990s, at her manager's suggestion, Clooney recorded a different holiday song each year on a small audiocassette. She sent copies to friends in lieu of Christmas cards—some years preparing up to three hundred tapes—after first recording a personal message to each recipient during the lull before the song's refrain. Mary kept nine of them. Clooney was surprised to learn during a 2000 interview for this book that Mary saved these cassettes, prompting her to mention it in the audio commentary she later recorded for a special *White Christmas* DVD release.

One October evening in the San Fernando Valley, Johnny Whitaker was sitting in a restaurant, making funny faces. The former child actor who found fame as fresh-faced little Jody in TV's *Family Affair* was contorting his mouth, raising his eyebrows, furrowing his brow, craning his neck, turning his head—in different ways feigning shock or horror. Far from being ill mannered, he was trying to illustrate how seriously Mary Wickes treated her comedy. During the run of the Saturday morning show *Sigmund and the Sea Monsters* in the 1970s, Mary taught Whitaker the five specific "reactions" that formed the cornerstone of her bag of tricks. She had a nickname for each expression, and each expression was carefully summoned at different moments in a Mary Wickes performance, sometimes more than once.

First, Whitaker illustrated, there was the "regular double take," a reaction registering great surprise after initial acceptance. The "pigeon double take" added stretching the neck when taking a second look. The "butterfly double take" was Mary's familiar shudder of multiple glances backward in quick succession. In the "triple take," Mary gazed at something three times, each time more intently. In "the one where you're caught," the actor quickly looks away in hopes of not being detected noticing what was noticed. Mary skillfully relied on these as staples of her comedy, which she viewed as a craft to be honed. Whitaker adored Mary and relished the times they sat together, she helping him refine these mannerisms. "I sat at her feet as an apt pupil, gleaning from everything she did and every word she said," he says. A decade after *Sigmund*, when Mary attended Whitaker's 1984 wedding at the Mormon temple in Westwood and reception at the Beverly Hills Hotel, she gave Johnny and his bride a simple bronze hotplate. "She wasn't out to impress me with what she could buy," he says. But the gesture touched him: The hotplate was in the shape of a butterfly to remind him of their practicing double takes together.

Mary's mentoring of Whitaker reflects her larger interest in teaching acting. While drawn to teaching, she was also apprehensive about it, so she tested the waters first in a setting she knew she could handle: the safe, protective environment of her alma mater. She became Washington University's first artist in residence in 1968, spending a month working closely with performing arts students there. She later taught a seminar on comic acting at American Conservatory Theater (ACT) in San Francisco, where she was part of ACT's acting ensemble (1972–73), and lectured on "The Thought and Feel of Comedy" at the College of San Mateo (1973). She returned to Washington University in 1977 to present a four-week course on acting in comedy, and she also taught a seminar at the College of William and Mary in Williamsburg, Virginia (1981).

Mary prepared carefully for these classes, doing library research, building a curriculum, and selecting texts (and, in some cases, costumes and set furniture). She designed courses that covered character development, timing, pace, concentration, and team work, as well as diction, makeup, and correct carriage and deportment in period clothes. She stressed the importance of staying fit and healthy, placing an almost turn-of-the-century emphasis on physical conditioning. The two pieces of advice she gave most often in detailed "notes" that she typed up for key performers were: Adhere carefully to the writer's original words, and don't think you're funny. "Going on stage thinking you are funny is fatal. Telegraphing it works like a wet blanket. You must be convinced the *part* has a comedic quality and that the audience will react, but not that *you* are funny," she wrote.

To be sure, these teaching gigs were no fly-in, fly-out celebrity appearances. "She was very excited about it. And nervous," recalls Jack O'Brien. "She was a self-styled repository of a certain kind of humor and a style of comedic acting. She felt she had something to give a company like [ACT]. She wanted that clean, acerbic, almost mechanized style of comedy that George S. Kaufman did so brilliantly. She wanted it sustained and honored, and she was eager to be a communicator of it." "She was so quintessential, so true to herself. She knew her gifts, she knew her timing. She worshipped—literally worshipped—George S. Kaufman. When he said, 'Turn, count three and say it,' she turned, counted three and said it. Her skill and technique confirmed by it, but not from an intellectual point of view. She was an intuitive actress," O'Brien says. "She didn't leave anything to chance. She wanted everything very clearly worked out for her. She was just a consummate, kind of tunnel-vision professional. She was used to being in an ensemble and used to doing what she was told. And she was not wildly secure: She worried a lot when she rehearsed—she wanted to make absolutely certain that *that* would be there and she would be standing *over here*, not over there. They were not unreasonable requests, but they were very specific. She was not a breezy person and she wasn't a ray of sunlight in those rehearsals. She worried, she ferreted, she rumbled a lot.

Mary respected her craft enormously, and she wanted others to respect it, too. When she was to be seen in a film or TV show, she frequently alerted colleagues in advance by mail and phone. She did this not as one might share good news with a friend, but more as a child who felt overlooked and needed to call attention to her accomplishments. It's as if the work did not matter if it was not seen by anyone important to her. At ACT in 1972, when Mary played a lead role in Kaufman and Hart's *You Can't Take It With You*, she asked Anne and Irving Schneider to come from New York to see her. "When you see me do Penny, you'll see what I can really do," she told them enthusiastically. Anne and Irving didn't go. "To fly thousands of miles to see even a good friend in a play that you've seen a million times seemed silly," Anne says. Certainly Mary had nothing to prove, yet "it rankled her" that they did not fly out, Anne says. "Every time we saw her after that, she'd mention it. She never really got over the resentment. She was still mentioning it years later—'Oh, if only you'd seen me as Penny!'"

Her desire to impress her peers created some unusual situations. Mary took a small part in a 1974 Los Angeles production of *Juno and the Paycock* because the Irish tragedy was a chance to work on stage with Jack Lemmon, Walter Matthau, and Maureen Stapleton. But Mary went one step further—offering to be understudy for Stapleton in the lead role of Juno. Would any other actress of Mary's stature at age sixty-four understudy the lead role in a high-wattage production in Los Angeles? "You sure know how to bowl somebody over. The fact that you would stand by for Maureen leaves me a bit stunned," director George Seaton told her. Mary never had to go on for Stapleton, but she was prepared to do so. She took seriously both the play and Seaton's direction. "Oh, how much better it is when you play it not quite so broad. The new hairdo and cutting out some of the eccentricity makes you real instead of a comic character," he advised her after one performance. "Let Jack finish his line before you take your gulp of whiskey. Last night, you did it on the last few words of his and the audience was looking at him instead of you."

Taking her work seriously kept Mary's confidence strong, but her confidence could cause her to overstep her bounds. She sometimes refused to defer appropriately to others, and tried to exert greater control than she should have. "She gave me a rough time the first day or so," says

Clinton Atkinson, who directed Mary in *Meet Me in St. Louis* at the Muny in 1977. "She tested me [as if to say], 'Listen kid, you better prove your-self.' You know when you take a dog out on a leash, and it digs its heels in? That's what she was like. Let's just say she stood with her hands across her chest for a while. But I realized what she was doing. She had done the show many times and knew what she wanted. After about two days, she realized I knew what I was doing, and then she let go. Once the dam broke, it was smooth as pie. I don't blame her for what she did. And I liked working with her." On other occasions when Mary tried to exert control, she could be severe or haughty, like the characters she played. Dolores Sutton, who played Sister Rose Marie in the two *Trouble with Angels* movies, remembers Mary behaving during rehearsals like a school principal might. "One day, I had a car from the studio. My parents were taking a big trip and I was going to see them off. Mary stopped me and began asking questions: 'Now where are you going? What are you doing? What time will you be back?' I thought, this is silly," Sutton says, recalling her annoyance. On the set, too, Mary got on Sutton's nerves. "She bossed me around a little," saying things like "you move here" or "you stand there." Barbara Sharma, who performed with Mary on stage and in television, remembers a similar attitude: "She had a 'clippiness' about her and somebody could take it in the wrong way. But that was just her way. It had nothing to do with you."

Elliott Reid recalls an actress friend complaining after a rehearsal she had with Mary, who seemed to want to manage the scene: "Jesus, your friend Mary Wickes—she's like the *director*. She's got 'helpful hints' for everyone!" To director William Hammerstein, Mary "was the sort of person who in the middle of rehearsals will turn to one of the other actors and make a suggestion, which drives directors crazy." In January 1981, about five months after Mary's *Oklahoma!* run closed on Broadway, Hammerstein wrote Mary a warm note about having arranged a new touring production of the show to begin in Florida. "During Christmas week I had the flu and missed two or three days of rehearsal, discovering to my horror that everything went along just fine without me. It was the only time I was happy you weren't there, because you would, of course, have seized the opportunity to re-direct everything." Even Peter Walker, one of Mary's closest friends, observes, "I would hate to have been a woman comedian in her company, unless it was the top comedienne—and of course the top comedienne became her close friend. With anyone else, she would become that strange, silent Mary. She could be terribly short and rude. Isabella would *never* have allowed it. Where did she learn that behavior?"

One possibility is suggested by Lamont Johnson, director of such groundbreaking dramas as *That Certain Summer*, *The Execution of Private Slovik*, and *My Sweet Charlie*. Johnson, who directed Mary three times, views her behavior in a larger context. "Actors have to fight for their lives a lot in television and theatre. So you developed a charmingly defensive attitude. You couldn't go in and just be ugly but, with any experience at all, you developed a defensive mechanism that had some humor attached to it, that tried to make light of things but at its base still had a very genuine kind of resistance movement around it. A lot of what I sensed as 'edge' with Mary was that—not hostile or snotty but strong and opinionated and not to be trifled with," he says. "Mary had a kind of spikey little temperament. Because she knew her craft and had gotten a lot of kudos, she had her own opinions. I wouldn't say she was difficult—we always got along great—but she was not a little supine mousy creature who did everything she was told."

Throughout her career, Mary took the industry to heart, seeing its needs as one might see a family member's needs. When she fought producers, it was sometimes to advocate for others. "If she caught wind that anyone wasn't getting what she thought they were due, she spoke up," says Scott Kolden, part of the *Sigmund and the Sea Monsters* cast. "One time she thought Johnny's and my dressing rooms weren't warm enough. 'Someone has to be here at 5:30 in the morning so they can turn the heaters on. Those boys are going to freeze!' Or, 'How come all the doughnuts are gone? Johnny and Scott are going to get out of make up and they aren't going to get any doughnuts. Someone needs to go get them some.' She was always looking out for everyone else on the set: actors, crew, script supervisor. 'Can't you see you're running her ragged? Ease up on her, she's doing the job of ten men!'"

This same concern prompted her to devote time to industry charities. In 1971 she helped organize a benefit that helped establish the Actors Fund in California. For "The Actors Fund of America Honors Miss Helen Hayes," which took place in Beverly Hills on April 5, 1971, Mary put her journalism training to use and worked with Iggie Wolfington to prepare a special souvenir book on a tight deadline. She wrote some articles, did a lot of the research for other articles, and pieced it all together. "It was beautiful," Wolfington says.

Mary seemed compelled to build this sense of family chiefly because she was so dissatisfied with the relationships she had with her natural family. Cousin Brooks Adkins in Dayton? She had long ago pushed him away—permanently. The Wickenhauser families of Illinois, just across the river from St. Louis? For reasons we may never know, Mary long ago decided to ignore them (and would not have been amused to see genealogist Edward Wickenhauser quoted in a local paper upon her death—mis-identifying her father, no less—before he himself realized he and Mary were actually from different Wickenhauser clans). Cousin Bill Dorsam in St. Louis? He indulged Mary out of loyalty to his mother but had little interest in a relationship, which was all too evident to Mary. Cousin Mary Ann Dorsam Baker, Bill's sister in Indiana, had even less interest and no contact. Even with their mother, Elizabeth, Mary's relationship was not always smooth because it was always on Mary's terms. "She would allow [only] so much time for my mom and that would be it, and my mom would have to see her when it was convenient for Mary. My mom would be on pins and needles when she was going to call. Mary would come see my mom for maybe an hour or two and then we wouldn't see her any more while she was here," says Bill Dorsam. "Any time she came to town, we always had the impression that she was only going to give you so much time because you were family, that it was just an obligation." Dorsam says the family many times tried to help Elizabeth see that Mary was being unkind, "but she'd always make excuses for Mary." This, despite Mary having made clear to Elizabeth that she did not approve of her husband, Waldo Dorsam. The feeling was apparently mutual: When Mary was in town, he would leave before her scheduled visit. "He wouldn't ever be at the house when she'd come," Bill says.

So it was colleagues and friends who became Mary's family. In the 1930s, she found familial comfort in people like Clifford Newdahl, Barbara Wolferman, Garson Kanin, Bob Wallsten, and Bob Thomsen. In the 1940s, she turned to Lester and Felicia Coleman, Kendall Clark, and the Sardi family, owners of the Times Square restaurant. In the 1950s, she relied on Max Showalter and Peter Walker. In the 1960s, especially after Isabella's death in 1965, in addition to Showalter, Walker, and Lucille Ball, Mary valued her close relationship with Vincent Price and his family. In the 1970s and '80s, the families of Lucille Ball, Vincent Price, and Rev. Richards filled the bill. In the '80s and '90s, family meant the Richards, Madelyn and Dick Davis, Emily Daniels, Rita Pico, and Dolly Wageman. Over the years, these were the people Mary spent holidays with, celebrated special occasions with, and considered her family, with all the simple gestures that relationship entails; Mary occasionally dropped off homemade baked goods at the Price home. These are the people who provided Mary with comfort and company, and in return, they could rely on Mary to bring good humor into their homes. When the children's table got rather quiet at a holiday dinner at the Davis home one year, Mary quipped, "Maybe it was the rum I put in the Jello."

For several Christmases near the end of her life, Mary stayed with Janet and Pete Lewis in Pebble Beach, California. Janet is a former model and Pete a former executive at Hilton Hotels. They had come to know Mary during the years they lived in Cheviot Hills, when Janet volunteered at Mary's church. The Pebble Beach home impressed Mary—it represented a grand way of living that had never been available to her—and she stayed for five or six days at a time. The main house, on the fourteenth fairway of a golf course, was a stunning five-thousand-square-foot property whose formal dining room overlooked the Pacific. Adjacent were three separate smaller buildings: a studio, a "laundry house," and guest quarters (Mary always stayed in the main house). Gatherings at the Lewis home were large and festive, accompanied by visits to a country club and caroling at the Lodge at Pebble Beach resort. "Mary *made* our Christmases. She had a funny bone that didn't stop," Janet Lewis says. Mary raved similarly to Emily Daniels about these holiday visits. No doubt the experience reminded Mary of the Wolfermans' Carmel home, which she so enjoyed in the 1940s.

It was important for Mary to feel needed, and for that, she turned to hospitals and her church. She spent several thousand hours volunteering at Los Angeles area hospitals, regularly visited residents of the Motion Picture and Television Fund hospital and retirement home in Woodland Hills, California, and, for a working actress, she was unusually active in her church. If Isabella and Lucy had been the anchor relationships in Mary's life—and acting its driving passion—then her church and her hospital work were its defining institutions. She made them a part of her life as if they were family, and in return, they provided all those things family provides. They gave her a sense of belonging and a sense of purpose. They gave her comfort when she might otherwise be reminded she was alone. ("Sometimes you get so lonely your back teeth hurt. I know. But I also know that those times can get much fewer and far between if you get busy and get out and do for other people," Mary said once.) They allowed her to feel needed, for she genuinely was. And, like all families, they sometimes made her angry.

Mary's devotion to hospital volunteerism can be traced to her youth. Isabella taught her that helping the sick was an important part of religious service. Isabella documented her own patient visits—by patient's name, the date and time of the visit—introducing Mary to a methodical approach to life's details. "From the time I was able to notice anything at all, I saw that when a friend of ours was ill or had a tragedy in the family, my mother and father did not telephone. They put on hats and coats and went to the house, presented themselves at the door and said, 'How can we help?' That was instilled in me," Mary said. As an adult during World War II in New York, she volunteered with the Hospital Committee of the American Theatre Wing War Service. In her early years in Los Angeles, when she lived on Crescent Heights, she volunteered at Good Samaritan Hospital. Later, living in Century City, she gave her time to UCLA Medical Center, which was closer.

Often, simply recognizing Mary put patients in better sprits. "I hesitated at first when she wanted to be a volunteer. I thought she would be slapstick," said Good Samaritan chaplain Bertrand Hause. "But I think she has been the most fantastic volunteer I have ever had. She is sensitive to people and she knows when to be funny and when to be serious." Later, Mary joined the board of directors of the medical auxiliary at UCLA's hospital, where she advocated for large clocks on patient room walls and more hangers in closets. Not surprisingly, she sometimes overstepped her bounds. This was especially true in matters related to cancer, because, having survived cancer herself, Mary felt a special responsibility to help. "One time, she'd heard that colon cancer could be diagnosed by a blood test from the stool. She decided there was no reason UCLA couldn't make that a standard procedure [where all physicians] just do it," explains Dick Davis, the retired UCLA surgeon who was Mary's friend. Mary knew that the hospital's director, Ray Schultze, had come from St. Louis, so she set out to see him about the matter because, to her, such testing made such sense. "He didn't want to tangle with her, because you can never get away from Mary. So Ray sent her to his assistant. The assistant said to me, 'You know Mary Wickes? She is a *bear!* I couldn't get her out of my office.' He had said, 'Well, Ms. Wickes, we'll take that up.' She said, 'You'll do more than that—you'll put it in!' He said [to Davis, later], 'Would you take her off my back?'" It fell to Davis, who was amused by this encounter, to ask Mary to drop this issue and let administrators handle it. It was a medical decision best left to hospital policy, after all.

Sometimes Mary's two worlds collided, such as when she encountered fellow performers in the hospital. Mary Jackson, who played Miss Emily Baldwin on *The Waltons*, was hospitalized at Good Samaritan in 1965, and was surprised to find Mary assisting patients. She remembers Mary as "extraordinary" there. Jane Wyatt ran into Mary at Good Samaritan when her husband Edgar was hospitalized. "I admired her so for doing it. She was awfully good at it, and it was great fun to see her there." In 1974, almost twenty years after Marjorie Lord worked with Mary on *Make Room for Daddy*, she encountered Mary at UCLA Medical Center. Lord's husband, theatrical producer Randolph Hale, was dying of lung cancer. "Whenever she was there, she'd spend time with him. He loved animals and was a Leo so one day she came in with a great big poster of a lion and put it up on his wall. He loved the lion poster. And she'd take me out to dinner when I was going back and forth to the hospital all the time." Hale spent his last fifteen days at home. Mary went to be with Lord and Hale on his last day, and knew exactly what to do when he passed away. Since Hale was well known in society circles in Los Angeles and San Francisco (he was part of the Hale family in the Carter-Hawley-Hale retail interest), Mary knew it would be important to notify people. She picked up the phone at Lord's house and called the *Los Angeles Times* to report his passing. "There was a huge article on him, more than you'd usually get, due to Mary. Whenever I think of Mary, I think of what she meant to me in those last days of my husband's life, because she was there for me right at the end," Lord says.

Peter Walker was in intensive care at UCLA in 1970, being treated for pneumonia. "Mary was coming to visit me and Lucy was going to see Gypsy Rose Lee, who was in the same hospital with cancer, dying. So Lucy said, 'Well, I like Peter, I'll come and visit and it may cheer him up.' That shows her generosity as a person," Walker says. But as he was talking with Lucy, he began to experience a psychotic episode, a severe toxic reaction to an overdose of tetracycline. "It just threw my system out, threw my body into convulsions. Lucy backed out of intensive care and said, 'Mary, I don't think pneumonia is the only thing Peter has. He's zonko.' Lucy was the first one to discover that my brain had been frazzled by a toxic poisoning from the tetracycline."

In addition to UCLA, Mary frequently made visits to the Motion Picture and Television Fund retirement home, where many elderly entertainers live. Harve Presnell thinks this "came out of loneliness and a sense of belonging there and not belonging in the real world. I think that got increasingly the case with her." Presnell says this is partly because "nobody would listen to Mary. Everybody just kind of said, 'Yeah, right.' She had a way of 'instructing' [younger] people, which is right and proper. But that's difficult for beginners or people who are not really interested in being in Akron doing *Oklahoma!*"

Mary did not limit her visitations to Los Angeles. While working on location, she often stopped in at local hospitals. While shooting *Father*

Dowling episodes, Mary volunteered at what was then called Denver General Hospital. "Mary's holiday regimen remains one of the great singular things I remember about her: She spent Christmas in the hospitals," says Jack O'Brien. "Of course, she had no immediate family, but what an amazingly positive thing to do for—forgive me—a salty broad. She had every right to feel forlorn, forgotten, with nobody in particular to cuddle up with." Instead, Mary found hospital volunteerism so rewarding—and made it seem so appealing—that she persuaded Lucie Arnaz at fourteen or fifteen to apply for a candy-striper position. "Mary was so proud of the work she did in the hospital. She said, 'You should volunteer! It's a wonderful job and it's great fun.' I thought, Wow, what a great idea. They gave me a uniform and my candy-striper apron and I spent about half of a morning with my little booklet and clipboard learning all the expressions, like *Stat!* At the end of the first day, they set me in a room and said, 'So-and-so had to leave. Could you please finish giving this older man his bath?' says Lucie, laughing raucously at the recollection. "They left me in this room with this naked old man in a bath tub and I started to shake. I called for some nurse and said, 'I have to go back downstairs, where I left something.'" Lucie, who tells this story with some embarrassment, went downstairs and never came back. She immediately confessed to Mary. "I said, 'Mary, [hospital volunteering] is not me. It's you.' She crossed her arms in front of her with this pretend-stern face and then she just cracked up. She thought it was the funniest thing she'd ever heard."

If her hospital work provided laughter, Mary was decidedly more serious about religion. In December 1949, Mary found herself in a New York rehearsal hall, preparing for her second episode of the live television show *Studio One*. This was the episode that featured her as Mary Poppins. Because the episode would air on a Monday, rehearsals continued through Sunday. That afternoon, Mary approached Iris Mann, the child actress who played one of Poppins's wards, and posed a question that Mann found so peculiar she remembers it more than fifty years later. "Did you go to church this morning?" Mary asked. Mann, who is Jewish, remembers being taken aback by the question, which she finds as odd in retrospect as she did at the time. "That's the one thing that stands out in my mind about her. Most of the people I grew up with were from the theatre in New York, and this was something nobody in the industry had ever asked me. I looked at her and said, 'No, I don't go to church.'" Mary just nodded.

Certainly, positioning her faith and volunteerism so prominently in her life set her apart from other performers. Elliott Reid remembers dining with Mary in 1976 to celebrate the end of their week together on *Tattletales*, a game show they considered embarrassingly bad. (The series initially featured husbands and wives trying to predict each other's answers to odd questions, but later paired contestants in all manner of relationships, like the non-romantic friendship Mary and Reid shared.) "We were being a little serious about life in general. I said, 'Mary, you live in Century City, which is kind of sanitized—there's something antiseptic about it.' She said, 'Oh, tell me, God, yes!' I said, 'What do you *do*, really, around here?' She said, 'It's not what I do around here—although everything is here, all the stores, good theatre—but what I'm doing that interests me is working closely now with All Saints'.' And we had a talk about her interest in the Episcopal Church in Beverly Hills. She was quite serious about this. She said, 'It gives me pleasure and gives me something I want to do, which is to be involved in the community, not just Beverly Hills but Los Angeles.'" Reid, who was raised Episcopalian but is not a churchgoer, felt Mary was trying to engage him in church activities. "I don't know if it was even conscious on her part. She said, 'Well, you might like this church. It has a really progressive point of view, it functions in the community.' She told me all the wonderful things they do, like for the poor. But I'm just not by nature a very religious person. I respect it, but it doesn't seem to be my way to show up every Sunday *anywhere*."

Mary told the *Denver Catholic Register* in 1989, "I was an only child and have no close relatives, so the church becomes your family. My really close friends, other than Lucy, are from church." Church was so important to her that, while she was away, Canon Richards occasionally mailed her the programs prepared for Sunday services so she could feel connected. In 1977, Mary began teaching Sunday school, which she would have done more often but for location shooting. Other well-known people belonged to All Saints', but none jumped in like Mary, who rolled up her sleeves for the church rummage sales. When the church printed new prayer books that Mary felt were difficult to follow, she created bookmarks with instructions—cutting them and gluing them into the prayer books herself.

All Saints' was not far from Lucille Ball's house, so Mary often stopped at Lucy's after church. Lucie remembers many of these visits, and always sensed that the church provided Mary with a strong support system.

"She was very religious, but not in a weird, born-again, annoying kind of way. There was a lot of joy in her church going, which *I* didn't pick up. The Catholic religion, to me, as a kid . . . it was a pain to go to church, and all the guilt they threw at you and 'the stand-up, sit-down, fight-fight-fight' aura of the Catholic Church. But she would come back from church with these wonderful, joyful stories about the fun they had."

Mary's faith shaped the way she saw things in all parts of her life. Although they were not close, she and actress Natalie Schafer stayed in touch in Los Angeles after their early New York stage days. They met for dinner one night at the New York apartment of Kaufman biographer Malcolm Goldstein in about 1980. Later, Goldstein told Mary that he and Anne Kaufman Schneider had been speculating about Schafer's 1991 death, partly because, though she had been very rich, late in life she had not been happy. "We thought she might have committed suicide. I mentioned this to Mary, who was quite shocked at the idea, [saying], 'I'm sure she never took her own life.' It was something Mary couldn't contemplate. It would have been against her religious beliefs. Natalie was not religious. The idea seemed to be outrageous or reprehensible or unthinkable from Mary's point of view."

CHAPTER FOURTEEN

Becoming the Characters She Played

SOMETIMES ACTORS STRUGGLE TO EMBRACE THE CHARACTERS THEY play. Other times, they struggle to leave their characters behind. In Mary's case, over time, she became more and more like her characters. A vibrant, adventurous woman became increasingly rude and with-drawn—even imperious—ultimately blurring the distinction between her personal and professional identities. This transformation surfaced in her interactions with friends, colleagues, and the media—with whom-ever she happened to encounter.

People in Mary's life trace this change to Isabella's death in 1965. The passing of the person Mary loved more than anyone else left a huge void in her life. Isabella's death marked the first time in Mary's fifty-four years that Mary would live alone, except for a brief period early in her career in New York. Isabella had been a reliable, affirming presence reminding Mary that she was making the right decisions, that she had selected the right friends, that she was leading a good life. No longer would someone else cook for her, keep her home tidy, guide her schedule, maintain her scrapbooks, support her in all ways. In Isabella's absence, Mary bothered less with other people, sometimes shut out friends who reached out to her, and invested less time in the manners she had always embraced, even while preaching them to others. These changes suggested more than the rigidity that sometimes accompanies aging.

"I think she felt she had to fend the world for herself, because Isabelle had been right there with her—and anything that bothered Mary, Isa-belle could analyze and handle. With Isabelle, she felt a strength and was able to give more of herself," says Max Showalter. "But when Isabelle died, Mary put a steel thing around her. She found out that she had to protect herself, and that's when the more caustic moments happened. The caustic [attitude] and the brittleness—that wasn't there at the begin-ning," he says, remembering a cheerful young Mary in New York. Those caustic qualities, present in so many of the characters she played, "got to be more and more the real Mary Wickes as time went on," he says. "Keeping people at arms' length, afraid of what might happen, never giving in to something that could have changed her life. At times, I feel terribly sorry for Mary that she just wasn't capable of opening up, really and totally."

Conversations between Mary and Showalter in the last few years of her life, after he moved from Los Angeles to Chester, Connecticut, in 1985, offer some insight into her behavior. "She could put people off rather quickly, even those she cared for. I'd call and say, 'Hello, my dear.' [Loud, gruff:] 'Who is this?!' 'This is Max.' [Harried:] 'Max, I'm very busy, I've got so much to do, I can't talk.' I'd say [nicely], 'All right, Mary, then I'll hang up. I don't want to bother you if you're *that* busy.' Then she'd reconsider, realize she'd been caustic, and say [less gruffly], 'No, no, wait a minute. Now, what's on your mind?' But still, it wasn't, 'Oh, how wonderful to hear from you.' The initial thing in contacting Mary was cold and a put-off. We'd talk for a while, and then I'd say, 'Mary, it's been wonderful to talk with you.' 'Well, mind your manners!' Never 'Thank you for the call' or anything. It was very strange." One time, Showalter called her on her behavior. "I said, 'Mary, this isn't you. Why are you doing this to me?' She said, 'What?' I said, 'Mary, where's the warmth that I knew from you?' Then she would melt and would come down." To Mary, it was as if Max's move from Los Angeles was a personal rejection. For thirty years, he had been only minutes away—he lived in the Hollywood Boulevard house that had been Carole Lombard's between her marriages to William Powell and Clark Gable—and Mary had come to rely on his company for so much, especially at parties and on holidays. Mary now resented that he would no longer be part of her life in the same way, so she would invest in him no more. She spoke to him only when he phoned her; she no longer phoned him.

Jack Pirozzi, who knew Mary for the last eleven years of her life, had the same experience. "Every time I'd call Mary, she'd start off with this persona. She'd be this curmudgeon. She was too busy to talk with you. Or too busy to meet with you. But as you talked, her time became much more available. She eventually became lovable [and] conciliatory." This edginess did not surface only in phone conversations. "She was at our home several times for dinner, and she did the same thing there," Pirozzi says. "She would start out in the same way, but by the end of the evening she had you eating out of her hand. She was so charming, so generous— but it had to be on her terms. Regardless of what our last conversation was, which generally ended [positively], when I contacted her again, I'd have to start all over from ground one with the game that she would play."

Why would friends accept that kind of behavior? "I knew what was beneath it all, I guess," Showalter says. "I knew that she did love me and that it was a thing of the moment." What makes Mary's behavior especially puzzling is that she often resented others who took on airs. Showalter remembers Mary complaining about changes in Vivian Vance that, for a time, cooled relations between the two women. "Viv did get rather grand and that upset Mary. She said, 'She's trying to be something she isn't. I don't think Viv is herself.'"

The changes in Mary that were occasioned by Isabella's death grew more pronounced over time, making Mary even haughtier. "Queenly" is how friend Dolly Reed Wageman puts it. Casting director Ethel Winant, who worked with Mary many times and respected her greatly, nonetheless says, "Mary was impossible, stubborn, difficult to work with, very opinionated, and wanted to do what she wanted to do." For some, Mary's abrasiveness was easier to accept because she was usually sorry about it later. "She was like Lucy in that way. They'd say something and you'd think, *My!* And then later [they would apologize]," says Madelyn Pugh Davis. "Sometimes Mary was too abrupt for her own good. Part of her was very caring and very nice. And that part of her would say [to herself], 'What would you say that for?!' Then she'd go back and make it all right." A few years before Mary died, Pugh Davis was driving them both to a baby shower in the San Fernando Valley when their conversation en route turned to the Academy of Motion Pictures' practice of sending Oscar-nominated films on videocassette to academy voters. "I'm not a member, because I didn't do enough movies. I said something like, 'Maybe I could borrow some of the tapes?' She had so many that she didn't know what to do with them, and I'm very good about returning things. But she said [curtly], 'I'm not finished with them yet.' I was taken aback. I'm not a person to ask many favors but I didn't think borrowing a couple of movies was too much." (Pugh Davis performed many favors for Mary, and had in fact driven her to a social gathering that day.) "Three or four days later, Mary said, 'You wanna borrow any of my tapes from the movies?' She knew she'd been abrupt and later she felt badly about it. That's the way she was." Mary loved receiving these videos, and not just because they were free. Says Bill Givens: "Every time we'd go to a movie, she'd complain that the movie screens were too dark, so she could see the videos better at home."

A similar dynamic surfaced when Mary appeared as a society matron in a 1987–88 episode of the series *You Can't Take It With You*. Executive Producer Chris Hart first offered the role to his mother, Kitty Carlisle Hart, but obligations in New York that week prevented Moss Hart's widow from performing in California. No doubt Mary was genuinely moved at the prospect of working with the Harts' son almost fifty years after she worked with Moss Hart on *The Man Who Came to Dinner*. But that feeling did not mean all would be smooth. During rehearsals at KTLA Studios, Hart was paged in his office. "They said, 'Get down here, Mary's throwing a fit.' Mary was causing some sort of ruckus on the set and, because of our connection, I was called down to straighten things out. She could be quite imperious, but by the time I got down there—it took me ten or fifteen minutes to get from my office to the stage—everything was cool." He doesn't recall the issue, but thinks it might have been about her costume or her dressing room. Mary subsequently baked chocolate chip cookies for cast and crew, "and by the end of the week everybody loved her. That was a very sweet thing that everybody found charming."

Though Mary enjoyed sharing stories of Moss with his son, in general she was less and less interested in reminiscing. She had always focused on activities that lay ahead, but rejecting the past now seemed more important. Alfred Gellhorn, a prominent Manhattan physician who grew up with Mary, was rebuffed when he went to see her backstage after a performance of *Oklahoma!* in New York. He expected Mary to be delighted to encounter an old friend, but that's not what happened. "It was very, very interesting. Mary had absolutely no interest in recalling any of the earlier period. She didn't want to talk about it at all. I was surprised, because it really was our major point of contact. I think she felt she'd outgrown that and was a person of some prominence in the theatre world." Clearly Mary remembered him and his wife, Olga, so her reaction was not due to failing memory. Not only had they spent considerable time together during her most formative years, but Gellhorn's was a prominent family. His mother was well known in St. Louis society and civic affairs, his sister Martha was the pioneering war correspondent who became Ernest Hemingway's third wife, and he himself built a distinguished clinical and research career.

Mac and Helen Morgan had a similar encounter. Mac had been an opera singer at the Tanglewood Music Center in Lenox, Massachusetts, in the 1950s and 1960s, when he and his wife spent time with the Berkshire Playhouse crowd in nearby Stockbridge. The couple became part of the gang, opening their home to each summer's theatre company, and they came to know Mary when she returned to Stockbridge to play in *The Great Sebastians*. In 1987, they were living in Atlanta when Mary appeared at the Alliance Theatre for six weeks in the comedy *The Foreigner*. The Morgans went backstage to greet her. While Mary was courteous and said, "I'm very glad to see you," it was clear she no longer knew them. The Morgans were disappointed, but they understood that this sort of thing happens; after all, they had known Mary only casually thirty years earlier. But they were stunned at what happened next. Trying to trigger Mary's memory, Helen reminded Mary of their encounters at the Berkshire Playhouse, where Mary had played so many years for director Billy Miles. Mary adored Miles—the theatrical legend who helped launch her career, the man spoken of so often in Stockbridge that he became one word, "Billymiles"—but she now claimed never to have heard of him. Not remembering Miles "was just extraordinary," says Helen, who was taken aback. "She couldn't remember anything. There was just a hole where that experience should have been. It seemed as though it wasn't an important part of her memory."

In these instances, perhaps Mary was impatient, or simply preferred to be left alone. She visited Miles in a Lenox, Massachusetts, nursing home in 1982 and spoke in detail about him for an oral history that year; if she had forgotten him in 1987, her memories had disappeared only recently. Maybe she was consciously avoiding reminders of her true age. Perhaps she was skirting conversations that might lead to argument. Talk with Gellhorn could easily have turned to the liberal anti-Hoover activities that so many Little Theatre folks were engaged in during the Depression years. Or possibly, Mary was beginning to show some signs of mental decline. "She got very peculiar at the end. She never even spoke to me the few times I went to church. I have no idea why," says Bill Frye, who was so favored by Mary that he had been one of Isabella's pallbearers. It is unlikely that her deteriorating eyesight prevented her from recognizing him, since he always accompanied Jim Wharton, who was even closer to Mary than Frye was. "She became more eccentric looking with her clothes and her dress, [like] putting on a coat if you're hot, you know. But that's normal for anybody who's that age, living alone, eccentric anyway—and an actor, to make it worse."

"Mary was very proper in public until, I'd say, the last twelve or fifteen years of her life," says Dolly Reed Wageman. "She could be quite imperious—[for example] with a meal check in a restaurant, checking out the figures and finding out that they were not exactly what she expected. Or not getting the courses delivered as quickly as she thought they should have been." Sometimes, she was simply inappropriate. Once, in the early 1990s, when she phoned friend Barbara Wolferman in New Jersey, Barbara's son, Peter A. D'Auria Jr, then in his late forties, picked up the phone. D'Auria's voice is naturally high, causing some callers to assume a woman has answered. When Mary realized she was speaking to a man, she decided his voice was something that needed to be fixed—and quickly told him so. She advised him to go to a voice coach "to straighten that out," D'Auria says. "I was dumbfounded. She went on and on about it. I didn't know how to respond."

In about 1994, after her deteriorating eyesight forced her to relinquish her car, Mary found herself on a Los Angeles city bus beside a woman who was struggling to remember how she knew Mary. Studying her face, the passenger told Mary, "I *know* I know you." She began guessing where she recognized Mary from: Was it from this part of her life, from that part of her life? Mary was dismissive and finally said curtly, "I'm an actress, maybe that's how you've seen me." Then she stepped off the bus. This anecdote is interesting less for Mary's reaction than for who observed it. By sheer coincidence, the passenger sitting directly opposite Mary during that ride was Iris Mann, the former child actress who co-starred with Mary in "Mary Poppins" in 1949. Mann could not help but listen as the other woman attempted conversation with Mary. It was the first and only time Mann had seen Mary in the forty-five years since the "Poppins" broadcast. Given all that "Poppins" had meant to Mary, there's no doubt Mary would have relished an opportunity to talk with Mann. Mann could not have known this, since Mary's demeanor certainly did not invite conversation, so she said nothing. "I just felt like it had been so long ago that she wouldn't remember me. Why start anything?"

Mary's impatience was especially evident with the press. She had embarrassingly little patience when she perceived reporters to be careless, and often adopted a smug, authoritative air with them. In interviews, she frequently talked down to reporters, sometimes correcting them, other times speaking in almost combative tones. Some examples from Jerry Berger: *Why* do you keep mentioning such and such? Didn't you *really* mean to ask me about such and such? *No*, it wasn't that show. "She was barking," recalls Berger. "Anyone else, Carol Channing [for example], would say, 'That's funny, ha, ha, ha. But it really was *this* show.' I remember working with Joan Crawford in the late fifties. In the few interviews she did, it was always very elegant, with a big smile. Very cool, very pleasant, almost like fluid, very receptive. [She'd say,] 'You know, if you see [this film], I might point out such-and-such.' She didn't go to college but she learned through the years how to handle an interview. She was very enlightening."

Mary, having had some journalism training, had a keen sense of the importance of getting facts right and a strong impulse to control what should appear in print. But she never learned to handle such things gracefully. In 1973 the small *Film Fan Monthly* published an appallingly error-ridden profile of Mary's career, getting the most basic, easy-to-check facts wrong. That the article was made the cover story was no consolation. Mary sent an angry three-page account of twenty-one inaccuracies to writer Don Stanke. Though she was right to ask for corrections, her approach was also to scold the author, schoolmarm-like. The mistakes were never corrected and were repeated when the article was reprinted in 1979 in Leonard Maltin's *The Real Stars* collection. The original *Film Fan* version was sold until very recently by Maltin's online publishing company.

When *The Aglaia*, the national magazine of Mary's Phi Mu sorority, was preparing a profile of Mary in 1982, its reporter sent Mary written questions as a follow-up to a phone interview. Mary shot back: "Some of these questions sound a bit 'plastic.' Let's not get trite and maudlin or 'dumb.' I'm intelligent and I am sure you are writing it for intelligent readers."

Chastising reporters is one thing, but chastising fans is another. When a San Francisco fan wrote her in 1986 wanting to add to his collection of photos of retired performers, an annoyed Mary responded that her retirement "is very far from fact." She repeated the same lie about her age that she had always told, and said his having misunderstood her true age "may account for what seems to you, obviously, as a career ready for retirement . . . When I do retire—and I doubt that a retirement is ever contemplated—I shall send you a photo." It's hard to imagine another performer of her stature replying to a fan's photo request with a scolding instead of a picture.

But Mary feared the business was passing her by. In a way, it was. Jerry Berger says, "She paid her dues and was starring on Broadway, but ask ten people on the streets of Manhattan who Mary Wickes is and maybe one person could say. But ask ten people, 'Who's Susan Lucci?' and nine could tell you." And when the current owner of the home where Mary lived while in college sought to explain to a neighbor why Mary Wickes's biographer was touring the house, she resorted to, "Did you ever see *Rear Window*? The housekeeper lady? Well that wasn't Mary Wickes, but she was like that, like Thelma Ritter." This in Mary's hometown, no less. Before appearing in *Damn Yankees* and *Oklahoma!* in the 1978 Muny season,

Mary flew to St. Louis for advance publicity work. Barbara Mahon, who managed Muny public relations for seven years, worked intensely with Mary over a three-week period. Mahon was surprised at how different Mary was from the scores of other celebrity performers she had worked with. "Do you want the truth? She was not an extremely pleasant person. She was kind of cranky and a little imperious—high on herself, rather egotistical. She was not amusing, and she didn't try to be. 'Crabby' isn't really the word, but she wasn't a warm, fuzzy person. I got along with her absolutely fine, but I didn't feel tremendously comfortable with her." To put this encounter in context, Mahon describes another actress who also played many wisecracking characters—Eve Arden—as "precious, just the most fantastic person I ever met."

Part of Mary's difficulty was that she could not let go when something went in a direction she did not like. For instance, something about the way her appearance was handled on the *Charlotte Peters Show* in St. Louis in 1965 upset her so much that she raised a fuss about it. Mary asked Howard F. Baer, a St. Louis civic leader, to intervene on her behalf, but Baer, like many others in Mary's life, recognized a fool's errand where Mary did not. "If you feel that you would like to make a cause celebre out of it and would like me to do something I will, but I suppose the best thing to do is let it alone," he replied. "You have a very busy schedule ahead of you with marvelous people, and I am sure that your life is so full of hard, constructive work and pleasant things to do, you have very little time for bitterness." *Ouch.* Mahon, who was unfamiliar with this flap, but who arranged a subsequent appearance by Mary on that program, says, "Most people would write a gracious letter to the host of any TV show and say thank you, or ignore the whole thing." Interactions like this might explain a seeming lack of enthusiasm for Mary among sponsors of the St. Louis Walk of Fame, a sidewalk of brass stars and bronze plaques that celebrates St. Louisans of significant cultural accomplishments. Friends had lobbied the organizers for years to include Mary while she was alive, but it didn't happen until nine years after her death. She was inducted in 2004, joining Betty Grable, Agnes Moorehead, Shelly Winters, Tina Turner, Vincent Price, and about one hundred others who came before her.

In 1982, when Mary returned to Stockbridge to appear in *The Palace of Amateurs,* local historian Polly Pierce sought to interview her for a Berkshire Playhouse oral history project. Director Billy Miles and actor Bill Roerick had recorded their experiences thoughtfully, but Mary could not be persuaded to sit for an interview. In the end—determined, as always, to do things on her own terms—Mary insisted on receiving questions from Pierce in writing. Then she rounded up a tape recorder, and, alone in her room one night at the Red Lion Inn, Mary recorded some random thoughts. Even this she did begrudgingly, her tone barely hiding her annoyance at the whole task. She dismissively refers to Pierce as "this historian lady." She is disdainful of the Playhouse's name change (to the Berkshire Theatre Festival) and rails against other changes that she perceives have all been for the worse. She blames "some rather ditzy people" and "different little minds and sticky fingers, some of them intelligent and some not," for changes made since the reign of Billy Miles.

"Time had passed her by and she was a sad lady," says Harve Presnell, recalling the last time he performed with Mary, in the Florida and Ohio productions of *Oklahoma!* in 1979. But Mary's cynicism was directed mostly at changes in the broader entertainment business, rather than the work itself. She resented it when so many younger performers in touring companies treated their assignments as mere way stations on the path to something grander. "They're always looking ahead instead of taking care of the moment. That was very disturbing for Mary. Every time you perform, because of respect for the material and your fellow actors, you have to give it your best shot. Even if that doesn't work, then you have to give it your best shot for yourself. So that's the way she was. She never lost her passion for working in the theatre," Presnell says. "Never."

Change in general was difficult for Mary to accept, in Stockbridge and elsewhere. By 1982, when the Muny was preparing yet another production of *Show Boat*, Mary had developed a sense of entitlement about Parthy Ann, Cap'n Andy's domineering wife, whom she had played at the Muny on three previous occasions. But this time, she was not offered the role. "She was livid," says Jerry Berger. Berger was told by producers that Mary wanted too much money, but Mary complained to producer Edwin Lester that she had never stated an amount and was never made an offer. She went to war. She began a letter-writing campaign to the board of directors of Muny's governing body, the Municipal Theatre Association, something Berger can't recall another performer ever doing. The folly of this move was lost on Mary, who presumably reasoned she had some influence. But when board members got her letter, "They scoffed at it. For some reason, she didn't know they had nothing to do with casting," Berger says.

The Muny ultimately decided against presenting *Show Boat* that season. But Mary never forgot the slight and remained bitter toward the Muny—and not merely for this casting decision. "She was critical of the producer, critical of the plant, critical of the improvements, critical of where the entertainment industry was going, critical of the high salaries television performers were getting. She was a bitter woman toward the end," Berger says. In 1980, he met Mary for lunch at New York's May-flower Hotel, where she was living during the Broadway run of *Oklahoma!* "She was almost intolerable. She sniffed at everything. And just spouted off—about high salaries, and do you think so-and-so really did a good job in such-and-such?" He contrasts her mood then with her mood during her early runs at the Muny, when she was "bouncy, happy, ecstatic to be back in St. Louis." Indeed, in 1965, when Mary led a film crew on a tour of the Muny for the TV program *America*, she practically gushed. "The productions here are absolutely divine—100 percent pro-fessional, beautiful lighting, beautiful sound," she said in the broadcast. "On a full-moon night, with that fifty-piece orchestra in the pit, *it's to die!*" At that time, for Mary, the Muny—with seats for twelve thousand and a proscenium larger than Radio City Music Hall's—was still the space that introduced her to the wonders of theatre, that had been magical to her as a child, that she came to love as an adult, that felt like home for so many years.

Her resentment toward the Muny later on might explain why she never returned to her graduate thesis, which she began in 1969. She was writing "The St. Louis Municipal Opera: Alone in its Greatness" for a master's of theatre arts degree at UCLA. Many times over the years, she mentioned this task—chronicling the Muny's history, architecture, man-agement structure, finances, and production schedule—but the project ultimately lost its attraction for her. By 1982 she had completed only four chapters of what was intended to be a much larger effort. She could not force herself to devote time to something that would promote an organization she felt no longer appreciated her. And with Isabella gone, there was no one to persuade her to do so.

Later still, as Mary's loneliness grew, her thoughts increasingly turned to St. Louis. In the late 1980s and early 1990s, she sought out conver-sations with Jane Sutter, a daughter of Mary's classmate Betty Sutter. "When she was bored or had nothing to do, she'd call and we'd have hysterical telephone conversations. We'd entertain each other and just laugh about everything. The ridiculous, the sublime, hypocrisy, the day's news. She had a very sharp eye," Jane said. In June 1991, Mary re-turned to the city to serve as honorary chair of a fundraiser to restore St. Louis's famed Forest Park. This role gave her a chance—maybe her last—to prove to St. Louis that she could still cut a figure as one of the city's important people. She arrived for the luncheon in wide-brimmed white hat, pearls, and a floral, matronly garden party dress.

Several times, Mary considered leaving Los Angeles permanently and, for her, St. Louis was the only option. Her affection for the city is remarkable, partly because of the very different feelings held by some other St. Louisans of the same generation who pursued careers in entertainment. Edmund Hartmann, just a year younger than Mary, was a third-generation St. Louisan who left to work for the Shubert theatre organization in New York, after which he became a television producer (*My Three Sons, Family Affair*) and screenwriter (five Abbott and Costello films). To him, "St. Louis was a very dullish place and I couldn't wait to get out." In New York and Los Angeles, "I made my own world." The attitude of four-time Oscar nominee Agnes Moorehead, who grew up in St. Louis, was similar: "When's the next bus leaving?" Mary explored retirement homes because she knew she would be unable to live as independently in St. Louis as she had in Los Angeles, especially in the winters. She visited LeClede Oaks and One McKnight Place, home at the time to Louis Westheimer, who had been so important to her in her youth. After touring these properties several times, accompanied by friends like Judy Hinrichs, she put her name on a waiting list at One McKnight. When a space became available, Mary decided she was not ready to move. To keep her position on the list, One McKnight requested a deposit. She let the spot go. "I'd still like to go to McKnight, but I don't want to put all that money down if I don't know when I'm going to be ready," she told Stella Koetter Darrow. In fact, physically, Mary was more than ready for an assisted living environment: She had increasing difficulty managing on her own and at this point could hardly see.

"There was something about it that put her off," says Elizabeth Danforth. "She never said the reason. Maybe it was just a bunch of old people and she wasn't putting herself in that category. Maybe it was her friends getting older. Maybe she thought there was more to do in California year long." But for Mary the most important consideration was that job offers would slow dramatically if she left Los Angeles, and she resisted the notion of no longer working. "Sometimes there's only one week between the time a script is finished and [the time] they cast it and start shooting. There's no way that you could live this far away from either coast and be in the thick of things," Mary told a reporter. She told Darrow in their last conversation, "I still would like to be back home in St. Louis, but I just can't give up my work." Looking at options closer to home, she considered the Motion Picture and Television Fund's retirement home, where she had for many years visited aged colleagues and in whose hospital she herself had been treated. In the end, she decided against this as well.

It was during this period that Mary began preparing her autobiography, which friends had long encouraged her to write. "She worked all those years—radio, television, movies, stage—and was like a walking encyclopedia of show biz. She had total recall of everything she ever did. She remembered the name of every theatre she was in and every play and the cast, even in the last few years," says Madelyn Pugh Davis. "She was the only person I ever told they should write a book. Well, you couldn't get Mary to do anything she wasn't in the mood for. She'd say, 'Well, I gotta do that.' She had an ancient little manual typewriter and she was going to write on that. I said, 'Mary, maybe you could dictate.' 'No, I have to see it written.' I said, 'They could write it out and then you could see it,' but she was going to do it her way, which was pretty much Mary. I could have organized it for her, but I didn't push. Finally, she started." She intended to call it "In the Draft of an Open Mind," the same title she used for a speech she once delivered at Washington University. At the time of her death, Dick Davis thinks Mary had completed about eighty pages. The document is not among Mary's official papers. Canon Richards has the only copy, which he says is much shorter than eighty pages, but which he declined to make available for this book.

In the face of disappointments, Mary grew even more demanding in her relationships. When Mary's cousin Elizabeth Dorsam died on January 29, 1994, just before her ninety-first birthday, her son Bill received an odd request. Mary, who considered Elizabeth her last living relative, naturally expected to attend the funeral. But because Mary preferred not to travel to St. Louis in harsh January weather, she asked Bill to cremate Elizabeth and have her remains kept at the funeral home until Mary could safely make the trip in the spring. "Mary wanted me to 'hold her' for about three months so she could come to the funeral," Bill says. To Bill, this request was beyond unreasonable. Elizabeth was his mother, after all, and she had never spoken to him about cremation. Besides, his sister Mary Ann Baker and her family had already made plans to travel from Indiana for the service. "I didn't see any point in cremating her just to [satisfy] Mary's wishes," he says. Mary was angry over Bill's decision and did not come to the service. Mary's own health quickly spiraled downward, and neither Bill nor Janice saw her again.

Inappropriate as Mary's request may seem, it is understandable in the context of the deep anxieties she experienced in 1994. When Elizabeth died, Mary lost more than a favored cousin. She lost the only connection to family who mattered to her, forcing her to face her own isolation. She had never bonded well with Bill's family, had never expressed interest in the Wickenhauser side of her family, and had long ago rejected her only other relative, Brooks Adkins in Ohio. Mary's behavior a few weeks before Elizabeth's death gives some indication of how vulnerable she felt as Elizabeth began slipping away. For years, whenever Elizabeth heard something in the news about trouble in Los Angeles, "My mom would hurry up and call to make sure Mary was OK, even if it was a train wreck five miles away," said Bill. When the 6.7 magnitude Northridge earthquake struck the Los Angeles area on January 17, Bill knew Mary would expect the same response from him, "but my mother was dying at the time and I didn't really think about Mary." Bill phoned Mary about a week after the earthquake and asked if she was OK. The quake had left Mary badly shaken and her apartment a mess, and she yelled angrily, "No, I'm not OK! You don't show concern for me, you never did, and you never did like anything I was in!" Bill says, "It hurt her that I didn't show concern. And she let me know."

With Elizabeth gone and many of Mary's friends dead, Mary's final years were often lonely, so maintaining a sense of family was especially important. Regular contact—especially dinner outings—with Emily Daniels, Rita Pico, and Dolly Reed Wageman helped. Daniels says a cornerstone of her friendship with Mary in the 1990s was an almost-daily telephone conversation about their evening meals. Late in the afternoon, one would call the other and each would report what they were preparing for the meals that they would later eat alone. Even late in life, when older people living alone often stop preparing meals, Mary made full dinners. This regular conversation is remarkable less for its content than for its regularity and for what it came to mean to Mary. "I'd say, 'I'm having half a chicken and a salad.' And she'd say, 'Well, I'm having so and so.' She ate very well. She always had meat or fish or salad, and fruit and potatoes and vegetables. And for dessert, she always had a chocolate sundae. She loved that," Daniels says. "I don't know whether it worked in reverse, but those conversations made me be sure [to eat well]. So that I didn't lie to Mary, I had to have that salad, even though I didn't want it."

CHAPTER FIFTEEN

Success Returns

MARY'S INVOLVEMENT IN THE 1980 *OKLAHOMA!* PRODUCTION ON Broadway began two years earlier, when she signed on to play Aunt Eller in two back-to-back, week-long performances in July 1978, first at the St. Louis Muny, and then at the Starlight Theatre in Kansas City. She was paid $1,750 per week. This was her first time playing Eller, the rural matriarch who in many ways is the heart of the show. Mary claimed she had never seen *Oklahoma!* before performing in it, but this is hard to believe. She lived in New York during the entirety of the musical's groundbreaking 1943–48 run, when its particular combination of drama, music, and dance was the talk of the performing arts world. On March 31, 1943, while in Boston for *Dancing in the Streets* tryouts, Mary sent a congratulatory telegram to Richard Rodgers in New York on the opening night of the original *Oklahoma!* at the St. James Theatre. It was an evening that changed the nature of American musical theatre, and he wrote her back. Three decades later, her denials of having seen the show were probably driven by wanting to avoid any suggestions that she patterned her performance on that of Betty Garde, the original Eller.

Oklahoma! is a sentimental tale about romantic rivalries that surface around a town social in the pioneer Midwest, just the kind of homespun storytelling that Mary liked. The part resonated with her, so in November 1978, when she was asked to play Eller in a short Florida tour being assembled by producer Zev Bufman, she quickly agreed. Just four months after playing the role in Kansas City, this job would pay less—$1,500 per week—but it would last ten weeks. She began rehearsals on December 4, 1978, in New York, before performing at the Miami Beach Theatre, Parker Playhouse in Fort Lauderdale, and the Royal Poinciana Playhouse in Palm Beach.

At this point, just shy of seventy, Mary—who never had trouble projecting her voice—struggled to establish a presence on stage. "When we were rehearsing, she was perfect. It was subtle and she was the absolute epitome of Aunt Eller. I couldn't think of anybody righter for the role. I thought, 'Boy, she's gonna just kill in this,'" says Lewis Stadlen, who played the peddler Ali Hakim. "But I was surprised that she lost a little energy on stage. She didn't have the right amount of energy to score, to show all the subtle aspects of her performance, and I think it may have frustrated her that it was somehow going to take a little more energy than she knew she had. Her performance in these big theatres didn't go beyond those first fifteen or twenty rows."

Harve Presnell played the wholesome cowboy Curly in the Florida shows. He and Mary bonded immediately around their lack of confidence in director Stone "Bud" Widney. "Mary came to me and said, 'Look, to protect us and to protect the show and so that the composer and lyricist don't turn over in their grave, we better make sure we do this right. We've both done it before, so let's do it our way.' So we did and the director just finally went along with it." That they had now established a rapport helped later when Presnell objected to Mary's efforts to guide his own performance. "She had done a lot of research in the characters and I got a lot from her. But she said, 'Well, *that* Curly . . .' and I said, "I don't care about the other Curlies. I do it my way. The reason they did it that way is because they couldn't sing.'" Mary had little patience with performers who were "perennial amateurs or with people not willing to do their homework. She was pretty short with some of those people," Presnell says. "But she was not domineering and she didn't interfere with the choreographer or the director. She'd say to me, 'What are they doing?!' [I'd say,] 'I don't know, maybe we'd better tell them.' 'You tell them.' 'I don't want to tell them—you tell them.'" Another cast member, who prefers not to be named, says he confronted Mary about her complaints to management about fellow cast members. "I went to her at one point and said, 'If you have a problem, tell me, or tell the stage manager, but don't do it behind my back.' She basically denied it."

Contretemps of this sort would be the least of the challenges presented by the Florida production. Alexander Orfaly, who was playing a lead role, the mysterious farm hand Jud, was killed in a horrific auto accident after the opening night party in Fort Lauderdale. The car he was driving was broadsided by a police vehicle during a chase. Orfaly died instantly, and one of his passengers—a female dancer in the show—also was killed. Bufman was asked to identify Orfaly's body. Late that night, he called both Presnell and Mary, who had developed a nice rapport with Orfaly, to give them the news and seek their advice. Bufman was worried about whether the cast would be able to continue and, if so, whether he could quickly find a suitable replacement for Orfaly. "I said, 'Look, we've got a job to do. You gotta leave it up to the cast, what they decide. But I think with Mary and I together, they'll do the show. We have a lot of this tour left,'" Presnell said. "So Mary and I came to work the next day knowing about this, but the rest of the cast didn't know. It was announced by the producer while we were there, and they were all upset. [Orfaly] was a terrific guy, wonderful. Of course, they were already thinking who we could get to replace him, not being sentimentalists, but knowing that the show has to go on. Why should we have to give all the tickets back?"

"Mary was very strong and did not allow the rest of the cast to fall apart. In fact, she told me a wonderful story about a dear, sweet friend of mine who was like my father, Hank Fonda. He was doing a matinee and his wife committed suicide in Connecticut. [Frances Seymour Brokaw, the second of Funda's five wives and the mother of actors Jane and Peter, took her life in 1950.] They said, 'Well, you need to go home.' And he said, 'What good will that do? This is too bad, but no, I'll do the show and then I'll go home.' So he stayed and did the show. And that attitude is the way Mary went." It was Mary who suggested the ultimate replacement for Orfaly. Bufman said at the time, with utter seriousness, that whenever he had doubts about the show, "I find myself speaking to Alexander, who's watching over us, and I know everything's going to be all right. We read and see and hear a lot about strange phenomena, but I've never believed any of it until now."

One reason Orfaly's death affected Mary is that it heightened her loneliness on the road. She was in a dance-oriented show surrounded by people decades younger with whom she had trouble finding common ground, so she was not close to many in the cast. She was in the mainstream of everything that was good about theatre, but she lacked contemporaries to share it with. "The dancers didn't know who she was or what she was talking about. *The Man Who Came to Dinner*? That's lost on twenty-year-olds," says Stadlen. "I sensed it must have been very frustrating. She was isolated and had nobody to really run with. She seemed extremely unhappy." Still, the remainder of the Florida tour went well. "People couldn't get seats. Oh, my lord, it was an incredible success," Presnell says. Mary was nominated for South Florida's Carbonell Award for Best Supporting Actress in the 1978–79 season. She did not win, but Orfaly won posthumously for Best Supporting Actor.

Mary had been back in Los Angeles only a month after the Florida tour, when she got a call about a new, larger *Oklahoma!* tour. Producers were hastily assembling a replacement for a *Seven Brides for Seven Brothers* tour starring Howard Keel that had fallen apart. Producer James Nederlander, who joined Bufman after the Florida run ended, needed something to present in the venues that had been booked. Mary was the only principal from the Florida shows who was brought on board for this tour, though many of the dancers were retained. The director was also replaced. For this production, William Hammerstein, lyricist Oscar Hammerstein II's son from his first marriage, directed. Hammerstein was known primarily for his work in the 1950s as managing director of the New York City Center Light Opera Company.

A nine-city tour began in Los Angeles and was to move on to San Francisco, Oklahoma City, Tulsa, Dallas, Chicago, Washington, Philadelphia, and Detroit. New York was added later, when the show proved successful on the road. Rehearsals began April 14, 1979, in Los Angeles. Mary's weekly salary was $1,750 during the Los Angeles production, which opened at the Pantages Theatre on May 5, and rose to $2,000 after that. She received first choice of dressing room along the tour, as well as first class air travel. The cast featured Christine Andreas as the farm girl Laurey, Laurence Guittard as Curly, Marty Vidnovic as Jud, and Christine Ebersole as the flirtatious Ado Annie. Mary received third billing after Guittard and Andreas, the leads.

While the show was staggering to its feet in Los Angeles, Lucille Ball visited backstage one night. "She was there for Mary, but she came to my room, which I found thrilling. That was the first time I met her," says Guittard. Guittard, who originated the role of the count in *A Little Night Music* just a few years before, was now so broke he had to borrow money to get from New York to Los Angeles for the audition. He and Mary did not like each other at first. "She had done it already and knew what she was going to do, and I didn't want to do it the way she had done it. We came to loggerheads at the very beginning. But we were both very serious, honorable workers and, at the heart of it, we were coming from the same place as actors." He would remain one of Mary's favorite people and a trusted confidant for the remainder of her life.

The early rehearsals were difficult because Mary gave Hammerstein the same hard time she often gave directors at the start of a production. "She didn't trust me as a director the first few days and she made that quite obvious. In fact, if things hadn't changed after those few days, we would have had a terrible time. She was unfriendly and resisted everything. I realized that I had a problem on my hands and I had to defeat the problem by getting her confidence, which eventually I did."

Hammerstein tried complimenting Mary and giving her opportunities to discuss whatever she wanted to talk about regarding the part. That tactic was not effective, but two other things finally did the trick. One day in rehearsals, he had the cast sit in a semi-circle, with him sitting in front of them. "I said, 'We're not going to rehearse today. We're going to go over the play *Green Grow the Lilacs* (on which *Oklahoma!* is based) and examine these characters, the way they were originally, before my father got hold of them.' Mary thought that was just great, particularly because I had Aunt Eller read her speech in the play, which is very long. And it reveals a lot more about her than there is time to reveal in the musical. It helped her to probe the part. That was the breaking point. After that, she was very cooperative," Hammerstein says. Eller's speech is a revealing text about a strong woman's perseverance against being sick and poor and alone and afraid. Guittard remembers, "Mary read it with absolutely devastating effect. It was so beautifully done, so simple and honest. I honestly think that was part of her, that Yankeeism. She was all of that."

Hammerstein's second strategy was to withhold direction from Mary: "I did this with Robert Morley in London. He was very resistant because he was a big star. So I just didn't tell him anything. I went about three days without giving him direction except "cross here, move there." He became very upset and spoke to me about it, and after that he was more accepting. We had a good time, in fact. I remembered that, so I did sort of the same thing with Mary. I just didn't say much to her, and she began to feel uncomfortable. If you do that with an actor in a rehearsal situation, eventually they come to you almost on their knees saying, please, tell me something. It didn't get to that point with Mary, but she got more cooperative and friendly.

The tour began well, with Mary and others receiving strong notices. In a rave review, the *Los Angeles Times* said, "The fact that Mary Wickes' singing powers are definitely limited was no deterrent—she is a veteran comedienne who can talk her way through anything—songs included. And she brings an unexpected tenderness to the gun-totin' old lady." Mary enjoyed the tour, which left her with some strong impressions, especially in the Midwest. In Oklahoma City, audiences stood and put their hands over their hearts when the cast sang "Oklahoma," which Mary found thrilling. She struggled with some of the physical demands of the show, especially because midway through the tour, an inner-ear problem made it difficult for her to keep her balance. She felt confident enough to leave the company for six weeks for a film role. In *Touched by Love*, she played a good-hearted teacher's aide at a school for children with cerebral palsy. Shot in Banff, Canada, the film featured Deborah Raffin, John Amos, and Clu Gulager, a team that had all worked together in a recent TV movie called *Willa*, in which Mary played a short-order cook. The roles allowed Mary to play two serious characters in quick succession.

The tour was never expected to be such a success; in fact, it was never intended to reach Broadway. "That production is the most interesting story of anything I've ever worked in," says Guittard. "It was given no chance, just something thrown into the mill as a stop-gap for something else. We had borrowed sets from Artpark [an outdoor summer theatre near Niagara Falls] and sort of slap-dash costumes and two weeks of rehearsal, and somehow it turned into an extraordinarily good show. We did so well that we *earned* New York. When they saw that we sold out everywhere and that we got these ecstatic notices, for the most part, when we were in Chicago, they gave us new sets and costumes. The company on the road found itself with something to be proud of. It really was an effort of an extraordinary company, if you think about who was in it. We had Agnes DeMille, which was thrilling for everybody." DeMille, who choreographed the original 1943 show, helped mount this show and rehearsed with the performers but did not travel with them.

While notices were good, business was not as good as Guittard remembers. "We would open on Monday night in some town and had practically no business at all. There would be nights when people would come out, and by the weekend we had good business. Then all we could count on was weekend business in every town. So it really never made much money," Hammerstein says. Nederlander began to press for bigger names in the cast to increase business before considering a New York run. This would mean replacing one or more performers who had committed to the tour. When Hammerstein gathered the cast in the last days of May 1979 to share this news, he created an uproar. Guittard remembers "having a shit-fit in front of everybody," though he did not feel his own job was threatened. Mary wrote Hammerstein an unusually angry letter. "I have a lot invested in this show and I think I have contributed enough to be heard," she said. She was especially annoyed at his having told the cast, "There are no stars in this company, begging your pardon," and proceeded to remind him of her own publicity value. She decried the production's poor public relations efforts, "directed by unpleasant and incompetent people," noting that she sought to promote the show on *Match Game* and *Password* during the Los Angeles run, but had to turn down those appearances when the publicity agency was not organized enough to shuttle her to the TV tapings between matinee and evening performances. Mostly, she reminded him the company was dedicated and committed and that "it would be a real tragedy" if it was not kept intact.

Hammerstein conceded to Mary that his remarks to the company had been disastrous, but pointed out that producers were only trying to protect the show. It was the star power of Yul Brynner that sold out the *King and I* on the road, he explained to her, and the power of Zero Mostel that sold out *Fiddler on the Roof*. But it was not Hammerstein who wanted cast changes, he explained later. "Nederlander wanted a star in the show, and I resisted that completely because that's not what the show is about. It's not made for stars. It's made for people who are cast properly in each part. Anyway, I won: We had no stars—and did no business."

The publicity staff was changed immediately, the tour continued with modest changes (Jamie Farr was replaced by Bruce Adler as Ali Hakim), and the show arrived in New York to great anticipation. But cast members' first impression of their new home—the Palace Theatre, a grand showplace renowned in vaudeville's heyday—was disappointing. The thick dust on the rafters made Guittard think the theatre had not been cleaned backstage in fifty years. "There were rats in the dressing room. It was horrible. We refused to occupy the theatre in the condition it was in, so they re-did it before we came in. I think Mary was behind that," Guittard says. Mary was given the star dressing room, which friend Warner Shook remembers was "huge—the size of a football field. She loved that."

From the first night, Mary shined. The *New York Post* found her performance "the most authentic," observing that "her pioneer presence and no-nonsense lovability illuminates the whole show." The *New York Times*, in a review full of positive comments, found Mary as Eller "just dandy. And if Miss Andreas, say, is enough of a puppy to take everything in earnest good faith, Miss Wickes is enough of a trouper to summon up what the original audiences took on faith. Quite apart from the hand-on-hips 'Hmphs!' that she regularly makes her own, she actually drives suspense into the open-air auction, under strings of Japanese lanterns, of the girls' basket lunches. Impossible? Not at all, not with the wary, tart-tongued actress rigging the bidding and keeping a sharp eye on the menacing Jud."

In many ways, Mary was now back where she started, walking many of the same streets she had walked forty-five years earlier, and she relished the attention the role brought her at this point in her life. For most of the run, she stayed at the Mayflower Hotel on 61st Street and

Central Park West, just a few blocks from where she lived throughout the 1940s. This was Mary's first Broadway role in more than thirty years, and its high profile brought her back into contact with people she had long ago lost touch with. At Sardi's, Vincent Sardi Jr. sometimes greeted Mary with, "Ahhh, Miss Wickes, your usual table." Malcolm Goldstein attended a small gathering there with Anne and Irving Schneider after the opening night performance of *Oklahoma!* "We all got there before Mary did. It was very clear that she wanted to make an entrance. She came in alone and got a round of applause, and she wanted that. It was great fun." She received a congratulatory mailgram on opening night from Lucy: "Take charge, Aunt Eller. The troops need you." She sent postcards to people like Jimmy Stewart, declaring, "I'm in *Oklahoma!* at the Palace Theatre in New York and we are a big fat hit! I know 1980 will be a good one for me!" Isabella was no longer here to share this triumph with, but no doubt Mary was mindful of another family connection: Her Aunt Hes performed in vaudeville at the Palace shortly after it opened in 1913, walking on this same stage.

Being in New York enabled Mary to spend time with friends from her early theatre days. She had lunch with Anna Crouse, whom she roomed with on the road during *Stars in Your Eyes* tryouts in 1939. Crouse was struck by Mary's recall of that period forty years later. That show featured a beautiful prop, a gray English pram, "none of this stuff you fold up and put in the taxi, but a really gorgeous baby carriage. When Mary came to lunch, she said, 'I always remember you pushing this baby carriage around backstage. You just couldn't take your hands off it.' I'd forgotten about this entirely. All my life, though I thought I wanted a career, what I really wanted was a family. I realized that I'd had this problem of what I wanted to do with myself for a long time," says Crouse. She was single when she and Mary worked together, working as Anna Erskine, but she later married playwright Russel Crouse (*The Sound of Music*) and raised two children, the actress Lindsay Crouse and the writer Timothy Crouse.

In May 1980, Mary's weekly salary jumped to $2,500, the most she would ever receive for stage work, but surprisingly little for a working actress with as much experience and as many credits as she had. Mary was to receive another bump to $2,750 in September, but she never saw it: The cast was notified on August 19 that the show would close at the end of the matinee on Sunday, August 24. Hammerstein had declined to give permission to videotape the show, so no visual record of it exists, but there is an excellent cast album. Made in January 1980 for RCA with the show's original conductor, it received a Grammy nomination.

When the show ended its nine-month run in August, Mary had hoped to do more than return to the occasional TV episode guest-star offer. But after putting herself before audiences for almost five decades, she found herself dependent on a generation of casting professionals who were only peripherally familiar with her work. Her career had stalled, and searching for work became humiliating. She talked with Columbia Artists Theatricals about mounting a touring one-woman show, but nothing came of those discussions. "She went through a very bad patch for about five years—a long, long stretch—where she didn't do anything," says Guittard. "She was down about not having a job. No one knew who she was anymore." Sometimes being overlooked stung more than others. During this period, Mary met Anne and Irving Schneider for lunch in the theatre district with their daughter, Beatrice Colen. Beatrice, or Betsy, was visiting from Los Angeles, where she was pursuing an acting career; with help from Natalie Schafer, Betsy had quickly landed a small, regular role as the waitress Marsha on *Happy Days*. This afternoon, the maître d' peered up at their party from his podium, looked straight past Mary and the Schneiders, and said excitedly to Betsy, "Aren't you in *Happy Days*?!" His reaction was especially striking, because Mary was wearing full theatrical make-up, as the meal took place between a matinee and an evening performance.

A year after *Oklahoma!*, Mary was one of about forty people who received an appeal from Max Wilk, who was creating a playwriting scholarship at the Yale School of Drama in honor of Audrey Wood. Wood was half of the prominent theatrical agency Liebling-Wood. She represented playwrights like Tennessee Williams and William Inge, while her husband William Liebling represented actors. Together, they built a devoted following, and now Wood was seriously ill. Responses came in quickly, many like that of Katharine Hepburn, who sent $1,000. Mary wanted to contribute for two reasons: Wood and Liebling (who died in 1969), had been among her first agents, and it was Wilk's father, Jacob Wilk, who brought Mary out from New York for *The Man Who Came to Dinner* at Warners Bros. From Mary, "I got back a letter that said, 'Dear Max: Things are not good. I'm not well, I'm not working a lot and I'm sort of broke. But I couldn't let this one go by. I'm sending you a check. It may not be a big check, but it's just as heartfelt as if it were.' She sent me a check for fifty bucks. And I knew how much that meant. I knew her well enough to know she was not kidding. Ups and downs, she probably wasn't making any money. I was so touched that she had to be part of it," Wilk says.

Mary returned to Hollywood and—grateful for work, but disappointed to have nothing more significant—took episodic work on *The Love Boat* (1981), *The Waltons* (1981), *Trapper John, MD* (1981, 1982 and 1984, playing a different character each time), and *Matt Houston* (1984). She played Lady Bracknell in *The Importance of Being Earnest* for a week in Williamsburg, Virginia (1981), followed by brief runs in *Henry IV, Part I*, with Christopher Walken at the American Shakespeare Theatre in Stratford, Connecticut (1982), and in *Palace of Amateurs* at the Berkshire Theatre Festival in Stockbridge (1982), her first time there in almost three decades. That work was followed by a three-week run in *Light Up the Sky* at the Coconut Grove (Florida) Playhouse in November 1983. She had been invited by Jose Ferrer, the theatre's new artistic director, whom Mary had known since the 1930s. She jumped at the chance to work again—in a Moss Hart play no less, and as Stella, the stage mother, a role full of bluster. Opening night must have felt to Mary like stepping back to the 1940s, since Kitty Carlisle Hart, Josh Logan, and even George Abbott traveled to see the production, but this audience of luminaries only made the lack of sparkle on stage more apparent. The production did not do well. The *Miami News* criticized Ferrer's direction, virtually every element of the show—which the reviewer said "literally plods for nearly two and a half hours"—and most of the performances, but not Mary's. "It is only when Wickes is on stage as Irene's mother does this comedy live up to its expectations. She shows a determination to bring some life to the carcass on stage that is admirable and which succeeds splendidly because this strong actress knows what to do even if nobody else does. Such a situation would be unnerving to a lesser talent, but if Wickes is fidgety in the company in which she finds herself, she doesn't show it," the paper wrote.

Even with reviews like that, Mary's frustration grew. In 1983 and 1984, she wrote at least three times to Robert Fryer, artistic director of the Ahmanson Theatre in Los Angeles, seeking work. "You are a most distinguished actress and I have long been a big admirer of your work," he responded in April 1983. "I promise you that we will bring your name up next season for each play in which there is a part appropriate for you." Mary was now seventy-three, an age when other actresses might consider retiring. "Mary wanted to work more than she wanted money. The career took over her whole life. It became her marital relationship," says Iggie Wolfington. So she continued assembling a patchwork of jobs, some in television, some on stage, but none in film. On television, she appeared in *Murder, She Wrote*, which meant a trip to Hawaii for location filming (1984); *The Canterville Ghost*, in which she was brilliant as the dour, humorless housekeeper (1985); and the *Christmas Gift*, an overly sentimental TV movie about a small town's belief in Santa Claus (1986). The latter starred John Denver and required location shooting in Georgetown, Colorado, a quaint mining town that must have reminded Mary of the streets of her childhood. On stage, she played for several months in *Detective Story* with Charlton Heston and Mariette Hartley in Los Angeles and Denver (1984). With Alice Ghostly, she played an elderly murderer in *Arsenic and Old Lace* at the Burt Reynolds Jupiter Theatre (1985), the only time her weekly salary for stage work ever reached the $2,500 she was making when *Oklahoma!* closed. When she played a slow-witted fishing resort owner in the comedy *The Foreigner* for six weeks at the Alliance Theatre in Atlanta (1987), she was the biggest name in the cast—and took the assignment so seriously that she took lessons from a voice coach to capture the character's rural Georgia accent. She hoped to appear a year later in a West Coast revival of *Strike Up the Band*, a 1927 musical comedy by George S. Kaufman and the Gershwins, but the role, originally played by Edna May Oliver, went to Faye DeWitt.

Within a couple of years, it became clear that, for Mary, working on the stage was no longer safe. She had such trouble getting around that performing nightly on a stage with a lot of movement taking place was risky for her physically. After he brought Mary to a matinee of his stage production of *You Can't Take It With You* in 1991, director Warner Shook sensed "a bit of melancholy that she knew in her gut that she couldn't do that anymore. She couldn't really work on the stage anymore because of her eyes and her health."

She re-focused her sights on film and television, but reaching out to casting directors would no longer be enough. "She felt there was a whole new breed in Hollywood who didn't know who she was. That was hard on her because she had worked so hard," Shook says. Mary now made a conscious decision to be seen at Hollywood parties, premieres, exhibit openings, and award shows. She liked dressing up, even if she often wore the same beaded gold and red jacket over a black dress, always with Tea Rose perfume. One event in particular, the American Cinema Awards, was little known outside of the industry, but was lavish, with big name entertainment (Liza Minnelli and Shirley Bassey have both performed there) and high-profile guests, especially of a certain generation. At this point in her life, Mary took pleasure in being around people she remembered from the heyday of her career. "Mary and I would go every year and have so much fun. She liked the camaraderie. These were

people she had worked with and could relate to. Every other time somebody would stand up, it was someone we thought was dead," jokes Bill
Givens, her frequent escort.

More frightened than she had ever been about a drop in income,
Mary reluctantly prepared an audition tape to circulate among casting
agents. Yes, Mary Wickes was reduced to arranging a twelve-minute collection of video clips to find work. She chose excerpts of her scenes in
White Christmas, *The Man Who Came to Dinner*, *The Lucy Show*, *Doc*, *Father
Dowling Mysteries*, and *You Can't Take It With You* (the TV series). "She was
very conflicted about whether she should do it," Guittard says. "She was
proud of what she accomplished and didn't feel she should beg for a job
in that kind of way. But when she did it, she started working like crazy.
It definitely turned her career around."

Postcards from the Edge, released in 1990, broke Mary's dry spell, and she
worked continuously in high-profile films after that. In *Postcards*, Mary
played the strong-willed but weary—and sometimes wearying—grandmother in a celebrated but dysfunctional Hollywood family. Written by
Carrie Fisher, the film is a clever, knowing look at Hollywood through
the lens of one family's mother-daughter angst. Fisher is the daughter
of actress Debbie Reynolds, and Mary's character was loosely based on
Reynolds's own mother. "I lived in dread that Debbie's mom would come
on the set and have her two cents worth. I never met her, but Debbie
said she liked the performance," Mary said. Grandma Pearl is a non-stop
chatterer, blowsy but endearing. She is the mother of a once-famous
actress who represents Old Hollywood glamour (Shirley MacLaine, who
spends much of the film in ermine and pearls) and the grandmother of
a young woman who struggles to emerge from a family filled with egos,
alcohol, and secrets to find her own identity (Meryl Streep, in one of
her most understated roles). Loving and ultimately lovable, Grandma
is the grounded, sane one in this three-generation relationship, completely without pretense. She wears cat-eye spectacles, saddle shoes,
and heavy embroidered sweaters long after all these items went out of
style. She knows her daughter drinks too much, so she wants to leave
a party before wine causes MacLaine to start babbling. She speaks with
a daffy southern manner that must have faded in subsequent generations. Greeting Streep lovingly, she says, "Let me look at'cha, Lovebug,
before your fat ol' grandmother hauls her rear off to bed. Give me a big
hug," she says. "You sure do stink pretty." Mary is given other wonderful
lines, usually delivered in knowing asides. In the hospital after MacLaine
crashes her car, Mary steals the scene by muttering, "I don't know what

I'm doing in this family. I got a wino daughter and a doped-up grand-daughter." She offers MacLaine some homespun advice: "Cry all you want. You'll pee less, as my grandma used to say." Her snappy comments never sounded so genuine. In that same hospital scene, Mary's character initially was to sit on MacLaine's bed while she spoke to her. But Mary's years of hospital volunteering had taught her that, for all sorts of reasons, it is best if visitors do not sit on patients' beds. So she raised this concern and was permitted to deliver her lines standing by MacLaine's bedside. "She knew better—you don't sit on the bed of a sick person," says Madelyn Pugh Davis, who heard about this from Mary.

The role fit Mary like a glove. But deciding to do *Postcards* must have caused her a lot of soul-searching, since the film prominently features drug use, drunkenness, random sexual encounters, and more. The chance to work with director Mike Nichols was a big opportunity to revive her career, so Mary found a way to put her objections aside. The irony, of course, is that when Mary finally accepted a film with story elements that she stayed away from her entire career, she found one of her greatest successes, a role that produced her strongest notices in years and, not surprisingly, more film offers.

Not wanting Nichols to discover how poor her eyesight had become, she purchased a large-screen magnifying machine that would allow her to memorize the entire part. This way, she could perform any scene he might want during the audition. But at the audition, Nichols unexpectedly offered her the role without asking her to read for it, a gracious gesture of confidence that Mary never forgot. "She told us she had a wonderful interview and he was great to her and he said, 'I'm just thrilled you're doing the picture.' She said, 'Don't you want me to read for you?' And he said, 'No, of course not. I'm honored you're going to do it, I don't want you to read for it.' She said, 'Well, I want to do the scene.' So she got up and did the scene because she had learned it," says Anne Kaufman Schneider.

What *Postcards* did to revive Mary's film career, *Father Dowling Mysteries* did for her television career. Tom Bosley, who signed on early to play the title role on this lightweight mystery series, attended auditions for Marie, the earthy rectory housekeeper. He was seated with producers when Mary read for the role. After she left, he turned to the others and said, "What are we kidding ourselves for? I don't think you have to look for anyone else." So Mary became the housekeeper who keeps tabs on a middle-aged priest with a penchant for sleuthing (Bosley), a young crime-solving nun (Tracy Nelson), and an ambitious, full-of-himself priest who has no patience for any of this (James Stephens). The series ran from 1989 to 1991. Set in Chicago, *Father Dowling Mysteries* was filmed in Denver for the first eighteen months and in Los Angeles thereafter. Denver's severe weather, snow, and winds exacerbated Mary's existing health and vision problems, but she was a trouper. She stayed in a residential hotel with a little kitchen where she prepared her own meals, and she did not socialize much. "All the time we were in Denver, she never came home for a holiday. When Thanksgiving or Christmas rolled around, she was cooking food for the homeless and visiting hospitals. I get kind of a glow when I think about her and everything she stood for," Bosley says. That same caring extended to the Dowling set. "She was like the ringleader. If the set was too cold, she'd make sure it was heated. If it was too hot, she made sure the AC was working. She was our drill master," he said.

The series was driven by a homespun ethos that Mary liked, especially its respect for religious life. Marie is simple and unsophisticated—and almost doddering. The role consists largely of her shuffling around the rectory in apron and sweater, driving Dowling around Chicago, passing phone messages among the others as they squeeze time for crime-fighting activities from their religious duties ("It's for you, Sister," she hollers into the living room), and cooking. Most of her dialogue revolves around food: what she is preparing for dinner, what dishes houseguests prefer, how long Latvian pudding must sit, what went wrong in the kitchen, lines like "I think I hear the soup boiling." Here, too, Mary learned her lines using sides, but now producers prepared them for her in enlarged type.

Dowling allowed Mary to do more than simply keep house. Marie was sometimes pulled into the week's detective activities, such as when she dons a dark overcoat and hat to resemble Dowling, allowing him to escape a threatening situation. And, twice widowed, Marie was occasionally allowed romantic feelings. In one episode, she becomes smitten with a dashing younger priest (alas, a hit man in hiding); in another, a kindly minister expresses interest in her company, which clearly pleases her. When she declares they can never become serious, he assumes she is referring to their color differences—he is African American—but she says, it is simply because he is a Baptist and she is a Catholic.

But Mary must have cringed at some of the show's production values and eye-rollingly bad writing. In at least two episodes, Bosley plays not just Father Dowling but Dowling's evil twin brother, while in another, Tracy Nelson, too, plays double roles: Sister Stephanie and her look-alike,

Lady Cara, a princess whom she impersonates. Dowling's confidence at one point is so shaken by having caused the wrong person to be arrested for stealing church candlesticks, he begins consulting with an apparition, a ghost-like Dr. Sherlock Holmes. Endings were sophomoric. How many times can Sergeant Clancy surface to arrest the bad guy at just the right moment? Worse, how often must wooden extras in police uniforms burst in to arrest the criminals without uttering a word or asking any questions? Story continuity, too, was problematic. In production materials, Marie's last name is Murkin, but in some episodes, it is Brody and in others it is Gillespie. Even the sets lack credibility; the walls of a jewelry store that has been burgled are inexplicably lined with law books. In one especially ridiculous episode, Marie is kidnapped, held for $6 million ransom and stuffed upright into a coffin-like crate. The kidnapper tapes her mouth and tells her to shut up—but does not tie her hands, so of course she removes the tape when the lid is closed. The telephone rings, even though Marie had just taken it off the hook. *Columbo*, this wasn't. Nor did it even approach the more polished *Murder, She Wrote*, with which it is sometimes compared and on which Bosley sometimes appeared. But it was a prime time role with good visibility. And it pleased Mary that she was appreciated both by those in religious life—she received letters from priests praising her character as someone they knew all too well—and by the show's producers, who paid tribute by calling one of the episodes, "The Man Who Came to Dinner Mystery."

But the opportunity that brought the biggest boost to Mary's career was neither Grandma in *Postcards* nor Marie in *Dowling*. It was a sarcastic, aging nun by the name of Mary Lazarus, who surfaced in 1991. At eighty-one, Mary found herself signing onto one of the most successful films of her career—and certainly the most lucrative she had known. She was paid $150,000 for her role in *Sister Act*, more than she had received for any other piece of work to that point, and a long way from the $25 she earned for her first Vitaphone short in 1935.

Sister Mary Lazarus is a cynical, suspicious nun who finds her role as longtime director of the convent choir challenged by the upstart Sister Mary Clarence (Whoopi Goldberg), who is actually a lounge singer hiding in disguise from the mob. Since audiences seem to find nuns funnier in threesomes, Mary is again paired with two good-hearted sidekicks, the excessively cheerful Sister Mary Patrick (Kathy Najimy) and the more solemn and sheltered Sister Mary Robert (Wendy Makkena). *Sister Act* is a big, loud, feel-good movie, popular with audiences but less well received by critics because of plot and dialogue elements that stretch credulity. For instance, after Mary Clarence reassures the trio that "we're always going be together," Mary Lazarus chimes in with her best seen-it-all voice, "That's what Diana Ross said." How many octogenarian nuns are conversant on the back-story of pop music groups? The *New York Times* criticized the nuns as "walking sight gags rather than real people," describing Mary Lazarus as "half-nun, half-marine." Yet Mary herself mostly received good notices. "The stage and screen stalwart Mary Wickes displays marvelous deadpan sovereignty as a proud battle-axe," the *New Yorker* said. "Wickes outdoes all the comedians who parody codgers reminiscing about the good old bad old days—she never breaks character and winks at the audience."

Mary Lazarus has served under four popes and clings to the old ways, a trait that gives her some wonderful lines. Reacting to a reference to a progressive convent, she declares, "Sounds awful. I liked my convent in Vancouver, out in the woods. Wasn't all modern like some of these new-fangled convents. We didn't have electricity. Cold water, bare feet—those were nuns. It was hell on earth. I loved it." Later, asking Mother Superior to help rescue Mary Clarence from gangsters, she snarls, "We can't leave it up to the Feds," as if she has lots of experience with crime stings.

One reason Mary is so effective is that her pallor suggested she was every bit the veteran nun who had seen it all in life—a little tired, a little pale, and a lot wise. Michael Germain, the film's make-up artist, says, "I didn't cover up any imperfections—what you saw is pretty much what you got. All the nuns had a very natural foundation, including Mary. Everything I did was minimal. I just put on a foundation so they wouldn't be ghost-white. The older ones 'got it' but the younger ones tried to cheat. Kathy Najimy and Wendy Makkena would sneak on lipstick, or sometimes sneak on mascara, but if I could catch it, I'd make them take it off."

The film gave Mary her first appearance on the *Tonight Show*, a segment on the *Today Show*, countless feature stories in magazines and newspapers (including an appearance in an *Entertainment Weekly* special cover story, "What is Cool?"), and even TV commercials for the film. This renewed attention meant others would be looking more closely at her career. When press materials from Disney described her as having "worked in motion pictures and television for more than six decades," she quickly objected. Her first film appearance was in 1935 so, at best, "almost six decades" would have been accurate. But, ever conscious of not appearing old, Mary never in her career mentioned that 1935 short film and always considered *The Man Who Came to Dinner* (1941) her first film. Disney revised the reference.

So many things about film marketing were new to her now. She was asked to appear in a music video to push the movie, but music videos were another world. For one thing, they place the emphasis on the music, not the words, which constituted Mary's comfort zone. She was to appear with a group called Lady Soul, singing "If My Sister's in Trouble." Mary assumed she would be given a script to work from, but instead, when she showed up with Najimy and Makkena, the actresses were told, "Now get up on the platform, this is the music, and think of something funny." Clearly, this was not how Mary preferred to work. In the end, Mary's contribution to the video is to look up from a prayer book and shoot disapproving glances as Najimy and Makkena, in habits, danced with Lady Soul's three young, svelte performers dressed in sexy outfits.

To familiarize herself with conducting a choir, Mary attended several choir rehearsals at All Saints' Episcopal Church in Beverly Hills. But preparing for her scenes would be the easy part. The production required travel (some scenes would be shot in San Francisco, some in Reno, and others in Los Angeles), which was now difficult for her. The script was in a constant state of flux owing to a succession of writers who worked on it after a draft was written by Paul Rudnick. And there were personality adjustments to be made. For one thing, Mary was not accustomed to actors who worked like Whoopi Goldberg. She was so uncomfortable with Goldberg's language during filming that she seriously considered leaving the project. It would have been only the second time in her career to have left a production because of exasperation, after *The Adventures of the Black Girl in Her Search for God* at the Mark Taper Forum in 1969. Jane Sutter remembers Mary being "horribly offended" by Goldberg. "Mary could not get over her foul mouth. Whoopi's language just appalled her. Mary came very close to leaving the set, but I think she felt that sometimes you just hold your nose. She would never say anything to anyone in Hollywood, but she just couldn't understand it," Sutter says. Madelyn Pugh Davis, too, remembers Mary being unnerved by Goldberg during shooting. "Whoopi was being Whoopi Goldberg, you know, the star. And Mary would get all nettled about something and she wasn't afraid to speak up. I remember telling her, 'You have to take into account that she had a terrible life. She was homeless and she's made something of herself. So give her a little slack. And she did—because she was a kind person, really."

One of the things that made Mary uncomfortable might have been Goldberg's very public accusation of racism on Disney's part reflected in certain elements of the film, such as a scene in early drafts in which

Goldberg's character steals. At a Friars Club Roast of Richard Pryor, Goldberg announced, "Working for Disney, I do feel like a nigger again and I'm not afraid to say it." She showed up on the *Sister Act* set the next morning with a T-shirt featuring Mickey Mouse in blackface that proclaimed, "Niggerteer." She passed extra shirts around the set. Bill Givens puts Mary's relationship with Goldberg in perspective. "Mary was a bit of a prude, but they liked each other," he says. "At one of the Comedy Awards that I went to with her, the one where Whoopi won, Whoopi came over to the table and talked. Mary may have been a little upset [during filming], but it wasn't the kind of thing that got in the way. She liked her. I never heard her say snide things about Whoopi Goldberg." Indeed, publicly Mary was very careful not to disparage her co-star. If Goldberg was upset with Disney over stereotypical traits given to her character, "She never gave any evidence that she was unhappy" on the set, Mary told a reporter. "She's very professional. She comes on, she knows her lines and she's very appreciative if you have something funny to do. I just loved her." Germain, the make-up artist, who has done Goldberg's make-up on almost all of her pictures, says, "Mary was old school and I guess you could say Whoopi was new school, but I don't recall any conflicts."

"She liked Whoopi Goldberg personally but I doubt that Mary would have been very friendly with her because Whoopi Goldberg is black. Mary was a little antediluvian in her attitude toward blacks. Like the way she talked about the director of the second film (Bill Duke, whom Mary did not like). 'Oh, those blacks, that *black* director—he didn't know what he was doing.' It wasn't 'that *director*' didn't know what he was doing.' Maybe if she lived a little longer . . . ," observes Dolly Reed Wageman. Wageman believes Mary would have been drawn not to Goldberg but to Maggie Smith, who played Mother Superior. Mary did, in fact, like Smith very much and told Givens that "the best thing that came out of the *Sister Act* movies was that she became close to Maggie Smith." But this apparently did not last. Wageman recalls Mary making "some slightly catty remark" about Smith one day, after the film was over. "Maggie was coming into town and Mary called her up to see if she wanted to have dinner, and she said, No, she didn't think so." Mary inferred Smith did not want to spend time with her and was hurt. She told Wageman in a self-protective way, "Well, you know, if *that's* the way she feels."

Of course, it is possible that Mary simply had less in common with Duke than with the director of the first film, Emile Ardolino. Duke's acting credits included roles in the Arnold Schwarzenegger films *Commando* and *Predator*, both pretty far removed from Mary's world. Mary grew especially close to Ardolino, who had previously directed *Chances Are* and *Dirty Dancing*. When he died of AIDS shortly after the film was made, Mary attended his memorial in Los Angeles and was disappointed to miss his funeral in New York.

The *Sister Act* cast and crew screening at the Academy of Motion Pictures in Beverly Hills happened to be on the same night as Johnny Carson's final evening as host of the long-running *Tonight Show*, on which Bette Midler was a guest. Midler, for whom Goldberg's part had originally been written, came to the *Sister Act* screening following the taping. "As soon as the lights came up at the end of the screening, we're adjusting ourselves and all of a sudden we hear, '*Mary Wickes!* I've always wanted to meet you!' And here comes Bette Midler charging across the room. She was still wearing the costume she wore on Carson, that funny little skirt. Mary was delighted. She enjoyed the attention of her peers," says Givens, who escorted Mary that night. She responded graciously and introduced them formally: "Miss Midler, this is Mr. Givens."

At the American Comedy Awards in February 1993, Mary and Najimy were among the five nominees for Funniest Supporting Female in a Motion Picture, and Goldberg was nominated as Funniest Actress. Mary had known she would not leave with an award that night, since winners were revealed in advance, but she attended the evening as a gesture of support for her co-workers. Najimy and Goldberg both won.

Even a film this successful brought Mary some disappointment. When she learned cousin Bill Dorsam had never gone to see *Sister Act*, Mary sent him a tape, which he never made time to watch. "She told me that it bothered her that I didn't make a special effort" to express interest in her work. "She said, 'You never did like to see anything I was in,' and that really wasn't the case. I just wasn't interested in much of her stuff. I like documentaries, like one recently on the Hubbell telescope. To me, that's interesting. It wasn't that I had anything against her. I don't change the channel when I see her on TV," he says. But contrast this attitude with the support Mary received from friends, and it's easy to understand why she resented Dorsam's indifference. Anne and Irving Schneider made plans to see the film on the afternoon it opened in New York, specifically so they could report back by phone right afterward. During this screening, the audience broke out in applause after one of Mary's scenes. "I couldn't believe it. I rushed home and called her up and said, 'You'll never believe what just happened. You got a hand!' She was absolutely thrilled," Anne says.

The film did so well that it inspired a sequel in quick order—perhaps too quick. *Sister Act 2: Back in the Habit* brought back most of the original cast, but it had little of the first film's spark and was not received as well by audiences or critics. Mary has a much smaller role and was mostly relegated to knowing facial expressions. Producers may not have known quite what to do with her in this story—what could she bring to a plot driven by rap lyrics?—but they were unwilling to change a casting formula that worked well the first time. So the film has clerics barricade a school administrator in a closet by sliding a salami through the door handles (shades of *Dowling*'s inanity here). Mary was further out of her element than she had ever been in a film, and she did not enjoy the experience as much as she had the first time around.

But the sequel produced two good things: another large salary and sustained visibility. Her role in this film meant she would perform briefly at the social event of the season in January 1994, the Commitment to Life fundraising dinner for local HIV services, keeping her in front of a who's who of Hollywood decision-makers. The event featured Elizabeth Taylor, Barbara Streisand, Liza Minnelli, Bruce Springsteen, Whitney Houston, Hillary Clinton, and others—and an appearance by the nuns. During an *Entertainment Tonight* news report on the event, Mary is caught on camera during rehearsals in a stairwell before the performance. Unfortunately, at that moment, she is snapping at another actress who has stepped on her line. She looks annoyed that the cameras are there, catching her with her hair up in kerchief and without makeup.

Postcards, *Dowling*, and *Sister Act* had together brought Mary's career full circle. "When all this happened, it was a professional shot in the arm. She was back in the public eye in a big way in very, very successful movies. I could tell this was gratifying to her," says Warner Shook. At least one more opportunity would come her way. In 1993, a film version of Louisa May Alcott's *Little Women* was being assembled and producers were casting the monied, critical Aunt March. They offered the role to Katharine Hepburn, who turned it down, saying she "would never even think of competing with Edna May Oliver," who played Aunt March in George Cukor's 1933 film version. (That would have been clever casting: Hepburn, eighty-seven in 1993, had played Jo in the original film.) Mary had no such reservations and accepted the part, perhaps the only one in her career that had been presented to Katharine Hepburn first. *Little Women* had been one of Mary's favorite books as a child, filled as it was with earnest, loving characters who depend upon each other for family support. The film was bolstered by a strong ensemble cast, including

Susan Sarandon, Winona Ryder, Clare Danes, Kirsten Dunst, and Christian Bale. It received wide distribution at Christmas 1994, quickly found an audience, and received solid notices.

Not much is required of Aunt March in the film, but Mary nonetheless found the job difficult, since much of the picture was shot on location. Even the few steps up to the hairdressing trailer were a challenge for her, so hairdresser James Brown went to her dressing room instead. Worse, she was even more isolated and alone than she had been during *Oklahoma!* fifteen years earlier. Warner Shook returned to his Seattle home one day in 1994 to find this comic plea from Mary on his answering machine: "Pushface, it's Mary Isabella. I'm up here in Canada with no one to talk to but Winona Ryder—help me!" It wasn't just that younger colleagues were unfamiliar with her body of work, her age and her place in the industry made people reluctant to approach her socially. "She spent more time alone than she should have. You easily could have phoned her up," Brown says. He remembers thinking once during the production of asking Mary to join him in his evening plans, but he assumed she would decline. The next morning, he was telling her about the prior night, and she said "So why didn't you call me?!" He found her easy to talk with and full of Hollywood stories—but only if she was asked. "With a lot of old stars, it's like they're still on the *Johnny Carson Show*, but she wasn't like that. She lived in the present, not in the past. Mary was, 'This is today, this is now, this is what we're doing.'"

Her last years also brought Mary to the single lowest point of her career. It came in the form of a TV pilot called *Weldon Pond*, starring Jason Bateman. The project began on an unpleasant note, when Mary initially did not understand that she would be expected to read for the role, and things never recovered. At this point in her career, Mary was willing to audition for film roles, but she resented having to read for a supporting part in a sitcom. To help calm her, a representative of her agency, the House of Representatives, accompanied her to the reading.

The role was humiliating. She was to play a Chicago ad agency receptionist who lives with an animated sheep—not just any animated sheep, but a talking sheep who mocks her by calling her things like "the wrinkle with lips." Mary was offered the part and accepted it, but why? Was her desire to generate income so great at this point that she would stoop to this? Denny Sevier at the House of Representatives concedes that perhaps he pushed her too hard to sign, swept up in the enthusiasm that surrounded *Babe*, the feature film about a talking pig. *Babe* was not yet released when CBS taped *Weldon Pond* in March 1994, but the film was already creating a buzz and would go on to earn seven Oscar nominations. *Weldon Pond*, on the other hand, was rejected by network executives in May 1994 and never aired. After this debacle, Mary changed agencies again—something she did often in her career—and other opportunities surfaced quickly.

Determined not to let her decreasing mobility restrict her work, Mary turned to jobs that would not require memorizing camera angles or marks on a stage floor: She would seek voice work for animated entertainment. Mary's raspy, expressive voice and clear enunciation made this a natural path. In October 1994, with the premier of *Little Women* just two months away, Mary accepted a voice-only role in a Disney animated film, *The Hunchback of Notre Dame*, playing a gargoyle originally named Quinn, but later renamed Laverne. Delays in that production postponed her first dialogue session to June 1995. The delay meant Mary's first voice-over work now would be on television instead: In the interim, she accepted the voice role of Grandma in comedian Louie Anderson's animated sitcom *Life with Louie*, alongside other distinctive-voiced performers such as Edie McClurg. The half-hour series, a semi-autobiographical look at Anderson's own childhood with ten siblings, debuted in January 1995 and developed a strong following. "When I first heard Mary's voice, I just felt it was a midwestern grandmother-type of voice, the kind of woman who, if her husband was sick, would take over the plowing chores and run the farm," Anderson said. "Mary really understood that character and played that part so well."

CHAPTER SIXTEEN

Physical Deterioration

FORCED TO GIVE UP DRIVING AND HER TRUSTED, FOUR-DOOR BLUE Ford Fairlane, Mary found herself for the first time in her life depending on others for help. And she hated it. For social events, the Davises (who lived in nearby Bel Air) or Emily Daniels (who lived in what is now called Valley Village) often picked her up and drove her home. For work, she now sometimes asked production companies to send a car. For errands, she often turned to public transit, surely making her one of the few established actresses who relied on Los Angeles County's bus system. Only occasionally did Mary take taxis because, naturally, she found them too expensive. Practical as ever, she purchased booklets of discount taxi fare coupons through a public program for senior citizens. Having to rely increasingly on taxis "was a blow to her pride and to her pocketbook. But it was also her independence. Having to rely on a taxi driver or a friend was just something she could not bear," Dolly Reed Wageman says.

For grocery shopping, Mary sometimes imposed upon Mary Jane Croft, the actress who played the Ricardos' Connecticut neighbor on *I Love Lucy*. Croft lived in the same complex as Mary, in a much larger apartment on a higher floor, with a small dog. Croft drove to Gelson's market on Saturday mornings promptly at nine, and if Mary wanted a ride, she made sure to be downstairs on time. The sight of these two sit-com war-horses comparing melons at Gelson's must have startled more than a few shoppers. Alice Urist from Mary's hospital volunteer circle drove her to hospital auxiliary board meetings, and friend Nelle Gillespie, the widow of special effects pioneer Arnold Gillespie, frequently drove her on errands. Mary's need for help made her so uncomfortable that she rarely asked for rides outright; instead, as she did with Wageman, Mary would complain about not being able to drive, prompting Wageman to offer a lift. Mary would then protest, "No, no, it's out of your way," at which point Wageman would insist.

Failing eyesight may have forced Mary to give up driving, but it wasn't going to separate her from her heavy manual typewriter. For sixty years, Mary was a frequent correspondent who did virtually all her own typing, but her letters became harder for recipients to read over time. "You could see from her typing that her sight was getting progressively worse. A lot of words were misspelled, and Mary just wasn't that kind of person," Janice Dorsam says. In what must surely amaze today's users of word-processing software, when Mary chose to update her list of credits to reflect a recent performance—something she did regularly in hopes of impressing producers and casting directors—she methodically retyped the entire list each time. It was three to five single spaced pages. In her last years, Mary's typing was so error-ridden that she would have been mortified had she been able to see her mistakes. With odd spacing and offset letters, Mary noted playing "Aunt Elker," co-starring with "Bzrnard Hughes" and "Charlton Hewton," and appearing in "the Cnaterville Ghost."

While health problems would have caused others to give up, Mary was intent on finding solutions. Determined not to lose job offers just because she could no longer read scripts, she sought help from a Santa Monica organization for the visually impaired. There, she was directed to a $3,000 projector-like appliance that magnified the pages of books placed on its glass until the text was large enough for her to read. She had it installed in her small bedroom, and it was this "VTEK" machine that helped her memorize her lines for *Postcards from the Edge*. She was forced to find small ways to cope, too. Because she had trouble distinguishing denominations of paper currency, she folded her bills differently according to their value; this way, she knew that if her purchase called for a ten-dollar bill, she needed to extract one that was folded over at the top right corner.

Her deteriorating sight made her other health problems harder to manage. Her shoulder ached from arthritis. Her feet were a constant source of pain. At one point, she sought a referral to a podiatric surgeon from Jane Wyatt, but ultimately underwent no procedure. She especially suffered from arthritic legs and knees; she had almost no cartilage left. In her last few years, not only could she not see clearly where she was walking, she could not walk steadily. This unsteadiness began to affect her performances. In the 1986 TV movie *The Christmas Gift*, her difficulty walking becomes hard to overlook; in the play *The Foreigner* a year later, her movement prompted a critic to observe that she "sort of marches without lifting her knees." Her stiff gait is especially apparent in a 1992 *Tonight Show* appearance when, on camera, Jay Leno must help Mary maneuver the single step up to his set. By this point, Mary's walk had deteriorated from a conventional one-leg-in-front-of-the-other to an awkward side-to-side shuffle.

By early 1995, Mary could not rise from a chair without assistance. At an April matinee of *Beauty and the Beast* at the Shubert Theatre, Mary arranged house seats down front for herself and Emily Daniels because she knew two of the lead performers (Tom Bosley was Mary's co-star in the *Dowling* series, and Beth Fowler appeared with her in the *Sister Act* pictures). "Mary sat down and stayed down until the end of the show, which was quite a long time, and she *could not* get up," Daniels says, remembering her astonishment. "She could not!" Daniels waited until most of the audience had left and then sought the help of an usher. Together, each grabbing one of Mary's arms, they pulled Mary upright until her legs could support her. Moving once again, Mary had no trouble in the following hours, when she and Daniels joined Bosley and Fowler for dinner at a Century City restaurant.

It wasn't just arthritis and stiff joints that troubled Mary. An inner-ear ailment was so severe that she could not always maintain her balance; at least twice during the *Oklahoma!* tour, inner ear attacks kept her from going on. Dental problems plagued her in the 1980s. And breast cancer was never far from her mind. She went for regular exams and, in 1993, some forty years after her mastectomy, made plans to see Dr. Susan Love, the breast health expert who had been lured from Boston to UCLA Medical Center to start a new clinic the year before.

Having seen how her father coped so stoically with his poor hearing, Mary simply came to accept that she was losing control over her body. "The last few years of her life, she was in a lot of pain all the time," Rita Pico says. "That lady was a champion. It bothered her tremendously that her eyesight was not as good as it should be, but she just did not feel that any of us has a right to complain." In those moments when her body failed her, as it did at the Shubert, she responded defiantly, as if this was simply a nuisance to be overcome. Says Joe Ross, "She had that attitude of 'I've got a 106 fever but I'm going on, no matter what. Open up those curtains—I'm on!'" As Lucie Arnaz remembers, "It wasn't like with some other people, where they get older and feeble, and they become Old People. I never got the sense that Mary was an Old Woman. But 'getting-old stuff' would happen to her. As she became a little frailer [but] was still trying to be the same old Mary, it was extremely frustrating to her. Her attitude was just, "Dammit, I can't do this now and I can't do that now, and that's irritating. I gotta deal with *this* now, and *that's* irritating. And I can't cook, because I'm chopping my hand off because my eyes are [failing]. But you'd never hear a whine come out of this woman," Lucie says. "Sometimes that's bad if you don't tell anybody or share it. Sometimes it's good to bitch a little, get it off your shoulders, let somebody support you. She wasn't going to do that."

Because Mary was so well informed about health matters—in part because of what she learned volunteering in hospitals—she was not a passive patient through any of this. Mary looked at friend Dick Davis, a surgeon who retired in 1990, as something of an unofficial consultant on all things medical. "She never talked to a doctor when she didn't call me later and say, 'This is what he told me. Is it all right?'" he says.

When Mary arranged a tea for Lucie's visit in 1995, Lucie arrived at Mary's apartment before the other guests. Watching Mary prepare, Lucie thought to herself, "'Gee, she's aged. She's failing on me.' In my mind, I could see it—add it up, it's been this many years since I'd hung out with Mary. Five years is a big difference sometimes. She looked frailer to me, and it was harder for her to get around, but she was fighting it even more." Lucie thinks Mary suspected the end was near. Mary was surrounded that day by more clutter than Lucie had remembered, but Mary offered an explanation: "She said she had been cleaning out storage bins and going through things, which, looking back on it, is interesting. She might have had some premonition: 'I'm failing, and I gotta get this stuff in order and take care of my papers.'"

As Mary's health worsened, her thoughts did in fact turn to planning her estate. She had always intended to leave a significant amount to Washington University, but now she had to decide how much and which particular part of the university would benefit. Meanwhile, could the school remain in her good graces long enough to secure an agreement? The university had courted Mary for years. It hosted a luncheon in her honor (1947); named her one of its distinguished alumni and invited her to speak at the accompanying convocation, following U.S. Chief Justice Earl Warren (1955); appointed her the university's first artist-in-residence (1968); presented her with an honorary doctorate (1969); named her mistress of ceremonies for the opening of Mallinckrodt Center and the school's first proper theatre (1973); made her a visiting artist who taught a four-week class in comedy acting (1977); selected her as grand marshal of the homecoming parade and arranged a reception in her honor (1986); invited her to give the school's first Adele Starbird Lecture (1988), an annual event that subsequently featured Susan Sontag, Anna Quindlen, and Anna Deveare Smith; and invited her to return later to teach a week-long master class. Even these overtures couldn't seal Mary's affection. She was easily upset when the university disagreed with something she thought was best. Mary's ruffled feathers date at least to the cold shoulder she received from the administration of Thomas Eliot, chancellor from 1962 to 1971—and probably earlier. She especially resented that her views were not given greater attention in the early 1960s, when architectural plans for a new campus theatre were developed. That design was ultimately scrapped.

When Richard Palmer was brought on as English instructor in 1964, part of his job was to bring Mary back into the fold. He largely succeeded (among other things, Mary decided to fund an annual $500 drama prize for freshmen in 1977), but Palmer left in 1980 for the College of William and Mary. Any decisions Mary would make at that point, at age seventy, would be critical if the school was to receive her estate. When the university hired Jack Pirozzi as a development officer four years later, one of his first assignments was to repair the institution's rocky relationship with Mary once and for all. "Mary dangled her estate in front of [various university departments] for years. And fell in and out of love with the arts department, depending on who was chairman, what their intention toward her was, and how they listened to her," Pirozzi says. "We all recognized that this donor, who was as successful as she was for sixty-some-odd years and lived modestly as she did, had the potential to make an impact on the institution." But the task was not easy. "There are some [alums] who were as difficult as Mary, but none who were as overtly complicated. She is certainly among the most challenging alums I've worked with and, at the same time, one of the most endearing." Among other things, Mary was disappointed in how the school handled her funds for the student prize. She intended the money to be used as a stipend of sorts, living expenses to help a young performer build a career in film, TV, or theatre; however, without a proper performing arts department, the school was not positioned well at the time to nurture such careers, and Mary felt her gift wasn't appreciated. In the late 1980s, she was frustrated when she and the school could not reach terms for her to appear as Madame Armfeldt in a university production of *A Little Night Music*.

In each period, administrators seemed to presume Mary had greater assets than she really did. "Washington University could never understand that actors don't make that much money, even successful ones, and that even when they have money, they're very insecure about it," says Palmer, now in Williamsburg, Virginia. "Mary was a bread and butter actress. She worked a lot, but didn't necessarily have particularly high-paying roles. The university couldn't understand why she wasn't more forthcoming on an ongoing basis." When Mary mentioned she would like to present the school with a special gift for the opening of its Edison Theatre in 1973, she had something lovely and ornate in mind, such as a decorative drinking fountain for the lobby. The school proposed pricier, more utilitarian items, such as the stage manager's electronic console. In the end, Mary purchased a large framed lithograph that, for her, was much more than a congratulatory gesture. She researched artists and gave careful thought to what the print should convey, even seeking advice from Vincent Price, who had become an expert in the visual arts. Judy Sutter Hinrichs accompanied Mary as she went from gallery to gallery in San Francisco considering possibilities (this was during Mary's time with the American Conservatory Theater there). Ultimately, Mary chose an 1893 Jules Cheret rendering of Loie Fuller, the dancer who symbolized the art nouveau movement in Paris. Mary arranged the framing, crating, and shipping of the artwork, which was appraised at $750 at the time. She was almost giddy about all this, but to the university, the gift was a disappointment. The school dutifully hung it in the Edison entry foyer, but when Mary arrived from Los Angeles for the theatre's dedication, she was stunned to find the lights out in the foyer. "No one could see my poster!! The cry was that no one knew where the switch was! After the 'performance,' I found the janitor and he turned on the lights!!! Darn it! I'm not sure the university knows what it has, but we don't care because *we* know!" Mary wrote William G. B. Carson at the time.

By 1995, having watched Mary suffer so many ailments in the previous year, Emily Daniels decided Mary's birthday should be something special. Daniels was not sure how old Mary was, but she arranged a dinner party one June evening at her spacious home, surrounded by trees and with a pool in the back yard. She allowed Mary to draw up the guest list. Mary selected Canon Greg and Debbie Richards, Dick and Madelyn Davis, Dolly Reed Wageman, and Maury Hill, an actor friend of her generation who later became a travel agent. The evening began with drinks and hors d'oeuvres on the lawn. Mary had her usual Campari, and Daniels remembers thinking how nice it was "to get her out of an apartment and into a backyard." The group moved indoors for dinner, and Mary asked Canon Richards to say grace. "We all held hands," says Wageman, "and it was one of the loveliest evenings I've ever spent because it was Mary with her 'residual' family, so to speak—those of us who'd survived. There was a feeling of such love and admiration for Mary from all of us, and she basked in it. It's the first time I ever saw her relax and accept the fact that all of us loved her very much."

CHAPTER SEVENTEEN

Fade Out

A TUMBLE THAT MARY TOOK ON THE *FATHER DOWLING* SET IN DECEM-
ber 1990—tripping over a cable and making "a perfect three-point landing on my nose and knees"—was a bit of foreshadowing in the truest
theatrical sense. Mary was not hurt badly, but in her final years, arthritic
knees and deteriorating vision conspired against her in devastating ways.
On at least three subsequent occasions in her eighties, alone in her apartment, Mary tripped over things she did not see, fell to the floor, and
blacked out. The events surrounding these three incidents, more than
anything else, shaped the last eighteen months of her life. This period
was marked by severe physical pain and domino-like medical complications, ultimately resulting in her death.

These things might not have happened had Mary made a different decision in the early 1990s, when she considered purchasing a larger, two-
bedroom condo that became available in her building. That move would
have allowed her to live in less cramped surroundings, possibly avoiding
injury. Bill Herz remembers an apartment so cluttered that "walking into
her bedroom was like an obstacle course." But she chose not to spend
more money on herself, reasoning that remaining in the smaller unit
would allow her to leave a larger bequest to her alma mater, which she
had now decided would receive the bulk of her estate.

In the first incident, in early December 1994, Mary regained consciousness to find herself prostrate on the floor of her apartment. The
phone cord, which may have been what caused her to trip, was within
her reach, and she used it to drag the phone closer. She called Greg Richards, told him she had hurt herself at home and was going to get herself
to the hospital. He insisted on coming to get her, but she prevailed. She
phoned the building's trusted lobby attendant, who came to help her off
the floor. Scared and upset, she nonetheless showed typical independence and arranged a cab to the hospital. The injury she sustained was

only a cut on her leg, but it developed into a severe case of cellulitis, a bacterial infection that caused the skin on her lower leg to become red, inflamed, and painful. It did not heal well and, after several days at UCLA Medical Center, Mary was transferred to the skilled nursing unit at the Motion Picture and Television Fund Hospital. Though she had a private room with a little terrace, she was uncomfortable from the very beginning. "She complained a lot about the ambulance ride out there from UCLA because, according to her, the road was too rough and it was bumpy and she was miserable and she kept telling them to slow down and they wouldn't. She was pretty miserable at the Motion Picture Home, really complaining and fussing and in pain and mad at all the doctors and disappointed that they couldn't relieve her more," says Emily Daniels, who remembers Mary's feet being swollen and painful. "She bitched a lot about being out there. She had a lot of problems and didn't feel they were curing her quickly."

Mary remained there for about five weeks, a stay that kept her from attending Christmas celebrations and the premiere of *Little Women*. Daniels and the Richards each brought Mary an eighteen-inch artificial Christmas tree with little lights to brighten her room. Rita Pico was among the few others who visited. Mary preferred that no one know she was unwell so, again, she was admitted as "Mary Shannon" and spoke only vaguely about the nature of her condition. Mary phoned Anne Kaufman Schneider, reassuring her that she was improving, *"whatever the real problem was,"* says Anne. "The problem with Mary being alone is that it was hard to call somebody and say, 'What is the real thing?'"

Mary's penchant for privacy meant that did not benefit from the love and support that friends could have shown. Anna Crouse tried to phone Mary at home at the holidays and was puzzled when she could not reach her. She grew concerned when her Christmas card to Mary was returned. Only later did Crouse learn Mary had been hospitalized. Bill Givens, who talked to Mary on the phone during this stay, said she insisted she did not want visitors. When Mary returned home on January 16, 1995, she was using a cane.

Her second fall was more frightening. One evening that spring, Rita Pico phoned Mary at home. There was nothing special about her call; the two women regularly spoke by phone simply to check in. But this night Pico was worried. "The phone was busy, busy, busy. I had an uncomfortable feeling about it. I called her until nine or nine thirty at night. I called her the next day and the phone was still busy. I knew Mary wouldn't have let the phone stay off the hook. I really panicked. Did she go someplace and not tell me? I called the front desk and said there's something wrong with Miss Wickes—someone's got to go up and knock on the door." Front desk attendants at first speculated that Mary had simply gone out, but Pico insisted Mary would not have left the phone off the hook ("she was too precise for that"). They then went to her fifth floor unit, put their ear to the door and told Rita they heard the television on, so all seemed to be well. Increasingly worried, she told them, "I don't care if you hear the television set! I'm telling you, the phone would not be busy that long. Call paramedics. Break down that door!" They did, and found Mary on the floor, where she had apparently lain for about twelve hours. She had tripped over something in her apartment, hurt her mouth and head, and lost a lot of blood. The phone had been knocked down in her fall and it appeared that Mary had tried to drag it toward her before losing consciousness. Pico waited at home until she could hear from the paramedics, who talked with her from Mary's phone once they entered her apartment. She then drove immediately to Century City Hospital's emergency department, where she found Mary hallucinating, saying things like "Rita, you've got your hair on backwards." Pico phoned Greg Richards and Dick Davis to report what happened.

Mary was stabilized and transferred to UCLA. Shortly after she recovered, an appreciative Mary called Pico and said, "My friends want to take you out to dinner. They feel you saved my life." Emily Daniels and Dolly Reed Wageman treated Pico to dinner at Shutters, an upscale hotel on the water in Santa Monica. "That was their way of thanking me for helping Mary, which I thought was so sweet," Pico says, insisting that "anybody would have done" what she did.

In June, as Mary continued to deteriorate, actress Lana Turner died at seventy-four in Mary's apartment complex, where she occupied a penthouse. In September, Joe Ross visited Mary in her apartment. "She didn't look well. She was bloating up a bit, and she looked very, very tired. She must have been in a lot of pain." In early October, Wanda Clark visited and the women had tea.

Later that month, Mary fell a third time. At home one evening, she tripped over a lightweight, collapsible wire cart on wheels, the sort that city dwellers often use to bring groceries home. She blacked out, but regained consciousness shortly thereafter and phoned Dick Davis. "She said she was having trouble breathing. It was nine or ten o'clock at night. I said, 'Mary, you ought to go to the hospital.' She said, 'I'll take care of it!'" Though she was in medical distress, she called a cab, not an ambulance, and had the presence of mind to grab her booklet of senior-citizen taxi discount coupons. She went to the emergency department at UCLA, again as Mary Shannon.

This time, she would not return home. Davis met her the next morning in the ICU, where Mary stayed about three days. Her condition improved, but she was not strong enough to care for herself at home, so she was moved to a private room. She was "still wobbly," Davis says, when, shortly after being moved there, she rose from bed one afternoon to go to the bathroom and fell to the floor. She had broken her hip. Hip replacement surgery was scheduled for the following morning. Rita knew none of this, as she was on a cruise to Greece with her sister and brother-in-law. She arrived home that night to receive a phone call from Mary at the hospital. "I was absolutely flummoxed," says Rita, who went to the hospital early the next morning. "She gave me her wrist watch to take care of while she was in surgery. After she got out of surgery and I knew she was OK, I came home." The next morning, Mary phoned, gruff and grouchy, "Rita! I don't have my wristwatch!'"

Emily Daniels, who had just had her own hip replaced about three weeks before at Century City Hospital, was home recuperating when Mary underwent hip surgery. Having successfully received a prosthetic hip, Mary was brought back to the ICU, one leg suspended in a huge cast. She was there for about three days and recovering well, even getting up for movement exercises. But then the unexpected happened: Mary suffered a stroke that caused left-side paralysis, and she immediately lost consciousness. "I got there about seven o'clock the next morning and lo and behold the whole ICU was in her room," Davis says. He was there again the following day, trying to see if Mary would respond, when the phone rang in her room. "I picked it up and it was Little Lucie. She was calling for Mary. She was really broken up," Davis says. Mary could not speak, but Davis held the phone to Mary's ear so Lucie Arnaz could tell Mary she loved her.

On the third day, a familiar pattern began developing. In the mornings, Davis would check in on Mary when he made his hospital rounds, after which he would phone Pico and the Richardses with an update. In the afternoons, Pico and the Richardses took turns sitting with Mary each day. "I'd just hold her hand and talk to her, 'Guess what so-and-so did today?' like you're supposed to do [with people in a coma], and a couple of times I thought she responded and opened her eyes a little bit," Pico says. "It was very sad. I remember saying, it's OK, Mary, to let go. You've had a lovely life and God is up there waiting for you."

Mary's close circle was soon confronted with a decision about medical heroics. "One day, I called Greg and told him there was a total change. She was slipping," says Debbie Richards. A doctor asked Pico if Mary wanted extreme measures taken. Pico turned to Greg, who did not know. Debbie had a vague recollection that, after Mary's blackout in the spring, Mary had signed "some sort of document. She had said to Greg as she was leaving Easter dinner, would you do something about my will, help handle things?" Canon Richards says, "It was more like, 'Would you *really* do that?' confirming that I would really be willing to help." Mary had begun to fear no one would be there to care for her if she became seriously ill or to handle her affairs when she died. Instinctively, Richards said yes, of course, he would do whatever Mary wanted, but they never spoke about it again. Now, from the hospital, Richards had to phone Mary's lawyer to ask if Mary had signed a living will or made any arrangements regarding extreme measures. "He said, 'Yes, I can fax it to you, but you can decide that—you have her medical power of attorney.' I said *I* didn't know that. 'Oh, yes,' he said, 'You're everything—you're her medical power of attorney, power of attorney for health care, you're her trustee and you're her power of attorney. I gave her a whole packet to give you.'" Until that conversation, Debbie says, "We had no idea, absolutely none." Similarly, Pico was unaware until this hospitalization that Mary had named her as back-up trustee.

Leaving these issues unresolved was unlike Mary. But she was so uncomfortable asking the Richardses to assume this role—it would be a favor, after all, and an extremely personal one at that—that she hoped her brief mention of it would suffice. Certainly, she made clear to others that she intended to rely on the Richardses completely in such matters. Before this recent health episode, she had told Emily Daniels, "I have nothing to worry about because when I die, Greg's going to handle everything and I don't have to worry about anything. It's wonderful." Daniels remembers Mary spoke "like it was all taken care of, written down and that he knew." Dick Davis helped the Richardses make the medical decisions. Davis says Mary's stated wish "was never to be incapacitated, ever. Richards was there and Rita was there and the three of us took care of it. We did what she wanted done—just took care of her, basically. No heroics of any kind. There was no reason to do anything."

Mary lasted four or five days but never woke up. On Sunday, October 22, 1995, her vital signs worsened. Michael Richards, Mary's godson, read her the 23rd and 121st Psalms, and his father gave her a final blessing. Mary died at five minutes after seven in the evening. "I think she knew she was dying, but she waited for me to get there," Canon Richards says. "When I got there, I held her hand and she just *looked* at me, like, 'Where in the hell have you been?' and 'I sure hope you're going to handle this right. Don't screw this up.' I didn't know she had died because she was still looking in my eyes." Four others were present: Debbie Richards, sons Michael and Matthew, and Rita Pico. Pico, who had devoted herself to Mary in her last weeks, says, "It was very important to me to be there. I had this love for Mary. She was like my mom. I would never in five million years have said that to Mary because we were kind of pals—she wouldn't have wanted me to think of her as that much older. She could have been my mom, but I never thought about that until after she died and I realized how much I missed her advice." When Mary died at eighty-five, Pico was sixty-four, more than twenty years younger. Just as Lucie thought Mary sensed that her death was close, so did Debbie. "When we went to her safe deposit box, we learned she had been there the day before she went into the hospital," Debbie says. It's unclear if Mary put something in or took something out, but bank employees told Debbie that Mary had been there a long time.

Few other people in Mary's life knew she had been hospitalized, let alone that she was dying. Bill Givens is just one of many who never got to say goodbye. He had no reason for concern, since normally he and Mary spoke only every few weeks. "Except for Greg, I don't think even her closest friends knew she was in the hospital," he says. Madelyn Davis did call Anne Kaufman Schneider to let her know of Mary's condition, but Pico was frustrated by the Richards' wish to keep Mary's condition so quiet. She believed others would want to know and that Mary would benefit from their support. When Mary was in a coma, "Nobody knew! It drove me crazy. I know she was a private person, but if you're sick and people want to know about you . . . I thought she could be having a lot of prayers from people all over the world, but with Greg, really, there was just no [wavering]. I honestly feel Greg did not think Mary was as ill as she was. It was not my place [to challenge him], but I remember saying, 'Can't we let people know?'" With the Richards' permission, she did call Larry Guittard, who was appearing with Judi Dench in *A Little Night Music* in London. "When I spoke to him, he said, 'When I left, I felt I would not see her again,'" Pico says. Certainly, others wondered if something was wrong. In early October, Bill and Janice Dorsam had mailed Mary an invitation to the December wedding of their daughter Beth. "It wasn't like Mary to not respond. It was two or three weeks and I had not heard anything when I got the first phone call [from Rita] that she was in the hospital and that things didn't look good. Then she called a couple of days later to let us know that Mary had died," Janice says.

Officially, the cause of death was acute renal failure due to a massive gastrointestinal bleed, severe hypotension (low blood pressure that, in Mary's case, lasted several weeks), and ischemic cardiomyopathy, or clogged arteries. Contributing factors cited on the death certificate were myocardial infarction, breast cancer, peptic ulcer, and anemia.

The day after Mary died, her agent, Jimmy Cota, phoned her apartment to tell her she was wanted for additional post-production voice work on *Hunchback of Notre Dame*. Cota had not heard the news and had no reason to suspect what had happened. Just the previous month, Mary had done a photo shoot for Disney to promote the film. Cota learned of Mary's death when, by coincidence, Givens called to gather information about her for a tribute. Madelyn Pugh Davis jokes that if Mary had known there was an offer of more work, she might have come back for it.

Disney, faced with the death of a principal player in a major film just months from release, could not afford to begin anew with another actress. Instead, the studio sought someone to mimic Mary's voice well enough to complete the unfinished dialogue. Earlier, while Mary was ill, the studio had turned to singer Mary Stouts to do some brief mimicking of Mary's voice on the song "A Guy Like You." But now, only days after her death, the studio approached Betty Garrett. "They said, 'Someone suggested you'd be able to imitate Mary's voice.' I said, 'Send me the tapes [of Mary as Laverne] and let me see if I can do it.' I'm pretty good at doing that, but I just didn't feel I got it well enough. At the time, I just didn't have time to work on it—and I'm not sure I could have really captured it anyway. I called them and said I wouldn't want to try because I just love that delivery and I wouldn't do justice to it," she says. The studio next turned to Jane Withers. Best known for her twenty years as Josephine the Plumber in Comet commercials, Withers began her career doing voices in Looney Toon and Warner Bros. cartoons as a child. This work included the *Willy Whooper* series, in which her vocal skills were so strong that she created voices for virtually the entire cast: "Willy, his girlfriend, the mother, the father, the bird, the dog and the cat," she laughs years later. Disney told her, "We need to do this as quickly as possible. We hope it won't be an imposition, but could it be today?" Withers asked them to send a driver over with a tape—"so I can listen to the ups and downs in Mary's voice"—along with a tape recorder and a script. She offered to listen to Mary and, on the same tape, record some of Laverne's dialogue as Mary might have spoken it. She would send the tape back with the driver for Disney to review.

A driver brought a tape over immediately. He waited outside on Withers's porch, where she offered him coffee and cookies. Withers listened to Mary's voice and tried to envision her mannerisms and movements ("that's the way I've always done everybody, since I was three years old"). She prayed ("before I do anything, that's what I always do"), and then spoke into the recorder. Twenty minutes later, she returned the tape to the driver. "He said, 'My goodness, that was quick!' I said, 'Well, it'll either be right or not and we won't know until they get it back.' The minute he got back to the studio, they played it and they were so excited they said, 'We can't tell where she stops and you begin! How soon can you begin with us?'"

Contrary to some reports, Withers and Mary were not lifelong friends; in fact, Withers says they had never met, even though they had attended some of the same events over the years. But Withers was a fan of Mary's, and once even bought a script at a charity auction specifically because it was donated by Mary, who had arranged for the show's cast to sign it.

The first day Withers worked on the film, she completed twenty to thirty pages of dialogue. "Mary didn't have many lines in any one scene, so they clumped them all together. In three sessions, I did everything in the film I had to do, and then was called back twice because they changed some of the lines. So it only took five times to complete everything. One day, I went and did less than a sentence. I said, 'That's it?!' They said, 'That's it!' Oh, dear Gussie!" Withers peppers her conversations with the same sort of dated expressions Mary favored.

Most of what Withers recorded was new dialogue that Mary had not yet received, but Withers also re-recorded six or seven lines that Mary had already spoken. Then a song was added. "I was so tickled to get to do that," she says. Withers recorded her *Hunchback* lines at three different studios but always performed alone. She never met the others who brought the gargoyles to life, Jason Alexander and Charles Kimbrough. (For that matter, Mary did not meet Kimbrough either.) Withers also became LaVerne's voice in the related Disney merchandise, including toys, books, and a game on CD-ROM, all work that Mary would have done—and been paid nicely for—had she lived.

❖

The chapel at All Saints' Episcopal Church in Beverly Hills was so full on Saturday, October 28, 1995, that some mourners had to strain to hear the service while standing outside. Mary had so many disputes with this church in her last years that she had recently begun attending a church in nearby Westwood, but it was only fitting that her final goodbye take place at the church that had been her second home for more than four decades. Mary had said she wanted her funeral there because All Saints' was where Isabella's funeral took place.

The mourners who filled the chapel for the three o'clock service on this sunny afternoon mirrored the different parts of Mary's life. The front pews were occupied by Lucie Arnaz, the Richards family, Rita Pico and her daughter, Dick and Madelyn Pugh Davis, Emily Daniels and her daughter (Daniels using crutches her first time out since her hip surgery), and Dolly Reed Wageman, who cut a trip to Northampton, Massachusetts, short to be at the funeral. Two of Madelyn's five children attended as well. Actresses Kathy Najimy and Susan Johnson were there from *Sister Act*, as was the film's music producer, Marc Shaiman. Binnie Barnes, in a wheelchair, came with her son. Producers Bill Frye and Jim Wharton, who were pallbearers for Isabella thirty years before, were in attendance. Tracy Nelson came to pay respects to her *Father Dowling* co-star, whom she regarded with the kind of fondness reserved for grandmothers. George S. Kaufman's granddaughter, the actress Beatrice Colen, came with her husband, actor Patrick Cronin. Hal Kanter from Mary's *Julia* days came. Wanda Clark was there, as was Lucy's long-time houseman, Frank Goering. Mary Jane Croft, Maury Thompson, and Tommy Thompson, who had worked on Lucy's various TV series, came, too. Director Warner Shook and his partner arrived from Seattle, where Shook was artistic director of the Intiman Theatre. *General Hospital*'s David Lewis attended, as did comedian Rip Taylor, who played with Mary in *Sigmund and the Sea Monsters*. Alice Urist and Mary Holmes, from Mary's hospital volunteer guild, attended. Janie Miller, who had never met Mary, flew in from Memphis because she so appreciated Mary's unsolicited support when Miller had breast cancer.

The church did something rare at Mary's funeral: It placed the casket on the altar. Mary's friends from the St. Clare's Group, a support group for older women in the church, sat in chairs around her casket. Covering Mary's casket was a striking funeral pall that Mary herself made by hand, on her tiny sewing machine. She presented it as a gift to All Saints' in the late 1970s, and it had become part of the church's liturgical life, helping grieving families avoid the expense of flowers that were expected to rest atop a coffin. Mary made the pall from a gold-colored church vestment fabric called coronation tapestry, which she adorned with a large, red image of a cross. On the underside, she embroidered a dedication to Debbie Richards.

Surrounded by flowers representing the spectrum of people in Mary's life—an arrangement from Whoopi Goldberg stood beside one from UCLA hospital volunteers—Greg Richards read a loving homily about Mary's life. It was just outside the doors of this chapel where he met Mary twenty-two years earlier. He spoke from the heart about four qualities he admired: her humor, her dignity, the hospitality she offered, and the way in which she built family around her. But it was the eulogy delivered by Lucie Arnaz that those present remember best. Lucie flew in from New York to offer a witty remembrance that captured Mary's cantankerous, independent spirit. "Lucie did a beautiful job. Everybody was laughing, and that's nice at a funeral. I think Mary would have liked that," says Emily Daniels. Lucie also read a reflection by Tom Bosley, who could not attend but who wrote remarks that his wife handed a surprised Richards at the church.

Lucie closed by revealing that at her mother's service six years before, mourners gave Lucille Ball a big round of applause—and that a pleased Mary said at the time, "I like that. I'd like that at my funeral." So Lucie led Mary's friends, extended family, and colleagues in loud, cheering applause and a standing ovation. It was an emotional moment whose recollection moved Bill Givens to tears several years later.

Mary's pallbearers included Givens (who jokes that, having accompanied Mary to so many events over the years, he was her escort at the end as well), young Matthew Richards, attorney John Tucker, and David Littler, an active member of the church. As they carried the coffin outside the chapel, tears streamed down Matthew's face and dropped softly onto the cloth that Mary created in his mother's honor. Joe Ross, seated on an aisle, softly put his hand on the coffin as it passed by and whispered, "Goodbye, Sweetheart. Save me two seats near the orchestra." As the casket moved toward the chapel doors, Givens saw comic Rip Taylor coming up the aisle and thought, "I hope to God he didn't bring confetti."

The service the Richards arranged was very close to what Mary wanted, partly because they knew her Episcopal preferences and partly because Mary had critiqued many funerals at All Saints'. It wasn't *exactly* what Mary wanted—it lacked some musical pieces she requested, for instance—because Mary left her funeral instructions in her safe deposit box, which the Richardses were unable to access until after the funeral. A small reception took place in the courtyard outside the chapel. Lucie then retired to the lobby bar of the Beverly Wilshire Hotel to reminisce with Wanda, Frank Goering, and Johny Aitchison, Desi's former secretary. Givens, his sister Janie Miller, and Susan Johnson (in poor health, with an oxygen tank) had lunch in Mary's honor at one of her favorite eateries, the Hamburger Hamlet on Beverly Drive at Wilshire Boulevard.

Although the *Los Angeles Times* and the *New York Times* published generous obituaries, each with a photograph, many friends and colleagues remained unaware Mary had died. Johnny Whitaker was crestfallen to have missed the service, which he learned about later from Rip Taylor. Iggie Wolfington also felt awful about not being there; he learned of her death about a month later, but even then did not know who to call to express condolences. Rita Pico believed Mary wasn't in the end shown the respect that she deserved: "I was angry because I felt there should have been an outpouring of ka-jillions of people there, actors and actresses. I thought, 'This was a darn great lady and where are all of you?!' I almost took it as a personal affront that there weren't more, but it goes back to the fact that a lot of people didn't even know she had died." The Academy of Motion Pictures ignored Mary in its annual video montage of lives lost, shown during the Oscar broadcast, but one TV program did acknowledge her passing. Louie Anderson dedicated an episode of *Life with Louie* ("The Thank You Note") to her memory, a story about a boy who feels bad after his grandmother dies because he had put off thanking her.

Mary's Los Angeles friends were not alone in feeling caught off guard by her death. As Mary Jane Ax asks repeatedly, a tone of frustration in her voice, "Why were none of us back here in St. Louis told *anything*? It just amazed us, really." They learned of her death through the newspaper but had no other information about her affairs. And they had no idea who to contact for more information. "We just figured that whoever took over and took charge didn't care," she said, unaware of how hard the Richardses worked to honor Mary's wishes—and how lovingly they treated Mary's memory. In the coming years, Canon Richards even continued replying to fan mail from people unaware Mary was dead. He did not simply send a form letter, but wrote personal notes to some who shared personal stories, and often included photographs.

Because her death certificate incorrectly records her age as seventy-nine, most media got Mary's age wrong. The *Washington Post, Chicago Tribune, San Francisco Examiner, Time Magazine*, and the *Hollywood Reporter* reported her to have been seventy-nine when she died. The *New York Times*, *Los Angeles Times*, *People*, and *Entertainment Weekly* accurately reported her age as eighty-five, the latter lamenting the loss of "one of Hollywood's most celebrated sourpusses."

Mary had chosen to be cremated and, attending to details as usual, had pre-paid her funeral with Pierce Brothers. The mortuary shipped her ashes to Shiloh Cemetery in St. Clair County, Illinois, which held a strong geographical pull for Mary. It was a bleak, cold day there on November 18, when about sixteen people gathered for a burial of her urn in lot twenty-six. They had no trouble finding the spot: Mary had long before arranged for her headstone to be in place. Canon Richards came from California to officiate. Others present included Washington University President Bill Danforth, who gave a homily; his wife Elizabeth; Harriet Switzer, who drove with them to the service that morning from St. Louis; Danforth's brother, then-Senator John Danforth, who would later officiate at the funeral of former President Ronald Reagan; Jane Sutter, who read a poem at the service; Edward L. Wickenhauser, a genealogy buff from Godfrey, Illinois, who tried to document Mary's ties to the Illinois branch of Wickenhausers despite her indifference; and cousins Bill and Janice Dorsam. The Dorsams recall a woman introducing herself as a cousin on the Wickenhauser side, but they remember neither her name nor how she might have been related. "Nobody here was interested enough to ask. I just wasn't interested in her or her family, and that really used to burn Mary," Bill Dorsam says.

Mary now rests among those most important to her. Her headstone is directly beside those of Isabella, Frank, and Aunt Hes, in the same lot as her great grandparents, Captain John Randolph Thomas (d. 1880) and his wife Hester McLean Thomas (d. 1899). Even in death, Mary prevented others from learning her age: The headstone above the urn with her ashes bears no years, only "Mary Isabella, Daughter of Frank A. [and] M. Isabella Wickenhauser."

Mary approached her estate with the same forthrightness that she lived her life. She left an estate worth approximately $2 million and named Canon Richards her trustee. This amount might appear small for an actress who worked often and lived frugally, but for many of the years she worked, performers were not paid today's large sums. Much of her film and television work took place in the years before residuals, and Mary did not invest in stocks.

Washington University's courting of Mary paid off. Though several other institutions had sought Mary's papers—most notably Boston University, the New York Public Library, and the University of Wyoming—and although she had considered UCLA, in the end she chose to leave Washington University all her scripts, photos, correspondence, books, videotapes, playbills, and other professional memorabilia. Material consuming about sixty cubic feet of space arrived there in February and March of 1997. Today, her materials are part of the university's Department of Special Collections, joining scripts and papers that belonged to alumni Tennessee Williams and A. E. Hotchner. The papers are housed in what was formerly St. Louis's Famous Barr department store.

Mary also left the university 94.5 percent of her estate, including all future residuals due her under various performance contracts. Mary's money did not go to the university's School of Arts and Sciences, where it would have supported performing arts programs, but instead went to the university's library. The funds are to be used to maintain her papers for scholarly use and to purchase theatre and film books in memory of her parents. The university has since established the Isabella and Frank Wickenhauser Memorial Library Fund for Television, Film and Theater Arts, introduced in a ceremony in St. Louis on April 16, 1998. "In many ways, she had the guilt of someone who had succeeded and hadn't realized how much other people who loved her had done to get her there, until later in life. That's the missing link. That's what the gift to Washington University is about—'Payback Time,'" says Canon Richards.

Mary left 2.5 percent of her estate to her godson, Michael Richards, to be administered by Debbie Richards. In helping secure his future, Mary was also giving something valuable to the entire Richards family, whom she loved so much. She left 1 percent each to All Saints' Episcopal Church and to the St. Louis Mercantile Library, which brought her such pleasure as a girl. The final 1 percent she left to Bill Dorsam. This bequest is quintessential Mary: She and Bill Dorsam did not care for each other, but even in death Mary could not ignore her strong sense of family loyalty. Bill's mother, Elisabeth, had been Mary's only real connection to family after Isabella died. But Mary's loyalty was not without limits. She left nothing to her two other living relatives: Elizabeth's older child, Mary Ann, who lived in Indiana and had no contact with Mary for many years, and Brooks Adkins of Ohio, whose existence Mary ignored her entire life.

Mary left her family antiques—mostly nineteenth-century American Empire furniture from the Midwest—to the Missouri Historical Society in St. Louis. This bequest surprised Amy Jane Ax, who says Mary told her the Belleville Historical Society in St. Clair County, Illinois, where many of the pieces originated, would receive her furniture. Some of these items were the 1834 wedding furniture of Mary's maternal great-great-grandparents, Mary W. Johnston and Milton N. McLean, a nephew of Supreme Court Justice John McLean. Many others belonged to their daughter, Hester McLean Thomas, Mary's great-grandmother. Mary lived amidst this severe furniture her whole life, moving it first to New York and then to Los Angeles. It includes a mahogany sleigh-bed with matching bureaus and mirrors, a pair of ornate Victorian loveseats, and a Jenny Lind day bed that in earlier days had a corn shuck mattress. Mary's confusion over the role of Justice John McLean in her family carried over to the Missouri Historical Society. The Missouri History Museum still represents an oil portrait bequeathed by Mary as a "painting of Hester McLean Thomas, daughter of Mary and John McLean," when in fact Hester was John's great niece, not his daughter.

Mary also left the society one of her favorite possessions, a large doll-house built for her as a girl. It is an elaborate wood creation painted gray with two chimneys and an internal staircase that extends from the first to the third floors. Obviously crafted with great care, the house features unusually detailed individual pieces, like the kitchen stove and lace curtains on many of its nineteen glass windows. Mary so prized this touchstone to her childhood that she kept it in her bedroom her entire life—surely an odd attachment for an adult, especially in her senior years. It was put on view in 1999 when the society lent it to a St. Louis exhibit of historical dollhouses.

Mary singled out few other possessions. She left Rita Pico a rectangular, forty-carat topaz stone she received in the 1940s from a writer who was grateful for a story idea Mary gave him. She left her V-TEK appliance for the visually impaired to St. Barnabas Senior Center in Los Angeles. To young Christian Hinrichs, the son of Judy Sutter Hinrichs, whose friendship Mary enjoyed while in San Francisco with ACT in the 1970s, Mary left the St. Louis Mercantile Library perpetual membership that had belonged to her father since 1915. This gift would keep Frank's spirit alive in a boy who also had strong St. Louis roots. Mary left her remaining possessions and the contents of her household to the Richards family.

Actor Barnard Hughes was disappointed Mary left nothing to the Episcopal Actors Guild, a charity founded more than seventy years before by Douglas Fairbanks, Mary Pickford, and others. The charity's president for many years, Hughes had pointedly reminded Mary of the support it gave to performers in financial need, in hopes that she would remember the guild. Bill Herz similarly talked to Mary about leaving money to the Actors' Fund. Anna Crouse was amused that she was not willed Mary's set of china; when the two women discovered years before that they had the same pattern of English china, they made a pact that whoever died first would leave her set to the other.

A few years after the Beverly Hills funeral service, Lucie Arnaz experienced something peculiar. A friend had been so impressed with John Edward, the spiritual medium who claims the ability to communicate with the dead, that she persuaded Lucie to request a reading from him. Edward has since built a fan base around his television programs, on which he tells surviving families what he has learned from "conversations" with their departed loved ones. Most people discount such things—and Lucie herself is not sure she believes in them—but she was stunned by something he said during her reading. "He apparently was in touch with my mother [from the after-life]," she says. "And one of the things that came through was that 'Mary is with us.' He said, 'Do you know who this is?' I said, 'I think so. Unless they mean the Blessed Virgin, [Mary Wickes] is the only Mary I could think of.' Not long after he said those words, he said, 'I'm getting a sense that you were with your mother at some type of a memorial for someone—your mother is not there, but it's *like* she's there with you. She's telling me she was there with you, but she's not there. Did you represent her somewhere?' I said yes. And he said, 'Well, she's telling me she *was* there.'" Lucie wonders how Edward could have known about Lucie's eulogy, and she is intrigued by the prospect of her mother having been present at Mary's service. "I was representing *her* that day, because if she had been alive, of course it would have been her and not me doing that eulogy. And everything I said [at the service] was 'My mother and I,' and 'If my mom was here, she'd tell you' . . . I was trying the best I could to represent her that day. Most everybody in that room knew how close they were. For my mother, it would have been like losing the closest relative she had."

The Roles of Mary Wickes

MARY'S FILM, TELEVISION, AND STAGE ROLES ARE PRESENTED IN chronological order. For films, the relevant year used reflects the date each was first released in the United States. For television series on which she had a regular or semi-regular role, the years listed are those in which Mary appeared, not the years the series aired. Episodic television appearances are listed by original broadcast date, as best can be determined from reference books, newspapers and magazines of the period, Mary's performance contracts, and her own records. Where a precise airdate could not be identified, the episode appears in its most likely place in the sequence. Stage performances are listed by opening night only; Mary's theatre jobs lasted for weeks, months, or (in a couple of cases) years—and some were one-time performances. Only her radio performances are listed alphabetically, because the original broadcast dates are difficult to verify. Details on airdate and her role are provided where confirmation was possible.

FILM PERFORMANCES

Watch the Birdie, 1935, silent passenger in deck chair on cruise ship
Too Much Johnson, 1938 (unreleased), Mrs. Battison, stern mother-in-law
Seeing Red, 1939, Mrs. Smith
The Man Who Came to Dinner, 1942, Miss Preen, nurse
Blondie's Blessed Event, 1942, Sarah Miller, bossy maid
Private Buckaroo, 1942, Bonnie-Belle Schlopkiss, overbearing man-hunter
Mayor of 44th Street, 1942, Mamie, unlucky-at-love wardrobe mistress
Now, Voyager, 1942, Dora Pickford, private nurse
Keeping Fit, 1942, nagging housewife
Who Done It?, 1942, Juliet Collins, wise-cracking secretary

How's About It?, 1943, Mike Tracy, wise-cracking secretary
Rhythm of the Islands, 1943, Susie Dugan, brash fiancée
My Kingdom for a Cook, 1943, Agnes Willoughby, spinster secretary
Happy Land, 1943, Emmy, small-town pharmacy clerk
Higher and Higher, 1943, Sandy Brooks, former vaudevillian
June Bride, 1948, Rosemary McNally, magazine journalist
The Decision of Christopher Blake, 1948, Clara, housekeeper
Anna Lucasta, 1949, Stella, caustic, hen-pecking wife
Petty Girl, 1950, Professor Whitman, sour spinster schoolmarm
On Moonlight Bay, 1951, Stella, housekeeper
I'll See You in My Dreams, 1951, Anna, cook and maid
Young Man with Ideas, 1952, Mrs. Gilpin, overbearing stage mother
The Story of Will Rogers, 1952, Mrs. Foster, landlady
Bloodhounds of Broadway, 1952, frazzled mother in the bowery
By the Light of the Silvery Moon, 1953, Stella, housekeeper
Half a Hero, 1953, Mrs. Watts, overbearing wife
The Actress, 1953, Emma Glavey, athletics instructor
Ma and Pa Kettle at Home, 1954, Miss Wetter, "maiden lady librarian"
White Christmas, 1954, Emma Allen, housekeeper
Destry, 1954, Bessie Mae Curtis, wife of boozy doctor
Good Morning, Miss Dove, 1955, Miss Ellwood, grade school teacher
Dance with Me, Henry, 1956, Miss Mayberry, officious social worker
Don't Go Near the Water, 1957, Janie, Navy nurse
Proud Rebel, 1958, Mrs. Ainsley, nosy frontierswoman
It Happened to Jane, 1959, Matilda Runyon, small-town telephone operator
Cimarron, 1960, Mrs. Hefner, upper-crust wife in the Old West
One Hundred and One Dalmatians, 1961 (live action model for Cruella De Vil)
The Sins of Rachel Cade, 1961, Marie Grieux, housekeeper in Belgian Congo
The Music Man, 1962, Mrs. Squires, town biddy
Fate is the Hunter, 1964, Mrs. Llewlyn, gossipy landlady
Dear Heart, 1964, Miss Fox, lonely postmistress
How to Murder Your Wife, 1965, drunken secretary
The Trouble with Angels, 1966, Sister Clarissa, nun
The Spirit is Willing, 1967, Gloria Tritt, cleaning lady
Where Angels Go Trouble Follows, 1968, Sister Clarissa, nun
Open Window, 1972, Mrs. Sappelton, homeowner in English countryside
Napoleon and Samantha, 1972, employment office clerk
Snowball Express, 1972, Miss Wigginton, conspiring secretary
Touched by Love, 1980, Margaret, earnest teacher's aide
Postcards from the Edge, 1990, Grandma

Sister Act, 1992, Sister Mary Lazarus, nun
If My Sister's In Trouble (music video), 1992, Sister Mary Lazarus, nun
Sister Act II: Back in the Habit, 1993, Sister Mary Lazarus, nun
Little Women, 1994, Aunt March, wealthy family matriarch
The Hunchback of Notre Dame, 1996, Laverne, a gargoyle (voice only)

TELEVISION PERFORMANCES, REGULAR OR RECURRING ROLES

Inside U.S.A. with Chevrolet, 1949–50, featured comedian in skits, often the maid
The Peter and Mary Show,[1] 1950–51, housekeeper
Bonino, 1953, Martha, housekeeper
Dennis Day Show, 1953–54, featured comedian in skits
Halls of Ivy, 1954–55, Alice, housekeeper
Annette, 1958, Katie, housekeeper
Dennis the Menace, 1959–62, Esther Cathcart, man hungry neighbor
Make Room for Daddy, 1956–57, Liz O'Neal, Danny's press agent
The Danny Thomas Show, 1957–58, Liz O'Neal, Danny's press agent
Zorro, 1958, Dolores Bastinado, new woman in town
Mrs. G. Goes to College,[2] 1961–62, Winona Maxfield, landlady
Temple Houston, 1963–64, Ida Goff, Texas frontierswoman
Julia, 1969–70, Melba Chegley, nurse and physician's wife
Jimmy Stewart Show, 1971, Jo Bullard, rigid neighborhood woman
Sigmund and the Sea Monsters, 1973–74, Zelda Marshall, housekeeper
Doc, 1975, Beatrice Tully, nurse
Father Dowling Mysteries, 1989–91, Marie, rectory housekeeper
Life with Louie, 1995, Grandma (voice)

TELEVISION PERFORMANCES, EPISODIC APPEARANCES

NBC Dramatic Sustainer, "Ring on Her Finger," 1945, Daisy
The Actor's Studio, "The Catbird Seat," Oct. 24, 1948, Ulgine Barrows, office efficiency expert
Studio One, "The Storm," Nov. 7, 1948
The Actor's Studio, "Good Bye, Miss Lizzie Borden," Nov. 21, 1948
Colgate Theatre, "Fancy Meeting You Here," Jan. 3, 1949

---

1. Series name later changed to the *Peter Lind Hayes Show with Mary Healy*
2. Series name later changed to the *Gertrude Berg Show*

Ford Theatre, "The Man Who Came to Dinner," Jan. 16, 1949, Miss Preen, a nurse

Philco Television Playhouse, "Dark Hammock," Jan. 30, 1949, Amelia Coop, scientist's spinster assistant

Studio One, "Mary Poppins," Dec. 19, 1949, a whimsical nanny

Chevrolet Tele-theatre, "The Schartz-Metterklume Method," May 22, 1950, Lady Carlotta, eccentric traveler

Mama, May 26, 1950

Star Spangled Revue, Sept. 14, 1950, maid

All Star Revue with Danny Thomas, "A Christmas Carol," Dec. 22, 1951, Mrs. Cratchit

I Love Lucy, "The Ballet," Feb. 18, 1952, Madame Lamond, a ballet instructor

Studio One, "Mrs. Hargreaves," March 24, 1952, Connie Hargreaves, an eccentric imaginary woman

Hollywood Opening Night

Studio One, "The Runaway," Jan. 4, 1954

Life with Father, Jan. 24, 1954, explorer who returns from Africa with drums

Shower of Stars, "Time Out for Ginger," Oct. 6, 1955, Lizzie, meddlesome housekeeper

Alcoa Hour, "The Small Servant," Oct. 30, 1955, Sally Brass, villainous employer

Matinee Theater, "The Catbird Seat," Feb. 17, 1956, Ulgine Barrows, office efficiency expert

Alfred Hitchcock Presents, "The Baby Sitter," May 6, 1956, Blanche Armsteader, gossipy neighbor

Schlitz Playhouse of Stars, "The Bankmouse," July 20, 1956

Alfred Hitchcock Presents, "Toby," Nov. 4, 1956, Mrs. Foster, no-nonsense landlady

Playhouse 90, "Circle of the Day," May 30, 1957, Grace, woman's sister

Lux Video Theatre, "Dark Hammock," Aug. 1, 1957, Amelia Coop, scientist's spinster assistant

Matinee Theatre, "The Sure Thing," Dec. 12, 1957

The Thin Man, "Bat McKidderick, Esq.," June 12, 1959, Sally, in Native American festival costume

Ford Startime, "Cindy's Fella," Dec. 15, 1959, Myrtle Parks, mean-spirited stepmother

Buick-Electra Theatre, "The Gambler, the Nun and the Radio," May 19, 1960, a nurse

No Place Like Home, 1960, housekeeper (failed pilot featuring Gordon and Sheila MacRae as show biz couple)

Shirley Temple's Theatre, "Little Men," Oct. 23, 1960, Hannah, a maid

The Dinah Shore Chevy Show, "Autumn Crocus," Feb. 12, 1961, Edith Gunther, spinster traveling companion

Shirley Temple's Theatre, "The Princess and the Goblins," March 19, 1961, Lootie, nurse to medieval princess

Ichabod and Me

Bonanza, "The Colonel," Jan. 6, 1963, Martha, operator of boarding house

The Lucy Show, "Lucy and the Runaway Butterfly," April 22, 1963, Mrs. Wickenhauser, courtroom witness

Our Man Higgins, "Love is Dandy," May 15, 1963, Madame Amethyst, visiting cousin from England

The Lucy Show, "Lucy Plays Cleopatra," Sept. 30, 1963, Frannie

The Lucy Show, "Lucy and Viv Play Softball," Oct. 14, 1963, Frannie

The Lucy Show, "Lucy Puts Out a Fire at the Bank," Dec. 2, 1963, Frannie

Kraft Suspense Theatre, "The Machine That Played God," Dec. 5, 1963, Mrs. Pike, blowsy courtroom witness

Bob Hope Presents the Chrysler Theatre, "It's Mental Work," Dec. 20, 1963, hospital nurse

The Donna Reed Show, "First Addition," Jan. 2, 1964

My Three Sons, "The Caribbean Cruise," Sept. 17, 1964, Jeri Schronk, manhungry cruise passenger

The Red Skelton Hour, "Be it Ever So Grumble, There's No Place Like Home," Oct. 13, 1964, Ruby

Ben Casey, "The Day They Stole County General," April 26, 1965, Miss Brink, hospital supply clerk

The Decorator, 1965, Viola, interior designer's assistant (failed pilot starring Bette Davis)

The Red Skelton Hour, Episode #15-9, Nov. 9, 1965, schoolteacher

The Lucy Show, "Lucy and the Sleeping Beauty," Nov. 15, 1965, Mary Jane's annoying Aunt Gussie

The Lucy Show, "Lucy and Clint Walker," March 7, 1966, Mary Jane's annoying Aunt Gussie

Pruitts of Southampton, "Phyllis, the Upstairs Girl," Nov. 15, 1966, Amelia Pembroke, snobby neighbor

Mrs. Thursday, 1966 (failed pilot with Joan Blondell as maid who inherits a fortune)

Bonanza, "A Christmas Story," Dec. 25, 1966, Hattie Manwearing, lonely society matron

The Lucy Show, "Lucy the Baby Sitter," Jan. 16, 1967, Mrs. Winslow, a woman raising chimps

F Troop, "Marriage, Fort Courage Style," March 9, 1967, Samantha Oglesby, a matchmaker

The Red Skelton Hour, "The Nag and I," May 9, 1967, Mrs. Applebee, homely wife

The Lucy Show, "Lucy and Robert Goulet," Oct. 30, 1967, Miss Hurlow, Goulet's assistant

The Lucy Show, "Lucy's Mystery Guest," Nov. 13, 1967, overbearing Aunt Agatha

The Beverly Hillbillies, "The Social Climbers," Nov. 8, 1967, Adaline Ashley, man-crazy hillbilly

I Spy, "Shana," March 8, 1968, Mildred, unwitting tourist used to smuggle rocket fuel

Here's Lucy, "Lucy Goes on Strike," Jan. 20, 1969, Isabel, a secretary and friend of Lucy

Doris Day Show, "The Buddy," Feb. 4, 1969, Major Emma Flood, a take-charge Marine

The Queen and I, "Requiem for Becker," Feb. 6, 1969, Hazel Becker, money-hungry wife

Here's Lucy, "Lucy Gets Her Man," Feb. 24, 1969, Isabel, a secretary and friend of Lucy

The Monk, 1969, Mrs. Medford, chatty apartment neighbor (failed pilot with George Maharis as a detective)

Here's Lucy, "Lucy and Harry's Tonsils," Oct. 20, 1969, Nurse Hurlow

Mr. Deeds Goes to Town, "Revolt of the Bucket Brigade," Dec. 19, 1969, Molly

The Headmaster, "Old Man Moe Ain't Dead," 1970, Cynthia Fleming

Debbie Reynolds Show, "Advice and Dissent," Jan. 20, 1970, Aunt Harriet

Here's Lucy, "Lucy and the Diamond Cutter," Nov. 16, 1970, maid

Here's Lucy, "Lucy and Her All-Nun Band," Nov. 1, 1971, Sister Paula, nun

The Man and the City, "Running Scared," Nov. 3, 1971, Cora

Columbo, "Suitable for Framing," Nov. 16, 1971, busy-body landlady

Don Rickles Show, unnamed premiere episode, Jan. 14, 1972, hospital nurse

Here's Lucy, "Lucy's Big Break," Sept. 11, 1972, Miss Ogilvie, nurse

Here's Lucy, "Lucy and Eva Gabor are Hospital Roomies," Sept. 18, 1972, Miss Ogilvie, nurse

Hallmark Hall of Fame, "The Man Who Came to Dinner," Nov. 29, 1972, Miss Preen, nurse

Sanford and Son, "The Light Housekeeper," Dec. 22, 1972, Mary, inept housekeeper

Here's Lucy, "Lucy Plays Cops and Robbers," Dec. 31, 1973, Violet Barker, hen-pecked wife

Here's Lucy, "Lucy the Sheriff," Jan. 28, 1974, Clara Simpson, eccentric small town character

Ma and Pa, March 7, 1974, Ma (failed pilot starring Mary as the matriarch of a complicated family)

Kolchak: the Night Stalker, "They Have Been, They Are, They Will Be," Sept. 27, 1974, Bess Winestock, scientist

M*A*S*H, "House Arrest," Feb. 4, 1975, Colonel Rachel Reese, man-hungry Army nurse

Tabitha, "Halloween," Nov. 12, 1977, Casandra, influential witch

Lucille Ball Special, "Lucy Calls the President," Nov. 21, 1977, Aunt Millie

Tabitha, "Tabitha's Party," Jan. 14, 1978, Casandra, influential witch

Willa (TV movie), March 17, 1979, Eunice, greasy spoon operator

Sesame Street, 1980, the Plant Lady

Love Boat, "Maid for Each Other," May 9, 1981, Mrs. Randolph, wealthy woman with maid

The Waltons, "The Hostage," May 28, 1981, cousin Octavia, legal secretary and kleptomaniac

Trapper John, "Hate is Enough," Oct. 25, 1981, Miranda, wise-cracking hospital patient

Trapper John, "The Good Life," Nov. 28, 1982, Hazel, small-town nurse

Matt Houston, "Wanted Man," Sept. 21, 1984, Nellie Cochran, retired secret agent

Punky Brewster, "Take Me Out to the Ball Game," Oct. 21, 1984, Sister Bernadette, nun

Trapper John, "Of Cats, Crashes and Creeps," Nov. 18, 1984, Rocky Flanagan, eccentric widow

ABC Afterschool Special, "First the Egg," March 6, 1985, Helen Crandall, schoolteacher

Murder, She Wrote, "Widow, Weep for Me," Sept. 29, 1985, Alva Crane, wealthy widow

WonderWorks, "The Canterville Ghost," Nov. 17, 1985, Mrs. Umney, dour Irish housekeeper

The Christmas Gift (TV movie), Dec. 21, 1986, Aunt Henrietta Sawyer, hotelkeeper

WonderWorks, "Almost Partners," April 11, 1987, Agatha Greyson, grandmother

Alf Loves a Mystery, Sept. 11, 1987, Agatha Megpeace, maid

We Got It Made, "Hello, Dolly," Oct. 16, 1987, Rose, cranky old art student

You Can't Take It With You, "Like Mother, Like Son," Nov. 28, 1987, Elizabeth Kirkbottom, society matron

Fatal Confession: A Father Dowling Mystery (TV movie), Nov. 30, 1987, Marie, rectory housekeeper

Punky Brewster, "So Long, Studio," Dec. 2, 1987, Mrs. Dempsey, longtime photo store customer

Highway to Heaven, "Country Doctor," Jan. 13, 1988, Minnie, mail carrier and town gossip

Weldon Pond, 1994, Ella Michalek (failed pilot with Mary as busy-body receptionist)

STAGE PERFORMANCES

Reunion in Vienna, Shubert-Rialto Theater, St. Louis, Jan. 22, 1933, Sophia, faded aristocrat

Another Language, Shubert-Rialto Theater, St. Louis, March 8, 1933, Helen Hallam, spinster sister

No, No, Nanette, Fox Theatre, St. Louis, September 1933

Queen High, Fox Theatre, St. Louis, Sept. 22, 1933

Her Master's Voice, Berkshire Playhouse, Stockbridge, Mass., 1934, Phoebe, the maid

Craig's Wife, Berkshire Playhouse, Stockbridge, 1934, Mrs. Harold, the maid

Saturday's Children, Berkshire Playhouse, Stockbridge, 1934, Mrs. Gorlick, landlady

Romance, Berkshire Playhouse, Stockbridge, 1934, Mrs. Rutherford

Good-Bye Again, Berkshire Playhouse, Stockbridge, 1934, maid

Biography, Berkshire Playhouse, Stockbridge, Aug. 13, 1934, Minnie, German maid

As You Like It, Berkshire Playhouse, Stockbridge, Aug. 20, 1934, Audrey, country wench

Fly Away Home, Berkshire Playhouse, Stockbridge, Aug. 27, 1934, Penny, nurse

The Farmer Takes a Wife, Garrick Theatre, Philadelphia, Oct. 15, 1934, Mary Howard and understudy as Lucy Gurget, a cook and gossip

The Farmer Takes a Wife, Colonial Theatre, Boston, Oct. 22, 1934, Mary Howard and understudy as Lucy Gurget, a cook and gossip

The Farmer Takes a Wife, 46th Street Theatre, New York, Oct. 30, 1934, Mary Howard and understudy as Lucy Gurget, a cook and gossip

Cat and the Canary, Berkshire Playhouse, Stockbridge, July 8, 1935, Aunt Susan Sillsby, sportswoman

Trelawney of the Wells, Berkshire Playhouse, Stockbridge, July 15, 1935, Miss Trafalgar Gower

Meet the Prince, Berkshire Playhouse, Stockbridge, July 22, 1935, overbearing Mrs. Faithful

All This While, Berkshire Playhouse, Stockbridge, July 29, 1935, Parker

Declassee, Berkshire Playhouse, Stockbridge, Aug. 5, 1935, servant

Accent on Youth, Berkshire Playhouse, Stockbridge, Aug. 12, 1935, Miss Darling, vain actress

Berkeley Square, Berkshire Playhouse, Stockbridge, Aug. 19, 1935, Lady Anne
  Pettigrew
In Old Kentucky, Berkshire Playhouse, Stockbridge, Aug. 26, 1935, Miss Alathea
  Layson, spinster aunt
Swing Your Lady, Shubert Theatre, New Haven, Conn., Nov. 15, 1935, Mabel
Swing Your Lady, National Theatre, Washington, D.C., Nov. 18, 1935, Mabel
Larger than Life, Court Square Theatre, Springfield, Mass., March 16, 1936,
  Miss Lathrop
One Good Year, Ambassador Theatre, New York, April 1936, Sarah
Spring Dance, Cape Playhouse, Dennis, Mass., July 6, 1936, Mildred, long-suf-
  fering maid
Mary, Mary Quite Contrary, Berkshire Playhouse, Stockbridge, July 13, 1936,
  Miss Mimms, Scout mistress
Topaze, Berkshire Playhouse, Stockbridge, July 20, 1936, Baroness
  Pitart-Verginolles
Kind Lady, Berkshire Playhouse, Stockbridge, July 27, 1936, Lucy Weston, sis-
  ter to crime victim
Spring Dance, Ridgeway Theater, White Plains, New York, Aug. 17, 1936, Mil-
  dred, long-suffering maid
Spring Dance, Empire Theatre, New York, Aug. 25, 1936, Mildred, long-suffer-
  ing maid
Stage Door, Forrest Theatre, Philadelphia, Sept. 28, 1936, Little Mary
Stage Door, New Haven, Oct. 4, 1936, Little Mary
Stage Door, Music Box Theatre, New York, Oct. 22, 1936, Little Mary
Hitch Your Wagon!, Washington, March 29, 1937, Donnelly, wise-cracking nurse
Hitch Your Wagon!, 48th St Theatre, New York, April 8, 1937, Donnelly, wise-
  cracking nurse
Mariette, Berkshire Playhouse, Stockbridge, June 28, 1937, Clotilde
Candida, Berkshire Playhouse, Stockbridge, July 5, 1937, Proserpine Garnett,
  secretary
Tonight at 8:30 (*Fumed Oak, Hands Across the Sea, Ways and Means*), Berkshire
  Playhouse, Stockbridge, July 9, 1937
Storm Over Patsy, Berkshire Playhouse, Stockbridge, July 26, 1937, Lisbet
  Skirving, publisher's wife
Many Mansions, Berkshire Playhouse, Stockbridge, Aug. 2, 1937, Miss Law-
  rence, comic character
Becky Sharp, Berkshire Playhouse, Stockbridge, Aug. 9, 1937, Old Miss Crawley,
  wealthy English relative
Patience, Theatre by the Sea, Matunuck, R.I., Aug. 24, 1937, Lady Jane, plain-
  looking lovesick maiden

Patience, Berkshire Playhouse, Stockbridge, Aug. 30, 1937, Lady Jane, plain-looking lovesick maiden

Father Malachy's Miracle, St. James Theatre, New York, Nov. 17, 1937, Annie, Scottish maid

Father Malachy's Miracle, Nixon Theatre, Pittsburgh, 1938, Annie, Scottish maid

Father Malachy's Miracle, Harris Theatre, Chicago, March 14, 1938, Annie, Scottish maid

We, the Willoughbys, Berkshire Playhouse, Stockbridge, June 27, 1938, Prudy Willoughby, comic character

Lightnin', Berkshire Playhouse, Stockbridge, July 4, 1938, Mrs. Moore, comic character

Enter Madame, Berkshire Playhouse, Stockbridge, July 18, 1938, Bice, Italian maid

Best Dressed Woman in the World, Berkshire Playhouse, Stockbridge, July 25, 1938, Phyllis, hotel maid

Stage Door, Berkshire Playhouse, Stockbridge, Aug. 1, 1938, Judith Canfield

Too Much Johnson, Stony Creek (Conn.) Theatre, Aug. 16, 1938, Mrs. Battison, stern mother-in-law

Danton's Death, Mercury Theatre, New York, Nov. 2, 1938, Christine

Stars in Your Eyes, Shubert Theatre, New Haven, Conn., Jan. 11, 1939, actors' voice coach

Stars in Your Eyes, Shubert Theatre, Boston, Jan. 17, 1939, actors' voice coach

Stars in Your Eyes, Majestic Theater, New York, Feb. 9, 1939, actors' voice coach

Merton of the Movies, Cape Playhouse, Dennis, Mass., June 26, 1939, Mrs. Patterson, society woman

Spring Meeting, Cape Playhouse, Dennis, Mass., July 17, 1939, Aunt Bijou Furze, gambling spinster

Skylark, Cape Playhouse, Dennis, Mass., Aug. 14, 1939, Lucille

The Man Who Came to Dinner, Bushnell Memorial Auditorium, Hartford, Conn., Sept. 23, 1939, Miss Preen, nurse

The Man Who Came to Dinner, Plymouth Theatre, Boston, Sept. 25, 1939, Miss Preen, nurse

The Man Who Came to Dinner, Music Box Theatre, New York, Oct. 16, 1939, Miss Preen, nurse

The Man Who Came to Dinner, American Theater, St. Louis, Nov. 3, 1940, Miss Preen, nurse

British Relief benefit performance, New York, March 29, 1941

George Washington Slept Here, Bucks County (Penn.) Playhouse, June 6, 1941, Annabelle Fuller, bitter wife

George Washington Slept Here, Berkshire Playhouse, Stockbridge, July 7, 1941, Annabelle Fuller, bitter wife

Dancing in the Streets, Shubert Theatre, Boston, March 19, 1943, Louella Briggs, newspaper columnist

Jackpot, Shubert Theatre, New Haven, Conn., Dec. 2, 1943, Nancy Parker, defense plant worker

Jackpot, Forrest Theatre, Philadelphia, Dec. 7, 1943, Nancy Parker, defense plant worker

Jackpot, Alvin Theatre, New York, Jan. 13, 1944, Nancy Parker, defense plant worker

Naughty Marietta, St. Louis Municipal Opera (Muny), July 10, 1944, Lizette, husband-seeking French girl

Dark Hammock, Forrest Theatre, New York, Dec. 11, 1944, Amelia Coop, scientist's spinster assistant

Hollywood Pinafore, Shubert Theatre, Philadelphia, May 14, 1945, Miss Hebe, the secretary

Hollywood Pinafore, Alvin Theatre, New York, May 31, 1945, Miss Hebe, the secretary

Apple of His Eye, McCarter Theatre, Princeton, New Jersey, Jan. 11, 1946, Nina Stover, greedy daughter-in-law

Apple of His Eye, Baltimore, Jan. 14, 1946, Nina Stover, greedy daughter-in-law

Apple of His Eye, Walnut Street Theatre, Philadelphia, Jan. 21, 1946, Nina Stover, greedy daughter-in-law

Apple of His Eye, Biltmore Theatre, New York, Feb. 5, 1946, Nina Stover, greedy daughter-in-law

The Late George Apley, Berkshire Playhouse, Stockbridge, June 24, 1946, Amelia, the sister-in-law

Blithe Spirit, Berkshire Playhouse, Stockbridge, July 1, 1946, Madame Arcati, a medium

Rebecca, Berkshire Playhouse, Stockbridge, July 15, 1946, Beatrice Lacy, Maxim's kind older sister

Elizabeth the Queen, Berkshire Playhouse, Stockbridge, July 29, 1946, title role

My Sister Eileen, Berkshire Playhouse, Stockbridge, Aug. 5, 1946, Ruth

Park Avenue, Shubert Theatre, New Haven, Conn., September 1946, Mrs. Betty Nelson

Park Avenue, Shubert Theatre, Boston, Sept. 23, 1946, Mrs. Betty Nelson, society wife

Park Avenue, Shubert Theatre, Philadelphia, Oct. 7, 1946, Mrs. Betty Nelson, society wife

Park Avenue, Shubert Theatre, New York, Nov. 4, 1946, Mrs. Betty Nelson, society wife

Heyday, Shubert Theatre, New Haven, Conn., March 13, 1947, Molly Pepper, nagging wife

Town House, Colonial Theatre, Boston, Sept. 2, 1948, Esther Murray, intellectual housewife

Town House, National Theatre, New York, Sept. 23, 1948, Esther Murray, intellectual housewife

New Moon, Muny, St. Louis, June 9, 1949, Clotilde Lombaste, oft-married 18th-century French trollop

The Late Christopher Bean, Berkshire Playhouse, Stockbridge, July 4, 1949, Abby, maid

The Torch-Bearers, Bucks County (Penn.) Playhouse, July 25, 1949, Mrs. Pampinelli, pretentious stage director

On Approval, Berkshire Playhouse, Stockbridge, Aug. 15, 1949, Maria Wislack, spoiled wealthy widow

New Moon, Houston Lyric Theatre, June 19, 1950, Clotilde Lombaste, oft-married 18th-century French trollop

Bloomer Girl, Houston Lyric Theatre, June 26, 1950, Aunt Dolly Bloomer

The Late Christopher Bean, the Woodstock (New York) Playhouse, July 25, 1950, Abby, maid

On Approval, the Woodstock (New York) Playhouse, Aug. 1, 1950, Maria Wislack, spoiled wealthy widow

Dandy Dick, the Woodstock (New York) Playhouse, Aug. 8, 1950, Georgiana Tidman, gambling widow

Ring Around the Moon, La Jolla (Calif.) Playhouse, July 3, 1951, Capulet, companion to Madame Desmermortes

Show Boat, Muny, St. Louis, June 5, 1952, Parthy Ann, shrewish wife of a riverboat captain

The Open Window, Sombrero Playhouse, Phoenix, Ariz., March 22, 1954, Buckle, maid

The Great Sebastians, Berkshire Playhouse, Stockbridge, 1957, Essie Sebastian, vaudeville mind reader

Leave It to Little People, Huntington Hartford Theatre, Los Angeles, March 31, 1960, Agatha, switchboard operator

Meet Me in St. Louis, Muny, St. Louis, June 9, 1960, Katie, housekeeper

Antigone, Theatre Group at UCLA, Oct. 23, 1962, nurse

Shakespeare's Way with Women, Beckman Auditorium, Pasadena, Calif., May 16, 1964, Mistress Ford

Show Boat, Muny, St. Louis, June 22, 1964, Parthy Ann, shrewish wife of a riverboat captain

Show Boat, Melodyland, Anaheim, Calif., September 1964, Parthy Ann, shrewish wife of riverboat captain

Meet Me in St. Louis, Muny, St. Louis, June 7, 1965, Katie, housekeeper

Music Man, Muny, St. Louis, June 6, 1966, Eulalie MacKechnie Shinn

High Spirits, Houston Music Theatre, July 19, 1966, Madame Arcati, a medium

High Spirits, Valley Music Theatre, Woodland Hills, Calif., Aug. 9, 1966, Madame Arcati, a medium

Glass Menagerie, Brown Hall, Washington University, March 14, 1968, Amanda
Wingfield, troubled matriarch of dysfunctional family

Show Boat, Muny, St. Louis, Aug. 5, 1968, Parthy Ann, shrewish wife of riverboat captain

Show Boat, Starlight Theatre, Kansas City, Aug. 12, 1968, Parthy Ann, shrewish
wife of riverboat captain

Adventures of the Black Girl in Her Search for God, Mark Taper Forum, Los Angeles, March 12, 1969, missionary in Africa (withdrew during rehearsals in
February)

Los Angeles's 188th Birthday Fiesta, the Hollywood Bowl, Sept. 8, 1969, typist
in one-woman skit

Music Man, Muny, St. Louis, July 26, 1971, Eulalie MacKechnie Shinn

Student Prince, Muny, St. Louis, Aug. 21, 1972, Grand Duchess

American Conservatory Theater, San Francisco, member of company, 1972–73
season, appearing in: *Mystery Cycle* (Noah's wife), *You Can't Take It With You*
(Penny, the eccentric mother), *The Crucible* (Rebecca Nurse), *House of Blue
Leaves* (Mother Superior). She also directed two one-acts from Noel Coward's *Tonight at 8:30*, *Hands Across the Sea*, and *Ways and Means*

Dorothy Parker and Other Funny Ladies, Geary Theatre, San Francisco, November
1973, one-woman show

Juno and the Paycock, Mark Taper Forum, Nov. 7, 1974, Maisie Madigan, hard-
drinking Irish widow

Wonderful Town, Curran Theatre, San Francisco, May 6, 1975, Mrs. Wade,
neighbor's visiting mother

Wonderful Town, Dorothy Chandler Pavilion, July 1, 1975, Mrs. Wade, neighbor's visiting mother

Meet Me in St. Louis, Muny, St. Louis, June 27, 1977, Katie, housekeeper

Oklahoma!, Muny, St. Louis, July 17, 1978, Aunt Eller, earthy frontier woman

Oklahoma!, Starlight Theatre, Kansas City, July 24, 1978, Aunt Eller, earthy
frontier woman

Damn Yankees, Muny, Aug. 7, 1978, Sister Miller, funny friend

Damn Yankees, Starlight Theatre, Kansas City, Aug. 14, 1978, Sister Miller, funny friend

Oklahoma!, Miami Beach (Fla.) Theatre, Dec. 20, 1978, Aunt Eller, earthy frontier woman

Oklahoma!, Parker Playhouse, Fort Lauderdale, Fla., Jan. 2, 1979, Aunt Eller, earthy frontier woman

Oklahoma!, Royal Poinciana Playhouse, Palm Beach, Fla., Feb. 5, 1979, Aunt Eller, earthy frontier woman

Oklahoma! National Tour, nine cities in eight months, beginning in Los Angeles in April 1979, Aunt Eller

Oklahoma!, Palace Theatre, New York, Dec. 13, 1979, a nine-month run as Aunt Eller, earthy frontier woman

Importance of Being Earnest, College of William and Mary, Williamsburg, Va., Oct. 1, 1981, Lady Bracknell

Dorothy Parker and Other Funny Ladies, Ojai, Calif., fall 1981, one-woman show

Henry IV, Part I, American Shakespeare Theatre, Stratford, Conn., July 6, 1982, Mistress Quickly

Palace of Amateurs, Berkshire Playhouse, Stockbridge, Aug. 8, 1982, Rosemary, hotel operator

Light Up the Sky, Coconut Grove Playhouse, Miami, Oct. 28, 1983, Stella Livingston, sarcastic stage mother

Detective Story, Ahmanson Theater, Los Angeles, Feb. 4, 1984, Willie, janitor

Detective Story, Denver Center for the Performing Arts, April 1984, Willie, janitor

Arsenic and Old Lace, Burt Reynolds Jupiter Theatre, April 2, 1985, Martha Brewer, kindly murderer

The Foreigner, Alliance Theatre, Atlanta, Jan. 14, 1987, Betty Meeks

Wizard of Oz, Fox Theatre, St. Louis, Dec. 27, 1987, Wicked Witch of the West

ON TELEVISION AS HERSELF (SELECT LIST)

The Gloria Swanson Hour, Oct. 21, 1948

News and Views, Dec. 11, 1948

Quizzing the News, Dec. 15, 1948

Quizzing the News, Dec. 29, 1948

Video Village, 1961

Here's Hollywood, 1962

Your First Impression, 1962

America, "Twin River Titan," 1965

Girl Talk, 1966

Password, Sept. 19, 1966

Merv Griffin Show, March 17, 1969

Tattletales, 1976
Match Game, recurring panelist in 1976, 1977, 1978
Wil Shriner Show, 1988
The Today Show, June 18, 1992
The Tonight Show, July 13, 1992

TELEVISION COMMERCIALS

Some of Mary's commercials, like one for Cudahy Meats, were brief, limited promotions. Some, like a Snowy Bleach commercial that fared badly with test audiences, never made it to broadcast. Others, like an Era detergent commercial, were popular campaigns that ran for several years. When Rosalind Russell replied to get-well wishes from Mary in 1975, she closed with, "Much love—and I adore you with the soap powder!! A riot." These appearances are listed by date of initial employment agreement.

Ford Automobiles—February 1969
Cudahy Meats—November 1969
Snowy Bleach—November 1970
Era Laundry Detergent—September 1972
Crisco Oil—September 1980

RADIO PERFORMANCES

Mary appeared in numerous live radio broadcasts. Some performances were as part of a regular series cast, while others were appearances in a single episode. Most were broadcast from New York, some from Los Angeles, and a few from St. Louis.

ACLU Celebration of the Bill of Rights, Dec. 13, 1950
Cavalcade of America
Colonel Stoopnagle and Budd
Crime Does Not Pay, "Escort for Hire," Oct. 30, 1950
Doris Day Show, April 18, 1952
Ellen Randolph
Heart-to-Heart Club (St. Louis), 1933
Henry Morgan Show

Hollywood Radio Theatre, 1973

Hollywood's Open House, "The Cursed Concerto," June 3, 1948

Hour of Romance

Jack Carson Show

Lorenzo Jones, Irma Barker, wife of Lorenzo's boss

Lux Radio Theatre, "On Moonlight Bay," May 5, 1952, Stella, housekeeper

Martha Deane Show, December 1946

Meet Corliss Archer, 1942–43, Louise, the maid

Mercury Theatre on the Air, "Life with Father," Nov. 6, 1938, employment office
    manager

Mercury Theatre on the Air, "Pickwick Papers," Nov. 20, 1938, Rachel Wardle

Mercury Theatre on the Air, "Seventeen," Oct. 16, 1938, Mrs. Partcher

Moon Mullins

Portia Faces Life

Report to the Nation

Stars Over Hollywood

That's My Pop, wife of the lazy Pop

Theatre Guild on the Air, "Alice Adams," Nov. 5, 1950, Malena, maid

Theatre Guild on the Air, "June Moon," March 27, 1949, Lucille

Theatre Guild on the Air, "The Man Who Came to Dinner," Nov. 17, 1946, Miss
    Preen

Theatre Guild on the Air, "Minick," May 28, 1950, Marge Diamond

Theatre Guild on the Air, "Rip Van Winkle," Dec. 26, 1948, Dimmick

Theatre Guild on the Air, "Another Language," Jan. 15, 1950

Tribute to St. Louis (from New York), Feb. 23, 1940

Vic and Sade

Victory Belles

NOTES

Where an interview was conducted in person, the city appears in the notation; otherwise, the interview was conducted by telephone. Where an interview date is different from a prior notation attributed to the same source, more than one interview was conducted with that person.

Repositories that appear frequently in these notes:

AMPAS—Margaret Herrick Library at the Academy of Motion Picture Arts and Sciences, Beverly Hills, California
LOC—Manuscript Division, U.S. Library of Congress, Washington, D.C.
MWP—Mary Wickes Papers, University Archives, Department of Special Collections, Washington University Libraries, St. Louis
SLA—the Stockbridge (Massachusetts) Library Association
WBA—Warner Bros. Archives, School of Cinematic Arts, University of Southern California, Los Angeles

CHAPTER ONE: PARDON ME LADY, BUT DID YOU DROP A FISH?

3 most popular film of 1954—*White Christmas* grossed $12 million, more than any other release that year, based on figures reported in *Variety*, per Gene Brown, *Movie Time: A Chronology of Hollywood and the Movie Industry from its Beginnings to the Present*, Wiley, 1995, p. 221

3 "knocked over two pews"—telephone interview with Rosemary Clooney, March 8, 2000

3 "really bothered her"—interview with Bill Givens, Los Angeles, April 9, 1999

4 "I don't think anybody"—interview with Dolly Reed Wageman, Studio City, Calif., Dec. 3, 1998

4 live talk show—this episode of *The Gloria Swanson Hour* was broadcast on Oct. 21, 1948

4 one of her first— on of Lucille Ball's first TV appearances was on the variety show *Inside U.S.A. with Chevrolet*, on which Mary was a regular, on Nov. 24, 1949

4 Montgomery Clift—in August 1934, Mary co-starred with Clift at the Berkshire Playhouse in Stockbridge, Mass., in *Fly Away Home*, Clift's first professional acting assignment

4 Grace Kelly—in July 1949, Mary co-starred with Kelly at the Bucks County (Penn.) Playhouse in *The Torch-Bearers*, Kelly's first professional acting assignment

4 Frank Sinatra—Mary appeared with Sinatra in *Higher and Higher* in 1943

4 as a cook—Frank's mother first appears in Gould's *St. Louis Directory*, a precursor to today's city telephone books, in 1883, listed as widow of August and "cook, Memorial Home." Neither the home's successor property nor the Western Historical Manuscript Collection at University of Missouri at St. Louis, which has many of the home's records, has more information.

5 one of nine children—William L. Thomas, "Thomas A. Hetherington," *History of St. Louis County, Missouri*, Vol. II, S. J. Clarke Publishing Co., 1911, pp. 341–42

5 a clerk at Glaser Brothers—per Gould's *St. Louis Directory*, 1898 edition

5 destroyed by fire—Albert Nelson Marquis, "Glaser, Adolph," *The Book of St. Louisans: A Biographical Dictionary of Leading Living Men of the City of St. Louis and Vicinity*, Second Edition, A. N. Marquis & Co., 1942, p. 229

5 Simmons Hardware Company—per Gould's *St. Louis Directory*, 1899 edition

5 Hargadine-McKittrick Dry Goods—per Gould's *St. Louis Directory*, 1900–1903 editions

5 American Central Trust Company—per Gould's *St. Louis Directory*, 1904 edition

5 tall, thin and slightly bent over—this description is drawn from photos of Frank and from recollections of ten people who had clear memories of him at the time this book was researched

5 "withdrew from conversations"—interview with Sally Higginbotham, St. Louis, Sept. 19, 1998

5 "not a very warm person"—interview with Jim Alexander, St. Louis, June 12, 1999

5 "seemed so much older"—telephone interview with Ruth Alexander Stubbs, June 18, 1999

5 at a dance—their first meeting is documented in Isabella's small "Bride's Booklet," MWP

6 mayor of East St. Louis—from notes about Isabella in MWP

6 dyed her hair red—interview with Amy Jane Harrison Ax, St. Louis, Sept. 25, 1998

6 treacly inspirational truisms—Mary saved many of Isabella's clippings, MWP

6 "best and happiest"—this message was in a Christmas 1934 telegram to Mary at the American Women's Association Clubhouse in New York, but numerous other examples appear in MWP

6 "your manners!"—friends say Mary used this expression, picked up from Isabella, her entire life

6 joined Mercantile Trust—Gould's *St. Louis Directories* indicate Frank was employed by the bank beginning in 1905, first as bookkeeper, then as teller, then assistant auditor and assistant comptroller—until 1930, when he begins appearing merely as "clerk." This change may reflect the salary cut that he was asked to take during the Depression.

6 Andrew Hetherington died—per death notice in the *St. Louis Post-Dispatch*, Aug. 21, 1905

6 engaged in April 1906—from Isabella's small Bride's Booklet, now in MWP

6 married in April 1908—per Frank and Isabella's wedding invitation, MWP

7 in the downstairs unit—per Gould's *St. Louis Directory*, 1909 edition

7 larger, single-family home—Gould's *St. Louis Directories* report the Wickenhausers living on 5017 Garfield Ave. from 1910 through 1918. The house still exists, but its address has changed to 5017 Locust Ave.

7 a full nine pounds—from the small, handwritten baby book in which Isabella chronicled Mary's every move as a newborn, MWP

7 "like a little boy"—letter from Aunt Hes in Barberton, Ohio, to Isabella in St. Louis, Oct. 25, 1910, MWP

7 her first laugh—from the small, handwritten baby book in which Isabella chronicled Mary's every move as a newborn, MWP

8 "black as can be"—interview with Mary Beresford Vahle, Webster Groves, Mo., Sept. 15, 1998

8 "nigger heaven"—interview with Louis Westheimer, St. Louis, Nov. 7, 1998. Actor John Loder, who appeared with Mary in *Now, Voyager*, recalls the same phrase for theatres' practice of segregating African American and white patrons: John Loder, *Hollywood Hussar: The Life and Times of John Loder*, H. Baker, 1977, p. 143

8 cooking was done by coal—descriptions of St. Louis life in this period benefit from "That's the Way It Was, 1914–1930," an unpublished personal history by Mary Margaret Ellis. Ellis was a second-generation Irish American born in St. Louis only a year after Mary, so her life parallels Mary's in many ways. The 1980 manuscript was accessed at the Western Historical Manuscript Collection at the University of Missouri at St. Louis.

8 "a woman is to be seen"—interview with Judy Sutter Hinrichs, St. Louis, Oct. 17, 1998

8 "proper kind of existence"—telephone interview with Virginia Weber Hoffmann, May 19, 1999

9 fond of outings—the descriptions are drawn from family snapshots from the 1910s that Isabella saved in a scrapbook called "Wickenhauser News and Views," MWP

9 "took their own lunch"—from an audiocassette of anecdotes that Mary recorded in 1990 in preparation for a possible autobiography, MWP

9 "that old stuff"—from an audiocassette of anecdotes that Mary recorded in 1990 in preparation for a possible autobiography, MWP

9 "My Doll Wedding"—photos are in the "Wickenhauser News and Views" scrapbook, MWP

10 "my childhood"—"Mary Wickes Home for First Park Role," *St. Louis Star-Times*, July 10, 1944

10 "stay awake without a nap"—Mary's Adele Starbird Lecture at Washington University, April 12, 1988, a copy of which is in MWP

10 "crunch of snow"—Mary was one of twenty-two personalities to record reflections on a special "Christmas in Saint Louis" record album in 1977 for the St. Louis Christmas Carols Association

10 leadership positions—over the years in St. Louis, for the women's clubs eighth district, she was press and publicity chair, community service chair and president

10 "at the Gellhorns"—interview with Louis Westheimer, Oakland, Calif., Oct. 19, 1999

10 "devoted"—interview with Mary Beresford Vahle, Webster Groves, Mo., Sept. 15, 1998

11 "Everybody liked Wick"—telephone interview with Eugene Fincke, Jan. 17, 1999

11 "When I went to the bank"—interview with Louis Westheimer, St. Louis, Nov. 7, 1998

11 "heard every word"—letter from Frank to Mary in Los Angeles, May 18, 1943, MWP

12 chocolate—from Mary's speech to Forest Park Forever in St. Louis, May 30, 1991, MWP

12 "great privilege"—from the "Who Reads What?" campaign by the Gardiner, Maine, Public Library promoting the favorite books of well-known people. Mary responded to the 1993 survey.

12 "entertaining was done"—interview with Sally Higginbotham, St. Louis, Sept. 19, 1998

12 "more in common"—interview with Sally Higginbotham, St. Louis, Sept. 19, 1998

12 "much younger than I"—from an oral history of the Berkshire Playhouse, recorded by Mary on Aug. 25, 1982, and preserved in the Historical Room of the Stockbridge Library Association

13 Cupples—from Mary's enrollment records in the Archives of the St. Louis Public Schools

13 "Carry Me Back"—the lyrics, in Mary's childhood handwriting, are in MWP

13 2104 Harris Avenue—per Gould's St. Louis Directories (editions 1919 to 1923) and the address where Mary's childhood report cards were sent, the family lived here from 1918 to 1924

13 *Harrison Weekly*—the little magazine exists in MWP

13 "gladly recite it"—Mary's handwritten note to Mrs. Elizabeth Noble, Feb. 12, 1919, MWP

13 "very sweet of you"—reply from Mrs. Elizabeth Noble, MWP

14 "Iama Nutt"—from copies of Mary's childhood academic forms, MWP

14 playing with dolls—interview with Dorothy McCauley, Granite City, Ill., Sept. 17, 1998

14 "Wicken-trousers"—telephone interview with Mary Jane Moise, Jan. 12, 1999

14 "walk across"—interview with Mary Beresford Vahle, Webster Groves, Mo., Sept. 15, 1998

14 "a wardrobe trunk"—"Mary Wickes Returns to the University, Reminisces: 'St. Louis Was Always Home,'" *Washington University Alumni News*, March 1968

14 she should remain—in speeches over the years, Mary said she had been accepted by Radcliffe College in Massachusetts but that her parents decided she was too young to be away from home

15 Frank declined—from Mary's Starbird Lecture at Washington University, April 12, 1988, MWP

15 $250 per semester—from the Washington University class reunion brochure, "You Should See 'Em Now: That Great Class of 1930 or Some '50 Years Later,'" June 7, 1980, MWP

15 forced to drop out—telephone interview with Virginia Weber Hoffmann, May 19, 1999

15 "in mourning"—telephone interview with Helen Margaret Aff-Drum, Nov, 4, 1998

15 third and fifth grades—interview with Stella Koetter Darrow, Clayton, Mo., Sept. 22, 1998

15 skipped two grades—interview with Lois Haase Mares, Washington, D.C., Nov. 11, 1998

15 "grew up a lot"—telephone interview with Dorothy Conzelman Nash, Oct. 30, 1998

15 "an unusual person"—telephone interview with Mary Jane Moise, Jan. 12, 1999

16 "drop a fish?"—telephone interview with Mary Jane Roach Masters, Feb. 12, 1999

16 "a baseball bat"—telephone interview with Ruth Alexander Stubbs, June 18, 1999

16 "almost eager"—interview with Sally Alexander Higginbotham, St. Louis, Sept. 19, 1998

16 "invaluable" preparation—Clark Clifford with Richard Holbrooke, *Counsel to the President: A Memoir*, Anchor, 1992, p. 31

17 "from a mold"—telephone interview with Virginia Weber Hoffmann, May 19, 1999

17 "a marvelous pianist"—telephone interview with Edmund Hartmann, July 21, 1999

17 6180 Pershing Avenue—the family lived here in 1928 and 1929, per Gould's *St. Louis Directories* and per correspondence addressed there, now in MWP

17 "to relax more"—interview with Mary Beresford Vahle, Webster Groves, Mo., Sept. 15, 1998

18 a B student—Mary's transcripts show she uniformly received B grades in college, with only occasional deviation, such a C in French literature and an A in English literature

18 became homeowners—the certificate of title to 6380 Pershing Avenue, dated Oct. 3, 1929, referencing the deed of trust that Frank and Isabella took out on Sept. 18, 1929, is in MWP

18 its particular floor plan—interview with Cyrus St. Clair, the high school teacher who owns the house today with his wife, Elizabeth, University City, Sept. 20, 1998

18 an unobstructed view—from Mary's Adele Starbird Lecture at Washington University, April 12, 1988, a copy of which is in MWP: "From my bedroom, if you had good binoculars, we could see a petty girl calendar on the walls of a room in the Beta House."

19 Sunday nights—Mary offered up this anecdote many times, including in a 1956 speech to a Phi Mu sorority gathering in Los Angeles and in her 1988 Adele Starbird Lecture in St. Louis, MWP

19 "from the dorm"—from Mary's speech to Phi Mu sorority in Los Angeles in 1956, MWP

19 "ran that household"—interview with Louis Westheimer, St. Louis, Nov. 7, 1998

19 "beam on us"—interview with Amy Jane Harrison Ax, St. Louis, Sept. 25, 1998

20 "solid and powerful"—Paul Finkelman, "John McLean: Moderate Abolitionist and Supreme Court Politician," *Vanderbilt Law Review*, Vol. 62, 1990, p. 565

20 Mary's true ancestor—sources helpful in clarifying this relationship include: "McLean, John," *Dictionary of American Biography*, Charles Scribner's Sons, 1933, p. 127; a summary of biographical sources on Justice John McLean at http://freepages.genealogy .rootsweb.ancestry.com/~dmcl/i/i1461.htm; biographical materials on John McLean at the Federal Judicial Center, Washington, D.C.; family trees of the Thomas family prepared by hand in MWP; "Information Concerning The Distinguished Careers of the McLean Brothers," a section in "Descendants of Thomas Entriken Hibben and Mary Jane McLean," part of an online book, *The Pioneer Hibben Family of Pennsylvania* by George C. Hibben at http://hibbengenealogy.org/Chapter_IV.aspx; entries for Milton N. McLean, Nathaniel C. McLean, Hester McLean, and Mary W. Johnston at "Hibben Family of Chester County, Pa., 1730 to early 1900s," a comprehensive genealogical history at this RootsWeb WorldConnect project: http://wc.rootsweb.an cestry.com/cgi-bin/igm.cgi?op=GET&db=ghibben&id=I1586

20 each received $25—correspondence documenting this payment is in MWP

20 "talked about the Thomases"—interview with Bill Dorsam, St. Louis, June 6, 1999

21 red quilt—from Isabella's notes chronicling gifts received for her 1908 wedding, MWP

21 "well-known fellow-citizen"—from obituary of Lorenz Wickenhauser that appeared in January 1901 in the *Union News*, a paper published for the German immigrant community in Highland, Illinois; translation by Joan Neumann Lowrey as part of genealogical research conducted by Edward L. Wickenhauser of Godfrey, Ill.

21 been called Berlin Avenue—Esley Hamilton, *Ames Place: A Brief History of its Planning and Development*, Historical Society of University City, Missouri, 1991, p. 6

21 grandfather Lorenz Wickenhauser—this connection was established by Edward L. Wickenhauser of Godfrey, Ill., with assistance from researcher and author Herbert Wickenhauser of Nenzigen, Germany, who traced Frank's lineage through parish baptismal records there

22 celebrations called "pageants"—Federal Writers Project, "The Theatre," *Missouri: A Guide to the "Show Me" State*, Duell, Sloan and Pearce, 1941, p. 157

22 "workman-like"—telephone interview with Mary Jane Roach Masters, Feb. 12, 1999

22 "Nobody had any money"—interview with Archer O'Reilly, St. Louis, Jan. 22, 1999

23 "pretty serious"—telephone interview with Marcella Wiget MacDermott, Jan. 16, 1999

23 "bull by the horns"—telephone interview with Dorothy Conzelman Nash, Oct. 30, 1998

23 "taking a test"—telephone interview with Julian Miller, May 20, 1999

24 "Where did she learn all this?"—telephone interview with Nelson Hower, Oct. 20, 1998

24 newspaper practice course—Mary's transcript is in MWP

24 "natural comedienne"—*St. Louis Star-Times*, March 6, 1933

24 one hundred—"Little Theater Star Turns Professional," *St. Louis Globe-Democrat*, Jan. 18, 1933

24 "I'd say No"—letter from Thomas Wood Stevens in Ann Arbor, Mich., to Mary in St. Louis, Aug. 27, 1933, MWP

25 "outstanding performer"—*St. Louis Post-Dispatch*, Dec. 6, 1933

25 "delightfully played"—Homer Bassford, "Humor Galore in 'Solid South' at Little Theatre," *St. Louis Star-Times*, Dec. 6, 1933

25 "invited to dinner"—Mary described this event many times, including in her Adele Starbird Lecture in St. Louis in 1988 and on the 1990 audiotape she made for a possible autobiography

CHAPTER TWO: FROM STOCKBRIDGE TO THE MERCURY THEATRE

26 "you are Mary Wickes"—letter from F. Cowles Strickland in Stockbridge to Mary in St. Louis, 1934 (undated), MWP

26 "change her characters' names"—*Here's Lucy* contracts signed by Mary show that her role in "Lucy Goes on Strike" was originally called "Jan Parker" and in "Lucy Gets Her Man" was originally "Mary." When the episodes were taped, both characters had become "Isabel." MWP

26 "proper theatrical trunk"—Mary's recollections of acquiring this trunk are on an audiocassette of anecdotes that she recorded in 1990 for a possible autobiography, MWP

27 "re-upholster the furniture"—Bill Roerick's recollections are from an oral history recorded Sept. 8, 1975, by the Berkshire Theatre Festival and preserved in the Historical Room of the SLA

27 "either a star or a first featured player"—from an oral history of the Berkshire Playhouse that Mary recorded on Aug. 25, 1982, which is preserved at the SLA

28 "slightly prestigious"—telephone interview with Jane Wyatt, July 24, 1999

28 "the same play"—from Jan. 28, 1974, oral history with Billy Miles, interviewed by Anna Smith for the SLA

28 "must surely be considered"—Berkshire Theatre Festival Records, 1886–1982, SLA, Susie Kaufman, 1983, p. 6

29 "live textbooks"—from anecdotes Mary told on the *Wil Shriner Show*, 1988 (date unknown)

29 "remember one thing"—from an oral history of the Berkshire Playhouse that Mary recorded on Aug. 25, 1982, which is preserved at the SLA

29 "picked and chose"—interview with Bill Swan, New York, Nov. 17, 1998

29 "invited back"—interview with Eleanor "Siddy" Wilson, Aug. 18, 1998

30 "door jamb"—from anecdotes Mary recorded in 1990 for a possible autobiography, MWP

31 "evening gowns"—Milton R. Bass, the "Lively World" column, *Berkshire Eagle*, Aug. 24, 1982

31 thirty chauffeur-driven cars—this recollection and that of coffee service are from a Jan. 28, 1974, oral history with Billy Miles, recorded by Anna Smith for the SLA

31 saluting passers-by—from an oral history of the Berkshire Playhouse that Mary recorded on Aug. 25, 1982, which is preserved at the SLA

31 "I was in heaven"—telephone interview with Andrea King, June 26, 2001

31 "That was brave"—telephone interview with Helen Margaret Aff-Drum, Nov, 4, 1998

31 "born in New York"—interview with Anna Crouse, New York, Nov. 18, 1998

32 "her mom was with her"—interview with Bill Dorsam, St. Louis, June 6, 1999

32 Frank insisted—Mary told Canon Richards that Frank wanted Isabella to help her get settled. "Dad insisted mother come"—interview with Canon Richards, North Hollywood, Calif., Dec. 11, 1998

32 "a hilarious summer"—from an oral history of the Berkshire Playhouse that Mary recorded on Aug. 25, 1982, which is preserved at the SLA

32 "it was madness!"—this and other observations from Lenka Peterson here come from interview with Peterson, Roxbury, Conn., Sept. 8, 1999

33 "you had to learn the cue"—Bill Roerick's recollections are from an oral history recorded on audiocassette Sept. 8, 1975, by the Berkshire Theatre Festival and preserved at the SLA

33 "scared pink"—telegram from Mary in Stockbridge to Isabella in St. Louis, Aug. 7, 1934, MWP

33 "a perfect understudy"—Ina Claire's original letter is preserved in MWP

34 "dance barefoot"—telegram from actor Eddie George (Edmund Baylies) to Mary at the Music Box Theatre on opening night of *Stage Door*, MWP

34 the value of Ina Claire's letter—Mary's use of the Ina Claire letter is chronicled in newspaper accounts from the 1930s through the 1990s, the events recounted in slightly different sequence and with slightly different elements each time. This chapter considers all that, as well as recollections from Mary's 1982 oral history at the

Berkshire Library Association, and her 1988 Adele Starbird Lecture, to arrive at the most likely sequence of events. News articles consulted include: George Ross, "So This is Broadway," *New York World Telegram*, Oct. 26, 1936; Reed Hynds, profile of Mary, *St. Louis Star*, June 29, 1937; Leonard Lyons, "Lyons Den" column, *St. Louis Globe-Democrat*, March 27, 1937; Helen Clanton, "Home from Broadway: Mary Wickes Returns Home," *St. Louis Globe-Democrat*, May 22, 1935; Gladys Hart, "St. Louis Girl in Case of Smash Hit on Broadway," *St. Louis Post-Dispatch*, Nov. 23, 1939; Joan McKinney, "Letter to 'Sam' Put Her on Broadway," *Oakland (Calif.) Tribune*, April 25, 1973

34 "dumb luck"—Gladys Hart, "St. Louis Girl in Case of Smash Hit on Broadway," *St. Louis Post-Dispatch*, Nov. 23, 1939

34 "Margaret Hamilton's grave"—Isabella wrote Mary on Oct. 9, 1934, at the James Hotel in Philadelphia that, having failed to reach Strick at the Philadelphia theatre, she reached him at his apartment. She repeated in the letter what Strick said to her on the phone.

35 Hamilton sent flowers—a floral arrangement gift-card with that date is in a scrapbook in MWP: "Good luck, darling—and don't you *dare* be *too* good!! Much love and *thank* you. Margaret."

35 "a most competent understudy"—from undated 1934 profile of Connelly, "Marc Connelly Not to Turn Actor, Yet," newspaper unknown, MWP

35 "at this stage of the game"—letter from Patricia Collinge to Mary, 1934, MWP

35 "should I write Miss Hamilton"—Oct. 9, 1934, letter from Isabella in St. Louis to Mary at James Hotel, Philadelphia, MWP

35 "more than okay"—from Oct. 22, 1934, review in *Variety* by Waters (first name unknown): "This reviewer caught Mary in the role of Lucy, programmed for Margaret Hamilton. Miss Wickes was more than okay."

36 "surprising poise"—from an un-bylined review in an unidentified newspaper clipping, MWP

36 "girl with the letter"—George Ross, "So This is Broadway," *New York World Telegram*, Oct. 26, 1936

36 Oct. 15, 1934—Mary wrote the un-bylined "'Bundling' Drama to be Presented at Stockbridge: *Pursuit of Happiness* at Berkshire Playhouse This Week" that appeared in the *Knickerbocker Press*

36 Margaret Huston—Lawrence Grobel, *The Hustons*, Charles Scribner & Sons, 1989, pp. 189–90

36 her first performance on film—Mary signed a contract on Feb. 15, 1935, with Vitaphone Production Manager Samuel Sax for production #1839-40, MWP

36 $40 for one day's work—per original Vitaphone contract for Photoplay #B-194-195, MWP

37 became a dramatic coach—Mary's papers contain her Federal Theatre Project identification card (ID #400611) and her WPA dismissal notice, Feb. 17, 1936. Both are in the name of Mary I. Wickes. She was "Dramatic Coach Grade S."

37 $24 a week—from *It Was a Wildly Exciting Time: Milton Meltzer Remembers the New Deal's Federal Theatre Project*, an oral history conducted by Elizabeth C. Stevens in 1978: "Our pay was $23.86 a week, and everybody, the vast majority of us, got exactly the same money; the only people who got more were those in supervisory positions." http://historymatters.gmu.edu/d/132/

37 overwhelming majority of artists—*The WPA Federal Theatre Project, 1935–1939*, extracts from material in the Federal Theatre Project Archives, U.S. Library of Congress, Washington, D.C. http://memory.loc.gov/ammem/fedtp/ftwpa.html

38 "one who's had it"—interview with Archer O'Reilly, St. Louis, Jan. 22, 1999

38 "Wicksie got up"—interview with Anne Kaufman Schneider, New York, Nov. 21, 1998

38 Top Hat Café—Ruby Comer, "Cheryl Crane," *Arts & Understanding*, September 2006, pp. 18–19

39 in the front row—Reed Hynds, *St. Louis Star*, June 29, 1937

39 "grand combination"—*Hollywood Reporter*, Oct. 23, 1936 (article headline and byline unclear)

39 "The story is trash"—Douglas Gilbert, *New York World-Telegram*, date unclear

39 "I could not untangle"—Robert Benchley, *New Yorker*, Oct. 31, 1936, p. 26

39 "ten more than she did"—letter from George S. Kaufman to Mary, Sept. 2, 1955, MWP

39 Gielgud, Evans—"I have never seen an actor who had as good acting equipment," Mary observed about Gielgud to Reed Hynds in the *St. Louis Star*, June 29, 1937

39 "He was heaven"—from Mary's interview with Don Richardson on "Behind the Scenes," KCRW 89.9 FM at Santa Monica (Calif.) College, March 15, 1984

40 He offered her a role—interview with Bill Herz, New York, Feb. 18, 1999

41 "if I had a summer theater"—interview with Bill Herz, New York, Sept. 10, 1999

41 offered to send a car—the account of Welles's efforts to get Mary to rehearsals appears in "Orson Welles Demon of Energy, Says St. Louis Actress," *St. Louis Globe-Democrat*, Nov. 28, 1938

41 "a one-track mind"—interview with Bill Herz, New York, Sept. 10, 1999

42 "an imitation silent comedy"—Orson Welles and Peter Bogdanovich, *This is Orson Welles*, HarperCollins, 1992, p. 40

42 "the police came"—telephone interview with Ruth Ford, Nov. 8, 1999

42 "lots of jumping around"—telephone interview with James O'Rear, May 7, 1999

42 "feats of athleticism"—Charles Higham, *Orson Welles: The Rise and Fall of an American Genius*, St. Martin's Press, 1985, p. 119

42 the few existing still photos—these descriptions are taken from a photo in the Billy Rose Theatre Collection of the New York Public Library (folder: *Too Much Johnson, Cinema, 1938*) and from photos that appear in *Stage*, September 1938, pp. 30–31

42 Some of the actors, like Mary—interview with Bill Herz, New York, Sept. 10, 1999

43 "shoes would be green"—telephone interview with Arthur Anderson, Feb. 18, 1999

43 a film is a performance—Frank Brody, "The Lost Film of Orson Welles," *American Film*, November 1978, p. 68

43 two-week run sold out—interview with Bill Herz, New York, Sept. 10, 1999

43 "the paradox of the Mercury"—Weldon B. Durham, *American Theatre Companies, 1931–1986*, Greenwood Press, 1989, p. 371

44 staccato, vaudeville-like—telephone interview with Arthur Anderson, Feb. 18, 1999

44 fireproof projection booth—Frank Brady, "The Lost Film of Orson Welles," *American Film*, November 1978, p. 68

44 prepared the audience—review of *Too Much Johnson*, *Shoreline Times* (Guilford, Conn.), Sept. 18, 1938

44 "One of the most vivid things"—telephone interview with Ruth Ford, Nov. 8, 1999

44 "didn't know what hit them"—interview with Bill Herz, New York, Feb. 18, 1999

45 forfeit its negative—Bret Wood, *Orson Welles: A Bio-Bibliography*, Greenwood Press, 1990, pp. 152–53

45 fire—Orson Welles and Peter Bogdanovich, *This is Orson Welles*, HarperCollins, 1992, p. 344

45 "surreal"—Frank Brady, "The Lost Film of Orson Welles," *American Film*, November 1978, p. 69

45 "brow-beating mother-in-law"—review of *Too Much Johnson, Shoreline Times* (Guilford, Conn.), Sept. 18, 1938

45 she earned $25—"Orson Welles Demon of Energy, Says St. Louis Actress," *St. Louis Globe-Democrat*, Nov. 28, 1938

45 the headliners—their joint appearance at the Guild Theatre was announced in the *New York Times* that day, Nov. 11, 1938

45 barely an hour and fifteen minutes—John Mason Brown, *New York Post*, Nov. 4, 1938, and (un-bylined) *Women's Wear Daily*, Nov. 3, 1938

45 masks—Peter Noble, *The Fabulous Orson Welles*, Hutchinson & Co., 1956, p. 101

45 replaced the conventional stage—the dramatic, dangerous staging of *Danton's Death* is well documented in film history books, biographies and news articles of the day

46 "rat-ridden basement"—John Houseman quoted by Peter Noble, *The Fabulous Orson Welles*, Hutchinson & Co., 1956, p. 101

46 "death-trap of a set"—interview with Bill Herz, New York, Feb. 18, 1999

46 "underneath the stage"—interview with Betty Garrett, North Hollywood, Calif., Dec. 10, 1998

46 "Mister soldier, handsome soldier"—Betty Garrett and Ron Rapoport, *Betty Garrett and Other Songs: A Life on Stage and Screen*, Madison Books, 1999, p. 43

46 "We were waiting"—"Orson Welles Demon of Energy, Says St. Louis Actress," *St. Louis Globe-Democrat*, Nov. 28, 1938

46 policemen—Peter Noble, *The Fabulous Orson Welles*, Hutchinson & Co., 1956, p. 111

47 "the first place he would go"—interview with Bill Herz, New York, Sept. 10, 1999

47 a party given by Ford—interview with Elliott Reid, Los Angeles, Dec. 9, 1998

47 "Orson adored a Yiddish actor"—interview with Bill Herz, New York, Feb. 18, 1999

47 "more sound than scene"—Brooks Atkinson, "Orson Welles Frightening Little Playgoers in *Danton's Death*," *New York Times*, Nov. 13, 1938

47 "all stunt and no play"—John Mason Brown, *New York Post*, Nov. 4, 1938

47 "as it is indecisive"—"The Theatre: New Plays in Manhattan," *Time*, Nov. 14, 1938

48 "being totally crazy"—Dorothy Brockhoff, "The Mary Wickes Story," *Washington University Magazine*, Summer 1977, p 14–19

48 "Citizen Kane in person"—interview with Bill Givens, Los Angeles, April 9, 1999

CHAPTER THREE: ON STAGE AND ON AIR

49 "Prince Matchabelli's *Stradivari*"—theatre-goers found this notice in the playbill for *Hollywood Pinafore*, Alvin Theatre, the week of June 10, 1945

49 "new asbestos curtain"—When the Berkshire Playhouse re-opened after the war in June 1946, its playbill for opening week proclaimed, "When its new asbestos curtain rises on *The Late George Apley*, the Berkshire Playhouse will again be in operation after

four dark years, during which members of its staff, company and audience were en-gaged elsewhere in a variety of necessary but rather less entertaining activities."

49 "kind of knew each other"—interview with Max Showalter, Chester, Conn., Sept. 1, 1998

49 "very much a community"—interview with Anna Crouse, New York, Nov. 18, 1998

50 "heart sank"—Kaye Ballard, *How I Lost 10 Pounds in 53 Years*, Back Stage Books, 2006, pp. 50–51

50 "breakfast together"—telephone interview with Mary Jane Roach Masters, Feb. 12, 1999

50 $65 per week—from original contract signed Dec. 19, 1938, by Mary and Samuel Haring of Diversified Theatre Corp., MWP

51 "a strict budget"—interview with Anna Crouse, New York, Nov. 18, 1998

51 "I would have to type them"—interview with Anna Crouse, New York, Nov. 18, 1998

51 catered supper—Ralph Blumenthal, *Stork Club: America's Most Famous Nightspot and the Lost World of Café Society*, Little, Brown and Co., 2000, p. 147

51 "I knew that was tacky"—interview with Anna Crouse, New York, Nov. 18, 1998

51 offered Billingsley $500,000—Ralph Blumenthal, *Stork Club: America's Most Famous Nightspot and the Lost World of Café Society*, Little, Brown and Co., 2000, pp. 186–87

51 $2,500 to $5,000—April 26, 1939, letter from business manager John Del Bondio to director Josh Logan, Joshua Logan Papers, LOC. The letter outlines the ticket price reduction strategy.

52 "lackluster"—Geoffrey Mark, *Ethel Merman, the Biggest Star on Broadway*, Barricade Books, 2005, p. 71

52 "Food was very cheap"—interview with Bob Wallsten, New York, Feb. 22, 1999

53 "a homebody"—interview with Dr. Lester Coleman, New York, Nov. 20, 1998

53 the most Freedley coughed up—per a series of letters and telegrams between Mary, Audrey Wood of Liebling-Wood, Edie Van Cleve of MCA, and producer Vinton Freedley, written between Jan. 25 and April 20, 1943. Some are in MWP, and others were made available courtesy of the Ira and Leonore Gershwin Trusts Archives, San Francisco.

54 "a tendency to hang your head"—letter from Robert Edmond Jones, undated, MWP. Mary no doubt trusted his advice. He was not only the leading designer of the day, but was the husband of Margaret Huston, for whom Mary worked briefly in the late 1930s.

54 in Santa Rosa—Isabella wrote Mary at the Hotel Santa Rosa in Santa Rosa, Calif., updating her about life in St. Louis. It was postmarked the evening of June 20, 1943; Frank died the next day.

54 "She was devastated"—interview with Dr. Lester Coleman, New York, Nov. 20, 1998

54 "believe me"—letter from Frank in St. Louis to Mary in Los Angeles, March 11, 1942, MWP

54 "kept your word?"—letter from Mary in Los Angeles to Frank in St. Louis, April 11, 1942, MWP

55 hope chest—in a June 20, 1943, letter, Isabella reports winning a towel and six jars of preserves at a party and putting them in Mary's hope chest. Mary turned 33 the week before.

55 "devote my life to you"—this excerpt combines text from two emotional, rambling letters written a day apart (August 18 and August 19, 1943) and sent to Mary while she was staying with Barry and Marie Sullivan on Belden Drive in Los Angeles

55 $11,500, $9,250—letter from Isabella to Mary in Los Angeles, Sept. 17, 1943

56 the entire top floor—G. D. Seymour, "A New Yorker at Large," *Sarasota (Fla.) Herald-Tribune*, May 15, 1929, p. 4

56 "general maternalization"—interview with Dr. Lester Coleman, New York, Nov. 20, 1998

56 "deep companions"—interview with Louis Westheimer, St. Louis, Nov. 7, 1998

56 "two isolated ladies"—interview with Bob Wallsten, New York, Feb. 22, 1999

56 "sweet, gentle, non-intrusive"—interview with Dr. Lester Coleman, New York, Nov. 20, 1998

57 "didn't have enough liquor"—telephone interview with John Scott, Oct. 1, 1999

57 "always wore hats"—telephone interview with James O'Rear, May 7, 1999

57 most vivid memory—telephone interview with Mary Healy, May 19, 1999

57 some of the sets—Lee Davis, *Bolton and Wodehouse and Kern: The Men Who Made Musical Comedy*, James H. Heinemann, 1993, pp. 369–70

58 to split the difference—per nine pieces of correspondence (between June 16 and Oct. 14, 1943) between Mary, producer Vinton Freedley, and agent Edith Van Cleve, MWP

58 "bug-eyed with excitement"—from an Oct. 18, 1943, letter from Mary in Los Angeles to Vinton Freedley in New York, courtesy of the Ira and Leonore Gershwin Trusts Archives, San Francisco

58 "glamorized"—Oct. 4, 1943, letter from Vinton Freedley to Mary in St. Louis, MWP

58 "was of course wrong"—*New York Post*, Feb. 15, 1944

59 "a complete frost"—Louis Kronenberger, "A Big Musical and a Bad One," *Time*, Jan. 14, 1944

59 "cheap sex gags"—John Champman, "Audiences Now Like Jackpot Bit Better Than First-Nighters," *New York Daily News*, Jan. 22, 1944

59 "vulgar"—Robert Garland, *New York Journal-American*, Jan. 23, 1944

59 "pain in the ass"—interview with Nanette Fabray, Pacific Palisades, Calif., Oct. 25, 1999

59 "you took an elevator"—interview with Betty Garrett, North Hollywood, Calif., Dec. 10, 1998

60 the American Theatre—Louis Westheimer recalls bringing Mary to this show in their youth, interview, St. Louis, Nov. 7, 1998

60 "George S. and Saint mixing things up"—Jeff Warren, living in Melbourne, Australia, shared his recollections of *Hollywood Pinafore* with the author in a series of emails between November 2000 and January 2001, and shared other recollections that he had written to help the American Century Theatre in Arlington, Virginia, with a *Pinafore* revival in August 2000

61 "Don't go back"—letter to Mary, 1945, MWP

61 "hit of the century"—Gibson's recollections come from telephone interview, July 13, 1999

63 $1,000 a week—from the Warner Bros. files on *The Decision of Christopher Blake*, WBA

63 an offer to return—producer Joe Hyman telegrammed Mary in Los Angeles on Dec. 5, 1947, reporting he had found no one else satisfactory and encouraging Mary to join the company. The show was *Make Mine Manhattan*, which opened Jan. 15, 1948, and played for a year.

63 mustard-colored dress—Helen Ormsbee, "Mary Wickes Finds Career in Character Portrayals," *New York Herald Tribune*, Sept. 19, 1948

63 "the upstairs, the downstairs"—Robert Garland, "A Simplex Play in a Duplex Set," *New York Journal-American,* Sept. 24, 1948, p. 22

64 "Nothing happens"—Brooks Atkinson, "Gertrude Tonkonogy's *Town House* is Based on John Cheever's Short Stories in the *New Yorker,*" *New York Times,* Sept. 24, 1948

64 the most she had earned—Mary's original contract, signed by Max Gordon on June 21, 1948, paid her $600 per week, MWP

64 "sharp wisecracking thrusts"—review of *Town House, Boston Post,* Sept. 3, 1948

64 "a great deal with every line"—review of *Town House, New York Sun,* Sept. 24, 1948

64 "a trumpet"—John Cheever, "The Origin of Town House," *Boston Sunday Post,* Dec. 5, 1948

64 "big and bad"—"Tele Review: Ring on Her Finger," un-labeled, undated newspaper review, http://classicshowbiz.blogspot.com/2011/04/television-review-from-1945.html

65 a car's headlights—Cloris Leachman with George Englund, *Cloris: My Autobiography,* Kensington Books, 1999, pp. 89–94

65 "lots of mistakes"—interview with Emily Daniels, Valley Village, Calif., April 20, 1999

65 "I ever saw television"—telephone interview with Martin Manulis, Aug. 18, 1998

65 performed a second time—interview with Elliott Reid, Los Angeles, Oct. 27, 1999

65 "quite a fraternity"—telephone interview with Lamont Johnson, Aug. 27, 1999

66 "nobody was telling us"—telephone interview with Adrienne Luraschi, Aug. 31, 1999

66 "much fiercer now"—interview with Lenka Peterson, Roxbury, Conn., Sept. 8, 1999

66 CBS named its studios—this explanation is provided on various websites (such as Askville: http://askville.amazon.com/long-Captain-Kangaroo-tape-show-Studio-54/AnswerViewer.do?requestId=41226014), which generally cite Wikipedia's entry for Studio 54 as the source. http://en.wikipedia.org/wiki/Studio_54

66 "much of a line"—telephone interview with Mary Healy, May 19, 1999

66 blurt out her line—this segment appears in an undated episode preserved at the Paley Center for Media in New York. Neither the segment nor the episode is catalogued by name, but a script in MWP confirms the skit is called "Nostalgia Revisited."

67 "very snobby"—interview with Sheila Bond, New York, Sept. 17, 1999

67 its $26,000 budget—Peter Lind Hayes and Mary Healy, *Moments to Remember with Peter and Mary: Our Life in Show Business from Vaudeville to Video,* Vantage Books, 2004, p. 225

67 furniture and décor—from a script and outline of the episode in the Gloria Swanson Papers at the Harry Ransom Center at the University of Texas at Austin, the segment was called "Design for Living." It took place on a set intended to suggest Swanson's home, where the guests chatted over tea. It opened with Mary on the set with a butler, Pembroke. They are joined by Swanson for a discussion of Duncan Fyfe and English Adams chairs, a French tea table, and decorative items.

68 "and re-direct it"—telephone interview with Iris Mann, July 3, 2000

68 "it must be hoped"—Jack Gould, *New York Times,* Sept. 16, 1953

68 "I'm pregnant"—interview with Lenka Peterson, Roxbury, Conn., Sept. 8, 1999

69 "the damnedest collection"—interview with Anna Crouse, New York, Nov. 18, 1998

69 Americano—Robert Wahls, "Broadway's Favorite Aunt," *New York Daily News,* July 13, 1980

69 "a touch of dessert"—telephone interview with Joe Ross, July 15, 1999

70 "people standing in front"—interview with Elliott Reid, Los Angeles, Oct. 27, 1999

CHAPTER FOUR: ANATOMY IS DESTINY

71 "watch that height!"—telephone interview with Terry Fay, Nov. 24, 1998; the anecdote was told to Fay by Sarah Enright

71 disappointing show—Gottfried's *Women's Wear Daily* review, Jan. 5, 1966, panned the play: "even this extravagantly dull comedy deserved more than the botching it received last night."

72 costume fitting document—this refers to a one-page typed list of Mary's various measurements, used to prepare her costumes for the *Wizard of Oz* in St. Louis in 1987, MWP

72 "the wrinkle with lips"—from the pilot episode of *Weldon Pond,* a CBS sitcom taped in spring 1994 but rejected before it aired

72 "laughing out loud"—telegram from unidentified "Pat" to Mary at the AWA Clubhouse in Manhattan on Dec. 28, 1934, MWP

73 "I'll just go out"—Mari Cartel, "Talking with *Sister Act's* Veteran Character Actress," *Valley Vantage,* May 28, 1992

73 "used her suggestions"—Marc Davis quoted by John Province in *Hogan's Alley: The Online Magazine of the Cartoon Arts,* issues 1 and 2

73 One 1957 news article—from short promotional piece in *The Mirror* (unidentified newspaper supplement), June 16, 1957

74 "on the back of her neck"—from a Feb. 13, 1952, Warner Bros. press release, Warner Bros. Archives, School of Cinematic Arts, University of Southern California

75 "up and down and in and out"—letter to Mary from John van Druten, June 14, 1950, MWP

75 turned down for Gran—letter from supervising producer Christopher J. Brough to Mary, July 1, 1983, informing her that programming executives in Burbank had concluded a smaller actress was best for the character, MWP

75 "How else could she?"—telephone interview with Ethel Winant, May 18, 1999

76 "adjustment to her own personality"—interview with Betty Garrett, North Hollywood, Calif., Dec. 10, 1998

76 "a nose job!"—telephone interview with Joe Ross, July 15, 1999

76 "that chin of mine?"—these notations in Mary's hand appear on the back of two different publicity stills, one for *Here's Lucy* and one for *The Don Rickles Show,* MWP

76 "so isolated"—telephone interview with Jack O'Brien, July 14, 1999

76 "Homely Girls Doing Fine"—the article appeared first in the *Detroit News* in September 1941 (exact date unclear). Slightly different versions then appeared Oct. 5, 1941, in the *St. Louis Post-Dispatch,* and Nov. 9, 1941, in the *Milwaukee Journal*

77 unusual-looking performers—Mary is inaccurately placed in *Andy Hardy's Private Secretary* by *Quinlan's Illustrated Directory of Film Comedy Actors* by David Quinlan, Henry Holt, 1992, p. 290 (among others)

77 had seen her in *Bewitched*—Tony Perry, review of *You Can't Take It With You, Davis (Calif.) Enterprise,* Feb. 6, 1973

78 "stood up straight"—interview with Hal Kanter, Encino, Calif., Dec. 8, 1998

80 "with a torn pocket"—interview with Jerry Berger, St. Louis, June 23, 2000

80 a joke that surfaced—in interview with Bill Swan, New York, Nov. 17, 1998, Swan said he dined out on this story for years

80 "our eyes were very similar"—interview with Bob Wallsten, New York, Feb. 22, 1999

80 "the most wonderful eyes"—telephone interview with Alfred Gellhorn, June 21, 1999

81 "like lamps"—telephone interview with Janet Fox Goldsmith, April 1, 1999

81 to make a point—interview with Madelyn Pugh Davis, Bel Air, Calif., Dec. 4, 1998

81 "the older I get"—*Dallas Morning News*, July 29, 1979, p. 8-C

81 "insignificant little field mouse"—Marjory Adams, *Boston Globe*, Sept. 5, 1948

81 "never manage to forget"—Virginia MacPherson, "She Says Men Find Glamour Gals Tiresome," *Los Angeles Daily News*, Oct. 1, 1951

82 pomades, creams, and masks—Mary's six-page parody is in MWP

82 "thing she was stuck in"—telephone interview with Barbara Sharma, June 26, 1998

82 "only half-way up there"—interview with Anne Kaufman Schneider, New York, Nov. 21, 1998

82 "this tall, gangly person"—interview with Harriet Switzer, St. Louis, Nov. 7, 1998

82 "never pushed a button"—telephone interview with Jack O'Brien, July 14, 1999

CHAPTER FIVE: MISS BEDPAN

83 "ideal for you"—letter from Irving Schneider of the Sam Harris organization to Mary in Dennis, Mass., Aug. 9, 1939, MWP

84 paying her $75—original standard minimum contract signed between Mary and Sam Harris, Aug. 25, 1939, MWP

84 "extravagantly, terrifically funny"—Peggy Doyle, reviewing Boston tryout of *The Man Who Came to Dinner*, *Boston Evening American*, Sept. 26, 1939, p. 15

84 "first-night howls"—Ward Morehouse, "Broadway After Dark," *New York Sun*, Oct. 21, 1939

84 "theatrical royalty"—the names of opening night theatergoers are in an unlabeled news clip in Mary's scrapbook, MWP

84 opening night telegrams—these telegrams and many others are in MWP

84 his favorite comedienne—undated letter from George S. Kaufman in MWP: "You are my favorite comedienne. Those are not just polite words, by the way."

84 "never did that"—interview with Anne Kaufman Schneider, New York, Nov. 21, 1998

85 if Florence Nightingale—Kaufman and Hart knew, of course, that it was Clara Barton and not the British Florence Nightingale who founded the American Red Cross, but they also knew that Barton's name was unlikely to resonate with audiences—and simply did not sound funny, interview with Anne Kaufman Schneider, New York, Nov. 21, 1998

85 pausing twice—interview with Anne Kaufman Schneider, New York, Nov. 21, 1998

85 A petition—a copy of the letter exists in MWP

86 "two thousand five hundred"—the telegram was sent to Mary at the American Theatre on Nov. 6, 1940, MWP

86 "a swell arrangement"—*St. Louis Star-Times*, July 10, 1944

86 $50 was stolen—revealed in correspondence from managers of the touring company (Nov. 23, 1940) and from Morris Jacobs of the Sam Harris organization in New York (Nov. 28, 1940), MWP

86 increase in pay—original contract between Mary and Sam Harris, signed Aug. 19, 1940, MWP

86 Linda and Cole Porter—the Porters telegrammed Mary in Boston on Oct. 12, 1939, inviting her to a supper party in the Waldorf's Perroquet Suite on Oct. 16, MWP

86 cocktail party—Monty Woolley telegrammed Mary at 1 Christopher St. in late 1939, inviting her to a Jan. 14, 1940, party at the Ritz Carlton, MWP

86 surprise party—telegram in MWP

86 late-night party at the Kaufmans—telegram on Dec. 29, 1939, for a Jan. 6, 1940, party at the Kaufman's home at 14 E. 96th St., MWP

86 "Bernie would get the car"—Mary's recollections of weekends at New Hope were recorded on audiocassette in 1990 for a possible autobiography, MWP

86 "the Commodore"—from anecdotes Mary recorded on an audiocassette in 1990 for a possible autobiography, MWP

87 "The town is buzzing"—letter from Moss Hart, June 11, 1941, MWP

87 "telephoned you every day"—letter typed on White House stationery from Bill Chase but signed "Eleanor," date unknown, MWP

87 "the female operator"—letter from Bill Chase but signed "Igor," date unknown

87 Social Security card—The card remains in MWP. Mary's account of receiving it is recorded on an audiocassette she made in 1990 for a possible autobiography. MWP

87 American Red Cross—translated from this Spanish-language website devoted to Tangier's history: "Bares y Cafes de Tanger:" *Tanger y otras utopias, Diseno, textos y imnagenes por Domingo Pino*, http://www.tangeryotrasutopias.com/2009/08/bares-y-cafes -de-tanger.html

87 Parade Bar—Michael K. Walonen, *Writing Tangier in the Post-Colonial Transition: Space and Power in Expatriate and North African Literature*, Ashgate Publishing, 2011, p. 16. The Parade was even caught up in a bit of political intrigue when, in 1952, Chase was found to have some ink sketches of Lenin and Stalin that had been drawn in the bar by Guy Burgess, the British diplomat who had defected to Russia the year before, according to "The Police of Fourteen Countries Seek the Man Who Drew These Pictures—and His Name is Guy Burgess," *Sunday Express* (London), Jan. 6, 1952

88 "perfectly revolting"—interview with Anne Kaufman Schneider, New York, Nov. 21, 1998

89 "got very forthright"—telephone interview with Don Knotts, Aug. 7, 1998

89 "His Highness"—Collins's account of the *Hallmark Hall of Fame* production appears in her memoir, *Past Imperfect*, Berkley, 1985, pp. 243–46

89 "pathetic to see Welles"—interview with Iggie Wolfington, New York, Oct. 12, 1998

89 one of the five worst—John J. O'Connor, "The Best of 1972 . . . and the Worst," *New York Times*, Dec. 31, 1972

90 "biggest star I could get"—telephone interview with Martin Manulis, Aug. 18, 1998

90 mousey-looking—interview with Canon Greg Richards, North Hollywood, Calif., Dec. 11, 1998

90 to play Preen—D. J. Hobdy, "'Miss Bedpan' Stays Cheerful," *Houston Chronicle*, Sept. 12, 1966

90 called *Sherry!*— A studio album of *Sherry!* was recorded in 2004 with Nathan Lane, Bernadette Peters, and Carol Burnett. Siobhan Fallon was Miss Preen.

90 did not make it to the screen easily—the description of *The Man Who Came to Dinner's* path to the screen—costs, salaries, delays, legal action, casting decisions—is drawn from dozens of letters and inter-office memos in the official Warner Bros. records of the production, WBA

91 "mad about her"—telephone interview with Max Wilk, Aug. 8, 1999

92 "most impressive performance"—"Bucks County Comedy Funnier at New Hope," *New York Post*, June 9, 1941

93 "gee, this is living"—Mari Cartel, "Talking with Sister Act's Veteran Character Actress Mary Wickes," *Valley Vantage*, May 28, 1992

93 "I just saw the rushes"—letter from Jerry Wald to Mary, Aug. 27, 1941, MWP

93 "took me under her wing"—Michael Welsh, "Mary, Mary, Quite Extraordinary," *Faces*, Fall 1991, p. 305

94 work from Russel Crouse—Mary wrote Crouse asking if Lindsay and Crouse might have a role for her. Crouse had nothing to offer, but replied with good humor, "the casting couch doesn't look the same without you," Nov. 17, 1941. MWP

94 offer from Max Gordon—the offer is detailed in separate telegrams to Mary from producer Max Gordon and from agent Edith Van Cleve on Sept. 6, 1941, MWP

94 "Don't you think"—from a Sept. 8, 1941, telegram from Edith Van Cleve at MCA in New York to Mary at Chateau Elysee in Los Angeles, MWP

94 Olive Higgins Prouty—from a Sept. 23, 1942, telegram from Prouty in Brookline, Mass., to Mary at the Villa Carlotta in Hollywood, MWP

94 "put up a booth"—from stories Mary told on the *Wil Shriner Show*, 1988 (exact date unknown)

95 "three very strange scripts"—an addendum to one of many typed, undated summaries of her credits that Mary prepared over her career, MWP

96 *Born Yesterday*—the job offer came in a July 4, 1950, telegram to Mary in New York from Al Melnick, her agent at the Louis Shurr Agency in Beverly Hills, WFP

96 only $250 per week—on May 8, 1950, Mary signed contracts with Edward Choate of the Woodstock (N.Y.) Playhouse for *On Approval* and *The Late Christopher Bean*, MWP

CHAPTER SIX: LOS ANGELES, MOTHER IN TOW

97 "out of Edward Gorey"—interview with Betty Garrett, North Hollywood, Calif., Dec. 10, 1998

97 "far more satisfactory"—Walter Ames, "Comedienne Says Live Video Tops Film; Rosalind Russell in Suspense Thriller Today," *Los Angeles Times*, May 3, 1951, p. 26

98 *One Touch of Venus*—letter from Mary Martin, Feb. 14, 1945, telling Mary why she was not chosen: "I don't really think there was any misunderstanding. From what I was told, it had something to do with that old stuff—money. And I do keep out of that. I was told the show just couldn't go on tour with *all* the salaries asked unless some compromises were made. I am really sorry. Both Richard [Halliday, her husband] and I would so love to have had you." MWP

98 producers refused to offer—this fact is referenced in a Jan. 12, 1954, letter from actor Charlie Ruggles to Mary, MWP

98 "They were a duet"—telephone interview with Mary Grant Price, Feb. 24, 2001

98 sold her fur coat and hat—Mary's copious notes about the move are saved in MWP

99 disagreements with doctors—a series of letters in March and April 1951 between Mary (closing out the apartment in New York) and Isabella (hunting for a new apartment in Los Angeles) chronicles Isabella's health problems and surgery at Hollywood Presbyterian Hospital

99 "so sorry I am not with you"—special delivery letter from Mary in New York to Isabella at Hollywood Presbyterian Hospital, March 1951, MWP

99 having undergone surgery—Isabella's surgery is referenced in letter to Mary from Rector Grieg Taber of the Church of Saint Mary the Virgin, New York, March 31, 1948, MWP

99 "makes me so sick"—letter from Barbara Wolferman at the office of Oscar Hammerstein II in New York to Mary at Villa Carlotta in Los Angeles, April 6, 1951, MWP

100 a new black Pontiac—Mary mentions this in a letter to George S. Kaufman, April 4, 1955, MWP

100 lived frugally—per careful notes that Mary kept in a black binder (now in MWP), she moved into the Voltaire in April 1952, got new carpeting in 1954, had the carpet cleaned in 1958, and had the apartment painted and re-carpeted in 1962

100 Marilyn Monroe would move in—"Places Where Marilyn Lived," http://marilyn monroepages.com/facts.html#residences

100 wrote her into every play—letter to Mary from George S. Kaufman, July 22, 1959, MWP

100 "get you back here"—undated letter (post-1951) to Mary from George S. Kaufman, MWP

100 delays in shooting *On Moonlight Bay*—a Jan. 24, 1951, Warner Bros. press release announced that Mary was forced to withdraw from *Small Dark Hours* because filming was taking longer than expected. The play's name was later changed to *Small Hours*.

100 a repressed gay man—Nicholas de Jongh, *Not in Front of the Audience: Homosexuality on Stage*, Routledge, 1992, pp. 82–83

100 tempted by this—Sam Zolotow, "Eva Le Gallienne to Star in Play," *New York Times*, Aug. 27, 1957

101 "a law against"—letter from George S. Kaufman, 1951 (undated), MWP

101 twenty-seven round trips—Edward A. Harris, "Back to Campus for Mary Wickes," *St. Louis Post-Dispatch*, Aug. 1, 1954

101 inserted the resulting footage—the account of Mary's work on *I, Bonino* is culled from various sources: Sheila Graham, *Los Angeles Citizen News*, Sept. 7, 1953 (about the sponsors wanting Mary so badly that they altered the shooting schedule); *Los Angeles Times*, Oct. 31, 1955 (the long-distance telephone call); *Variety*, Oct. 5, 1953 (that she is away with her sister); *Hollywood Reporter*, Aug. 27, 1953 (number of episodes filmed before shooting *White Christmas*); and Tom E. Danson, unidentified TV column, Nov. 23, 1953 (Mary's feelings about returning to the cast)

102 "breadwinner"—interview with Iggie Wolfington, New York, Oct. 12, 1998

102 remember Mary Wickes's mother—telephone interview with Gene Reynolds, Jan. 19, 2000

102 "hard to forget"—telephone interview with Martin Manulis, Aug. 18, 1998

102 "dominated rooms"—interview with Mary Jackson, Hollywood, Calif., April 4, 1999

102 teas in her mother's honor—telephone interview with Ethel Winant, May 18, 1999

102 "looked alike, acted alike"—written statement from Doris Day to author, Feb. 22, 2000

102 "tables for twelve"—interview with Peter Walker, Chester, Conn., Sept. 1, 1998

103 "from the church"—interview with Max Showalter, Chester, Conn., Sept. 1, 1998

103 "like a Hollywood family"—interview with Peter Walker, Chester, Conn., Sept. 1, 1998

103 "gracious, uncomplicated"—interview with Iggie Wolfington, New York, Oct. 12, 1998

103 "power behind the throne"—interview with Louis Westheimer, St. Louis, Nov. 7, 1998

104 "did lots of things"—letter from Mary to Vincent Price, Feb. 22, 1965, Vince Price Papers, LOC

104 death certificate has been altered—Isabella's death certificate from the Los Angeles County Clerk's Office shows a year of birth that has been manually altered to read 1895; Isabella's record of birth, obtained from the St. Clair County (Ill.) Clerk's Office, properly reads 1885.

104 "source of strength"—letter from Mary to Vincent Price, Feb. 22, 1965, Vincent Price Papers, LOC

104 driving to the burial site—interview with Bill Dorsam, St. Louis, Sept. 16, 1998

104 "lived for that woman"—interview with Peter Walker, Chester, Conn., Sept. 1, 1998

105 never even shared a meal—interview with Herb Metz, St. Louis, June 6, 1998

105 "confront her"—interview with Canon Greg Richards, North Hollywood, Calif., Dec. 11, 1998

105 "an integral part of that"—telephone interview with Mary Grant Price, Feb. 24, 2001

106 "could have worked every day"—telephone interview with Ethel Winant, May 18, 1999

106 "That's what I did"—interview with Stella Koetter Darrow, Clayton, Mo., Sept. 22, 1998

106 "tiny little Victorian box"—telephone interview with Mary Grant Price, Feb. 24, 2001

107 some real estate expertise—in an interview with Nanette Fabray, Pacific Palisades, Calif., Oct. 25, 1999, Fabray recalls that Mary later phoned her several times, so "frantic" and "upset" about some "very traumatic" change at Century Towers that Fabray invited her to stay at her home and store her belongings in Fabray's garage until matters were sorted out. Mary declined.

107 "Lucy convinced her"—interview with Wanda Clark, Los Angeles, Oct. 31, 1999

CHAPTER SEVEN: LUCILLE BALL'S BEST FRIEND

108 had never met Lucy—Michael Welsh, "Mary, Mary, Quite Extraordinary," *Faces International Magazine*, Fall 1991, p. 307, and a longer, pre-publication version of that story that is saved in MWP. Mary relayed a similar account to journalist David Cuthbert in "Mary Wickes: From Barrymore to Bosley," (paper unknown), May 27–June 2, 1990

108 "lots of people around her"—Michael Welsh, "Mary, Mary, Quite Extraordinary," *Faces International Magazine*, Fall 1991, p. 307

108 "my mom's best friend"—interview with Lucie Arnaz, Katonah, N.Y., Feb. 17, 1999. All observations from Arnaz in this chapter come from this interview unless otherwise indicated.

110 "before she was famous"—telephone interview with Laurence Guittard, Sept. 30, 1999

110 "try to get something"—telephone interview with Mary Grant Price, Feb. 24, 2001

110 "both adored our mothers"—Geoffrey Mark Fidelman, *The Lucy Book: A Complete Guide to Her Five Decades on Television*, Renaissance Books, 1999, pp. 26–27

111 Rotary dial telephones—Lee Tannen, *I Loved Lucy: My Friendship with Lucille Ball*, St. Martin's Press, 2001, p. 45

111 "been through it"—telephone interview with Laurence Guittard, Sept. 30, 1999

111 "treated most people"—interview with Wanda Clark, Los Angeles, Oct. 31, 1999

112 "would hit it off"—interview with Iggie Wolfington, New York, Oct. 12, 1998

113 "I'd love to do with Desi"—interview with Sheila Bond, New York, Sept. 17, 1999

113 "Lucy's perfectionism"—Geoffrey Mark Fidelman, *The Lucy Book: A Complete Guide to Her Five Decades on Television*, Renaissance Books, 1999, p. 23

113 "never quite understood"—interview with Emily Daniels, Valley Village, Calif., April 20, 1999

114 Albertina Rasch—Mary's recollections of rehearsing "The Ballet" are on an audiocassette of anecdotes she recorded in 1990 for a possible autobiography, MWP

114 "absolutely everything"—interview with Emily Daniels, Valley Village, Calif., April 20, 1999

114 tongue-in-cheek—this was the "Lucy and the Runaway Butterfly" episode of *The Lucy Show*, April 22, 1963

114 "What are you doing this afternoon?"—Mary's account of shopping with the chimpanzee is on an audiocassette of anecdotes she recorded in 1990 for a possible autobiography, MWP

115 managed to spend $600—Patricia Ward Biederman, "Lucy—the Museum: If You Loved Lucy, Now There's 2,200 Square Feet of Enough Lucille Ball Memories to Keep You Happy Between Reruns," *Los Angeles Times*, March 10, 1991, p. 46

115 "it was dusk"—from anecdotes Mary recorded in 1990 for a possible autobiography, MWP

116 "cleaning out my closet"—from an audiocassette of anecdotes Mary recorded in 1990 for a possible autobiography, MWP

116 "and play cards"—telephone interview with Elizabeth Wilson, Sept. 24, 1999

116 "You know Dictionary?"—interview with Peter Walker, Chester, Conn., Sept. 1, 1998

117 "always wondered"—telephone interview with Richard Palmer, Aug. 4, 1999

117 "give us the high sign"—Coyne Steven Sanders and Tom Gilbert, *Desilu: The Story of Lucille Ball and Desi Arnaz*, William Morrow & Co., 1993, p. 344

117 "sort of 'guard' Lucy"—interview with Emily Daniels, Valley Village, Calif., April 20, 1999

117 wall against strangers—Kathleen Brady, *Lucille: The Life of Lucille Ball*, Hyperion, 1994, p. 324

118 going poorly—telephone interview with Sheila MacRae, Oct. 7, 1998

118 "screwed up the bookkeeping"—interview with Wanda Clark, Los Angeles, Oct. 31, 1999

118 ice bucket, a traveling jewelry case—from Mary's notes to herself, MWP

118 "only did it once"—interview with Wanda Clark, Los Angeles, Oct. 31, 1999

119 "distressing" to learn—interview with Bill Swan, New York, Nov. 17, 1998

119 "a mistake here?"—Coyne Steven Sanders and Tom Gilbert, *Desilu: The Story of Lucille Ball and Desi Arnaz*, William Morrow & Co., 1993, p. 327

119 Mary's phone rang—Mary's account of the flight and of her time in Hawaii are extracted from an audiocassette of anecdotes she recorded in 1990 for a possible autobiography, MWP

122 "usually because of time"—Coyne Steven Sanders and Tom Gilbert, *Desilu: The Story of Lucille Ball and Desi Arnaz*, William Morrow & Co., 1993, pp. 257–58

122 "guilty of dropping names"—interview with Bill Swan, New York, Nov. 17, 1998

122 "She's my pal"—interview with Jack Pirozzi, St. Louis, June 11, 1999

122 "dreary Tom Brokaw"—letter from Mary to Lucie Arnaz, Oct. 20, 1992, courtesy of Arnaz

123 "all *kinds* of presents"—interview with Iggie Wolfington, New York, Oct. 12, 1998

123 "hiring and firing"—telephone interview with Jerry Berger, June 15, 2000

124 "Everything going remarkably"—letter from Lucy to Mary at the El Cortez Hotel in San Francisco, Jan. 11, 1973, while Mary was working with the American Conservatory Theater, MWP

125 "feel quite at peace"—letter from Lucy at New York's Savoy Hilton, Aug. 22, 1960, MWP

125 "toughest work"—letter from Lucy at 150 E. 69th St., Dec. 23, 1960, MWP

125 "up to our neck"—letter from Lucy at Caesar's Palace, Las Vegas, to Mary in St. Louis, March 7, 1968, while Mary was performing in *Glass Menagerie*, MWP

126 "a real doll"—Letter from Lucy, March 14, 1962, MWP

126 "The weather so far"—letter from Lucy from aboard ship, May 16, 1959, MWP

126 "getting tired of traveling"—postcard from Lucy in Capri, Italy, June, 1959, MWP

126 "the mad, mad, mod group"—letter from Lucy at the London Hilton, Feb. 25, 1968, MWP

126 "gossip-hungry"—letter from Lucy at Hotel de Paris, Monte Carlo, Feb. 8, 1968, MWP

126 "a bored doll"—letter from Lucy at Hotel de Paris, Monte Carlo, Feb. 18, 1968, MWP

126 "let her get drunk"—letter from Lucy, Dec. 5, 1957, MWP

127 "they ask for you"—letter from Lucy, Jan. 11, 1973, MWP

127 "Holy Cow"—letter from Lucy, May 16, 1959, MWP

127 "an unmade bed"—letter from Lucy at Ilikai Hotel in Waikiki, Honolulu, Hawaii, May 1970, MWP

127 "Your Obedient Servant"—letter from Lucy, Dec. 24, 1971, MWP

127 "My future in pictures"—letter from Lucy, Jan. 11, 1973, MWP

127 "our little stockings"—letter from Lucy, Dec. 30, 1958, MWP

127 "Desiree's Daughter"—telegram from Lucy to Mary at Muny in St. Louis, Aug. 5, 1968, MWP

128 "readin', writin' and arithmetic"—letter from Lucy, Feb. 25, 1968, MWP

128 "playing house"—letter from Lucy, Jan. 11, 1973, MWP

128 "made me very happy"—letter from Lucy at Snowmass, Feb. 21, 1970, MWP

128 "hippy madhouse"—letter from Lucy at Ilikai Hotel in Waikiki, Honolulu, Hawaii, May 1970, MWP

128 "Think of you"—postcard from Lucy in Monte Carlo, Feb. 7, 1968, MWP

128 "wake-up pills"—letter from Lucy, Hotel de Paris, Monte Carlo, Feb. 8, 1968, MWP

129 "haven't forgiven you"—telegram from Lucy to Mary at Muny in St. Louis, Aug. 5, 1968, MWP

129 "find time to come down"—letter from Lucy, Jan. 11, 1973, MWP

129 "hate to think"—letter from Lucy, Feb. 18, 1968, MWP

129 "the hell you're doing"—letter from Lucy in London to Mary in St. Louis, Feb. 25, 1968, MWP

129 "Mary Isabella, hear this!"—letter from Lucy, March 7, 1968, MWP

129 "Just talked to you"—letter from Lucy, Feb. 4, 1971, MWP

130 laughed out loud—telephone interview with Lucie Arnaz, Feb. 19, 1999. Gary Morton died on March 30, 1999, less than six weeks after that conversation with Lucie, and was not interviewed for this book.

130 might refer to a problem—telephone interview with Lucie Arnaz, Feb. 19, 1999

130 "Lucy talked that way"—interview with Wanda Clark, Los Angeles, Oct. 31, 1999

130 "you'd never know it"—interview with Dolly Reed Wageman, Studio City, Calif., Dec. 3, 1998

131 "somebody at the door"—interview with Wanda Clark, Los Angeles, Oct. 31, 1999

131 "been turned away"—interview with Wanda Clark, Los Angeles, Oct. 31, 1999

132 "rather quiet"—interview with Emily Daniels, Valley Village, Calif., April 20, 1999

132 "a lot about Lucille Ball"—telephone interview with Michael Germain, Jan. 11, 2011

132 "the only one"—telephone interview with Lucie Arnaz, Feb. 19, 1999

133 "the empty house"—letter from Mary to Lucie Arnaz, Nov. 13, 1992, courtesy of Arnaz

CHAPTER EIGHT: COOKIES AND MILK WITH MOTHER

134 "cookies and milk"—interview with Bill Swan, New York, Nov. 17, 1998

134 "didn't even adjust"—interview with Dolly Reed Wageman, Studio City, Calif., Dec. 3, 1998

134 "her own standards"—telephone interview with Mary Grant Price, Feb. 24, 2001

134 as character—interview with Lucie Arnaz, Katonah, New York, Feb. 17, 1999

135 never "Ms."—one example: filling out a Marriott honored guest award enrollment form in 1984, she circled "Miss" instead of "Ms.," MWP

135 Talbot's—interview with Rita Pico, Los Angeles, April 19, 1999

135 "except the buttons"—the expressions in this section come from numerous friends of Mary interviewed for this book and from print interviews over the years

135 "Doctor"—interview with Anne Kaufman Schneider, New York, Nov. 21, 1998

135 "prim and proper"—interview with Jerry Berger, St. Louis, June 23, 2000

135 "a wider 'moral path'"—telephone interview with Janet Fox Goldsmith, April 1, 1999

136 "almost a little old-fashioned"—interview with Anna Crouse, New York, Nov. 18, 1998

136 "like Joan Crawford"—telephone interview with Warner Shook, Aug. 16, 2010

136 "a lot of principles"—telephone interview with Ethel Winant, May 18, 1999

137 "it was awful"—interview with Anne Kaufman Schneider, New York, Sept. 14, 1999

137 "acceptable today"—telephone interview with Jane Sutter, Oct. 17, 1998

137 "holier than thou"—telephone interview with Max Showalter, Aug. 19, 1998

137 "even slightly distasteful"—interview with Emily Daniels, Valley Village, Calif., April 20, 1999

137 "almost everything offensive"—telephone interview with Ethel Winant, May 18, 1999

137 "the dirtiest script"—telephone interview with Max Showalter, Aug. 19, 1998

137 "all the curse words"—interview with Bill Givens, Los Angeles, April 9, 1999

138 "wouldn't want my friends"—interview with Madelyn Pugh Davis, Bel Air, Calif., Dec. 4, 1998

138 "a ten-foot pole"—Jim McPherson, "Humor as Dry as Summer Sand," *Toronto Telegram*, June 14, 1969

138 "whole trend of comedy"—*St. Louisan*, April 1974, p. 12

138 "Mother warned me"—a three-stanza poem Mary sent George Seaton on Jan. 13, 1975, MWP

138 "parts that were mean"—telephone interview with Helen Margaret Aff-Drum, Nov. 4, 1998

139 "wildly innocent"—telephone interview with Elizabeth Wilson, Sept. 24, 1999

139 "she went as far as she did"—telephone interview with Barnard Hughes, Nov. 14, 1998

139 "harder comedy"—Pete Rahn, "TV-Radio Column," *St. Louis Globe-Democrat*, Aug. 31, 1976

139 two demands—Mary's demand and the producers' reaction are documented in correspondence between agent Don Wolff (Jan. 31, 1974) and Warner Bros. Vice President for Business Affairs Barry Meyer (March 22, 1974), MWP

140 "Campfire Girl rules"—interview with Mary Jackson, Hollywood, Calif., April 4, 1999

140 Snoopy items—interview with Canon Greg Richards, St. Louis, April 17, 1998

140 considered collaborating—interview with Canon Greg Richards, St. Louis, April 17, 1998

140 "you made it home"—telephone interview with Johnny Stearns, Aug. 6, 1999

140 "two ladies alone"—interview with Rita Pico, Los Angeles, April 19, 1999

140 "communal experience"—telephone interview with Jack O'Brien, July 14, 1999

141 "Now I Lay Me"—interview with Anna Crouse, New York, Nov. 18, 1998

141 in Jenny's bedroom—telephone interview with Jenny Sullivan, Feb. 9, 2000

141 "to pass off as new"—interview with Bill Dorsam, St. Louis, Sept. 16, 1998

142 she was cheap—interview with Rita Pico, Los Angeles, April 19, 1999

142 certificates—interview with Canon Greg Richards, North Hollywood, Calif., Dec. 11, 1998

142 "near with the buck"—interview with Bill Herz, New York, Feb. 18, 1999

143 "safety pins"—interview with Debbie Richards, North Hollywood, Calif., Dec. 11, 1998

143 never chatted long—interview with Rita Pico, Los Angeles, April 19, 1999

143 "reduced-rate clothes"—interview with Emily Daniels, Valley Village, Calif., April 20, 1999

143 "getting their own"—telephone interview with Harve Presnell, Oct. 10, 1999

145 chicken salad or chili—numerous of Mary's friends describe both her generosity as a host and her simple taste in foods served. Emily Daniels provided the ingredients for Mary's actor's pâté.

145 "a shock"—interview with Bill Herz, New York, Feb. 18, 1999

145 "my favorite songs"—telephone interview with Lee Roy Reams, July 13, 1999

145 The $2,900 passage—the receipts and journal for her cruise are in MWP

CHAPTER NINE: SHE KEPT IT TO HERSELF

146 "cantankerous"—interview with Iggie Wolfington, New York, Oct. 12, 1998

147 "an emotional outside"—interview with Nanette Fabray, Pacific Palisades, Calif., Oct. 25, 1999

147 "solace in secrecy"—interview with Lester Colman, New York, Nov. 20, 1998

147 "never really got that close"—telephone interview with Elizabeth Wilson, Sept. 24, 1999

148 "never allow herself"—interview with Peter Walker, Chester, Conn., Sept. 1, 1998

148 "pretend he hasn't died"—interview with Bob Wallsten, New York, Feb. 22, 1999

148 "never got to the point"—interview with Bob Wallsten, New York, Sept. 11, 1999

148 "all the secrets"—interview with Max Showalter, Chester, Conn., Sept. 1, 1998

149 "Part of the reason"—interview with Lucie Arnaz, Katonah, New York, Feb. 17, 1999

149 "questions like that"—telephone interview with Joe Ross, July 15, 1999

149 "never have broached it"—interview with Iggie Wolfington, New York, Oct. 12, 1998

149 "conclude certain things"—interview with Elliott Reid, Los Angeles, Dec. 10, 1998

149 "totally in awe"—telephone interview with Bonnie Happy, Sept. 10, 2001

149 "everybody's grandmother"—telephone interview with Richard Baratz, April 2, 1999

150 "wasn't really *giving*"—interview with Max Showalter, Chester, Conn., Sept. 1, 1998

150 "sort of ignored them"—interview with Amy Jane Ax, St. Louis, Sept. 25, 1998

150 "*Eeeeek!*"—interview with Jerry Berger, St. Louis, June 23, 2000

150 "damaged goods"—telephone interview with Wendy Borcherdt LeRoy, May 24, 1999

151 "a day's work"—interview with Richard Davis, Bel Air, Calif., Dec. 4, 1998

152 "I had breast cancer"—interview with Dolly Reed Wageman, Studio City, Calif., Dec. 3, 1998

152 "a pioneer lady"—telephone interview with Lee Roy Reams, July 13, 1999

152 "never mentioned it"—telephone interview with Larry Guittard, Sept. 30, 1999

152 "wasn't being paranoid"—telephone interview with Elizabeth Wilson, Sept. 24, 1999

153 "her only condition"—telephone interview with Jack O'Brien, July 14, 1999

153 "for sympathy"—telephone interview with Clinton Atkinson, Feb. 7, 1999

153 "tub of lard"—interview with Anne Kaufman Schneider, New York, Nov. 21, 1998

153 "look at your chest"—telephone interview with Janie Miller, Jan. 15, 2000

154 "the false bosom"—interview with Haase's daughter, Lois Haase Mares, Washington, Nov. 10, 1998. Mares says Mary "was really reassuring" to her mother.

154 "we have survived"—from a speech on volunteerism that Mary delivered at St. Vincent's Hospital, Los Angeles, Celebration of Life Day, June 5, 1988, MWP

154 "die-hard Republican"—interview with Peter Walker, Chester, Conn., Sept. 1, 1998

154 "your darned mouth shut"—telephone interview with Marjorie Lord, July 21, 1999

155 "in agreement"—telephone interview with Wendy Borcherdt LeRoy, May 24, 1999

155 "that old rule"—interview with Iggie Wolfington, New York, Oct. 12, 1998

155 "is don't ask"—interview with Madelyn Pugh Davis, Bel Air, Calif., Dec. 4, 1998

156 "held my tongue"—interview with Dolly Reed Wageman, Studio City, Calif., Dec. 3, 1998

156 "goes double for politics"—telephone interview with Jack O'Brien, July 14, 1999

156 "politics were virginal"—telephone interview with Janet Fox Goldsmith, April 1, 1999

157 "as an old lady"—interview with Elizabeth Danforth, St. Louis, June 2, 1999

157 pled with her alma mater—she wrote Chancellor William Danforth on Sept. 25, 1973, and asked him to omit any reference to her graduating class in publicity materials related to her upcoming appearance at the opening of the university's new theatre, MWP

157 success playing an old woman—"Young St. Louis Actress in Role of 65-Year-Old Housemaid," *St. Louis Daily Globe-Democrat,* Feb. 12, 1938

158 "still in her 30s"—*Lewiston (Maine) Journal,* magazine section, Feb. 16, 1957

158 as older women—"She's Young but Old," *Los Angeles Mirror,* May 27, 1957

158 "out of her teens"—from the summary of credits that Mary prepared in July 1964, MWP

158 "the Marcel wave"—these passages are taken from a travel diary that Mary kept beginning Oct. 2, 1977, during her cruise on the *Island Princess,* MWP

CHAPTER TEN: MARY'S SECRET COUSIN

All comments and observations from Brooks Adkins come from: a) a lengthy interview with him and his wife Mary at their Dayton, Ohio, home on July 10, 1999, and b) two pieces of follow-up correspondence from them dated July 14, 1999, and Sept. 12, 1999.

161 "when I'll be home"—Mary's grandmother Mollie, in Ohio caring for Hes, writing to Isabella at 5017 Garfield Ave. in St. Louis on June 15, 1910, just days after Mary was born

162 "High Class"—prominent display ad appeared in *The Billboard,* Feb. 25, 1911, p. 29

162 "the contralto and the violinist"—one of various notices promoting their appearances, this one at the Star Theater, Ithaca, New York, *Cornell Daily Sun,* March 16, 1914, p. 6

162 "they are not performers"—from reviewer "Jolo" in *Variety,* late April 1914, p. 16

163 a rooming house—the fourteenth census of the United States counts Hester M. Adkins as a lodger at 105 South Robert Boulevard, Dayton

163 a saleswoman at the Rike Kumler Co.—from Hester's death certificate filed with the State of Ohio Bureau of Vital Statistics, Jan. 27, 1920, file number 215

163 from pneumonia—Hester's death certificate says she died of "lob pneumonia"

163 though never finalized—the fourteenth census of the United States, taken just twelve days before she died, lists Hester M. Adkins as married

163 mention of Hes's two children—from an undated, unlabeled 1920 newspaper clipping in the folder at Missouri Historical Society, St. Louis, that chronicles Mary's bequest to the society

163 The 1920 census—the fourteenth census of the United States records Hester M. Adkins' age as 35 living in Dayton

164 Mollie and James were not married—per their Illinois marriage license in MWP, Mollie Thomas and James T. Shannon were married at the home of bride's mother in Illinois on Oct. 30, 1883

165 named guardian—Belle Rentchler was appointed guardian on July 16, 1926, in St. Clair County, Ill. Guardianship and related transfers of funds are documented in legal papers MWP

165 a frustrated trust officer—trust officer George Rinck wrote Isabella on March 1, 1943, saying the bank is "still holding" the amount due Brooks from Belle Rentchler, has been trying unsuccessfully to find him, and is "most anxious" to close the estate. He asks Isabella for help she sends Brooks' address on March 14. Letter in MWP.

166 "rings a bell"—interview with Bill Dorsam, St. Louis, Sept. 16, 1998

166 "tight-lipped"—interview with Bill Dorsam, St. Louis, June 6, 1999

167 "that kind of situation"—telephone interview with Bill Carson, July 12, 1999

CHAPTER ELEVEN: "NOT AN OUNCE" OF ROMANCE

169 "got all 'proper'"—interview with Mary Jackson, Hollywood, Calif., April 4, 1999

170 "beaus or gentleman callers"—interview with Bill Swan, New York, Nov. 17, 1998

170 a strong-willed girl—their undated outline for a teleplay called *Tish* is in MWP. Tish is a good-hearted young woman trying to save a summer camp for underprivileged boys from closure.

170 "I'm going to get married"—from an email exchange with Steven L. Rehl, John Patrick's co-executor and a close friend, March 18, 2012. Rehl and Bradley Strauman, Patrick's other executor, heard the story directly from Patrick, who died in 1995, two weeks after Mary died.

170 "Nobody knew"—interview with Anne Kaufman Schneider, New York, Nov. 21, 1998

171 "tarred and feathered"—interview with Bill Swan, New York, Nov. 17, 1998

171 "He's gay, you know"—interview with Hal Kanter, Encino, Calif., Dec. 8, 1998

171 "deep eyes, round cheeks"—the description of Newdahl is drawn from photographs: one printed in the "Only Human" column, *New York Daily Mirror*, March 8, 1938; two that Mary kept her whole life (MWP); and about a dozen at the Billy Rose Theatre Collection, New York Public Library, from his American Opera Company performances

172 traveled around China—"Only Human," *New York Daily Mirror*, March 8, 1938

172 for the Shubert organization—*Variety*, June 23, 1939, notes his upcoming appearance in the Shuberts' production of *Student Prince* at the Iroquois Amphitheatre in Louisville, Kent

172 frequently had engagements—Muny records document his appearances in nineteen productions in the 1931, 1932, and 1933 seasons

172 a nightclub career—numerous newspaper notices trumpeted Newdahl's appearances, including the *New York Evening Journal*, April 3, 1937 (for the Hotel St. Moritz) and the *New York Sun*, Dec. 18, 1939 (for the Number One)

172 "totally asexual"—interview with Dr. Lester Coleman, New York, Nov. 20, 1998

172 "does not seem possible"—letter from Clifford Newdahl to Mary, sent from Anti-aircraft Artillery Command, Eastern Defense Command, July 21, 1943, Portsmouth, Va.

173 "absolutely bereft"—interview with Bob Wallsten, New York, Feb. 22, 1999

173 "trunk is lovely"—from anecdotes Mary recorded in 1990 for a possible autobiography, MWP

173 well-built redhead—from a lengthier physical description of Thomsen in publicity materials distributed by MGM, May 24, 1951, AMPAS

173 "the only person"—telephone interview with Nancy Thomsen Brown, Sept. 26, 1999

174 "the hours at Bob Thomsen's"—letter from Garson Kanin to Mary, June 14, 1977, MWP

174 blacklisted—telephone interview with Nancy Thomsen Brown, Sept. 26, 1999

174 ghostwrote—telephone interview with Nancy Thomsen Brown, Sept. 26, 1999

175 maiden voyage—telephone interview with Nancy Thomsen Brown, Sept. 26, 1999

175 "must have known"—interview with Bob Wallsten, New York, Feb. 22, 1999

175 "never saw either of them"—interview with Anna Crouse, New York, Nov. 18, 1998

175 "death was knocking"—letter from Thomsen in North Africa to Mary in St. Louis, May 20, 1943, using the military's V-mail system, MWP

176 "paper into the typewriter"—letter from Thomsen in North Africa to Mary in care of Barry Sullivan in Hollywood, July 6, 1943, MWP

176 accidentally set fire—Ronald Martinetti, "The James Dean Story: A Myth-Shattering Biography of an Icon," *The Blacklisted Journalist*, www.blacklistedjournalist.com, 1975

177 "a shock to all of us"—letter from Patricia Collinge to Mary, Nov. 26, 1973, MWP

177 "most of her estate"—interview with Anna Crouse, New York, Nov. 18, 1998

177 "grieved beyond words"—letter from Garson Kanin to Mary, Feb. 16, 1984, MWP

177 "look you up?"—letter from Bob Thomsen in Africa to Mary in New York, July 4, 1943, MWP

177 magazine ads—Mary saved at least one, which features Raiser and John Cameron Swayze. The magazine is unclear, but its style is reminiscent of *Esquire*.

178 "he turned the project over to Bill"—Stewart Williams as told to Hal Meltzer, "Building a Reputation," *Palm Springs Life*, January 2000, pp. 78–83

178 "rumors about them"—telephone interview with Laurence Loewy, Jan. 17, 2000

178 "closer to Mary"—interview with Bob Wallsten, New York, Sept. 11, 1999

179 were killed—"Arthur Elrod Killed in Crash; Designer," *Los Angeles Times*, Feb. 19, 1974, section II, p. 4

179 "go up a day earlier"—telephone interview with Lee Roy Reams, July 13, 1999

179 "poor soul"—Jim McPherson, "Humor as Dry as Summer Sand," *Toronto Telegram*, June 14, 1969

179 "many men friends"—letter from Mary to Debora S. Bloom of Phi Mu's magazine, The *Aglaia*, April 23, 1982, MWP

180 extended her skirt—interview with Anne Kaufman Schneider, New York, Nov. 21, 1998

180 "so normal and married"—telephone interview with Joe Ross, July 15, 1999

180 "around Alan Handley"—letter from Lucille Ball to Mary, Dec. 24, 1971, MWP

180 "Hiya, Pinky!"—interview with Iggie Wolfington, New York, Oct. 12, 1998

181 a romantic relationship—telephone interview with Lee Roy Reams, July 13, 1999

181 "married Iggie"—letter from Lucille Ball to Mary, Feb. 4, 1971, MWP

181 "I can see why"—interview with Iggie Wolfington, New York, Oct. 12, 1998

181 they all understood—telephone interview with Paul Barselou, Aug. 17, 1998

182 "gave herself totally"—interview with Max Showalter, Chester, Conn., Sept. 1, 1998

182 "happy with her world"—telephone interview with Joe Ross, July 15, 1999

182 "cheerful, happy"—Vernon Scott, "TV Profile: Mary Wickes," *Houston Post*, Jan. 19, 1976

182 *Mike Douglas Show*—in a June 3, 1977, letter to Ruth Gordon and Garson Kanin, Mary says, "And here I sat, tears welling up in my eyes, while Mike Douglas sang the Anniversary Song to you!" Letter courtesy of Garson Kanin

183 "sad about going home"—interview with Malcolm Goldstein, New York, Nov. 17, 1998

183 "if I was married"—interview with Harriet Switzer, St. Louis, Nov. 7, 1998

183 "used to date a lot"—Frank Hunter, "Wickes Returns as Muny Hall of Famer," *Clayton (Mo.) Citizen Journal*, Dec. 22, 1987

184 "never happened to me"—interview with Herb Metz, St. Louis, June 6, 1998
184 "slightly foreign territory"—telephone interview with Jack O'Brien, July 14, 1999
184 "martyred herself"—interview with Lucie Arnaz, Katonah, New York, Feb. 17, 1999
184 "if she died a virgin"—interview with Max Showalter, Chester, Conn., Sept. 1, 1998
184 "world of deprivation"—interview with Dr. Lester Coleman, New York, Nov. 20, 1998
184 "the next eight thirty curtain"—telephone interview with Harve Presnell, Oct. 10, 1999
185 "certified virgin"—interview with Anne Kaufman Schneider, New York, Nov. 21, 1998
185 a virgin when they met—interview with Bob Wallsten, New York, Feb. 22, 1999
185 "Uncle Whit," "Uncle Bob"—interview with Bob Wallsten, New York, Sept. 11, 1999
185 he watched Mary—interview with Bob Wallsten, New York, Feb. 22, 1999
186 homes with a shared living space—telephone interview with actor Gordon Chater, a close friend of Sumner Locke Elliott, Aug. 31, 1999
186 "If you'd like to bring a girl"—interview with Bob Wallsten, New York, Feb. 22, 1999
187 "seated on a porch"—interview with Bob Wallsten, New York, Feb. 22, 1999
187 "kind of dewey-eyed"—telephone interview with Janet Fox Goldsmith, April 1, 1999
188 "a great wit"—Robert L. Daniels, "Glenn Anders: He Knew What He Wanted," *After Dark*, November 1977, p. 52
188 convinced she was in love—interview with Louis Westheimer, St. Louis, Nov. 7, 1998
188 included him in a dinner—from an undated, unlabeled news clip in one of Mary's scrapbooks, MWP, the other guests were Edith Barrett, who had just returned from New York, where husband Vincent Price was appearing in *Angel Street*; Barry and Marie Sullivan, with whom Mary would stay during a trip to Los Angeles the following year; and Barbara Wolferman, the actress Mary befriended at Stockbridge who now, during the war, was working in Los Angeles for Douglas Aircraft.
188 "to crime!"—from a telephone interview with Jane Sutter, Oct. 17, 1998: Mary offered this toast at a dinner after Richard Sutter shared a long story about a successful business deal. After Mary died, daughter Jane and a friend visited the Shiloh cemetery to plant a rose at her grave. Task completed, they raised their beverages and toasted Mary, "Here's to crime!"
188 a ground floor window—interview with Elliott Reid, Los Angeles, Dec. 10, 1998
188 "the most effete young man that ever existed"—Robert L. Daniels, "Glenn Anders: He Knew What He Wanted," *After Dark*, November 1977, p. 53
188 "I'm sure she understood"—interview with Elliott Reid, Los Angeles, Oct. 27, 1999
189 "Every time Miss Bankhead went out"—from anecdotes that Mary recorded on audiocassette in 1990 for a possible autobiography, MWP
189 "anti-gay cracks"—telephone interview with Laurence Guittard, Sept. 30, 1999
189 "an eight-dollar bill"—interview with Malcolm Goldstein, New York, Nov. 17, 1998
190 felt sorry for herself—interview with Mary Jackson, Hollywood, Calif., April 4, 1999
190 "talked about 'pansies'"—interview with Jerry Berger, St. Louis, June 23, 2000
190 "the parts you play"—interview with Iggie Wolfington, New York, Oct. 12, 1998
191 "sort of asked"—interview with Anne Kaufman Schneider, New York, Nov. 21, 1998
191 "here nor there"—interview with Lucie Arnaz, Katonah, New York, Feb. 17, 1999

191 "somewhere along the line"—telephone interview with Larry Guittard, Sept. 30, 1999

191 "she just accepted"—interview with Emily Daniels, Valley Village, Calif., April 20, 1999

191 "make her feel bad"—interview with Amy Jane Ax, St. Louis, Sept. 25, 1998

CHAPTER TWELVE: NURSES, NUNS, AND HOUSEKEEPERS

193 "nicer, braver, wittier"—Ronald Bergan, "The Nosy Nun Next Door: Obituary, Mary Wickes," the *Guardian* (London), Oct. 26, 1995

193 phone call from the set—interview with Bill Frye, Palm Desert, Calif., March 9, 1999

194 "card-carrying"—"Faces/Places: The Name is Mary Wickes," *Houston Post*, July 17, 1966

195 "pigeon-holed"—from a letter Mary wrote Bill Ball at American Conservatory Theater, in which she is unusually revealing about her feelings, July 21, 1973, MWP

196 "raising a laugh"—Wilella Waldorf, *New York Post*, Aug. 26, 1936

196 "I Played Maids"—Harriet Van Horne, *New York World-Telegram*, Oct. 7, 1955

196 "a maid *again*?"—telephone interview with Mary Healy, May 19, 1999

197 "given a face"—*Boston Sunday Herald Advertiser*, May 9, 1976

197 "great sweaters"—interview with Mary by Dave Otto, KRXY, 103 FM, Denver, December 1987

197 "total strangers"—from Mary's appearance on *The Doris Day Show* (radio), April 18, 1952

197 "with a refrigerator"—interview with Bill Frye, Palm Desert, Calif., March 9, 1999

197 "living down to reality"—interview with Bill Frye, Palm Desert, Calif., March 9, 1999

198 "and Norma Shearer"—telephone interview with Ted Donaldson, Aug. 14, 1998

199 "offending the public"—per the May 29, 1947, version of the script at WBA, p. 13, the boy pretends to hang himself with a dishtowel and tells Mary he is dead, to which she replies, "Not in my kitchen. Anyhow, you stop that. It makes me nervous." Memos establish that the scene was cut to avoid violating the Production Code and offending the public with the notion of teen suicide.

199 The Danny Kaye role—Ed Blank, "Oklahoma's Auntie Down-to-Earth," the *Pittsburgh Press*, June 22, 1980, p. G-1

199 a business-like set—all observations attributed to Rosemary Clooney are from a telephone interview with the author, March 8, 2000

199 a sandwich made by Isabella—Edward A. Harris, "Back to Campus for Mary Wickes," *St. Louis Post-Dispatch*, Aug. 1, 1954

199 "didn't get to know anybody"—all comments from Anne Whitfield are from a telephone interview with the author, April 14, 2001, unless otherwise indicated

200 "shooting had been postponed"—Donald Shepherd and Robert Slatzer, *Bing Crosby: The Hollow Man*, St. Martin's Press, 1991, p. 228

200 "Two girl have small tear"—letter from Anne Whitfield to the author, April 24, 2001

201 popped in a videotape—Bruce R. Miller, *Sioux City Journal*, June 5, 1992

201 insufficiently promoted—on-air interview with Mary by Dave Otto, KRXY, 103 FM, Denver, December 1987

201 $750 a week—salary figures here come from the Warner Bros. production files for *On Moonlight Bay*, WBA

201 "*Moonlight Bay* Strikes Back"—excerpt from a note from Rosemary DeCamp to Jack Warner, thanking him for flowers, in *By the Light of the Silvery Moon* production files, WBA

201 "pick up the bird"—from a 1982 speech Mary made to a group of hospital volunteers, MWP

202 "happened naturally"—from Mary's interview with Don Richardson on "Behind the Scenes," KCRW, 89.9 FM, at Santa Monica (Calif.) College, March 15, 1984

202 "steal some limelight"—*Rocky Mountain News,* April 5, 1984

202 an illustrated hardback—MWP contains a copy of *Mary Poppins* in which Mary has made notations by hand (*Mary Poppins* by P. L. Travers and illustrated by Mary Shepard, published by Reynal and Hitchcock, New York, 1947)

203 $500—from a letter of agreement on CBS letterhead, signed by Mary, Jan. 26, 1950, MWP

203 "wasn't expecting much"—telephone interview with Paul Nickell, July 24, 1998

203 "a thing of the past"—from a Dec. 19, 1949, telegram to Mary from Sherman Marks, MWP

203 "nobody did it"—interview with Max Showalter, Chester, Conn., Sept. 1, 1998

204 every consideration—letter from Hubbell Robinson Jr. at CBS Television to Mary, May 16, 1955, MWP

204 unavailable—letter from Dominick Dunne at CBS Television to Mary, June 11, 1957, MWP

204 "double A for effort"—letter to Mary from Martin Manulis, 1958, MWP

204 "and we chatted"—interview with Mary by Jim Brown, *Today,* June 18, 1992

204 she came to believe—in an interview by Dave Otto, KRXY, 103 FM, Denver, December 1987, Mary said, "I sold the idea to Mr. Disney . . . I'm not really getting the bends taking bows, but I did suggest it to him and he got in touch with the people and eventually he did Poppins."

204 already mentioned it—Mary's interview with Jim Brown, *Today,* June 18, 1992

204 first learned of the book—Bob Thomas, *Walt Disney: An American Original*, Simon & Schuster, 1976, pp. 315–16

204 "broke my heart"—D. J. Hobdy, "'Miss Bedpan' Stays Cheerful," *Houston Chronicle*, July 12, 1966

204 "She wasn't bitter"—interview with Judy Sutter Hinrichs, St. Louis, Oct. 17, 1998

204 "the Julie Andrews casting"—telephone interview with Paul Nickell, July 24, 1998

205 educator and politician—Richard Schickel recounts the dispute between school superintendent Max Rafferty and children's literature expert Frances Clarke Sayers in *The Disney Version: The Life, Times, Art and Commerce of Walt Disney*, Simon & Schuster, 1968, pp. 349–57

205 Disney did consider Bette Davis—Bob Thomas, *Walt Disney: An American Original*, Simon & Schuster, 1976, p. 319

205 "Is she dressing?"—interview with Malcolm Goldstein, New York, Nov. 17, 1998

205 Davis lying on a settee—still photos of this scene exist in two places, a scrapbook in the Bette Davis Collection at Boston University, and in the Ilka Chase folder at the Billy Rose Theatre Collection, New York Public Library

206 "her happiest experience"—telephone interview with Mary Kay Stearns, Aug. 6, 1999

206 $500 per week—per contract dated May 1, 1942, between Mary and Warner Bros., WBA

206 the scene initially—Paul Henreid, *Ladies Man: An Autobiography*, 1984, pp. 115–17

206 "on schedule"—inter-office memo from Irving Rapper to J. L. Warner, May 19, 1942, Warner Bros. production files on *Now, Voyager*, WBA

206 thirty costumes—from a Warners Bros. production note for *Now, Voyager*, WBA

206 *How, Now, Voyager*—first produced in 1997, it ran Off- Broadway in the 1999–2000 season

206 did not even warrant a mention—no mention appears in *Hollywood Hussar: The Life and Times of John Loder* (H. Baker, 1977)

207 "have to use Mary Wickes"—telephone interview with Gene Reynolds, Jan. 19, 2000

207 "a funny, funny character"—from Mary's interview with Don Richardson on "Behind the Scenes," KCRW, 89.9 FM, at Santa Monica (Calif.) College, March 15, 1984

208 to detract from the dignity—Bob Williams, "On the Air" column, *New York Post*, June 7, 1976

208 "nun wouldn't say"—interview with Madelyn Pugh Davis, Bel Air, Calif., Dec. 4, 1998

208 "might have been a nun"—interview with Harriet Switzer, St. Louis, Nov. 7, 1998

208 "they were slippery"—interview with Bill Frye, Palm Desert, Calif., March 9, 1999

208 "double-clutching"—from Mary's May 5, 1978, speech to the Beta Sigma Phi convention at Century Plaza Hotel, Los Angeles, MWP

209 more than $250,000—interview with Bill Frye, Palm Desert, Calif., March 9, 1999

209 "deliberate comics"—review of *The Trouble with Angels, New York Times*, April 7, 1966

209 "fluff reigns supreme"—review of *Where Angels Go, Trouble Follows, Variety*, April 3, 1968

209 transatlantic courtship—William Frye, "The Garbo Next Door," *Vanity Fair*, April 2000, p. 220

209 "her faith and her religion"—Tony Vellela, "Comedian Mary Wickes Holds Her Own," *Christian Science Monitor*, Feb. 15, 1994, p. 14

209 "a romance about it"—Susan King, "Mary Wickes Makes a Habit of Playing Nuns on the Run," *Los Angeles Times*, June 6, 1992

209 "loved playing a nun"—"Faces/Places: The Name is Mary Wickes," *Houston Post*, July 17, 1966

209 "you get quieter"—Susan King, "Mary Wickes Makes a Habit of Playing Nuns on the Run," *Los Angeles Times*, June 6, 1992

210 "in black or white"—interview with Bill Frye, Palm Desert, Calif., March 9, 1999

210 "During breaks"—Mary relayed these and similar anecdotes many times, including to Harry Bishop in "Father Dowling's TV Housekeeper," *Denver Catholic Register*, Feb. 8, 1989

210 "get rid of Ida"—interview with Bill Frye, Palm Desert, Calif., March 9, 1999

211 "everybody laughed"—telephone interview with Dolores Sutton, Aug. 17, 1998

211 "everything about the opening"—this description is from interviews and press clips, such as, "Thousands Jam Grand to See *Trouble With Angels* Stars: Red Carpet for Roz," by Beulah Schacht, *St. Louis Globe-Democrat*, March 31, 1966

212 "When they were looking"—interview with Jack Pirozzi, St. Louis, June 11, 1999

212 "with a capital 'B'"—excerpt from Mary's letter to Mike Frankovich, Jan. 16, 1966, MWP

212 "have no pull"—interview with Bill Frye, Palm Desert, Calif., March 9, 1999

212 "like a house-afire"—excerpt from a letter from Mary at the Philadelphia Marriott to Vincent Price, July 15, 1967: "Binnie Barnes is one of the greatest traveling companions and all-round nice person. We get on like a house-afire." The letter is in the Vincent Price Papers, LOC

212 "went about her business"—telephone interview with Marge Redmond, Aug. 6, 1998

213 "heart-to-heart talks"—interview with Jack Pirozzi, St. Louis, June 11, 1999

213 "instrumental"—interview with Jack Pirozzi, St. Louis, June 11, 1999

213 One of several notes from Russell—the notes are in MWP

213 "Oh, that's too bad"—interview with Jack Pirozzi, St. Louis, June 11, 1999

214 cast was told—Anna Parker, "Meet Mary Wickes," *Entre Nous Houston,* November, 1967, p. 45

214 "truly disappointed"—letter from Mary to professor William G. B. Carson in St. Louis, March 17, 1962, courtesy of son Bill Carson

214 with June Allyson—interview with Peter Walker, Chester, Conn., Sept. 1, 1998

214 clumsily—the awards show is archived for viewing at the Paley Center for Media in New York

214 *Rehearsal for Breakfast*—a copy of the script is in MWP

214 a Hildegarde Withers mystery—Mary's papers contain the first draft of the script, "The Riddle of the Green Ice," in which Mary envisioned herself starring opposite James Gleason

215 *Mary-Go-Round*—The outline is in MWP, along with a brochure from the actual business that inspired it, called Presents Unlimited

215 renamed it *Donna Quixote*—a copy of her Writers Guild submission is in MWP

215 Fontanne's original costumes—from an oral history of the Berkshire Playhouse that Mary recorded on Aug. 25, 1982, which is preserved at SLA

215 "I was terrified"—Marjory Adams, *Boston Globe,* Sept. 5, 1948

215 "pretty anxious"—interview with Lenka Peterson, Roxbury, Conn., Sept. 8, 1999

215 "things went wrong"—from an oral history of the Berkshire Playhouse that Mary recorded on Aug. 25, 1982, which is preserved at SLA

216 "a tendency to overshadow"—Kingsley R. Fall, *Berkshire Evening Eagle,* July 30, 1946

216 "hysterical"—from anecdotes Mary told on the *Wil Shriner Show,* 1988 (exact date unknown)

216 gymnasium teacher—Sept. 22, 1952, memo to Ruth Gordon from R. Monta at Metro-Goldwyn-Mayer on the status of securing releases for characters' names, Ruth Gordon Papers, LOC

217 "over-shot"—James Fisher, *Spencer Tracy: A Bio-Bibliography,* Greenwood Press, 1994, p. 53

217 halve her original script—memo from Lawrence Weingarten, executive producer at MGM, instructing Gordon and Kanin to reduce the story from one that would film at 15,000 feet to one that would film at about 8,500 feet, the length of *Pat and Mike,* April 7, 1952, Ruth Gordon Papers, LOC

217 her sherbet spoon—the description of the eliminated scene is drawn from the script of *Years Ago* (the original title of *The Actress*), pp. 63–68, Ruth Gordon Papers, LOC

217 Mary was paid $3,000—from records in Warner Bros. *Dear Heart* production files, WBA

217 a shock to both producer and director—efforts to obscure Page's pregnancy and delay her learning of President Kennedy's assassination are described in Delbert Mann's

unpublished memoirs, Part II, pp. 312–22, Delbert Mann Papers, Vanderbilt University Special Collections and University Archives, Nashville, Tenn.

219 hoped Bette Davis would accept—letter from Irving Rapper to Mary, May 11, 1949, MWP. Rapper shares his disappointment at having to turn down a chance to direct Greta Garbo in Rome because he was preparing for *Menagerie*. He was referring to *La Duchess de Langelais*, which never got beyond pre-production.

219 "sufficiently confident"—"It's Good to Be Home Again," *St. Louis Globe-Democrat*, May 29, 1949

219 "go after Irving Rapper"—note from Gertrude Lawrence to Mary, Sept. 28, 1949, MWP

219 "some concern"—telephone interview with Richard Palmer, Aug. 4, 1999

220 "he deferred to her"—interview with Jack Pirozzi, St. Louis, June 11, 1999

220 "I'm stunned"—letter from Mary to George Seaton, Jan. 13, 1975, MWP

CHAPTER THIRTEEN: WHEN ACTING IS EVERYTHING . . .

221 While taping—the contract for *The Jimmy Stewart Show* was signed May 27, 1971, by Mary and producer Bernard Wiesen, MWP. She earned $1,000 to play her recurring character, Josephine Bullard, in the "Period of Readjustment" episode.

221 her next job—Mary needed to be in St. Louis by July 19, 1971, to begin rehearsals for *The Music Man*, which opened July 26, 1971 at the Muny. She played Eulalie MacKechnie Shinn.

221 "from the bottom of her toes"—telephone interview with Joan Darling, Aug. 1, 1999

222 "grand old lady"—interview with Betty Garrett, North Hollywood, Calif., Dec. 10, 1998

222 "an actress and that was it"—telephone interview with Joe Ross, July 15, 1999

222 "put my toes into the water"—letter from Moss Hart to Mary, Feb. 1, 1949, MWP

222 "before you or I die"—letter from Moss Hart to Mary, June 25, 1952, MWP

223 "no need to trouble yourself"—letter from Michael Curtiz to Mary, Oct. 7, 1949, MWP

223 Mary's pursuit—Mary wrote Logan on May 13, 1963, he replied on June 3, and she wrote again on June 7, no doubt the very day she received his response, Joshua Logan Papers, LOC

223 He was encouraging—Rogers replied to Mary on Jan. 11, 1966, that he would recommend her to Henry Guettel, who was managing the theatre (and who had recently become his son-in-law)

223 "a new comedy"—letter from Mary to Garson Kanin, Nov. 24, 1984, courtesy of Garson Kanin

224 Eva Gabor—Gabor told Mary she decided not to mount the play after all, Jan. 18, 1978, MWP

224 Ruby the maid—in a Nov. 15, 1978, letter, Grant Tinker explained that producers' final choice was simply a matter of type: "Certainly no one is ever *better* than Mary Wickes."

224 "we can't use another girl"—letter from Jimmy Durante to Mary, Oct. 3, 1947, MWP

224 *Danny Thomas Show*—Thomas replied on Sept. 16, 1988, that Mary had a right to take umbrage but that she was directing it at the wrong person, as he had no role in the arrangements, MWP

224 protested directly—Mary wrote Frankovich on Jan. 16, 1966, MWP

225 "this is her livelihood"—Bill Vaughan, "Star Billing Beef by the Old Billpayer," *Kansas City Star*, Aug. 17, 1968

225 no claim was possible—the dispute is chronicled in correspondence between Mary and Actors' Equity Association representatives from July 10 to September 20, 1979, MWP

225 advertisements for a stage production—the dispute is chronicled in correspondence between Mary, agent Don Wolff, the Muny's Edward Greenberg and Karen McCrory, and the Actors' Equity Association, MWP. The apology appeared in the *St. Louis Post-Dispatch*, Nov. 22, 1987

226 he is surprised—telephone interview with Patrick McGoohan, Aug. 5, 1998

226 Dale has no recollection—telephone interview with Jim Dale, Aug. 27, 1999

227 simply acquaintances—interview with Bill Danforth at his Washington University office and Elizabeth Danforth at the Danforth home in St. Louis, both on June 2, 1999

227 "cooking in the bathroom"—letter from Doris Day to Mary, March 24, 1971, MWP

227 "marvelous"—note from Doris Day during *Jumbo* preparations at MGM, Dec. 27, 1961, MWP

227 "gone a year"—letter to Mary from Doris Day, Nov. 29, 1977, MWP

228 "meet you in Monterey"—note from Doris Day in Carmel, Calif., undated (post-1981), MWP

228 "like the best of friends"—interview with Janet Lewis, Aug. 29, 2005

228 "hit it off"—interview with Madelyn Pugh Davis, Bel Air, Calif., Dec. 4, 1998

228 "a real friend"—statement issued by Doris Day to author, Feb. 22, 2000

228 "wanting everybody to like you"—Joan McKinney, "Letter to 'Sam' Put Her on Broadway," *Oakland (Calif.) Tribune*, April 25, 1973

228 "B.D. is running"—letter from Bette Davis, fall of 1948 (undated), MWP

228 midnight supper—the invitation came by telegram April 16 for a dinner on April 21, 1949, MWP

229 "getting free"—letter from Bette Davis to Mary, 1950 (undated), MWP

229 "just up and married"—letter from Bette Davis to Mary, 1950 (undated), MWP

229 "decided not to like her"—Roy Moseley, *Bette Davis: An Intimate Memoir*, Donald I. Fine, 1989, p. 127

229 "Congratulations"—interview with Peter Walker, Chester, Conn., Sept. 1, 1998

230 "horrendous" emergency appendectomy—note from Vivian Vance at the Royal Poinciana Theater, Palm Beach, Fla., to Mary, Jan. 24, 1966, MWP

230 "state of shock"—letter from Gene Rayburn to Mary, March 28, 1979, MWP

230 "a kind of vindication"—letter from John Patrick to Mary, Jan. 14, 1954, MWP

230 "sit down and tell me"—letter from Maureen O'Sullivan to Mary, Feb. 4, 1992, MWP

231 a 2000 interview—the author interviewed Rosemary Clooney by telephone, March 8, 2000

231 "I sat at her feet"—Johnny Whitaker re-created Mary's five reactions during an interview with the author, Studio City, Calif., Oct. 26, 1999

232 two pieces of advice—from notes Mary prepared to guide her teaching, MWP

232 "excited about it"—telephone interview with Jack O'Brien, July 14, 1999

233 "thousands of miles"—telephone interview with Anne Kaufman Schneider, Nov. 29, 1998

233 "bowl somebody over"—letter from George Seaton to Mary, April 1, 1974, MWP

233 "how much better"—production notes from George Seaton to Mary, spring 1974, MWP

233 "a rough time"—telephone interview with Clinton Atkinson, Feb. 7, 1999

234 "Mary stopped me"—telephone interview with Dolores Sutton, Aug. 17, 1998

234 "clippiness"—telephone interview with Barbara Sharma, June 26, 1998

234 "helpful hints"—interview with Elliot Reid, Hollywood, Calif., Dec. 10, 1998

234 "one of the other actors"—interview with Bill Hammerstein, Washington, Conn., Sept. 8, 1999

234 "discovering to my horror"—letter from Bill Hammerstein to Mary, Jan. 12, 1981, MWP

234 "a woman comedian"—interview with Peter Walker, Chester, Conn., Sept. 1, 1998

235 "fight for their lives"—telephone interview with Lamont Johnson, Aug. 27, 1999

235 "If she caught wind"—David Holifield, "The Scott Holden Interview," *The Unofficial Sid & Marty Krofft Home Page*, a web link that apparently is no longer available

236 not have been amused—Jayne Matthews, "Film Star is Coming Home One Last Time," *Belleville (Ill.) News-Democrat*, Nov. 12, 1995

236 "time for my mom"—interview with Bill Dorsam, St. Louis, Sept. 16, 1998

236 "the children's table"—email to author from Michael Q. Martin, son of Madelyn Pugh Davis, March 16, 2010

237 "a funny bone that didn't stop"—telephone interview with Janet Lewis, Aug. 29, 2005

237 "Sometimes you get so lonely"—from speech Mary delivered at All Saints' Episcopal Church in Beverly Hills, date unknown, MWP

238 "when a friend of ours was ill"—Mary relayed this anecdote on multiple occasions, including a 1982 speech to hospital volunteers (location unknown), and a June 5, 1988, Celebration of Life Day speech at St. Vincent's Hospital, Los Angeles; copies of her remarks are in MWP

238 "she would be slapstick"—"The Many Faces of Volunteers," *Los Angeles Times*, Sept. 3, 1967

238 "colon cancer"—interview with Dick Davis, Bel Air, Calif., Dec. 4, 1998

238 "extraordinary"—interview with Mary Jackson, Hollywood, Calif., April 4, 1999

239 "awfully good at it"—telephone interview with Jane Wyatt, July 24, 1999

239 "Whenever she was there"—telephone interview with Marjorie Lord, July 21, 1999

239 "Gypsy Rose Lee"—interview with Peter Walker, Chester, Conn., Sept. 1, 1998

239 "sense of belonging"—telephone interview with Harve Presnell, Oct. 10, 1999

240 "Mary's holiday regimen"—telephone interview with Jack O'Brien, July 14, 1999

240 "You should volunteer!"—interview with Lucie Arnaz, Katonah, New York, Feb. 17, 1999

240 "church this morning?"—telephone interview with Iris Mann, July 3, 2000

241 "something antiseptic"—interview with Elliott Reid, Hollywood, Calif., Dec. 10, 1998

241 "church becomes your family"—Harry Bishop, "Father Dowling's TV Housekeeper," the *Denver Catholic Register*, Feb. 8, 1989

241 rummage sales—telephone interview with Wendy Borcherdt LeRoy, May 24, 1999

242 "born-again"—interview with Lucie Arnaz, Katonah, New York, Feb. 17, 1999

242 "suicide"—interview with Malcolm Goldstein, New York, Nov. 17, 1998

CHAPTER FOURTEEN: BECOMING THE CHARACTERS SHE PLAYED

243 "fend the world"—interview with Max Showalter, Chester, Conn., Sept. 1, 1998

244 "Mary, this isn't you"—interview with Max Showalter, Chester, Conn., Sept. 15, 1999

244 "start off with this persona"—interview with Jack Pirozzi, St. Louis, June 11, 1999

245 "what was beneath it"—interview with Max Showalter, Chester, Conn., Sept. 1, 1998

245 "rather grand"—interview with Max Showalter, Chester, Conn., Sept. 15, 1999

245 "Queenly"—interview with Dolly Reed Wageman, Studio City, Calif., Dec. 3, 1998

245 "impossible, stubborn"—telephone interview with Ethel Winant, May 18, 1999

245 "like Lucy"—interview with Madelyn Pugh Davis, Bel Air, Calif., Dec. 4, 1998

245 "screens were too dark"—interview with Bill Givens, Los Angeles, April 9, 1999

246 "throwing a fit"—telephone interview with Chris Hart, Oct. 6, 1999

246 "the earlier period"—telephone interview with Alfred Gellhorn, June 21, 1999

247 "Billymiles"—from an interview with Billy Miles conducted by Judy Salsbury for an oral history of the Berkshire Theatre Festival, Stockbridge, Mass., undated audiotape

247 Not remembering Miles—telephone interview with Helen Morgan, Feb. 4, 1999

247 spoke in detail—Mary makes many references to Miles in an oral history of the Berkshire Playhouse that she recorded Aug. 25, 1982; the recording is available at SLA

247 "very peculiar"—interview with Bill Frye, Palm Desert, Calif., March 9, 1999

247 "very proper"—interview with Dolly Reed Wageman, Studio City, Calif., Dec. 3, 1998

248 "dumbfounded"—telephone interview with Peter A. D'Auria Jr., Aug. 7, 2011

248 "I *know* I know you"—telephone interview with Iris Mann, July 3, 2000

248 such and such—interview with Jerry Berger, St. Louis, June 23, 2000

249 twenty-one inaccuracies—Mary wrote Don Stanke on Nov. 15, 1973, MWP

249 "plastic"—letter from Mary to Debora Bloom of Phi Mu's *The Aglaia*, April 23, 1982, MWP

249 "very far from fact"—letter from Mary to K. Robert Whittemore of San Francisco, July 3, 1986, author's collection

249 "paid her dues"—interview with Jerry Berger, St. Louis, June 23, 2000

250 "the truth?"—telephone interview with Barbara Mahon, May 26, 1999

250 "let it alone"—letter to Mary from Howard F. Baer, July 23, 1965, MWP

251 questions from Pierce—interview with Polly Pierce, Stockbridge, Mass., September 1998

251 "this historian lady"—the excerpts here come from the oral history that Mary recorded on Aug. 25, 1982. The recording is available at SLA.

251 "Time had passed her by"—telephone interview with Harve Presnell, Oct. 10, 1999

251 "She was livid"—interview with Jerry Berger, St. Louis, June 23, 2000

252 "telephone conversations"—telephone interview with Jane Sutter, Oct. 17, 1998

253 "a very dullish place"—telephone interview with Edmund Hartmann, July 21, 1999

253 "next bus"—interview with Jerry Berger, St. Louis, June 23, 2000

253 "go to McKnight"—interview with Stella Koetter Darrow, Clayton, Mo., Sept. 22, 1998

253 "put her off"—interview with Elizabeth Danforth, St. Louis, June 2, 1999

253 "there's only one week"—Amy Endrizal, "Wickes Discusses Time Spent on Hilltop," Washington University's *Student Life*, Sept. 30, 1986, p. 7

253 "to be back home"—interview with Stella Koetter Darrow, Clayton, Mo., Sept. 22, 1998

254 "a walking encyclopedia"—interview with Madelyn Pugh Davis, Bel Air, Calif., Dec. 4, 1998

254 "to 'hold her'"—interview with Bill Dorsam, St. Louis, Sept. 16, 1998

254 angry over Bill's decision—interview with Janice Dorsam, St. Louis, Sept. 16, 1998

255 "Mary was OK"—interview with Bill Dorsam, St. Louis, Sept. 16, 1998

255 "I'm not OK!"—interview with Bill Dorsam, St. Louis, Sept. 16, 1998

255 "half a chicken"—interview with Emily Daniels, Valley Village, Calif., April 20, 1999

CHAPTER FIFTEEN: SUCCESS RETURNS

256 She was paid $1,750—per contract signed by Mary and Muny president Bill Culver III, Mary performed July 17–23 at the Muny and July 24–30 at the Starlight Theatre in Kansas City, MWP

256 had never seen *Oklahoma!*—Mary made the claim in at least two interviews: Diane Werts, "Mary Wickes Moving Ahead by Earning Masters Degree," *Dallas Morning News*, July 29, 1979; and Ed Blank, "Oklahoma's Auntie Down-to-Earth," *Pittsburgh Press*, June 22, 1980

256 wrote her back—Rodgers's April 7, 1943, note is among about a dozen pieces of correspondence from him, spanning 1939 to 1966, that Mary kept, MWP

256 this job would pay less—per contract dated Nov. 27, 1978, between Mary and producer Zev Bufman, she was paid $1,500 per week, MWP

256 "When we were rehearsing"—telephone interview with Lewis Stadlen, Feb. 3, 1999

257 "Mary came to me"—telephone interview with Harve Presnell, Oct. 10, 1999

258 "speaking to Alexander"—James Lardner, "Tales of Bufman: From Israel to *Oklahoma!*," *Washington Post*, Sept. 9, 1979

258 "didn't know who she was"—telephone interview with Lewis Stadlen, Feb. 3, 1999

258 Orfaly won posthumously—Carbonell Awards Archives, 1978–79 season, http://carbonellawards.org/carbonell-award-history/1975-1979/the-4th-annual-carbonell-awards/

259 rose to $2,000 after that—per original contract dated March 30, 1979, MWP

259 "She was there for Mary"—telephone interview with Laurence Guittard, Sept. 30, 1999

259 "didn't trust me"—interview with Bill Hammerstein, Washington, Conn., Sept. 8, 1999

260 "absolutely devastating"—telephone interview with Laurence Guittard, Sept. 30, 1999

260 "definitely limited"—Sylvie Drake, *Los Angeles Times*, May 4, 1979

260 which Mary found thrilling—from Mary's interview with Don Richardson on "Behind the Scenes," KCRW, 89.9 FM, at Santa Monica (Calif.) College, March 15, 1984

260 inner-ear problem—telephone interview with Laurence Guittard, Sept. 30, 1999

261 "a lot invested"—letter from Mary to Bill Hammerstein, June 1, 1979, MWP

262 Hammerstein conceded to Mary—from a June 11, 1979, letter from Bill Hammerstein in Redding, Conn., to Mary at the Curran Theatre, San Francisco: "Several people have spoken to me since my disastrous comments to the group assembled to say
that they do want to stay on."

262 "wanted a star"—interview with Bill Hammerstein, Washington, Conn., Sept. 8,
1999

262 "there were rats"—telephone interview with Laurence Guittard, Sept. 30, 1999

262 "a football field"—telephone interview with Warner Shook, Aug. 16, 2010

262 "the most authentic"—Clive Barnes, "*Oklahoma!* is Still as High as an Elephant's
Eye," *New York Post*, Dec. 14, 1979, p. 31

262 "just dandy"—Walter Kerr, "Stage: *Oklahoma!* Returns to Broadway," *New York Times*,
Dec. 14, 1979, p. C5

263 "your usual table"—this is how Sardi greeted Mary when she arrived after an *Oklahoma!* performance with friends Jan and Lois Mares, per Lois Haase Mares, Washington, Nov. 11, 1998

263 "to make an entrance"—interview with Malcolm Goldstein, New York, Nov. 17,
1998

263 "Take charge, Aunt Eller"—mailgram from Lucy, Dec. 17, 1979, MWP

263 "a big fat hit!"—postcard from Mary in New York to Jimmy Stewart in Beverly Hills,
Dec. 17, 1979, posted for sale on e-Bay, Oct. 29, 2003

263 Aunt Hes performed—several pictures of Hester Margaret Shannon found for this
project, including at MWP, are labeled: Palace Theatre, New York, one from Lumiere
New York Studios, and another from Unity New York

263 "this stuff you fold up"—interview with Anna Crouse, New York, Nov. 18, 1998

263 jumped to $2,500—this increase and the scheduled increase to $2,750 were arranged in a contract and rider dated May 1, 1980, MWP

264 talked with Columbia—Mary talked with Ken Olsen, president of the organization, about fee structure and division of responsibilities if Columbia were to manage
Mary's tour, per correspondence from Olsen, Oct. 16, 1980, MWP

264 "in *Happy Days*?!"—interview with Anne Kaufman Schneider, New York, Sept. 14,
1999

264 Katharine Hepburn—the account of this fundraising effort comes from a telephone
interview with Max Wilk, Aug. 8, 1999

265 "literally plods"—Bill von Maurer, "'Light Up the Sky' Proves a Dim Bulb at Grover
Opener," *Miami News*, Oct. 29, 1983

265 "a most distinguished actress"—letter from Robert Fryer to Mary, April 14, 1983,
MWP

265 "than she wanted money"—interview with Iggie Wolfington, New York, Oct. 12,
1998

266 weekly salary for stage work—the original contract signed by Mary and Karen Poin-
dexter stipulates $2,500 per week, Oct. 9, 1984, MWP

266 a voice coach—audiotapes of Mary's recorded lessons are in MWP

266 *Strike Up the Band*—Mary turned to Edwin Lester, a leading force in musical theatre
on the West Coast, for advice on this part, and also wrote Lee (Mrs. Ira) Gershwin
about it, per 1988 correspondence between them in MWP

266 "a bit of melancholy"—telephone interview with Warner Shook, Aug. 16, 2010

266 gold and red jacket—interview with Bill Givens, Los Angeles, April 9, 1999

267 "very conflicted"—telephone interview with Laurence Guittard, Sept. 30, 1999

267 "lived in dread"—Bruce R. Miller, "Veteran Nunsense: Supporting Roles often Give Mary Wickes the Best Lines," *Sioux City Journal*, June 5, 1992

268 hospital volunteering—interview with Madelyn Pugh Davis, Bel Air, Calif., Dec. 4, 1998

268 without asking her—interview with Anne Kaufman Schneider, New York, Sept. 14, 1999

268 "kidding ourselves"—telephone interview with Tom Bosley, April 12, 1999

269 in enlarged type—telephone interview with Tom Bosley, April 12, 1999

270 paid $150,000—from agreement between Walt Disney Pictures and Mary, represented by The Artists Agency, Aug. 14, 1991, MWP

271 "half nun, half marine"—Janet Maslin, "Whoopi Goldberg on the Run, Disguised as a Nun," *New York Times*, May 29, 1992

271 "deadpan sovereignty"—Michael Sragow, "The Current Cinema: To the Rescue," the *New Yorker*, June 15, 1992, p. 88

271 "any imperfections"—telephone interview with Michael Germain, Jan. 11, 2011

271 revised the reference—in a March 31, 1992, memo, Richard Jordan of Disney's Buena Vista Pictures Marketing confirms to Mary that her bio will be revised, MWP

272 "up on the platform"—Mary shared this on *The Tonight Show with Jay Leno*, July 13, 1992

272 constant state of flux—Stephen Schaefer, "Difficult Birth for Disney Film," *Boston Herald*, May 29, 1992

272 "horribly offended"—telephone interview with Jane Sutter, Oct. 17, 1998

272 "being Whoopi"—interview with Madelyn Pugh Davis, Bel Air, Calif., Dec. 4, 1998

273 "feel like a nigger again"—the incident was widely reported at the time, including by Entertainment Weekly's www.ew.com, "Summer Movie Preview," May 22, 1992, and Stephen Schaefer, "Difficult Birth for Disney Film," *Boston Herald*, May 29, 1992

273 "they liked each other"—interview with Bill Givens, Los Angeles, April 9, 1999

273 "never gave any evidence"—Bruce R. Miller, "Veteran Nunsense: Supporting Roles Often Give Mary Wickes the Best Lines," *Sioux City Journal*, June 5, 1992. Mary made similar, positive comments about Goldberg to Mari Cartel, "Talking with Sister Act's Veteran Character Actress Mary Wickes," the *Valley Vantage*, May 28, 1992.

273 "old school"—telephone interview with Michael Germain, Jan. 11, 2011

273 "Goldberg is black"—interview with Dolly Reed Wageman, Studio City, Calif., Dec. 3, 1998

273 drawn not to Goldberg—Smith and Goldberg declined to be interviewed for this book

273 "close to Maggie Smith"—interview with Bill Givens, Los Angeles, April 9, 1999

273 "slightly catty remark"—interview with Dolly Reed Wageman, Studio City, Calif., Dec. 3, 1998

274 miss his funeral—interview with Bill Givens, Los Angeles, April 9, 1999

274 "didn't make a special effort"—interview with Bill Dorsam, St. Louis, Sept. 16, 1998

274 the afternoon it opened—interview with Anne Kaufman Schneider, New York, Nov. 21, 1998

275 "shot in the arm"—telephone interview with Warner Shook, Aug. 16, 2010

275 "with Edna May Oliver"—A. Scott Berg, *Kate Remembered*, Putnam, 2003, p. 347

276 "but Winona Ryder"—telephone interview with Warner Shook, Aug. 16, 2010

276 "more time alone"—telephone interview with James Brown, May 20, 1998

276 pushed her too hard—telephone interview with Denny Sevier, Aug. 10, 1999

277 first dialogue session—correspondence in 1994 and 1995 to Mary from Walt Disney Feature Animation (Kara Lord and producer Don Hahn, separately), MWP

277 "grandmother-type of voice"—Michael Starr, "Louie's Touching Tribute to 'Grandma,'" *New York Post*, Feb. 20, 1997, p. 90

CHAPTER SIXTEEN: PHYSICAL DETERIORATION

278 "blow to her pride"—interview with Dolly Reed Wageman, Studio City, Calif., Dec. 3, 1998

278 Gelson's market—interview with Emily Daniels, Valley Village, Calif., April 20, 1999

279 "No, no"—interview with Dolly Reed Wageman, Studio City, Calif., Dec. 3, 1998

279 "progressively worse"—interview with Janice Dorsam, St. Louis, Sept. 16, 1998

279 "Aunt Elker," "Bzrnard Hughes"—from the credit lists that Mary typed in her later years, MWP

279 folded her bills—interview with Canon Greg Richards, North Hollywood, Calif., Dec. 11, 1998

279 a podiatric surgeon—Jane Wyatt writes Mary in July (year unknown, but between 1971 and 1974) recommending a "Dr. Levy" as "fabulous," MWP

280 "without lifting her knees"—Linda Sherbert, "*The Foreigner* is Right at Home at the Alliance," *Atlanta Journal-Constitution*, Jan. 16, 1987

280 "*could not* get up"—interview with Emily Daniels, Valley Village, Calif., April 20, 1999

280 Dr. Susan Love—telephone interview with Janie Miller, Jan. 15, 2000

280 "a lot of pain"—interview with Rita Pico, Los Angeles, April 19, 1999

280 "a 106 fever"—telephone interview with Joe Ross, July 15, 1999

280 "never got the sense"—interview with Lucie Arnaz, Katonah, New York, Feb. 17, 1999

281 "This is what he told me"—interview with Richard Davis, Bel Air, Calif., Dec. 4, 1998

281 "*Gee*, she's aged"—interview with Lucie Arnaz, Katonah, New York, Feb. 17, 1999

282 given greater attention—telephone interview with Richard Palmer, Aug. 4, 1999

282 "dangled her estate"—interview with Jack Pirozzi, St. Louis, June 11, 1999

282 handled her funds—interview with Jack Pirozzi, St. Louis, June 11, 1999

282 could not reach terms—interview with Jack Pirozzi, St. Louis, June 11, 1999

283 "could never understand"—telephone interview with Richard Palmer, Aug. 4, 1999

283 appraised—Mary purchased the artwork at The Poster, a gallery in San Francisco, records at MWP

283 the gift was a disappointment—telephone interview with Richard Palmer, Aug. 4, 1999

283 "No one could see my poster!!!"—letter from Mary to Mr. and Mrs. William G. B. Carson in St. Louis, Oct. 18, 1973, courtesy of son Bill Carson

284 "into a back yard"—interview with Emily Daniels, Valley Village, Calif., April 20, 1999

284 "loveliest evenings"—interview with Dolly Reed Wageman, Studio City, Calif., Dec. 3, 1998

CHAPTER SEVENTEEN: FADE OUT

285 "three-point landing"—Charles Champlin, "Mary Wickes: Woman Who Came to Dinner," *Los Angeles Times*, Dec. 18, 1990

285 larger, two-bedroom—interview with Emily Daniels, Valley Village, Calif., April 20, 1999

285 "like an obstacle course"—interview with Bill Herz, New York, Feb. 18, 1999

285 In the first incident—Mary's medical records were closed to the author. The precise sequence of events that led to Mary's death—the falls in her apartment, the resulting complications and hospitalizations—as described in these pages are based on the recollections of those closest to her at the time. Their memories about specific details differ slightly, discrepancies that required the author to decide how to characterize certain incidents in the absence of documentation most accurately. But recollections of Emily Daniels, Dick Davis, Madelyn Pugh Davis, Bill Givens, Rita Pico, and Greg and Debbie Richards are consistent on the main points.

286 "ambulance ride"—interview with Emily Daniels, Valley Village, Calif., April 20, 1999

286 "real problem"—interview with Anne Kaufman Schneider, New York, Nov. 21, 1998

286 "busy, busy, busy"—interview with Rita Pico, Los Angeles, April 19, 1999

287 "didn't look well"—telephone interview with Joe Ross, July 15, 1999

287 "having trouble breathing"—interview with Dick Davis, Bel Air, Calif., Dec. 4, 1998

289 "slipping"—interview with Debbie Richards, North Hollywood, Calif., Dec. 11, 1998

289 "Would you *really?*"—interview with Canon Greg Richards, North Hollywood, Calif., Dec. 11, 1998

289 "nothing to worry about"—interview with Emily Daniels, Valley Village, Calif., April 20, 1999

289 "the three of us"—interview with Dick Davis, Bel Air, Calif., Dec. 4, 1998

290 "It wasn't like Mary"—interview with Janice Dorsam, St. Louis, Sept. 16, 1998

291 renal failure—from Mary's death certificate on file with the Los Angeles County Recorder

291 Cota learned—interview with Bill Givens, Los Angeles, April 9, 1999

291 offer of more work—interview with Madelyn Pugh Davis, Bel Air, Calif., Dec. 4, 1998

291 singer Mary Stouts—Raven Snook, "Stouthearted Woman: Jane Eyre's Mary Stout Chats with Raven Snook About Flop Musical, Swim Class and Cherry Jones," *TheaterMania*, Jan. 5, 2001, http://www.theatermania.com/broadway/news/01-2001/stouthearted-woman_1195.html

291 "immitate Mary's voice"—interview with Betty Garrett, North Hollywood, Calif., Dec. 10, 1998

291 "as quickly as possible"—all recollections from Jane Withers come from a telephone interview, March 11, 2000

292 Contrary to some reports—various articles reported that Withers was "a lifelong friend," when in fact she and Mary had not met. These articles include Jim Hill, "From the Archives," *LaughingPlace.com: Connecting Disney Fans Across the World*, April 5, 2001, http://www.laughingplace.com/news-PID115030-115033.asp

292 Kimbrough—Louis B. Hobson, "Dial M for Murphy," *Calgary (Alberta) Sun*, July 16, 1996

293 Northampton—from interview with Dolly Reed Wageman, Studio City, Calif., Dec. 3, 1998. Active in Smith College alumni affairs, she was there for the installation of Smith's president.

293 fondness reserved for grandmothers—from an interview with Lucie Arnaz, Katonah, New York, Feb. 17, 1999: "I remember Tracy stopping me and saying, 'She was just like a grandmother to me. She taught me so much.'"

293 casket on the altar—interview with Jim Wharton, Palm Desert, Calif., April 13, 1999

294 arrangement from Whoopi Goldberg—Janie Miller remembers the arrangement at the funeral; from a telephone interview with Miller, Jan. 15, 2000

294 four qualities of Mary's—from the three-page homily delivered by Canon Richards at Mary's funeral, a copy of which he shared for this book

294 "Everybody was laughing"—interview with Madelyn Pugh Davis, Bel Air, Calif., Dec. 4, 1998

294 Mary's casket—interview with Canon Greg Richards, North Hollywood, Calif., Dec. 11, 1998

294 dropped softly—interview with Bill Givens, Los Angeles, April 9, 1999

294 "two seats near the orchestra"—telephone interview with Joe Ross, July 15, 1999

294 "he didn't bring confetti"—interview with Bill Givens, Los Angeles, April 9, 1999

295 until after the funeral—interview with Debbie Richards, North Hollywood, Calif., Dec. 11, 1998

295 crestfallen—interview with Johnny Whitaker, Studio City, Calif., Oct. 26, 1999

295 Wolfington also felt awful—interview with Iggie Wolfington, New York, Oct. 12, 1998

295 "ka-jillions of people"—interview with Rita Pico, Los Angeles, April 19, 1999

295 "none of us back here"—interview with Amy Jane Ax, St. Louis, Sept. 25, 1998

295 wrote personal notes—fan letters and copies of some of Canon Richards's replies are in MWP

296 "most celebrated sourpusses"—Jessica Shaw, "Deaths," *Entertainment Weekly*, Nov. 10, 1995

296 "Nobody here was interested"—interview with Bill Dorsam, St. Louis, Sept. 16, 1998

297 94.5 percent—this account of distributions from Mary's estate comes from the outline of bequests in Mary's written estate plan. A copy of those plans, prepared by Beverly Hills attorney M. Alan Bunnage, rests in a folder concerning Mary at the Missouri Historical Society, apparently provided to the society in 1996 in connection with Mary's bequest of her furnishings.

297 "who had succeeded"—interview with Canon Richards, North Hollywood, Calif., Dec. 11, 1998

298 represents an oil portrait—the portrait is listed here on the museum's website: http://collections.mohistory.org/object/OBJ:1996+448+0005

298 perpetual—the original receipt for membership number 1359, dated Sept. 14, 1915, is in MWP

298 Hughes was disappointed—telephone interview with Barnard Hughes, Nov. 14, 1998

299 Mary's set of china—interview with Anna Crouse, New York, Nov. 18, 1998

299 "in touch with my mother"—interview with Lucie Arnaz, Katonah, New York, Feb. 17, 1999

INDEX